THE PSYCHOLOGICAL EFFECTS
OF WAR AND VIOLENCE
ON CHILDREN

Andrea Northwood

THE PSYCHOLOGICAL EFFECTS OF WAR AND VIOLENCE ON CHILDREN

Edited by

Lewis A. Leavitt
University of Wisconsin–Madison

Nathan A. Fox
University of Maryland at College Park

LEA LAWRENCE ERLBAUM ASSOCIATES, PUBLISHERS

1993   Hillsdale, New Jersey   Hove and London

Lawrence Erlbaum Associates, Inc., Publishers
365 Broadway
Hillsdale, New Jersey 07642

Library of Congress Cataloging-in-Publication Data

The Psychological effects of war and violence on children / edited by
   Lewis A. Leavitt, Nathan A. Fox.
         p.   cm.
      Based on papers from a conference held in Washington, D.C., May
   1991.
      Includes bibliographical references and index.
      ISBN 0-8058-1171-0 (alk. paper). — ISBN 0-8058-1172-9 (pbk. :
   alk. paper)
      1. War — Psychology — Congresses.   2. Children and violence —
   Congresses.   I. Leavitt, Lewis A.   II. Fox, Nathan A.
   U22.3.P775   1993
   305.23 — — dc20   92-43225
                                                                        CIP

Books published by Lawrence Erlbaum Associates are printed on acid-free paper, and their
bindings are chosen for strength and durability.

Printed in the United States of America
10 9 8 7 6 5 4 3 2 1

To our children:
Sarah and David Leavitt;
Rebecca and David Fox

Contents

PART III.   International Perspectives on Children and Violence

Part IV.   Perspectives on Intervention

Introduction

There is now substantial evidence that the legacy of family violence and trauma is passed down through generations. Adults who were abused as children are more likely to perpetuate this violence upon their own children (Cicchetti & Carlson, 1989). They face great difficulty in overcoming this history when dealing with their own families. Armed with this knowledge, psychologists and those involved in social policy have made great efforts to stop the cycle of violence within families. We as a society seem keenly aware that the violence within families can perpetuate violence on the next generation.

War and its attendant exposure to violence is something we visit on our children, as well. Around the globe, children are exposed to continuing internecine struggles. Even the end of the Cold War has not seemed to diminish the level of violence. Indeed, many of the ethnic tensions that lay dormant for so many years while Europe was divided into two major and opposing camps, have now come to the surface, often with a high degree of vengeance, violence, and savagery. And all this time, children are being exposed to the escalating brutality of war. Children are being socialized into a world where political violence and ethnic strife continue to be the means by which conflict is settled. If family violence perpetuates itself through a process of exposure, is it any wonder that larger scale violence continues to be present around the world, passed on from generation to generation?

Surprisingly, however, we know little about the effects of exposure of children to war and violence. Developmental research has investigated for some time the pattern of social and moral development in children, as well as children's changing understanding of ordinary events in their daily lives.

However, what are the effects of war and political violence on a 3-year-old child and how do they differ from the effects on a 10-year-old? What do children understand about their world when that environment is filled with chaos and violence? What happens to the development of the moral self and to the child's developing social competencies? Although it is obvious that war and exposure to violence cannot be good for children, it is imperative that we understand exactly what the short- and long-term behavioral effects are and what are the mechanisms by which socialization to violence occurs.

Research in the behavioral sciences has begun to confront the problems of children exposed to war and violence. Two general goals are apparent in this effort. The first is to understand the immediate and perhaps short-term psychological and physical effects of war and violence so that public health intervention can take place to deal with the acute and, if left untreated, chronic effects of exposure. The second is to understand the broader psychological context around which war and violence are presented and interpreted by children. In some sense we wish to know the mechanisms by which we continue to socialize our children to continued political violence and strife.

Recent work by clinicians and researchers has demonstrated the widespread and often long-term effects of exposure to violence on the psychological well-being of children. This work has revised past clinical understanding that children recover quickly and completely from exposure to natural and man-made disasters (Terr, 1983). It lends urgency to the need to develop wide-ranging public mental health measures in response to the profound exposure to violence that children around the world experience.

The context in which children are exposed to war and violence has also become the object of much study. Researchers have begun to study the manner in which conflict is politicized for children as well as the use and organization of children for ideological purposes. Children are no longer passive observers and recipients of the chaos of war but are sometimes socialized to be the vanguard of political change (Baker, 1991).

THE GULF WAR AS A CASE STUDY

The events surrounding the Gulf War serve as an interesting case study and example in which one can observe both the immediate and broader consequences of children's exposure to war and violence. This was a brief, though violent war, in which children in the Middle East were exposed to violence and danger and for which it is important to understand the immediate consequences thereof. In addition, these children live within the context of the Middle East, a region and area of the world known for its continued violence and political strife. So it is important not only to observe the acute effects of the war but also to examine how this conflict has been interpreted and presented to children within the broader context of the politics of their everyday lives.

During the gathering storm of military preparations for the Gulf War, Americans were confronted with the fear of a new global conflict with its attendant violence and destruction. When the fighting war began, television brought us images of physical destruction and human emotion that were powerful and upsetting. From a great distance Americans were made brutally aware of the physical dimensions of war. This war, fought by adults, as all modern wars, had as the greatest number of casualities — civilians. Among these civilians were a population all too forgotten in wars — children. Forgotten as well in the intense attention to physical injury to objects and people was the psychological injury to and suffering associated with war and exposure to violence.

The Gulf War was but one instance of the violence prevalent worldwide. The violence rife in American urban communities takes a large physical toll on adults but as well lays a heavy psychological burden on the youngsters in these communities.

This book grew out of a conference held in Washington, D.C. in May 1991 as a response to the need for researchers and clinicians to develop integrated plans for addressing the psychological trauma of children exposed to violence. Its goals were to summarize research on the psychological effects of exposure to violent conflict on children, with particular emphasis on the Gulf War, and to use this information to formulate an outline of what current knowledge suggests are reasonable approaches to public mental health intervention. An additional goal was that of developing an agenda for future research necessary for improving our clinical efforts in varying international conflicts. We have divided the book into four sections. The chapters have been segregated by common overall themes but frequently address questions germane to other sections. The authors have varied clinical and political commitments that exemplify important contested areas that future research and practice must address.

PART I: OVERVIEW

The first section presents three chapters that deal with the basic issues involved in the effects of war and violence on children. These chapters serve as a backdrop for the more detailed research on the psychological consequences of violence in the later sections. The first chapter, by Edward Goldson, a pediatrician at the University of Colorado, presents the stark implications of war on the physical trauma toward children. Goldson's chapter details the magnitude of physical injury to children within the theater of adult conflict. In his chapter, James Garbarino of the Erikson Institute summarizes some of the basic material gleaned from research during and after recent wars. Despite many important lacunae in what we need to know, there is a clear and present need to act now. This chapter helps prepare us for population-based clinical interventions, which must be assembled on an ad hoc basis. Dante Cicchetti, Sheree Toth, and Michael Lynch from the University of Rochester use research on child maltreatment as a model for examining the implications for children of exposure to war-related violence. They are sensitive to the dynamic changes in children's response to violence that are related to children's developmental status. These investigators emphasize the need to understand processes that interact at many levels that include individual, families, and communities. They outline as well how developmental theory can inform both research on and therapy for children exposed to the violence of war.

PART II: THE MIDDLE EAST CONFLICT: ITS EFFECTS ON CHILDREN

One impetus for the conference from which many of the chapters in this volume emerged, was the Gulf War, December 1990–January 1991. Although not one of the official combatants, Israel was directly involved in the conflict due to the Scud missile attacks launched from Iraq. Iraq had threatened to use chemical and biological weapons against Israel, and the entire population of that country was faced with the need to utilize countermeasures against this "unconventional" type of warfare. These measures included sealing off rooms in which citizens would stay during missile attacks and the use of gas masks and protective clothing in the event of use of chemical or biological weapons. Israeli citizens of all ages and in every part of the country were forced to respond due to the high degree of uncertainty of the situation. It was never clear whether such weapons would be used nor where these missiles would land. Young children as well were forced to wear the masks and to share with both parents the uncertainty of the times. This uncertainty was magnified by the fact that Israel remained an official noncombatant, never mobilizing her armed forces and not responding with military action even when directly attacked.

The threat of war and actual conflict are, unfortunately, not new situations for Israel or its citizens. There have been numerous conflicts and actions over the 40 plus years of the state. Surprisingly, there has been little study of the effects of war and violence on children. What literature there is, is reviewed in the chapter by Avigdor Klingman and Abraham Sagi from the University of Haifa and Amiram Raviv of Tel-Aviv University. Klingman, Sagi, and Raviv review work that occurred prior to the Gulf conflict and then present some of the newer studies that have recently taken place in Israel as psychologists and mental health workers study the effects of stress and war on Israeli children.

The responses of children to this "acute" episode of war, destruction, and uncertainty in their lives is the theme of three of the chapters in this section. Nurit Shilo-Cohen was the newly appointed curator of the Youth Wing of the Israel Museum in Jerusalem when the war broke out. Many of the modern, impressionist paintings were taken off the walls of the galleries in the main museum wing and stored in underground shelters for fear of destruction due to missile attack. Shilo-Cohen used the empty wall space in a highly creative fashion, putting large sheets of paper on the walls and inviting Israeli school children to paint large murals and pictures of their perceptions and views of the Gulf conflict. Some examples of their art may be found in her chapter.

Naomi Bat-Zion and Rachel Levy-Schiff, developmental psychologists at the Bar-Ilan University lived and worked in an area of Israel that was directly affected by the missile attacks. They witnessed firsthand the destruction produced by the Scuds and investigated the relation between proximity to this destruction and psychological reactions of young children. It is indeed remarkable that they had the foresight to organize themselves and begin data collection during the war. Their actions enable us to learn directly the responses of children to the stress of missile attacks.

In a similar study, Charles Greenbaum, Chedva Erlich, and Yosef Toubiana of the Hebrew University investigated the effects of proximity to damage on Israeli children. Greenbaum and colleagues, however, broadened their scope of inquiry to include the effects of exposure to Israeli–Palestinian violence occurring during the Intifada, as another setting in which children are exposed to uncertainty and violence. Greenbaum's decision to compare Israeli children of settlers (those living on land beyond the so-called Green Line of pre-1967) and nonsettlers is an interesting one for it adds the dimension of ideology as a force in determining the degree of stress response of children to war and violence. It is instructive in this respect to compare the responses of these two groups to the Israeli–Palestinian conflict.

The chapter by Shafiq Masalha, a clinical psychologist at Birzeit University, presents a view of the psychological consequences that violence has had on Palestinian children. Masalha makes creative use of the dreams of Palestinian children to explore the inner psychological reactions of these children to the Intifada. He also attempts to understand the reaction of these children and of the Palestinian population in general to the Gulf War. The chapter underlines both the power of ideology in constructing the perspectives of children toward violence as well as the common underlying responses of all children to the horrors of war.

The final two chapters in this section provide important approaches for the study of the effects of war on children. Roberta Apfel and Bennett Simon, child psychiatrists with Harvard University, interviewed both Israeli and Palestinian children during the Gulf War and 1 year later. They adopt a psychoanalytic approach to understanding children's responses to the war and afford us an interesting perspective on the psychic trauma that children undergo when exposed to acute conflict. Kathi Nader and Robert Pynoos from the Program in Trauma, Violence, and Sudden Bereavement at the University of California, Los Angeles were pioneers in the study of posttraumatic stress disorder in children. These researchers describe the methodological approach that they developed to study the effects of war on children, including the care in sample selection and choice of interview materials. Their study of Kuwaiti children after the Gulf War is remarkable for its rigor and the important data that it produced.

PART III: INTERNATIONAL PERSPECTIVES ON CHILDREN AND VIOLENCE

Part III brings together research on children and violence in a wide range of places and circumstances. Each of the chapters in this section represents a detailed empirical investigation into the effects of war and violence on the lives of children. The subject matter of these chapters range from the global problems associated with the threat of nuclear war to the specific problems of children growing up on the streets of the cities of the United States. A common theme across the chapters is the role of ideology as a mediator of children's response to violence. The effects of war and violence on children are in many ways modulated by the political ideologies of the environments in which these conflicts exist. Many times the manner in which this violence is perceived may buffer the traumatic effects of the experience. Political socialization of young children may exert a powerful force in forming the child's perception of violence. Examples of the role ideology may play in forming the perceptions of children may be found in the Liddell and Cairns chapters.

Christine Liddell, Jennifer Kemp, and Molly Moema of the Early Education Research Unit in Pretoria, South Africa describe the attitudes of young South African children in their struggle with apartheid. These studies clearly demonstrate the role that political organization and commitment can have as a means by which children interpret the daily violence that they see around them. They studied the effects of political ideology among Black South African youth and found it to be a powerful force in the construction of interpretation regarding both intercommunal and interracial violence.

Their chapter is a graphic reminder of the power of ideology in forming these perceptions even among young children.

Edward Cairns of the University of Ulster in Northern Ireland and Ignatius J. Toner of the University of North Carolina at Charlotte present a similar picture with their work on the youth of Northern Ireland. Here, again, the power of ideology is a primary motivating force for the continued participation of both Catholic and Protestant youth in the "Troubles." Cairns and Toner, however, have managed to transform this ideological rift into a force for reconciliation. They present an innovative program in which discussion regarding ideological differences takes place within the context of developing peer relationships.

Susan Goldberg of the Hospital for Sick Children in Toronto reports on her work on children's fear of nuclear war, extending our view of children's exposure to violence. Concern about nuclear war extends to children of all classes and is worldwide. However, concern about nuclear war may be associated in some children with optimism about the future and enhanced feelings of social efficacy. As Goldberg points out, the manner in which the issues are framed, the context and ideology of the debate, may lead to very different psychological outcomes in the children who are exposed to violence.

John Richters and Pedro Martinez from the National Institute of Mental Health bring the war "home" in their chapter. They document carefully the intensity of children's exposure to violence in a Washington, D.C. community school and the implications of this exposure to children's socioemotional distress. This chapter delineates the pervasiveness of children's exposure to community violence in urban America and indicates the range of social sequelae from such exposure.

PART IV: PERSPECTIVES ON INTERVENTION.

This section presents an overview of public mental health approaches to preventing and mediating the sequela in children exposed to community violence. Steven Marans and Donald Cohen of Yale Child Study Center describe a community-based initiative that links mental health professionals and community police. Their program suggests new directions for linking mental health professionals with community workers directly involved in confronting the effects of violence.

Tiffany Field of the University of Miami addresses in her chapter how an acute practical problem — Israeli children confronted by gas masks and peer separation — can be approached by an informed analysis of childhood developmental research, and outlines how "basic" research can be applied.

Amiram Raviv of Tel Aviv University describes the use of telephone hotlines and television during the Gulf War and how they provide the mental health professional practical access to large populations. Raviv shows how hotline and media interventions can be used to gather data on population effects of community violence as well as provide acute interventions for sequelae of community violence. He provides, as a result of the Gulf War experience, guidelines for effective use of media interventions.

In his chapter on Americans and the Gulf War, Charles Figley of Florida State University summarizes how previous work on war-related stress can be marshalled to plan systematic approaches to affected children and families. He notes the important role that mental health professionals must play in confronting the interacting needs of soldiers and their families.

Although there is still much vital information to be learned about the consequences of exposure to community violence on children's development, the work presented in this book reveals that mental health workers have available a wide range of recent studies whose findings can and should inform therapeutic efforts.

The work presented here outlines as well the complexity of performing and interpreting research on the effects of exposure to violence in children living under contrasting political and cultural conditions. Translation of findings from one community to another, from one age group to another, and from one historical period to another presents serious theoretical and practical challenges.

The work included here represents the burgeoning of a newly integrated field of study. Children, who arguably comprise a majority of the direct and indirect casualties of war and community violence, have so far been a relatively forgotten group. This book has attempted to bring together knowledge on children exposed to violence from diverse perspectives attending to a diversity of cultural and political contexts. In reading the individual chapters the reader will find many questions unanswered but also many common conclusions about important dimensions for understanding the effects of violence on children.

Regrettably, children all over the world will continue to be exposed to acute and chronic forms of violence, whether localized to their community or the result of a national war. The work presented here suggests informed approaches to public mental health efforts that can be implemented. It directs our attention as well to the need for interdisciplinary collaboration among researchers and clinicians to better understand the effects of exposure to violence on the psychological well-being of children and optimal modes of remediation on individual, family, and community levels.

ACKNOWLEDGMENTS

This book is the result of a conference held in Washington, D.C. in May 1991. The meeting was supported by funds from the National Institute of

Mental Health, the American Psychological Association, the National Institute of Child Health and Human Development, and the John D. and Catherine T. MacArthur Foundation. We are grateful for the help and support we received from Lewis Lipsitt, Robert Emde, Sumner Yaffe, Susan Solomon, and Alan Leshner.

Lewis A. Leavitt
Nathan A. Fox

REFERENCES

Baker, A. M. (1991). Psychological response of Palestinian children to environmental stress associated with military occupation. *Journal of Refugee Studies, 4,* 1–11.

Cicchetti, D., & Carlson, V. (Eds.). (1989). *Child maltreatment: Theory and research on the causes and consequences of child abuse and neglect.* New York: Cambridge University Press.

Terr, L. (1983). Chowchilla revisited: The effects of psychic trauma four years after a school bus kidnapping. *American Journal of Psychiatry, 140,* 1543–1550.

I OVERVIEW

1 War Is Not Good for Children

Edward Goldson
The University of Colorado and
The Children's Hospital, Denver

"War is not good for children and other living things," was a catch phrase of the 1960s. However, the effect of war on children and other living beings has been depicted graphically by ancient historians, as evidenced in the following passage by Josephus (1959) in his book, *The Jewish Wars*, telling of the Roman siege of Jerusalem:

> All human feelings, alas, yield to hunger, of which decency is always the first victim; for when hunger reigns restraint is abandoned. Thus it was that wives robbed their husbands, children their fathers, and — most horrible of all — mothers their babes, snatching the food out of their very mouths; and when their dearest ones were dying in their arms, they did not hesitate to deprive them of the morsels that might have kept them alive. . . . They showed no pity for grey hairs or helpless babyhood, but picked up the children as they clung to their precious scraps and dashed them to the floor. (p. 291)

People have been committing violence and waging war against one another for millennia. Even before the wars just described, the ancient Egyptians and Greeks waged war as did the most primitive of peoples. However, the character of war has changed. In ancient times war was fought with stones and clubs. We then advanced to spears and bows and arrows, and then to guns. We advanced to bombs, mines, and other armaments that enabled us not only to kill other combatants, but also to wreak devastation on civilians and the environment (Dudley, Knight, McNeur, & Rosengarten, 1968). We have finally achieved, with the development of nuclear weapons, the capacity to destroy entire populations

3

and, with even more advanced technology, to deliver devastating firepower "surgically" to very specific targets, as was demonstrated during the Gulf War in 1990. Moreover, it seems that throughout history the ultimate sufferers of war were the innocent: noncombatants, children, and the elderly.

What are the effects of war, defined by Eckhardt (cited in Zwi & Ugalde, 1989, p. 633) as "any armed conflict which includes one or more governments and causes deaths of 1000 or more people per year"? Since 1700, there have been 471 wars resulting in at least 101 million deaths, with more than 90% of these deaths occurring in the 20th century, but this may not include the 144 successful military coups that occurred between 1960 and 1986 (Zwi & Ugalde, 1989). There has been an increasing proportion of civilian casualties relative to combatants, with civilians accounting for 85% of war deaths in the 1980s (Sivard, 1987). Prior to the 20th century, the major casualties were soldiers, who died from both war injuries and infection. If one examines the average annual number of deaths per million population from wars in the past, it ranges from 19.0 in the 17th century to 10.8 in the 19th century. This increases drastically in the 20th century to 183.2 deaths per million (Garfield & Neugot, 1991), with a significant increase in deaths in the civilian population. In World War I, 19% of the deaths occurred among civilians; in the Spanish Civil War, 50% occurred among civilians; in World War II, 48% occurred among civilians; and in the Korean and Vietnam Wars, respectively, 34% and 48% of the deaths occurred among civilians (Sivard, 1985).

It seems possible that the long-term effects of war are probably more devastating than the immediate effects. This is particularly true for children. Sidel (1987) pointed out that during 1985, over $940 billion were spent worldwide on armaments. He noted that it would cost only 1 hour's worth of the world arms spending to eradicate smallpox, that the annual budget of the World Health Organization costs about 3 hours of arms spending, and that the cost to immunize the world's children against common infectious diseases would cost less than 1 day's expenditures on arms. He went on to report that 1 year's spending on Star Wars research could provide an elementary school education for 1.4 million Latin American children, and that the cost of one Trident submarine could fund a 5-year program for universal immunization against six major deadly diseases. These figures do not even consider some of the other sequelae of war, such as the effect of refugees on already stressed host countries, destroyed health facilities and schools, malnutrition, increased infant mortality and childhood morbidity, and the disruption of families.

The purpose of this chapter is to discuss the effects of war and political violence on children. The psychological effects are not addressed here, because they are covered in other chapters in this volume. Instead, my focus is on the physical effects on children. These effects can be divided into two categories: direct effects (i.e., the mortality and morbidity associated with armed conflict) and indirect effects, which include the various consequences of the physical conflict (i.e. the disruption of health care and education, infection, malnutrition, and the displacement of families). This chapter reviews these issues from a historical perspective, starting with conflicts during the early part of the 20th century and ending with the 1990 Gulf War. Obviously, it is impossible to review all 441 wars (as of 1989). Consequently, selected conflicts for which there are data are reviewed in order to describe what does happen to children during and after war.

WORLD WAR II

Prior to World War I, there were virtually no meaningful data on civilian casualties. Sivard (1985) reported that during World War I over 10 million noncombatants died. During World War II, 33 million civilians died, but the number of children was not specifically identified in those figures (Sivard 1985). However, there are some very provocative data describing the indirect effects of World War II on children in three different settings: Leningrad, Malta, and Holland. Antonov (1947) described the effect of the German siege of Leningrad from August 1941 to January 1943. During this period, there was incessant bombing of the city which was accompanied by no heat in homes, no transportation, and insufficient food. Drawing on the records from the Department for the Newborn of the Leningrad State Pediatric Institute, Antonov found that during 1942 there were 468 live births, 166 (35.5%) of which were premature. There were 25 stillbirths and 22 (7.3%) neonatal deaths, and 39% of the infants born prematurely died. During the first half of 1942, there were 414 births, whereas from July to December of that year, the number of births fell dramatically to only 79. Antonov suggested that this was the result of inadequate maternal nutrition. Because of the lack of food, there was significant amenorrhea among women in the city. During the latter part of the year, however, some women received adequate nutrition and did not suffer from amenorrhea, and therefore were able to conceive and carry to term healthier babies.

Antonov also reported that there was a fall in the average birthweight during 1942, and that children born in late 1941 and early 1942 had continuing weight loss in the perinatal period that lasted for 6 days instead of the usual 3 days. These children were described as being lethargic, sucking poorly, and having difficulty maintaining their temperature. Among the factors contributing to poor weight was also the decrease in the quantity (and probably quality) of breast milk and the decreased duration of lactation. From what we know today, these infants were deprived of the protective ingredients in breast milk. During 1942, 18.6% of the infants died in the neonatal period; 7.3% of term infants and 39% of preterm infants succumbed, with the mortality being worse during the first half of the year. These deaths were associated with scleredema, pneumonia, intracranial hemorrhage, prematurity, and congenital debility (not clearly defined in the study, but may represent infants born small for gestational age). Antonov attributed these difficulties to inadequate maternal nutrition, inadequate and a shorter length of lactation, inadequate heat in the pediatric institute, and the physical and emotional stress of living under siege.

The reproductive performance on the Maltese Islands, Malta and Gozo, during World War II have been described by Savona-Ventura (1990). Although the islands were not invaded, they nevertheless sustained heavy bombing from June 1940 to November 1942. As a result, food rations, water allowances, soap, and fuel had to be curtailed. The people subsisted mainly on vegetable soup, some tinned meat or fish, fat, oil, and beans. Any fresh meat that was available was reserved for the hospitals. Moreover, although most births prior to the war had taken place at home, during the war the rate of hospital confinement and hospital births increased.

During the war, the birthrate on both islands fell markedly. In 1940, the birthrate on both islands was about 32.53 per 1,000. In 1941, the birthrate on Malta fell to 27.39 per 1,000 and on Gozo to 25.02 per 1,000. The birthrate continued to fall in 1942, but increased with the cessation of hostilities. The changes during the war were attributed to the disruption in family life, such as communal living, and by the need for families to live in shelters to avoid the bombings. Also, male conscription may have contributed to the lowered birthrate, although the marriage rate was higher during the war than during the prewar years. There seemed to have been a reluctance to conceive during the war years. Poor nutrition of the population may also have interfered with reproduction.

Perinatal and infant mortality were significantly affected by the hostilities. Prior to the war, there had been a gradual decline in infant mortality, most likely associated with the improved organization of health care on the islands. Improved health care had led to the prevention and management of diarrheal diseases, which had been a major cause of death. Home nursing visits were established, which resulted in a leveling off of neonatal mortality. Support for needy mothers by the government was provided, and four infant health centers providing support to postpartum mothers were maintained on Malta. Despite these prewar measures, diarrheal diseases increased with the onset of the war, as did the prematurity rate and neonatal mortality. With the cessation of hostilities, the neonatal mortality rate fell, as did deaths from diarrheal diseases, measles, whooping cough, and diphtheria. These positive effects were the direct result of postwar improvements in the standard of living and an increase in marriages and births, primarily of first-borns, all of which allowed for better child care. Also, as already noted, there was an increase in the rate of hospital confinement, which may have contributed to the decline in stillbirths in the postwar years. In summary, it appears that the war directly and indirectly resulted in a decreased Maltese birthrate and an increase in neonatal mortality. However, it did lead to a change in obstetric care, with more mothers attending antenatal clinics and delivering their babies in hospitals. These obstetric changes persisted after the war, whereas the increases in neonatal mortality and deaths associated with diarrheal diseases were reversed with the cessation of hostilities.

Another aspect of war was addressed in a very extensive epidemiologic study by Stein, Susser, Saenger, and Marolla (1975) in which the authors asked the question, "Does extreme starvation affect the mental competence of adults?" Because of the way the Dutch health system was organized in the 1930s and 1940s, the authors were able to gather extensive and precise data on the degree of malnutrition that existed during the Dutch hunger winter of 1944–1945. Their hypothesis was that war can lead to famine and societal disorganization, which affect brain development and subsequently result in a decrease in mental competence. Although they did not demonstrate any cognitive impairment among the young adult men who survived that famine, they did uncover some striking effects on infants and young children born and living during the year of the famine.

They found that, despite severe rationing, particularly in the western part of the country and in urban settings, some groups had less food than others. This was reflected in increased numbers of deaths from malnutrition among adults in the lower classes and in decreased fertility among manual laborers and their families. Among women severely affected by the famine, there was evidence of ovarian dysfunction, demonstrated by increased menstrual irregularities, retarded menarche and amenorrhea. This was most prevalent in the laboring classes and in older and multiparous women. Among men there was a decrease in libido, potency, and sexual activity. These data suggest that the link between fertility and famine was both psychological and physiological. Among the higher classes fertility was better sustained as a result of better nutrition.

The famine's effects on the fetus during the first trimester included an increase in stillbirths, probably associated with maternal undernutrition as well as infection, and an increase in abnormal development of the central nervous system. The authors also quoted a 1952 German study that reported an increase in central nervous system malformations during the food shortages following the war in Berlin. There was also an increase in low birthweight and prematurity, which were associated with increased neonatal mortality.

Exposure to famine in late gestation resulted in retarded placental growth, intrauterine growth retardation, shorter infant length at birth, smaller head circumference, prematurity, and lower maternal weight at the end of pregnancy. These developmental disturbances were associated with an increase in the death rate up to 90 days after delivery, and were usually associated with gastrointestinal and respiratory infections.

In the introduction to this chapter, I noted that there were numerous civilian casualties during World War II, many of which were undoubtedly children. These three studies of the World War II experience raise broader issues concerning the indirect effects of war: famine, inadequate health care and services, and disruption of the social fabric. These resulted in a decrease in the fertility rate and increases in stillborns, in low-birthweight infants born prematurely or small for gestational age, in infant mortality associated with infection, and in developmental disturbances of the central nervous system.

POST-WORLD WAR II CONFLICTS

Since World War II, there have been numerous regional conflicts, some of which have involved all-out war, such as the Korean and Vietnam Wars; others have involved internal conflicts, such as those in Nicaragua and Eritrea. I focus here on some of these regional conflicts and their effects on children.

Southeast Asia

This part of the world has been the site of armed conflict for many years. The war in Vietnam is merely a prototype of what has occurred to civilian populations during these many years. Dudley et al. (1968) commented that since World War II, there have been small wars, insurrections, and peace-preserving actions that have inevitably involved civilians and physicians without prior military experience. In their report, they described the civilian battle casualties treated in the Bien Hoa Provincial Hospital from January 1966 to March 1967. Although their discussion focused on the technical aspects of war surgery, they also reported the number and nature of the civilian casualties. During the period under study, 137 civilian patients were anesthetized for surgical procedures related to war inflicted injuries; 46% of these surgeries involved patients between the ages of 0 and 19 years; 12% of these casualties were of individuals between the ages of 0 and 9 years. The authors reviewed 31 patients who sustained a variety of injuries to the thorax and/or abdomen. Thirteen of these patients were younger than 19 years of age; 12 of these young people survived the surgery.

Thus, during this brief period in this "limited" war, children represented a significant proportion of the civilian casualties.

Of further interest are the data reported by Vastyan (1971) on civilian war casualties and general medical care in South Vietnam. He noted that the death rate for combatants in Vietnam since World War II fell from 4.8% to 1%. However, the number of civilian casualties increased, and the medical care for civilians was appalling. Before 1967, there were no reliable statistics regarding civilian casualties. Since then, data have been gathered on the number of civilian casualties, and it appears that increasing numbers of civilians were admitted to the Ministry of Health system. Between 1967 and 1969, 100,000 to 300,000 civilians were killed or wounded each year. Of these, an estimated 25% were killed outright or died seeking medical care. Overall, there were approximately 1 million civilian casualties, with approximately 300,000 deaths during one decade of the war. In one report cited in the article, there were 105,200 disabled civilians, 20,000 orphans in registered orphanages and 85,000 in pagodas and churches (nonregistered orphanages), and 50,000 war widows.

As occurred during the Vietnam War and other conflicts, one of the most significant consequences of war is the number of refugees that move within and between countries. In Vietnam, there were an estimated 2,114,200 refugees who moved from the north to Saigon. This mass movement of displaced persons placed an enormous burden on existing health facilities, which were already less than optimal. Even prior to the war, the Vietnamese medical system was inadequate, having been developed by the French to meet only the needs of the colonial power. Medical equipment was sparse, maintenance capability was inadequate, and there were only 150 Vietnamese physicians available to care for 15 million civilians, because all other physicians either were in the armed forces or treated only paying patients. As a result, life expectancy was approximately 35 years, half the children born died before their 5th birthday, and the infant mortality was estimated to be 225 per 1,000 births. Malaria, tuberculosis, and enteric and parasitic disease were widespread, and typhoid fever was endemic. Trachoma, leprosy, and smallpox were very prevalent, as were cholera and plague. The response to these preexisting medical problems, which were complicated by the war and the influx of refugees, was to contain rather than eradicate disease and to provide essential care only to the acutely ill and injured. The aid provided by the United States was directed toward the psychological impact it would have in securing the population's loyalty to the South Vietnamese government. As a result medical care for civilians became highly politicized rather than being a response to the needs of the population. Thus, in a country with an archaic, inadequate medical system, the Vietnam War took a direct toll on the civilian population, took an indirect toll in the form of persistent infectious disease, and resulted in the displacement of more than 2 million refugees from the north. Families were disrupted, basic preventive medicine and child care were not available, and the impact on the civilian population, including children, was enormous.

With the termination of hostilities in Vietnam, the horror of Cambodia emerged, with the death of more than 2 million people under the regime of Pol Pot. Levy (1981) reported on his experiences in a refugee camp for Cambodians in Thailand where he worked in 1980. There were over 120,000 refugees in the camp, and although the precise number of children was not reported, he noted that there were 1,200 children living in camp orphanages, and many more were being cared for by relatives and friends. Prior to February 1980, 15% of the children had been malnourished; this number had fallen to only 1% at the time of Levy's arrival. A ward was established at the camp where 80 to 100 patients with a median age of 15 years were seen per day. Over three fourths of the patients had infectious diseases, the most common of which were respiratory and gastrointestinal. There were a number of cases of complicated measles, with 500 children being hospitalized during an outbreak of the disease. Obviously, these patients had not been immunized. The team saw numerous cases of meningococcal meningitis, malaria, and intestinal worms, and an average of two new cases of tuberculosis per day. Although severe malnutrition had decreased, they saw cases of kwashiorkor (protein malnutrition) as well as chronic undernutrition, with many women having amenorrhea. On the obstetric ward, 12 babies were delivered daily. Although on average they weighed 1 kg less than American-born babies, they did fairly well. The effect of the aid provided by the team, in conjunction with Cambodian workers, was to decrease deaths in the camp. Nevertheless, two or three patients (mostly children) died each day of pneumonia, malaria, diarrhea, or other preventable infectious diseases.

East Asia

As discussed in my introduction and in the section on the Vietnam War, one needs to consider both the direct effects of hostilities on children, which may be relatively short term, and the indirect effects, which may have significant long-term sequelae not only for children, but for the country in general. Bhatnagar and Smith's (1989) paper on trauma during the Afghan guerrilla war is instructive regarding what may occur to civilians exposed to direct conflict. They reviewed the cases of 1,373 patients admitted to a Pakistani border hospital from 1985 to 1987. Of the total number, 1,411 injuries were directly related to the war. The casualties ranged in age from 2 to 74 years, with 3.6% being 1 to 9 years and another 16.2% being 10 to 19 years. The injuries covered a wide range, but the most common were in the extremities and the thorax. Among the civilians admitted to the hospital (younger than 15 years or older than 50 years), the predominant injuries were caused by fragmentation weapons and burns; 75% of the burns occurred in children less than 15 years of age. Eleven percent of the fragmentation injuries and 5.5% of firearm injuries occurred in the civilian population. The clustering of these injuries in the civilian population reflects this group's "casual" involvement in the hostilities, because they were the result of the bombing of civilian villages and the subsequent fires and flying fragments.

During 1971, Bangladesh was the scene of a civil war. Mackay (1974) studied the effects of this war on a total resident population made up primarily of Hindus who worked in the tea gardens of the Consolidated Tea and Lands Company in the Balisera Valley of the Sylhet district. These workers had been recruited from other parts of the subcontinent four generations earlier to work in the tea gardens. At the time of the civil war, they were essentially indigenous to the region and completely settled in the tea garden areas. However, with the onset of the war, several events occurred: There was a large population movement out of the area to India starting in April 1971, with a return to the tea gardens in January 1972; there was a period when it was difficult to get money and so workers were not paid; there were difficulties getting food grains; because of increased tension there was irregularity of work and a lowering of work standards and discipline; there was a shortage of medical staff and supplies in the existing relatively well-established medical centers; and there was interruption of preventive programs as a result of a lack of materials and organization. During the population move, 8,441 out of a population of 40,402 went to India. It was reported that while in India 264 children and 265 adults died primarily of malnutrition and diarrhea.

Among those families that remained during the war, it was reported that even without birth control the birthrate fell, and the death rate rose by 45.3% over the previous 5-year average. These additional deaths were caused primarily by bacillary dysentery, pneumonia, tuberculosis, malnutrition, and anemia. Other causes included other gastrointestinal disorders and cardiovascular disease. Although children were not discussed separately from the general population, it is probably fair to assume that they were highly represented among those dying from dysentery, malnutrition, and pneumonia. There was a marked increase in the rate of stillbirths in 1972. Neonatal mortality rose from an average of 27.5 per 1,000 in 1966–1970 to 43.2 per 1,000 in 1972. Post-neonatal mortality rose from 21.8 to 47.1. Infant mortality rose from 49.2 to 90.3, and perinatal mortality rose from 74.7 to 95.6. Toddler mortality rose from 27.4 to 105, partly due to a striking increase in malnutrition in this age group. There were also some increases in the rates of tuberculosis and dysentery during 1972. Curlin, Chen, Babur, and Hussan (1976) reported very similar findings in a different rural area in Bangladesh. In summary, the effect of the war on the tea garden and other rural populations was that vital statistics in general deteriorated, toddler mortality increased, and the incidence of dysentery, anemia, and tuberculosis increased. Thus, in contrast to the Afghan report, although not exposed to the direct fighting, this population sustained significant morbidity and mortality as the result of the breakdown in the medical and social systems and the displacement of persons as refugees.

Africa

Africa is a continent that has experienced conflict since the beginning of the 20th century (UNICEF, 1989). Conflicts have existed between countries and within countries and have included civil wars, peasant uprisings, labor unrest, and student strikes (Ityavyar & Ogba, 1989). Moreover, these conflicts have taken place in an area of the world that is economically, technologically, and medically underdeveloped, and that has been subject to the whims of nature, including severe droughts. These conflicts, which require significant increases in military spending, have had a significant impact on health care and consequently on the lives of children. Factors such as less support for health care, the destruction of social infrastructures, and the creation of refugees all exacerbate the existing tenuous health conditions (Ityavyar & Ogba, 1989). With the advent of war, health policies become narrow and unidimensional, focusing on the war effort and the maintenance of health services for combatants rather than on issues of public health, preventive medicine, education, health programs, food, housing, water, and so on. Thus, the maintenance of child and welfare clinics and immunization programs have been compromised, with potentially horrendous outcomes for women, children, and other noncombatants. Malnutrition, which has existed throughout Africa even without war, becomes exacerbated under war conditions. Persistent diarrhea, pellagra, beriberi, rickets, and Vitamin A deficiency are common among refugee children, and result in significant mortality and morbidity, adding enormous stresses to existing inadequate medical systems.

Hughes (1969) described malnutrition in a bush area during the Nigerian Civil War in 1968-1969. A medical team was organized to treat starving members of the Ibo tribe in one of the eastern states. When the team arrived, 43% of the patients, mainly old men and young children, suffered from protein-calorie malnutrition. With the institution of appropriate nutritional therapy and measles immunization, many were saved and rehabilitated. Odling-Smee (1970) described the work of a team sent out to reopen a regional hospital that also served Ibo civilians. As in the case of Afghanistan casualties, civilians were usually innocent bystanders with little or no understanding of the war. Moving objects fired on by opposition soldiers were often found later to be women and children. A total of 338 casualties were seen: 54 (16%) were children, and of the 22 deaths, 4 were children. Thus, during the Nigerian Civil War, civilians were innocent casualties of the armed fighting as well as of the disruption of health services.

The scenarios described in Bangladesh and Nigeria have been similarly played out in other parts of Africa, such as Eritrea (Sabo & Kibirge, 1989), Zimbabwe, Southern Africa (Sanders, 1982; UNICEF, 1989), and the Ogaden (Henderson & Biellik, 1983), among others. First, there is the profound malnutrition that existed in these countries prior to the hostilities, which is then compounded by refugees and internally displaced persons. In Eritrea (Sabo & Kibirge, 1989), following the overthrow of Haile Selassie in 1975, the Eritrean People's Liberation Front (EPLF) was confronted with a country rife with infectious diseases, anemia, vitamin deficiencies, and malnutrition. In the lowland areas, 34% of the children had marasmus (protein and calorie starvation), 6% had kwashiorkor, and 52% died before the age of 5. This was the legacy of the Italian and British colonialization of these countries, which is reflected, among other ways, by inadequate medical services. Furthermore, when Selassie was replaced by Mengistu Haile Miram, the attempt to annex Eritrea continued, with a resulting war. Despite the war and bombings, the EPLF developed a needs-based health-care system that provides effective emergency services, primary care, and preventive health services, which has resulted in improvement of the health of the Eritrean population.

The second major problem in Africa, as well as in other war-torn regions, which was reviewed by Toole and Waldman (1990), has been the large number of refugees. The mortality rates for children under 5 years of age are higher (and often underestimated) than for any other age group. In 1985, there was a large Ethiopian refugee community in the Sudan. In eastern Sudan, the mortality rate for refugee children under 5 was 66 per 100 or 2.6 times greater than the mortality for children ages 5 to 14 and 7.6 times the mortality for persons 15 to 44. Within the birth to 5-year range, children under 1 year had a much higher mortality rate than those between 1 and 4. The causes for mortality in this age group generally included measles, diarrheal diseases, and acute respiratory infections, as well as malaria, particularly in the Cambodian refugee camps, as already noted. Within the refugee population, malnutrition increases the case-fatality rates for measles and other infectious diseases, diarrheal diseases, and vitamin deficiency disorders. The suggested solutions to these refugee problems have included the provision of adequate food, clean water, programs for disease prevention, malaria control, the provision of appropriate and adequate drugs, and the establishment of a health information system. The real solution is to stop the wars. In the Ogaden, a much disputed border area between Somalia and Ethiopia, the civilian population fled to Somali refugee camps or Ethiopian shelters. In response to this influx of refugees, both countries developed selective feeding programs, primary health care including immunizations, and preventive health measures such as waste disposal and a clean water supply, although these are still less than optimal (Henderson & Biellik, 1983).

In the discussion of Vietnam, I noted that the delivery of medical care to civilians was influenced by how effectively that care would generate loyalty to the South Vietnamese government. A similar situation has been reported with respect to the use of food as a weapon in Zimbabwe and Southern Africa during the War of Independence (Sanders, 1982). In 1980, after the War of Independence, it was determined that as many as 70% of children were undernourished, which was associated with a high infant and childhood mortality. A feeding program designed to meet some of the short-term needs of the population was instituted and was successful, to some extent. Initially, it was felt that the food crisis was a result of the influx of returning refugees putting an additional strain on the country's inadequate food reserves. However, on closer inspection, the most significant factors contributing to the food crisis were probably the previous regime's policy of "protected villages." The idea had been to isolate the civilians from the guerrillas by forcing them to live in compounds, often many miles away from their fields and subjected to rigid curfew hours. As a result, the people were unable to cultivate their fields, protect their crops from predators, and care for their livestock. An even more brutal policy, called Operation Turkey, was instituted, which empowered troops to destroy crops, livestock, huts, and personal property of those suspected of collaborating with the guerrillas. The purpose was to allow only the barest minimum of food to reach the local population so they would have none to share with the guerrillas. Thus, there was a marked dislocation of agriculture, a lack of grain stores to cover periods of shortage, and demoralization among the population, all of which were complicated by a drought two seasons prior to the War of Independence. Consequently, the food crisis after the war actually predated the arrival of the refugees, and was shown to be one of the direct results of the policies of the former White regime's use of food production as a weapon during the War of Independence.

Central America

The various wars in Central America bring into focus what has been occurring in other parts of the world. Conflicts in El Salvador, Guatemala, and Nicaragua have also influenced Honduras. Garfield and Rodriguez (1985) stated that, with the onset of the war, life expectancy among men in El Salvador fell, and civil strife became the most common cause of death in

Guatemala, El Salvador, and Nicaragua. The number of refugees living in the region also increased markedly. The medical system was and continues to be inadequate in Central America, partially as a result of the inequality of the distribution of wealth, but also because of the various conflicts, embargoes, and the need to direct resources toward the war effort.

Chelala (1990) reported that of 850,000 children born every year in Central America, 100,000 will be low-birthweight babies, and 100,000 will die before they are 5 years old. As is the case in Africa and Asia, the major causes of infant mortality are intestinal and respiratory infections. Moreover, as Geiger et al. (1989) reported, civilians have become the targets of the Salvadoran armed forces, who believe that the population supports and maintains the guerrillas. As of 1989, the civil war had caused nearly 70,000 deaths, and 27% of the children were malnourished (Geiger et al., 1989). It was reported that 43% of the child deaths in one of the "repopulated" villages was the result of army violence (Chelala, 1990). Furthermore, the Salvadoran army has targeted medical facilities and personnel of the guerrilla movement that have provided medical support to the rural population. Thus, among effects of the war are the killing and maiming of thousands of noncombatants, with thousands of children being orphaned and malnourished.

In Guatemala, Chelala (1990) wrote, the nutritional status of rural children has not improved in 20 years. UNICEF reported that 60% of the rural population has no access to health care, and there is a gross lack of immunization programs.

The war in Nicaragua has been a prototype for other low-intensity wars in the region as well as other parts of the world. *Low-intensity wars,* " . . . refers to conflicts short of conventional war, which intentionally subject the civilian population to a combination of psychological, economic, and military pressure to promote the adoption of the desired social system by the civilian population" (Nicaragua Health Study Collaborative at Harvard, CIES, & UNAN, 1989, p. 424). Among the tactics used in low-intensity war is torture, which serves not only to eliminate certain individuals but also to " . . . activate intense fear responses and disruption of the mental processes in the 'pueblo' in order to bring compliance with the strictures of the state" (Bendfeldt-Zachrisson, 1988, p. 303).

Since 1979, after the overthrow of the Somoza regime, there was a dramatic improvement in health care in Nicaragua (Braveman & Siegel, 1987). Health and education had been neglected by Somoza, such that 50% of the population was illiterate, the 1977 infant mortality was 121 of 1,000 live births, and services were not coordinated. The Sandinistas organized an integrated system with an increased budget that resulted in a decrease in infant mortality, an increase in life expectancy, increased immunizations, a decrease in polio, and the establishment of preventive health programs.

With the onset of the contra attacks, much of this changed (Garfield, 1989). Health facilities and personnel became the targets of attacks so as to destabilize the Sandinista regime. By 1987, 47 salaried health-care workers had been killed by the contras, 31 had been kidnapped, and 25 had been reported to have been wounded. During the first 2 years of the revolution, approximately 500 doctors left the country. From 1983 to 1985, another 1,000 health workers, half of them doctors, left the country.

Garfield (1989) reported that 67 schools were partially or completely destroyed, and 503 schools were closed. A total of 125 social service centers serving 17,000 children and elderly people have been partially or completely destroyed. The U.S. embargo resulted in serious shortages of medicine, pharmaceuticals, foodstuffs, journals, medical books, pens, medical re-agents, and so on.

By the end of 1986, a total of 5,714 war-related deaths were reported in Nicaragua, one third of them among civilians. These deaths included 331 children under the age of 15. Along with the deaths associated with fighting were the diseases of war, of which malaria was the most serious and widespread. Immunization programs developed by the Sandinistas were so compromised that there was a measles epidemic that lasted from late 1985 through 1986 in two war-zone regions.

An excellent example of the effect of the war was reported by the Nicaragua Health Study Collaborative at Harvard, CIES, and UNAN (1989). Two rural communities were studied: One was directly in the war zone, whereas the other was isolated from contra attacks. The results of the study revealed that food production, food availability, and nutrition were worse in the war zone, as was the prevalence of undernutrition in children 24 to 71 months of age (44% of the children in the war zone were undernourished, as compared to 19% in the isolated zone). Vaccination coverage was better in the more isolated zone. The contras had deliberately killed, kidnapped, and injured civilian health workers and destroyed health facilities. The disruption in the war zone of vaccination and malaria campaigns has been associated with an outbreak in measles and a reported increase in the incidence of malaria. In the country as a whole, of the 4,429 war-related deaths on the Nicaraguan side, one third were civilian noncombatants, including 210 children under 12 years of age. Finally, the war resulted in the displacement of about 250,000 Nicaraguans severely straining the health and social infrastructure of the country.

Since the Korean conflict, wars have taken on a different complexion. The difference between a low-intensity war and the more conventional wars of the past appears to be not in the numbers killed or in geographic booty captured, but in the focus on political objectives. In many ways, this kind of war may be far more destructive than conventional wars, because it focuses not on military objectives but rather on the civilian population and on the disruption of the social and economic infrastructure of the country.

The Middle East

The Gulf War is the most recent conflict on which there are some data on the effects of the hostilities (although as this is being written, there are wars in Somalia and Yugoslavia). It is also the Gulf War and its effects on children that inspired the preparation of this volume. On August 2, 1990, Iraq invaded Kuwait. The war was joined in January 1991, and raged for 6 weeks. It included massive bombings of Iraq, which ultimately led to its capitulation. This defeat brought about a widespread civil revolt, which was suppressed in March and April 1991, but led to the displacement of about 2 million people. The Harvard Study Team (1991) reported on the health consequences of this devastating conflict on the health and health care of Iraqi civilians, particularly children under the age of 5. Prior to the war, Iraq was an industrializing nation that had become increasingly urbanized and electrified. There had been improvements made in the health infrastructure, with the majority of the people having access to safe drinking water. Free primary health care was available to 93% of the population and infant mortality had been reduced to 42 per 1,000. The mortality among those under 5 years was 52 per 1,000 in 1990. At the end of the Gulf crisis, the entire water purification system had come to a standstill, and the sewage treatment system had been severely compromised. This affected not only the urban centers, but also the drinking water in southern Iraq. As a result of the destruction of the infrastructure that was so dependent on electricity, there was a marked increase in the incidence of water-borne diseases such as cholera, typhoid, and gastroenteritis, particularly in the pediatric population. In a number of hospitals, the rates of gastroenteritis among pediatric patients ranged from 38% to 91%, figures unheard of in the recent past. In addition, outpatient facilities were inundated with children with gastroenteritis. High levels of marasmus and kwashiorkor were reported among pediatric patients cared for in regional centers; this may be attributable to the epidemic levels of cholera, typhoid fever, and other gastroenteritides. The high cost of foods and the decrease in breast-feeding, combined with a shortage of infant formulas, may also have contributed to this malnutrition. The result of the country's disruption by the war was a decrease in hospital admissions, probably due to the breakdown in transportation services. On the other hand, there was a marked increase in the total number of deaths and a two- to threefold rise in hospital deaths. Iraqi physicians reported that there were even higher pediatric death rates in the community than in the hospitals.

Other effects of the war included the destruction of a number of health centers around the country. Even those that were not destroyed were not functioning adequately to meet the population's needs. Furthermore, there were grave shortages of personnel, laboratory and radiology services, and major drugs.

In summary, the combination of the military action, the UN sanctions, the civilian uprisings and the suppression of those uprisings have led to the destruction of the health and social infrastructure of Iraq. This has actually been more devastating to the country and, in particular, to the health infrastructure, than the actual direct damage to the population. Within this context, the group that has suffered the most is the children, who are dying of preventable diseases and starvation.

DISCUSSION

War is one of the four horsemen of the apocalypse; the others are pestilence, famine, and death (Lambert, 1991). Pestilence, famine, and death occur without war, yet, as has been described in this chapter, war, in and of itself, leads to pestilence, famine, and death. The nature of warfare has changed over the centuries from what we describe as conventional wars, which were global yet focused on military objectives, to low-intensity wars, which focus on the political, economic, social, and psychological disruption of a country. Both kinds of wars have direct and indirect effects on the population, particularly on children. For the purposes of this chapter, direct effects are those injuries and deaths that result from the actual fighting (i.e., bombing, mining of roads, and direct gunfire). The indirect effects include increases in infant mortality, resulting from inadequate hospitals and health care; in malnutrition; and in infectious diseases.

As noted in the introduction, there have been over 471 wars since the 17th century, which have resulted in the deaths of 101 million people, the majority in the 20th century. This chapter has described the effects of several wars — conventional and low-intensity — that have occurred during the 20th century for which there are data on children. Each of these conflicts is different, and each has taken place in its own context, yet they are strikingly similar with respect to the effects they have had on children.

The direct effects of war are that children are maimed and killed. Their injuries are no different from those of adults and are the result of weapons used. For example, during the wars in Vietnam and Afghanistan, children sustained severe burns and fragmentation injuries, consistent with the use of bombs, mines, defoliation, and the burning of villages. Children were injured when they were caught in the crossfire between adversaries in Africa and Central America. For the injured or disfigured survivors, there will be ongoing needs for rehabilitative services. These may be provided within the country or elsewhere, as occurred when children who has been burned or who had lost limbs were transferred to the United States for rehabilitation after the Vietnam War. Under these circumstances, families are further disrupted, which places even more psychological stress on the children as well as their families and communities.

When the indirect effects of war are considered, there are some striking commonalties across the various conflicts. Under virtually every circumstance, there has been severe undernutrition, if not outright famine, for the adult population, including women of child-bearing age, and for infants and children. In every conflict described in this chapter for which there were available epidemiologic data, there was a decrease in the birthrate, and increases in the number of stillborns, the number of low birthweight infants, and the incidence of perinatal and neonatal mortality. Thus, in addition to killing and maiming children outright, wars also result in reproductive casualty.

Associated with famine (or profound undernutrition) has been death from starvation and from infectious diseases that, under other conditions, might not have resulted in increased childhood mortality. This has been true of virtually every war in underdeveloped countries in the 20th century.

Wars disrupt societies. This has been particularly true of low-intensity conflicts of the middle and latter part of this century. Every war described has brought about the destruction, or at least the disruption, of the social, medical, economic, agricultural, and psychological infrastructure of the country. As a result, the maintenance of hospitals and outpatient clinics, and of maternal and child health programs has been compromised or discontinued, as have immunization, public education, and public health programs. Consequently, even when famine has not been a major issue, preventable infectious diseases have become rampant with increases in the morbidity and mortality among children. Children die of measles, diphtheria, polio, malaria, cholera, meningitis, and dysentery, which, by and large, are preventable and certainly treatable illnesses.

Moreover, there are those children who survive in countries where living conditions may be appalling. Schools are closed, food is inadequate, children may not grow adequately, and medical care may be nonexistent. What is to be the sequelae of these conditions? In the study by Stein et al. (1975), there were no adverse cognitive sequelae of the famine. After the war, however, Holland recovered, and the famine conditions no longer existed. This is certainly not the case in the underdeveloped countries of Asia, Africa, and Central America. In contrast to Holland, the conditions in these countries are atrocious. One wonders what is the loss of human potential as a result of war in these countries. Those data are not available and probably are not even being collected. Nevertheless, growing up under conditions of deprivation cannot lead to the achievement of the child's greatest potential in these disrupted societies.

Since World War II, new strategies of warfare have been developed. What seems to be most striking in our current era is the use of food and medical supports as weapons of war. Whereas in the past wars were fought between combatants, they are now waged in the civilian arena. Children, as innocent bystanders, become the victims. Adversaries now use food restriction, terrorization of the civilian population, and the destruction of medical capabilities and societal infrastructures to achieve their goals. Consequently, civilians, particularly children, become the most affected, because they are the most vulnerable members of society. They are the ones most significantly affected by the disruption of public health and maternal and child health programs, by the lack of immunizations, of adequate nurseries, hospitals, clinics, and medical personnel. This was true during the Vietnam War, and continued through 1991 in Latin America, Africa, and Asia. It was also the case in Iraq, where the "simple" planned destruction of the country's power system resulted in the most profound disruption of every aspect of the society's ability to meet its people's needs—from water purification and garbage disposal to electricity for hospitals and clinics.

Finally, there is the displacement of persons within (as well as outside of) the countries where hostilities are occurring. In many parts of the world where societies function on a marginal basis, the introduction of large numbers of homeless and impoverished people wreaks havoc on the existing fragile systems. As was noted earlier, it is again children, particularly the very young, who suffer the most. They have the greatest morbidity and mortality. Moreover, their families are frequently separated, their parents may be dead, their schooling is terminated, and their prospects for any meaningful life become minimal.

SUMMARY

This chapter has attempted to describe, using selected examples, the effects of war on children. The psychological sequelae have not been addressed, although they are of enormous significance; the emphasis has been on the physical effects. They include not only injury and death from weapons, but also the effect of the disruption of the basic infrastructures of the country: public health, medicine, education, and social services. Furthermore, as a result of war, families are disrupted, children are orphaned, and people are forced to become refugees either within their countries or outside them.

I have also pointed out that warfare has changed from being a battle between soldiers to being a battle that includes and focuses on civilians. Furthermore, the strategies of war have changed such that the goals are different, and the sequelae even more destructive than they were in the past. Is this acceptable as we approach the 21st century? Is it allowable to let the world's children—its most valuable resource—continue to suffer as they do because of war, even as this chapter is being written? Will someone heed the message that war is not good for children and other living things before it is truly too late?

ACKNOWLEDGMENTS

Appreciation is extended to Anne Klenk, Kathy Szabo, and Beverly Giordano for assistance in researching this chapter. Special thanks are extended to Dr. P. A. Campbell for critical review of the manuscript.

REFERENCES

Antonov, A. N. (1947). Children born during the siege of Leningrad in 1942. *Journal of Pediatrics, 30,* 250–259.

Bendfeldt-Zachrisson, F. (1988). Torture as intensive repression in Latin America: The psychology of its methods and practice. *International Journal of Health Services, 18,* 301–310.

Bhatnagar, M. K., & Smith, G. S. (1989). Trauma in the Afghan guerrilla war: Effects of lack of access to care. *Surgery, 105,* 699–705.

Braveman, P., & Siegel, S. (1987). Nicaragua: A health system developing under conditions of war. *International Journal of Health Services 1987, 17,* 169–178.

Chelala, C. A. (1990). Central America: The cost of war. *The Lancet, 335,* 153–154.

Curlin, G. T., Chen, L. C., Babur, & Hussain, S. B. (1976). Demographic crisis: The impact of the Bangladesh Civil War (1971) on births and deaths in a rural area of Bangladesh. *Population Studies, 30,* 87–105.

Dudley, H. A. F., Knight, R. J., McNeur, J. C., & Rosengarten, D. S. (1968). Civilian battle casualties in South Vietnam. *British Journal of Surgery, 55,* 332–340.

Garfield, R. M. (1989). War-related changes in health and health services in Nicaragua. *Social Science and Medicine, 28,* 669–676.

Garfield, R. M., & Rodriguez, P. F. (1985). Health and health services in Central America. *Journal of the American Medical Association, 254,* 936–943.

Garfield, R. M., & Neugot, A. I. (1991). Epidemiologic analysis of warfare: A historical review. *Journal of the American Medical Association, 266,* 688–692.

Geiger, J., Eisenberg, C., Gloyd, S., Quiroga, J., Schlenker, T., Scrimshaw, N., & Devin, J. (1989). A new medical mission to El Salvador. *New England Journal of Medicine 1989, 321,* 1136–1140.

Harvard Study Team. (1991). The effect of the gulf crisis on the children of Iraq. *New England Journal of Medicine, 325,* 977–980.

Henderson, P. L., & Biellik, R. J. (1983). Comparative nutrition and health services for victims of drought and hostilities in the Ogaden: Somalia and Ethiopia 1980–1981. *International Journal of Health Services, 13,* 289–306.

Hughes, S. P. F. (1969). Malnutrition in the field: Nigerian civil war 1968-9. *British Medical Journal, 2,* 436–438.

Ityavyar, D. A., & Ogba, L. O. (1989). Violence, conflict and health in Africa. *Social Science and Medicine, 28,* 649–657.

Josephus, F. (1959). The Jewish wars (G.A. Williamson, Trans.). Harmondsworth, Middlesex: Penguin Books Ltd.

Lambert, C. (1991). Roughriding with the four horsemen of the apocalypse. *Harvard Magazine* (September–October), *94,* 23–28.

Levy, B. S. (1981). Working in a camp for Cambodian refugees. *New England Journal of Medicine, 304,* 1440–1444.

Mackay, D. M. (1974). The effects of civil war on the health of a rural community in Bangladesh. *Journal of Tropical Medicine and Hygiene, 77,* 120–127.

Nicaragua Health Study Collaborative at Harvard, CIES, & UNAN. (1989). Health effects of the war in two rural communities in Nicaragua. *American Journal of Public Health, 79,* 424–429.

Odling-Smee, G. W. (1970). Ibo civilian casualties in the Nigerian civil war. *British Medical Journal, 2,* 592–596.

Sabo, L. E., & Kibirige, J. S. (1989). Political violence and Eritrean health care. *Social Science and Medicine, 7,* 677–684.

Sanders, D. (1982). Nutrition and the use of food as a weapon in Zimbabwe and Southern Africa. *International Journal of Health Services, 12,* 201–213.

Savona-Ventura, C. (1990). Reproductive performance on the Maltese Islands during the second world war. *Medical History, 34,* 164–177.

Sidel, V. W. (1987). Socioeconomic effects of the arms race. *Preventive Medicine, 16,* 342–353.

Sivard, R. L. (1985). *World military and social expenditures, 1985.* Washington, DC: Worldwatch Institute.

Sivard, R. L. (1987). World military and social expenditures, 1987–88. *World Priorities 1987,* 28–31.

Stein, Z., Susser, M., Saenger, G., & Marolla, F. (1975). *Famine and human development: The Dutch hunger winter of 1944–1945.* New York: Oxford Press.

Toole, M. J., & Waldman, R. J. (1990). Prevention of excess mortality in refugee and displaced populations in developing countries. *Journal of the American Medical Association, 263,* 3296–3302.

UNICEF. (1989). *Children on the front line.* New York: United Nations Children's Fund.

Vastyan, E. A. (1971). Civilian war casualties and medical care in South Vietnam. *Annals of Internal Medicine, 74,* 611–624.

Zwi, A., & Ugalde, A. (1989). Towards an epidemiology of political violence in the third world. *Social Science and Medicine, 28,* 633–642.

2 Children's Response to War: What Do We Know?

James Garbarino and Kathleen Kostelny
Erikson Institute for Advanced Study in Child Development

AN INTRODUCTION TO THE EXPERIENCE OF DANGER AND TRAUMA

In order to understand how children respond to war, perhaps the best place to begin is with a brief developmental perspective on danger and trauma. What does danger mean for a child? The dictionary definition indicates that *danger* is "liability to all kinds of harm"—injuries that may be physical, psychological, or moral.

At the outset, we must recognize that "objective" and "subjective" dangers may be weakly correlated, at best. This is true of children to be sure, yet even adults may be unaware of the objective dangers around them: They may feel safe when they "ought" to be afraid, or feel endangered when, in fact, they are at negligible risk of harm. This issue is important because war represents the coincidence of many dangers for children.

Perhaps danger is best approached along the lines developed for the study of child maltreatment, where the same mix of objective and (collectively) subjective criteria are faced (Garbarino, Guttmann, & Seeley, 1986). Child maltreatment constitutes a social judgment regarding treatment of a child that is determined to be inappropriate and to jeopardize the child's growth and development.

In this same sense, there is a social grounding to notions of danger—if not a lowest common denominator, then at least a low one. Danger is a judgment about the social meaning of risk and an authorization for effective and moral response. Subjective danger is the phenomenological construction (i.e., the recognition) of liability to injury or evil consequences; objective danger is an empirical determination regarding the probability of liability being translated into injury.

Those whose sensibility falls very much below the social standard—who see danger in and feel imperiled by what is socially defined as mundane, benign, or improbable—may be judged "neurotic," "phobic," or perhaps just "fearful." Those whose sensibility to risk is not activated until threats are (by common social standards) extreme, imminent, and terrifying are classified as "reckless," "numbed" or "pathologically brave." It has been hypothesized that both of these extreme patterns exist as the result of children experiencing war, as forms of adaptation to the experience of war.

One issue with which we are concerned is identifying and understanding the forces that push individual people away from the norms (in either direction). A second is understanding the forces that change those norms.

For example, in the 1950s, children never wore seat belts in the family car. Now, in societies like the United States, there is an expectation (one that is met in a slim majority of cases) that children and youth (and their parents) will "buckle up," and failure to do so has been called "child neglect" (Garbarino, 1988). Now, well-socialized children and youth feel endangered if asked to travel without being buckled up, even if for a brief time: Objective danger decreases (seat belts reduce injuries by 60% and deaths by 90%), and subjective danger may well increase.

Safety, like danger, has costs associated with it—costs that go beyond the financial and physical, to include the psychological and philosophical (Garbarino, 1988). The greater our awareness of the risks around us, the more we feel impelled to act safely, and the more guilty we may feel if harm befalls us.

Can someone become addicted to danger? Totally desensitized? Both appear to be consequences of childhood experience with war. In our observations of Palestinian children in the *Intifada*, for example, we have observed children who have developed a "bravery" in combatting Israeli soldiers that can be seen as a reckless disregard for their safety (Garbarino, Kostelny, & Dubrow, 1991).

Adopting a psychoanalytic perspective, one could see this as a caricature of the more common excitement that comes from playing in the zone between the life force (Eros) and the death force (Thanatos). Indeed, many people claim that they feel most alive when successfully challenging themselves by confronting danger, perhaps flirting with danger or even thumbing their noses at it.

How do we understand danger in the lives of children? How do we understand the origins, mechanisms, and coping processes employed by children in dealing with danger? In short, how can we understand danger developmentally?

A few preliminary observations:

- Most children can appreciate the thrill that comes with moderate danger and seek it out in their play (e.g., climbing games on the playground). Some children even seem to thrive on danger: They seek the thrill of it and may be incompletely aware of its possible ramifications for themselves and others.
- Some children seek extreme danger as an expression of psychopathology; a recent exploration of childhood suicide shows this clearly (Orbach, 1988).
- Some children are paralyzed by the slightest hint of danger, having become so through an unfortunate interaction of temperament and parental training (e.g., a timid 7-year-old boy who visits friends of his parents at their home on a lake and spends the entire time with his life jacket on, cataloguing the dangers to be found there, from the possibility of being bitten by the family's pet hamster to the chance of falling from the dock into the shallow water and drowning).

Danger is about risk, risk of injury or trauma. In contrast, trauma is a disordered psychic or behavioral state resulting from mental or emotional stress or physical injury. What happens when a child is hurt? The consequences can range from minor injury to death, with the outcome reflecting a host of organismic and situational factors. Physical disability has certain objective realities, of course, but the consequences of greatest concern are psychological and moral. They lie in the meaning of physical consequences.

The same physical consequences can have very different life course effects, as a function of cultural, social, and psychological influences. For example, it matters developmentally whether a child's leg is broken by a parental assault or through play, whether in the course of running away from a fight or in the course of standing up for a friend.

Of particular developmental interest is whether or not danger results in psychological disruption. The emergent field of traumatic stress studies is increasingly recognizing the importance of understanding the phenomenon of Post Traumatic Stress Disorder (PTSD) as a response to childhood trauma (Eth & Pynoos, 1985). This follows the inclusion of the PTSD as a category for official diagnosis in the third edition of the American Psychiatric Association's *Diagnostic and Statistical Manual* (1987). Diagnostic criteria for PTSD include:

1. Existence of a recognizable stressor that would evoke significant symptoms of distress in almost everyone.

2. Re-experiencing of the trauma, as evidenced by at least one of the following: (a) recurrent and intrusive recollections of the event; (b) recurrent dreams of the event; or (c) suddenly acting or feeling as if the traumatic event were reoccurring, because of an association with an environmental or ideational stimulus.

3. Numbing of responsiveness to or reduced involvement with the external world, beginning some time after the trauma, as shown by at least one of the following: (a) markedly diminished interest in one or more significant activities; (b) a feeling of detachment or estrangement from others; or (c) constricted affect.

4. At least two of the following symptoms that were not present before the trauma: (a) hyperalertness or exaggerated startle response; (b) sleep disturbance; (c) guilt about surviving when others have not, or about behavior undertaken for survival; (d) memory impairment or trouble concentrating; (e) avoidance of activities that arouse recollection of the traumatic event: or (f) intensification of symptoms by exposure to events that symbolize or resemble the traumatic event.

These developments have helped build a foundation on which to build our understanding of the relationship between danger and trauma, and thus to shed light on the experience of children in situations of war. One element of this foundation is the distinction between acute danger (e.g., when a deranged individual enters a normally safe school and opens fire with a rifle) and chronic danger (e.g., when soldiers regularly attack students and teachers in or around the school as a means of disrupting day-to-day academic life).

ACUTE AND CHRONIC DANGER: IMPLICATIONS FOR ADJUSTMENT

Acute danger requires a process of adjustment, through some measure of objective change in the conditions of life and/or subjective alteration of one's stance toward life events. Acute incidents of danger often require only *situational adjustment* by normal children leading normal lives, assimilation of the traumatic event into the child's understanding of his or her situation. The therapy of choice here is reassurance: "You are safe again; things are back to normal."

This is not to deny that traumatic stress syndrome in children and youth exposed to acute danger may require processing over a period of time (Pynoos & Nader, 1988). If the traumatic stress is intense enough, it may leave permanent psychic scars, particularly for children made vulnerable because of disruptions in their primary relationships (most notably with parents). These effects include excessive sensitivity to stimuli associated with the trauma and diminished expectations for the future (Terr, 1990).

Chronic danger, however, imposes a requirement for *developmental adjustment*, accommodations that are likely to include persistent Post Traumatic Stress Disorder, alterations of personality, and major changes in patterns of behavior or articulation of ideological interpretations of the world that provide a framework for making sense of ongoing danger (particularly when that danger comes from violent overthrow of day-to-day social reality, as occurs in war, communal violence, or chronic violent crime).

The therapy of choice in situations of chronic danger is one that builds on the child's primary relationships to create a new positive reality for the child, one that can stand up to the "natural" conclusions a severely traumatized child might otherwise draw about his or her self-worth, about the reliability of adults and their institutions, and about the safe approaches to adopt toward the world (Garbarino, Dubrow, Kostelny, & Pardo, 1992).

There is a growing body of research and clinical observation based on a concern that children and youth caught up in war and other forms of social crisis will adapt in adverse ways. Specifically, clinicians and researchers have noted that children who experience war and community violence are at greater risk for developmental impairment, physical damage, and emotional trauma, and, as a result, may be mis-socialized into a model of fear, violence, and hatred (Garbarino et al., 1992; Garbarino, Kostelny, & Dubrow, 1991; Goleman, 1986; Rosenblatt, 1983).

This growing concern is fueled by the recognition that the demographics of war dangers shifted as the 20th century progressed. According to a report from UNICEF (1986), the ratio of soldiers to civilians killed in armed conflict has gone from approximately 9:1 in the early decades (e.g., World War I) to 1:9 in recent conflicts (e.g., Lebanon). Some observers have noted a similar trend in the case of the high-crime neighborhoods of American cities: increasing victimization of women and children in situations of chronic community violence. Other research (cf. Garbarino et al., 1992) indicates that most children in violent community settings are exposed to potentially traumatizing violence on a regular basis. For example, Bell (1990) reported on a population in which one third of the children had witnessed a homicide and more than two thirds had witnessed a serious assault.

Political conflict, racism, and poverty create potentially dangerous threats to child development. Indeed, an accumulative model of risk (Sameroff et al., 1987) points to the special relevance of risk factors like community violence for children who already have to face substantial risk factors in their lives, and for whom community violence may be the proverbial "last straw" (Garbarino et al., 1992).

These evils provide a context in which we can seek to understand the dynamics of children in dangerous and stressful environments, and the relationship between danger and trauma, but the presumption that danger leads to developmental impairment is clearly not the whole story. A second theme in studies of children in danger emphasizes the role of social crisis in stimulating moral development.

Coles (1986) noted this in his study of the political life of children: Under conditions of violent political crisis, some children develop a precocious and precious moral sensibility. We can hypothesize that this process of "meaning giving" is an important mediator between danger and trauma, and between danger and moral development.

On the one hand, the common-sense assumption is that children exposed to danger are destined for developmental difficulties: War is not good for children and other living things. On the other, the fact is that children survive such danger, and some may even overcome its challenges in ways that enhance development.

Freud and Burlingham's (1943) reports on children exposed to trauma during World War II present this latter view (at least in the short run): Children in the care of their own mothers or a familiar mother substitute were not psychologically devastated by war-time experiences, principally because parents could maintain day-to-day care routines and project high morale.

A similar theme emerges from a recent study involving a number of safety issues for children in a public housing project in Chicago that is saturated with violence (Dubrow & Garbarino, 1988). Mothers in the project identified "shooting" as their major safety concern for their children, and sought to utilize a variety of coping mechanisms to protect their children from immediate harm.

This is not to say that such children escaped unscathed, however. Indeed, follow-up studies of severely traumatized children cared for by Anna Freud and her colleagues revealed a significant proportion who evidenced chronic and profound problems, despite receiving compensatory care. Recent longitudinal analyses of the impact of divorce on children suggest a similar "sleeper" effect, with life adjustment problems emerging 10 or more years after family dissolution (Wallerstein & Blakeslee, 1989).

Being a child in a highly stressful environment can lead to long-term mental health concerns, even for a child with access to parental protection in the short term. This is evident in economically stressful situations, even if they do not include acute danger. For example, Elder and Rockwell (1978) found that the effects of having been a child during the Great Depression of the 1930s in the United States were often seen decades later in the life courses of adults, particularly for males.

Convergent findings from several studies of life-course responses to stressful early experience suggest a series of ameliorating factors, factors that lead to pro-social and healthy adaptability (Losel & Bliesener, 1990):

- Active attempts to cope with stress (rather than just reacting).
- Cognitive competence (at least an average level of intelligence).
- Experiences of self-efficacy, and a corresponding self-confidence and positive self-esteem.
- Temperamental characteristics that favor active coping attempts and positive relationships with others (e.g., activity, goal orientation, sociability), rather than passive withdrawal.
- Stable emotional relationships with at least one parent or other reference person.
- An open, supportive educational climate and a parental model of behavior that encourage constructive coping with problems.
- Social support from persons outside the family.

These are the factors that have been identified as important when the stresses involved are in the "normal" range found in the mainstream of modern industrial societies (e.g., poverty, family conflict, childhood physical disability, and parental involvement in substance abuse). Nonetheless, they may provide a starting point for efforts to understand the special character of coping in the stressful circumstances of prolonged violence (war, communal conflict, and pervasive violent crime), where the risk of socially maladaptive coping is high (Garbarino et al., 1991).

SOCIALLY MALADAPTIVE METHODS OF COPING WITH DANGER

Children forced to cope with the chronic danger that war brings may adapt in dysfunctional ways. The psychopathological dimensions of such adaptation — most notably PTSD — are now widely recognized. The social dimensions are equally worthy of attention, however.

Children (and parents) may cope with danger by adopting a world view or a persona that may be dysfunctional in any "normal" situation in which they are expected to participate (e.g., school). For example, their adaptive behavior in the abnormal situation of chronic crisis may be maladaptive to school success if they defend themselves by becoming hyperaggressive (which stimulates rejection at school).

What is more, some adaptations to chronic danger, such as emotional withdrawal, may be socially adaptive in the short run, but may be a source of danger to the next generation (e.g., when the individual becomes a parent). This phenomenon has been observed in studies of families of Holocaust survivors (Danieli, 1985).

Even in the absence of this intergenerational process, however, the same links between danger and trauma observed in children may operate directly among parents. Their adaptations to dangerous environments may produce child-rearing strategies that impede normal development, as in the case of a mother who does not allow her child to play on the floor because there is poison on the floor to kill the rats that infest the apartment, but who, in doing so, may deprive the child of important opportunities for exploratory play.

Likewise, the parent who prohibits the child from playing outside for fear of shooting incidents may be denying the child a chance to engage in social and athletic play, as an undesirable side effect of protecting the child from assault.

Similarly, the fear felt by parents of children in high-crime environments may be manifest as a very restrictive and punitive style of discipline (including physical assault) in an effort to protect their children from falling under the influence of negative forces in the neighborhood (e.g., gangs).

Unfortunately, this approach is likely to have the result of heightening aggression on the children's part, with one consequence being a difficulty in succeeding in contexts that provide alternatives to the gang culture, and endorsing an acceptance of violence as the modus operandi for social control (which, in turn, rationalizes the gang's use of violence as the dominant tactic for social influence). Holding children back from negative forces through punitive restrictiveness is generally much less successful a strategy than promoting positive alternatives to the negative subculture feared by the parents (Scheinfeld, 1983).

In all three of these examples, the adaptation is well intentioned and may appear to be practically sensible, but its side effects may be detrimental in the long run. The onus here, of course, is on the social forces that create and sustain danger in the family's environment, thus forcing parents to choose between the lesser of two evils.

In addition, early adaptation may lead to a process of *identification with the aggressor*, in which children model themselves and their behavior on those powerful aggressive individuals and groups in their environment that cause the danger in the first place: gangs in the public housing project or enemy soldiers under conditions of occupation.

Children exposed to the stress of extreme violence (such as was the case in Cambodia) may reveal mental health disturbances years after the immediate experience is over (Goleman, 1986). For example, a follow-up study of Cambodian children who experienced the moral and psychological devastation of the Pol Pot regime in the period 1974–1979 revealed that, 4 years after leaving Cambodia, 50% developed PTSD.

Of particular interest for our concerns is that those children who did not reside with a family member were most likely to show this and other psychiatric symptoms (Kinzie, Sack, Angell, Manson, & Rath, 1986). This finding is consistent with the larger body of work exploring the consequences of war for children: Separation from family and destruction of attachment relationships is one of the most important and potentially damaging consequences of war for children (Garbarino, Kostelny, & Dubrow, 1991).

When coupled with political ideology reflecting communal violent conflict, the experience of chronic danger appears to be a primary force serving to generate recruits for participation in terrorist violence (Fields, 1987). More broadly, the experience of chronic danger appears to be associated with truncated moral development in which a "vendetta" mentality predominates.

Fields' research in Northern Ireland and the Middle East revealed children stuck at more primitive stages of moral development at ages when children in less violently conflictual communities had progressed to more advanced moral reasoning (e.g., among 11–14-year-olds in normal social environments, 27% typically respond at the "rational/beneficial/utilitarian" fifth stage in the Tapp-Kohlberg scheme; of the 11–14-year-olds studied in Northern Ireland and Lebanon, almost none did; Fields, 1987).

From what we know of the development of moral reasoning and ego development generally (cf. Loevinger, 1966), the most likely explanation for this difference is one that mixes cultural, temperamental, and social forces. For example, it may be that males and females are inclined to approach moral issues somewhat differently as a function of their characteristically different early experiences, cultural expectations, and perhaps even innately different sensibilities.

This is the basis for Gilligan's (1982) feminist alternative to standard "masculine" approaches to moral development that concentrate on morality as the assertion of objective principles and rights. In her view, such masculine models are too narrowly rational, and disregard the importance of moral reasoning based on empathy and attempts to sustain and repair relationships.

Given that feminine approaches to morality seek, as their primary goal, to minimize hurt, they may provide an important resource for children encountering extreme danger. In such situations, masculine models of asserting rights may lead directly to moral development arrested at the stage of vendetta. Movement beyond vendetta may depend on the social environment stimulating a process of dialogue that can move victimized children and youth to an appreciation of abstract principles that provide an intellectual basis for empathy.

Advanced moral reasoning of the type measured by the Tapp- Kohlberg assessment seems to reflect the degree to which children are supported in engaging in issue-focused discussions and social interactions. These interactions invoke the child's emergent cognitive capacities and stimulate perspective taking and intellectual encounters with values and principles.

More generally, Vygotsky (1986) referred to this process as operating in the *zone of proximal development*, the developmental space between what the child can do alone and what the child can do with the help of a teacher. Developmentalists have come to recognize that it is the dynamic relationship between the child's competence alone and the child's competence in the company of a guiding teacher that leads to forward movement.

This seems particularly important in the case of moral development. The key here is a process of *optimal discrepancy*, in which the child's moral teachers (adults or peers) lead the child toward higher order thinking by presenting positions that are one stage above the child's characteristic mode of responding to social events as moral issues.

When all this happens in the context of a nurturant affective system (e.g., a warm family), the result is ever-advancing moral development, the development of a principled ethic of caring (Gilligan, 1981). What is more, even if the parents create a rigid, noninteractive, authoritarian family context (and thus block moral development), the larger community may compensate: " . . . [T]he child of authoritarian parents may function in a larger more democratic society whose varied patterns provide the requisite experiences for conceptualizing an egalitarian model of distributive justice . . . (Fields, 1987, p. 5).

This becomes problematic, however, when we consider that only a minority of adults ever achieve the highest levels of moral reasoning in the Kohlberg system (or ego development in Loevinger's scheme). Thus, the issue of stimulating moral development beyond the lower levels becomes, in large measure, a social issue: Do adults in the community outside the family (most notably school teachers) demonstrate the higher order moral reasoning necessary to move children from the lower (rational/beneficial/utilitarian) stages to the higher (principled) stages?

This is one reason why ideology is so important to the process of moral development. If school teachers and other adult representatives of the community are disinclined to model higher order moral reasoning or are intimidated if they try to do so, then the process of moral truncation that is "natural" to situations of violent conflict will proceed unimpeded.

This appears to have happened in Northern Ireland, for example, as both Protestant and Catholic teachers learned that if they tried to engage their students in dialogue that could promote higher order moral reasoning they would be silenced by extremist elements (Conroy, 1987). The same prohibition against processing conflict and trauma in educational ways has been observed in other war situations (Garbarino et al. 1991; Rosenblatt, 1983).

Thus, situations of chronic danger *can* stimulate the process of moral development if they are matched by an interactive climate created by adults (and endorsed, or at least not stifled, by the larger culture through its political, educational, and religious institutions) and if the child is free of debilitating psychopathology (e.g., PTSD).

Families can provide the emotional context for the necessary processing to make positive moral sense of danger (and even trauma itself). Usually, it is communities that must carry things to the next step, stimulating higher order moral development. They do this by presenting a democratic milieu, perhaps beginning in schools. However, when danger derives from political conflict in an antidemocratic social context and also occurs in an authoritarian social climate within the family, the result is likely to be the truncated moral reasoning observed by Fields (1987), particularly among boys, who are more vulnerable to this consequence of living at risk, as they are to most other risks (Werner, 1989).

CONCLUSION

War represents a social challenge to children, families, and their communities. We have begun to understand the dynamics of PTSD in victims of war. We have begun to understand, however, that the long-term prognosis for children exposed to war hinges, in large measure, on the ability and motivation of the adult community to be psychologically available to children, to reassure and protect, to clarify and interpret. This joint function is challenging for adults, particularly those who face trauma themselves and often have strong needs to demonize the enemy as a way to justify themselves.

Situations of war and community violence are different from situations in which isolated events temporarily disrupt the social fabric and its ability to justify and rationalize day-to-day life. War and chronic community violence produce "social disaster," in which there is a dramatic and overwhelming destruction of the infrastructure of daily life at precisely the time when children need reliable social structures to reassure them and to offer moral interpretation.

Kai Erikson's (1976) study of an Appalachian community devastated by flood speaks to this point, because the flood went beyond "simple" physical damage and loss of life. It produced a breakdown in the social fabric and created massive adult inability to function. In this case, young children were confronted with vivid and concrete evidence of their vulnerability through the impotence of their community and their parents. Their homes were destroyed, and their parents were demoralized and (apparently) socially powerless: "The major problem, for adults and children alike, is that the fears haunting them are prompted not only by the memory of past terrors but by a wholly realistic assessment of present dangers" (Erikson, 1976, p. 238).

The quality of life for young children — and their reservoirs of resilience — thus becomes a social indicator of the balance of social supports for parents and the parental capacity to buffer social stress in the lives of children (Garbarino & Associates, 1992). This hypothesis emerges from a wide range of research and clinical observation, including Freud and Burlingham's (1943) work with children in England during World War II. It finds validation in other studies of World War II that showed that the level of emotional upset displayed by the adults in a child's life, not the war situation itself, was most important in predicting the child's response (Janis, 1951). It emphasizes the importance of phenomenological considerations in assessing the meaning and impact of "support" for children. Ideology is the public expression of phenomenology, and, as a world view, it figures prominently in successful coping under conditions of extreme danger.

Some observers have pointed to the importance of ideological factors in sustaining the ability to function under extreme stress. In his observations of life in Nazi concentration camps, Bettelheim (1943) noted that those who bore up best were those with intense ideological commitments (most notably the ultrareligious and the communists), commitments that offered meaning impervious to day-to-day brutalization.

Among inner-city Black Americans living in a racist society, and contending with crime-plagued environments, fundamentalist religious groups that offer a political ideology (e.g., the Black Muslims) serve the same function. In the Israeli–Palestinian conflict in the Gaza Strip and West Bank, Muslim fundamentalist groups (e.g., Hamas) may play this role for Palestinians, and extreme Zionist groups may do so for Jewish Israelis.

Support for this interpretation is to be found in a study in Israel reporting that ultra-Orthodox Jews were suffering less from stress as a result of the current Palestinian uprising than were more secular Jews (Pines, 1989). The former tended to see the issue in simplistic ideological terms (e.g., a necessary prelude to fulfilling their Zionist dream of "Greater Israel"), whereas the latter were suffering from the stress of being battered by their consciences as they sought to balance competing loyalties and values (their commitment to a democratic ethic and the ethical imperatives of Judaism, and their concern for national security). One dramatic expression of this conflict is the fact that hundreds of Israeli soldiers have refused, on grounds of conscience, to participate in the military/police activities involved in combatting the Palestinian uprising in the West Bank and Gaza Strip.

On the other side of the conflict, Palestinian Islamic fundamentalists take comfort in *their* extremist ideology, which promises an end to Israel and a return to them of lands they feel were taken by the Israelis in 1948. At the same time, democratic-humanistic Palestinians contend with the stressful moral ambiguities they face as they seek ethically acceptable ways to participate in the nationalist struggle that forces them to find a path that both acknowledges the historical and moral claims of the Zionists and asserts the national rights of Palestinians in an ethically tenable fashion, despite the imbalance of power.

Thus, stress and moral tension are the necessary price one pays for moral sensibility in the midst of extreme conflict. Ideology is a psychological resource, and the more powerful it is as a psychological resource the more it serves to truncate moral development and even be an impediment to political settlement, thereby possibly prolonging the situation of conflict.

This ideological dimension emerges repeatedly in accounts of families under stress. Political and religious interpretation can play an important role in shaping the consequences of experience, particularly when held to with fanatic intensity, which it often must be to defend against the crushing weight of reality in a concentration camp, a prison, or a refugee camp.

Punamaki (1987) saw exactly this process at work in the case of Palestinians under occupation and in refugee camps, where every feature of day-to-day stress and physical deprivation was met with a process of ideological response that mobilizes social and psychological resources.

> . . . [T]he psychological processes of healing the traumatic experiences drew strength from political and ideological commitment. Nationalistic motivation was present at all stages of the stress process: The meaning and harmfulness of an event as well as sufficiency of one's own resources to cope with stressors were approached in the wider social and political context of a victimized and struggling nation. (Punamaki, 1987, pp. 82–83)

The concept of determined struggle to persist (*sumud*) figures prominently in analyses of Palestinian culture and community life (Grossman, 1988), and in the resilience of children in the face of awesome stress, such as was experienced by Palestinian families under siege in the refugee camps in Lebanon (Cutting, 1988). In this, the parallels with Zionism as a sustaining ideology for Jews seeking to create the State of Israel is clear. It finds parallels of a sort in the several nationalist ideological movements among Blacks in the United States (e.g., the Black Panther Party and the Black Muslims).

Punamaki's report goes beyond simple formulations of the buffering model:

> Classical pronouncements that the mother functions as a buffer between traumas of war and the child's well-being assumes new dimensions when it is realized that it leads to an additional stress on the mother. The trend to

concentrate on the mothers' significance as the main determinate of their children's well-being, distorts our understanding of the psychological processes which (sic) are characteristic of a population exposed to political violence. . . . [T]he women's success in retaining their psychological integrity is related to their political and ideological commitment to the national struggle. (p. 83)

Ideology is a resource for adults, and thus may have important consequences for the care that children receive, as well as the interpretation offered to them of the meaning of events.

POSTSCRIPT: THE SPECIAL ROLE OF IDEOLOGY FOR ADOLESCENTS

The role of ideology in situations of war is even more evident in the psychosocial development of adolescents than of younger children, because as development proceeds, they are less and less dependent on the narrow confines of the parent–child relationship. More and more, children live in response to the world beyond their families. Thus, another hypothesis to emerge from a review of the available evidence concerns the role of adolescents as a kind of social weather vane.

The normal issues of adolescence, particularly as they are played out in identity formation, get bound up in the ideological events in the society in which those young people are growing to maturity. We take this for granted as a natural feature of political socialization in normal times and places, where the ideology of youth is normative, in the sense of being consonant with the political institutions that ultimately determine their fate (Coles, 1986). As such, it blends in with the cultural background and may even appear to disappear.

However, when children and youth are involved in struggles in which they are pitted against political institutions (e.g., the movement to end racial segregation in the American South in the 1960s), they participate in a much more articulated ideology and are much more likely to be articulate about it (Coles, 1986).

There is growing recognition among developmental psychologists that where one is developmentally has a lot to do with how and how much historical events in the society and the community influence one's personal development. For example, Stewart and Healy (1989) found that the effects of changed roles for American women during World War II "took" for women who came of age during the war to a larger degree than for their younger or older counterparts. Late adolescence is a time when sociopolitical influences on identity seem particularly powerful.

The openness to social redefinition that accompanies the role changes at the heart of normal adolescence makes adolescents acutely susceptible to the influence of ideology and especially able to make use of that influence as a personal resource and as a source of resilience (Elder, 1980). This is evident over and over again, as young people are the vehicles for social movements.

Social history is important for adolescents, because developmental outcomes for adolescents depend less on the day-to-day character of the infrastructure of families, and more on the ideologically driven activities available in the community and the larger society. It suggests that adolescents encounter social conditions and culture more directly than do young children, and that adolescents incorporate social events into their repertory of "identity alternatives" and then use them as resources as they form a coherent identity in early adulthood (cf. Stewart & Healy, 1989).

Studies of the life course of youth exposed to violent danger support this view in differentiating between the paths followed by criminals from those followed by terrorists. The two groups are similar in their experience with brutalization, but are differentiated by the ideological meanings available to the latter (Fields, 1987).

Although we think of adolescence as a time for focusing on the here and now, on the present, it is the relation of the present to the future that really drives most adolescents (Garbarino & Associates, 1985). In social movements and ideology, they seek to find a path to meaningfulness that fits into individual identity. Thus, one measure—perhaps *the* measure—of a "good society" for adolescents lies in its capacity to provide constructive social movements, movements that assist young people in developing identity without exploiting that need in the pursuit of narrow political or economic interests.

It is a matter for historians, political scientists, and moralists to evaluate the legitimacy of the social movements to which adolescents are attracted. Nonetheless, the psychosocial dynamic seems clear: Ideology plays to identity, and adolescent energy is mobilized through dramatic action that engages the critical process of identity formation.

REFERENCES

American Psychiatric Association. (1987). *Diagnostic and statistical manual of mental disorders* (3rd ed.). Washington, DC: Author.

Bell, C. (1991). Traumatic stress and children in danger. *Journal of Health Care for the Poor and Underserved, 2*(1), 175–188.

Bettelheim, B. (1943). Individual and mass behavior in extreme situations. *Journal of Abnormal and Social Psychology, 38,* 417–452.

Coles, R. (1986). *The political life of children.* Boston: Houghton-Mifflin.

Conroy, J. (1987). *Belfast diary.* Boston: Beacon Press.

Cutting, P. (1988). *Children of the siege.* London: William Heinnemann.

Danieli, Y. (1985). The treatment and prevention of long-term effects and intergenerational transmission of victimization: A lesson from Holocaust survivors and their children. In C. R. Figley (Ed.), *Trauma and its wake*. New York: Brunner/Mazel.

Dubrow, N., & Garbarino, J. (1989). Living in the war zone: Mothers and young children in a public housing project. *Child Welfare, 68*(1), 3–20.

Elder, G. (1980). Adolescence in historical perspective. In J. Adelson (Ed.), *Handbook of adolescent psychology* (pp. 3–46). New York: Wiley.

Elder, G., & Rockwell, R. (1978). Economic depression and post-war opportunity in men's lives: A study of life patterns and health. In R. Simmons (Ed.), *Research in community and mental health* (pp. 240–303). Greenwich, CT: JAI Press.

Erikson, K. (1976). *Everything in its path: Destruction of community in the Buffalo Creek flood*. New York: Simon & Schuster.

Eth, S., & Pynoos, R. (Eds.). (1985). *Posttraumatic stress disorder in children*. Washington, DC: American Psychiatric Association.

Fields, R. (1987, October). *Terrorized into terrorist: Sequelae of PTSD in young victims*. Paper presented at the meeting of the Society for Traumatic Stress Studies, New York.

Freud, A. & Burlingham, D. (1943). *War and children*. New York: Ernest Willard.

Garbarino, J. (1988). Preventing childhood injury: Developmental and mental health issues. *American Journal of Orthopsychiatry, 58*, 25–45.

Garbarino, J., & Associates. (1992). *Children and families in the social environment* (2nd edition). New York: Aldine.

Garbarino, J., & Associates. (1985). *Adolescent development: An ecological perspective*. Columbus, OH: Merrill.

Garbarino, J., Dubrow, N., Kostelny, K., & Pardo, C. (1992). *Children in danger: Coping with the consequences of community violence*. San Francisco: Jossey-Bass.

Garbarino, J., Guttmann, E., & Seeley, J. (1986). *The psychologically battered child*. San Francisco: Jossey-Bass.

Garbarino, J., Kostelny, K., & Dubrow, N. (1991). No place to be a child: Growing up in a war zone. New York: Lexington.

Gilligan, C. (1982). *In a different voice*. Cambridge, MA: Harvard University Press.

Goleman, D. (1986, September 2). Terror's children: Mending mental wounds. *The New York Times*, pp. 15, 19.

Grossman, D. (1988, February 8 & February 15). Report from Israel: The yellow rain. *The New Yorker*, 41; 58.

Janis, I. (1951). *Air war and emotional stress*. New York: McGraw-Hill.

Kinzie, J., Sack, W., Angell, R., Manson, S., & Rath, B. (1986). The psychiatric effects of massive trauma on Cambodian children. *Journal of the American Academy of Child Psychiatry, 25*, 370–376.

Loevinger, J. (1966). *Ego development: Conceptions and theories*. San Francisco: Jossey-Bass.

Losel, F., & Bliesener, T. (1990). Resilience in adolescence: A study on the generalizability of protective factors. In K. Hurrelmann & F. Losel (Eds.), *Health hazards in adolescence* (pp. 299–320). New York: Walter de Gruyter.

Orbach, I. (1988). *Children who don't want to live*. San Francisco: Jossey-Bass.

Pines, R. (1989, January). *Why do Israelis burn out?: The role of the intifada*. Paper presented at the International Conference on Psychological Stress and Adjustment, Tel Aviv, Israel.

Punamaki, R. (1987, April 27). Psychological stress responses of Palestinian mothers and their children in conditions of military occupation and political violence. *The Quarterly Newsletter of the Laboratory of Comparative Human Cognition, 9*, pp. 76–84.

Pynoos, R., & Nader, K. (1988). Psychological first-aid and treatment approach to community violence: Research implications. *Journal of Traumatic Stress Studies, 1*, 445–473.

Rosenblatt, R. (1983). *Children of war*. New York: Doubleday.

Sameroff, A., Seifer, R., Barocas, R., Zax, M., & Greenspan, S. (1987). Intelligence quotient scores for 4-year-old children: Social-environmental risk factors. *Pediatrics, 79,* 343–350.

Scheinfeld, D. (1983). Family relationships and school achievement among boys of lower-income urban Black families. *American Journal of Orthopsychiatry, 53,* 127–143.

Stewart, A., & Healy, J. (1989). Linking individual development and social changes. *American Psychologist, 44,* 30–43.

Terr, L. (1990). *Too scared to cry.* New York: Harper Collins.

UNICEF. (1986). *Children in situations of armed conflict.* New York: Author.

Vygotsky, L. (1986). *Thought and language.* Cambridge, MA: MIT Press.

Wallerstein, J., & Blakeslee, S. (1989). *Second chances: Men, women, and children a decade after divorce.* San Francisco: Ticknor & Fields.

Werner, E. (1990). Protective factors and individual resilience. In S. J. Meisels & J. P. Shonkoff (Eds.), *Handbook of early childhood intervention* (pp. 97–116). Cambridge, England: Cambridge University Press.

3

The Developmental Sequelae of Child Maltreatment: Implications for War-Related Trauma

Dante Cicchetti
Sheree L. Toth
Michael Lynch
Mt. Hope Family Center
University of Rochester

In response to the increased number of clinical and empirical investigations documenting the negative psychological, psychobiological, and psychosocial sequelae that often emerge as reactions to wartime stress (Dubrow & Garbarino, 1989; Garbarino, Kostelny, & Dubrow, 1991; Terr, 1990), the American Psychological Association and the Kent State University Applied Psychology Center convened a task force to address these issues. The goal of this task force was to propose recommendations for prevention and intervention directed toward these stressful reactions and "to develop guidelines for public policymakers, mental health professionals, and those persons directly affected by the stress of war" (Hobfoll et al., 1991, p. 848).

In their report, the task force emphasized that war-related traumatic reactions may occur simultaneously with other stressors (e.g., community violence, persistent poverty, and child maltreatment; cf. Cicchetti & Lynch, 1993) and/or reawaken the negative sequelae associated with earlier traumas. Importantly, the task force delineated an array of symptoms that may characterize *families* that are exposed to war: (a) unresolved conflict, (b) verbal and/or physical violence, (c) isolation among family members, (d) scapegoating of one or more children for family difficulties, (e) extreme dependency and clinging, and (f) discipline and school-related difficulties in the children (Hobfoll et al., 1991). In addition, the task force identified a variety of potential stress reactions that may occur in *individuals* in response to the trauma of war, including: (a) guilt and shame; (b) alcohol and substance abuse; (c) the inability to forget scenes of horror; (d) impairments in concentration; (e) intrusive thoughts; (f) depression, extreme fear, anxiety, and anger; (g) social isolation and withdrawal; (h) emotional blunting; (i) difficulty modulating arousal, especially anger and aggression; (j) excessive physiological startle; (k) dissociative reactions; and (l) suicidal ideations and plans (Hobfoll et al., 1991).

The task force underscored that special attention must be directed toward children who have been exposed to war. Because there are developmental differences in the ways adults and children of varying ontogenetic stages process information and react to the social world (Damon, 1977; Selman, 1980), it is essential that preventive and intervention efforts with children take into account their unique needs and characteristics (Cicchetti, 1990a; Hobfoll et al., 1991).

Unfortunately, despite the burgeoning amount of research on the symptoms and reactions of children exposed to the stresses of war, our knowledge about the direct and indirect effects of war on children's development is sparse. Although statistics on the amount of violence in the United States suggest that children are increasingly growing up in chronically violent environments, relatively little is known about how community violence affects the developmental process (Cicchetti & Lynch, 1993; Richters & Martinez, 1993). Clearly, more research must focus on the direct and indirect effects of growing up in violent environments on children's development.

One body of research that sheds light on how exposure to war might impact upon child development and family functioning is studies on the sequelae of child maltreatment (Cicchetti & Carlson, 1989; Cicchetti & Toth, 1993; Starr & Wolfe, 1991). In this chapter, we apply our knowledge of the developmental consequences of child maltreatment to issues relevant to the effects of war on children. Specifically, we believe that the trauma associated with both of these conditions may result in adverse effects on the ontogenetic process, and that methods of intervention designed to address the negative sequelae of child maltreatment may be modified to provide intervention strategies for children exposed to war.

MULTIFACTORIAL MODELS AND CHILD MALTREATMENT

Rather than relying on the historical emphasis on single etiological factors, such as parental psychopathology, persistent poverty, situational stress, or social isolation, theoreticians and researchers increasingly define the course of child maltreatment as being multifactorial (Belsky, 1980; Cicchetti & Rizley, 1981). Likewise, children's developmental outcomes are viewed as having multiple, interrelated causal factors, rather than as the direct outcome of singular antecedents (Cicchetti & Lynch, 1993; Sameroff & Chandler, 1975). Consequently, an adequate model for conceptualizing the consequences of trauma, whether attributed to maltreatment or war, must be complex and developmental, allowing for multiple pathways to both adaptive and maladaptive outcomes.

Research on normal and abnormal development, conducted within the organizational perspective (Cicchetti, 1990b; Cicchetti & Sroufe, 1978; Sroufe, 1979), has contributed considerably to our knowledge of how maltreatment experiences within the family affect the course of family and individual development. According to theorists who adhere to the organizational perspective, adaptation or competence, as opposed to maladaptation or incompetence, results from the successful resolution of the family and individual tasks most salient for a given developmental period. A hierarchical depiction of adaptation ensues, where the successful resolution of stage-salient issues increases the likelihood of subsequent successful task resolution and adaptive functioning (Sroufe & Rutter, 1984). Because early structures serve as the basis for the evolution of future structures, an early deviation or perturbation in functioning may be an enduring risk factor that causes much more significant disturbances to emerge in the future (Cicchetti, 1990b).

For example, because the multiproblem poor family struggles with multiple stressors and frequent crises, it has been described as having insufficient time to resolve the tasks of each life stage and, therefore, as experiencing increased difficulty in successfully resolving subsequent life stages (Colon, 1981). The overrepresentation of maltreating families among the multiproblem poor may be indicative of the kinds of links that exist between stress and difficulties dealing with these stages effectively. Furthermore, pathological family development can be conceptualized as a failure in hierarchical organization, where individual members have difficulty establishing their autonomy. In this regard, maltreating families are described as *disorganized*, with blurred boundaries between the parental and child subsystems (Boszormenyi-Nagy & Spark, 1973). The failure of parents in the system to initiate and sustain caregiver responsibilities and their propensity for creating role-reversals with their children (Carlson, Cicchetti, Barnett, & Braunwald, 1989) are excellent examples of a failure in hierarchical organization in the maltreating family. A similar breakdown in caregiving might be expected to occur in families grappling with the devastation of war. This can be elucidated through an examination of developmental issues that families encounter.

STAGE-SALIENT ISSUES OF FAMILY DEVELOPMENT

Both families and individuals must address a series of stage-salient issues across the course of development. Because the family's approach to developmentally relevant tasks fosters or impedes the individual child's resolution of individual stage-salient issues, we begin our discussion with family issues. The conceptualization of family tasks is commensurate with the work of family theorists who describe various aspects of the family life cycle (e.g., Erikson, 1950; Wynne, 1984). Most family theorists postulate an epigenetic sequence of family tasks; attempts to bypass any one of these core issues results in developmental impasses and dysfunctions (Wynne, 1984). Moreover, because both family and individual issues are believed to be hierarchically integrated, families who successfully resolve an early issue (e.g., attachment) have a greater likelihood of successfully negotiating subsequent issues (e.g., autonomy).

The following stage-salient issues that are relevant to individual development also can be considered at the family level.

1. *Attachment.* Attachment theory has generally focused primarily on individuals or on dyadic relationships (for exceptions, see Marvin & Stewart, 1990; Stevenson-Hinde, 1990). Just as dyadic relationships strive to achieve a "goal-corrected partnership" (Bowlby, 1969/1982), so, too, do families pursue shared plans and goals. In this regard, theorists have highlighted similarities in individual attachment organizations and family interactional styles. For example, Stevenson-Hinde (1990) noted the resemblances between secure, avoidant, and resistant attachment patterns; and adaptive, disengaged, and enmeshed family patterns.

Descriptions of adaptive, disengaged, and enmeshed families, from a family systems perspective, do not address the historical factors that contribute to the evolution of such systems. Attachment theory provides a framework within which to conceptualize an expanding relational network that is organized around explicit styles of interaction and that ultimately reflects, in relational style, the original family members (i.e., the parents) that set the emotional tone for subsequent family development (Sroufe & Fleeson, 1988).

Using maltreatment as an illustration, we observe role reversal, boundary dissolution, and victimization at the level of the caregiver–child relationship (Carlson et al., 1989; Cicchetti & Barnett, 1991; Crittenden & DiLalla, 1988). Similarly, a family network of relationships exists where the victim--victimizer dynamic pervades relationships and where members may assume either role in various family relations (Main & George, 1985; Troy & Sroufe, 1987). *Victim–victimizer* describes a family role or script for negotiating relationships. For example, the parent may be the victimizer (to the child) and the victim (of the spouse or partner), so the family is characterized by this form of relating. In effect, the family system condones violence and intimidation as a viable strategy (e.g., violence between spouses/partners and between parent and child are highly likely to co-occur; see Straus, Gelles, & Steinmetz, 1980).

The occurrence of such coherence across relationships suggests the existence of shared representational models of relationships among family members (cf. Sroufe & Fleeson, 1988). For example, individual family members generate mental representations of the self and of the self in relation to others, including attachment figures. The research on maltreating families suggests that family members develop shared expectations about themselves and about the safety and stability of the world they live in and the people they encounter (Rieder & Cicchetti, 1989; see also Reiss, 1981, 1989). Their representations of others may include not only dyadic relationships, but also representations of how the family operates as a system (cf. Reiss, 1981, 1989, for notions of family paradigms). As a result, family members may assume interchangeable roles within this system. We hypothesize that maltreating families develop shared expectations about themselves, others, and the world in which they reside (e.g., their communities) as unsafe and unstable (Cicchetti & Lynch, 1993). Similarly, families faced with the chaos, deprivation, and loss accompanying war may develop expectations that become integrated into the family system and affect interactions both among family members, and between those individuals and the broader environment.

2. *Emotion Regulation.* Regulating the emotions of its members is one of the shared goals and developmental tasks that the family system must address. Emotion regulation can be conceptualized at the individual, dyadic, or family level (Cicchetti, Ganiban, & Barnett, 1991).

In general, it appears that maltreating families experience particular problems with the regulation of negative emotions. For example, Burgess and Conger (1978) found that maltreating families display great amounts of conflict and reciprocal negativity. From a family-systems perspective, these results can be reconceptualized as indicative of a failure in family emotion regulation.

Although families living in conditions of war may not necessarily experience difficulties with the inhibition of negative affect, problems with emotion regulation are likely. During times of conflict, families faced with loss or ongoing fear may experience an emotional numbing, thereby decreasing their ability to process emotionally laden material. Conversely, extreme anger reactions might be expected to occur in families that perceive themselves as being victimized by the deprivation of a war-torn environment.

3. *Autonomy.* The development of autonomy is critical to the understanding of multigenerational organization and the adaptation of family members. The success of negotiating attachment and emotion-regulation issues is critical in predicting subsequent success in the emergence of autonomy.

Because maltreating family environments frequently have failed to foster the successful resolution of attachment and emotion regulation, the maladaptive interactional styles already present are also likely to impede autonomy. In a maltreating family, chaos, neediness, and poorly differentiated boundaries among family members contribute to the family's inability to foster autonomy among its members.

Similar difficulties may occur in families struggling with the emotional devastation of war. In these cases, parents may turn to their children for comfort. This may be especially likely to occur if a spousal partner becomes emotionally or physically unavailable, either through war-related trauma or service-related absences. Just as some instances of maltreatment result in child parentification, so, too, may the environments of war lead to poor parent–child differentiation and to the child's assumption of caregiving responsibilities.

On a broader level, family incompetence in fostering autonomy may contribute to the ontogenesis of multigenerational family systems without a clear hierarchy. Furthermore, family failures around the issue of autonomy may result in poorly developed individuals destined to try to solve their autonomy issues in subsequent relationships with mates and with children. This state of affairs may result in the cross-generational transmission of incompetence in fostering autonomy. In times of war, similar dissolution of family boundaries may occur as historically disparate generations are drawn into closer proximity because of either economic or emotional needs.

4. *Competence at school and work.* In order to gain competence, individuals must develop both intrafamilial relationships and relationships external to the family. Typically, this occurs in arenas involving task performance at school and work (Cicchetti, 1989). For successful adaptation to occur, families must encourage individual members to develop networks outside the home environment. In particular, the successful resolution of the family task of fostering peer, school, and work competence is reflective of a major transition out of the nuclear family and into a broader social network. Although all stage-salient family issues reflect developmental transitions, prior ones require reorganizations within the family. The facilitation of competence at school and work ushers in a whole new array of possibilities for the occurrence of reorganization outside of the family context. However, intrafamilial support is important if one is to seize the opportunities successfully.

Because war is likely to disrupt family functioning, the ability of family members to promote extrafamilial mastery experiences may be stultified. During times of war, families are likely to have fewer material and psychological resources, and their ability to devote their energies toward facilitating the involvement of members in competence-promoting endeavors at school or work is likely to lessen. Although empirical evidence is lacking, it is possible that families may withdraw from the broader social environment during periods of war, thereby decreasing the involvement of family members in arenas outside of the home.

Having explored the effects of maltreatment on family adaptation and, where possible, drawn parallels to the effects of war on family functioning, we turn our attention toward the resolution of individual tasks of development and the effects that the trauma of child maltreatment have been shown to exert on the ontogenetic process. Again, we are not suggesting invariant pathways to adaptation or maladaptation, but are articulating links between the literature on the sequelae of maltreatment and the possible adverse effects of war.

STAGE-SALIENT ISSUES OF INDIVIDUAL DEVELOPMENT

As with our formulation of family functioning, we see individual ontogenesis as consisting of an unfolding series of age- and stage-appropriate tasks that remain critical to the child's adaptation throughout the life span. As new tasks emerge, old issues may decrease in relative salience. Nonetheless, each issue requires continued coordination with and integration into the child's adaptation to the environment and to the stage-salient developmental issue of the period. These issues of development include: affect regulation, attachment, the development of an autonomous self, and peer relations/school adaptation.

1. *Affect regulation.* We define affect regulation as the intra- and extra-organismic factors by which emotional arousal is redirected, controlled, modulated, and modified to enable an individual to function adaptively in emotionally arousing situations. Affect regulation helps maintain internal arousal within a manageable, performance-optimizing range. Whereas emotions mediate a person's adaptive functioning by providing crucial information to the self and others about internal states, affect- regulatory systems are essential if the individual is to maintain a tolerable but flexible range of affective expressions necessary for adaptive functioning across the life span. Feedback components of the emotion system also serve a critical role in the development of self-evaluation and self-regulation.

In the maltreatment literature, abnormalities in the development of affective communication between maltreated infants and their caregivers have also been identified (Gaensbauer, Mrazek, & Harmon, 1980). These investigations have revealed four affective patterns that appear to represent the predominant mode of communication between maltreating mothers and their babies: (a) *affectively retarded*, characterized by lack of social responsiveness, emotional blunting, and inattentiveness to the environment;

(b) *depressed*, exhibiting inhibition, withdrawal, aimless play, and sad and depressed facial expressions; (c) *ambivalent/affectively labile*, showing sudden shifts from engagement and pleasure to withdrawal and anger; and (d) *angry*, manifesting active, disorganized play and low frustration tolerance, with frequent angry outbursts.

In further explorations of the development of affect in maltreated youngsters, Gaensbauer (1980, 1982) reported observations of a 4-month-old physically abused infant. Detailed codings of this infant's facial expressions revealed the precocious appearance of a number of negative affects, including fear. These findings are in striking contrast to those reported for nonabused babies. Fear, for example, does not normally emerge until approximately 8–9 months of age (Sroufe, 1979). Thus, it is conceivable that early maltreatment experiences may accelerate the development of fear in infancy.

Although very young babies are unlikely to possess the cognitive sophistication necessary to process fear-inducing stimuli during war, they certainly are likely to experience the heightened stress and vigilance of their caregivers. Therefore, it is possible that parental anxiety and safety concerns may act to accelerate the development of fear in infants exposed to war in a manner similar to the effects of fear-inducing situations on maltreated children. Fear reactions may also emerge at an accelerated rate simply because infants in conditions of war may be exposed to frightening events.

The role that fear plays in eliciting patterns of affective communication, as well as the impact that its early emergence may have on the infant suggests that there may be a severe impairment in the regulation and organization of affect in maltreated youngsters. In fact, maltreated children exhibit a profile of symptoms similar to that of individuals suffering from chronic stress, including anxiety, low tolerance to stress, depression, and helplessness (Kazdin, Moser, Colbus, & Bell, 1985; Toth, Manly, & Cicchetti, 1992; Wolfe, 1985). The chronic stress of war may result in a similar form of dysfunction. The loss of the attachment figure as a secure base and haven of safety, whether through maltreatment or war, is a devastating psychological insult that may lead to long-term psychobiological impairment such as those found in posttraumatic stress disorder (PTSD; van der Kolk, 1987).

In addition to these findings with infants, physically abused children manifest the later vestiges of these early affect- regulatory problems in the coping patterns they evidence when they are exposed to inter-adult anger. For example, physically abused boys who witnessed an angry simulated live laboratory interaction directed at their mothers by an adult female, evidenced greater aggressiveness and more coping responses aimed at alleviating the distress of their mothers than did nonabused boys (Cummings, Hennessy, Rabideau, & Cicchetti, 1992). Rather than habituating to others' hostility as a result of their history of exposure to familial violence, these abused children appeared more aroused and angered by it, and more motivated to intervene. Moreover, because level of arousal is related to one's subsequent propensity for aggressive behavior (Cummings & Zahn-Waxler, in press), hypervigilance and arousal in response to aggressive stimuli among abused children could contribute to the development of aggressive patterns, particularly if conflict in the home is chronic.

In a related study, Hennessy, Rabideau, Cicchetti, and Cummings (1992) presented physically abused children with videotaped segments of adults in angry and friendly interactions and asked children questions about their responses following each episode. Abused children reported greater distress than nonabused children in response to various forms of inter-adult anger, particularly in response to anger that was unresolved between adults. Physically abused children reported greater fear in response to different forms of angry adult behavior. Similar to the findings reported by Cummings et al. (1992), these results support a sensitization model whereby repeated exposure to anger and familial violence leads to greater emotional reactivity. Likewise, the distress responses to different forms of inter-adult anger exhibited by the abused children in this study may provide an early indication of the potential for developing internalizing problems in children exposed to high levels of familial violence (cf. Kazdin et al., 1985; Toth et al., 1992).

These patterns of affective interactions and expectations impact on how maltreated children's affect regulation continues to differentiate with development. The internal, experiential components of affect become divorced from the outward expressions of affect, allowing for the adoption of specific affect-regulatory strategies consistent with the qualities of the child's environment. Thus, affect regulation may also play a role in the disorganization found in maltreated children's attachment relationships. (Disorganized and disoriented attachments are described further on.)

Finally, we see some of the coping skills that maltreated children acquire in the types of cognitive control functioning that they use in the service of affect regulation. Rieder and Cicchetti (1989) found that maltreated children were more hypervigilant to aggressive stimuli and recalled a greater number of distracting aggressive stimuli than did nonmaltreated children. Maltreated children also assimilated aggressive stimuli more readily, even though this may result in less cognitive efficiency and impaired task performance. Hypervigilance and ready assimilation of aggressive stimuli may have developed originally as an adaptive coping strategy in the maltreating environment, alerting the child to signs of imminent danger and keeping affects from rising so high that they would incapacitate the child. This strategy may also help the child to identify specific elements of the current situation that will help determine the most adaptive response. However, this response pattern becomes less adaptive when the child is faced with nonthreatening situations, and may even undermine the child's ability to function adaptively under normal circumstances.

We believe that the hypervigilance, increased sensitivity, and tendency to try to de-intensify angry situations observed in maltreated children might also be present in children exposed to war. Although they do not necessarily experience intrafamilial threat, the children of war may directly witness acts of extreme aggression that sensitize them to potential violence. In the most severe conditions, children may experience PTSD. However, even less traumatic situations involving the constant threat of violence may heighten anxiety, impair performance, and lead to the development of coping strategies that are atypical and, in the long run, maladaptive.

2. *Attachment.* Although the capacity for attachment originates during early affect-regulation experiences and interactions with the primary care-givers, overt manifestations reach ascendancy near the end of the first year of life, when the infant learns to coordinate a broad variety of behavioral responses into an adaptive and flexible repertoire of goal-corrected re-sponses (Sroufe, 1979). Dyadic interactions, marked by relatedness and synchrony, resilience to stress, and appropriate affective interchange, are associated with successful adaptation during this stage. The knowledge that a caregiver is reliable and responsive is also critical, because inadequate response-contingent stimulation is likely to exert a negative impact on the infant's ability to develop a secure attachment relationship (Sroufe & Waters, 1977).

Although maltreated children clearly do form attachments, the main issues with which we are concerned relate to the quality of their attachments and the nature of their internal representational models of their attachment figures, the self, and the self in relation to others. Children form represen-tational models of attachment figures, of themselves, and of themselves in relation to others based on their relationship history with their primary caregiver (Bowlby, 1969/1982). Through these models, children's affects, cognitions, and expectations about future interactions are organized and carried forward into subsequent relationships (Sroufe & Fleeson, 1988).

Several studies have shown that the attachments maltreated children form with their caregivers are more likely to be insecure than those of nonmal-treated children (Crittenden, 1988; Egeland & Sroufe, 1981; Schneider-Rosen, Braunwald, Carlson, & Cicchetti, 1985). Moreover, a number of investigators have observed patterns of behavior in the assessment of maltreated children's attachments using the Strange Situation, a standard-ized series of infant–mother separations and reunions covering eight 3-minute episodes in a laboratory playroom (Ainsworth & Wittig, 1969), that did not fit smoothly into the traditional classification scheme. For example, Main and Solomon (1990) noticed some unusual patterns of attachment behavior in their observations of samples of maltreated children from laboratories around the country. They found a combination of moderate-to-high proximity seeking, moderate-to-high avoidance, and moderate-to-high resistance in many of their maltreated children. Unlike the secure (Type B), anxious avoidant (Type A), and anxious resistant (Type C) children, these children consistently lacked organized strategies for dealing with stressful separations from and reunions with their caregivers. Main and Solomon described this pattern of attachment as "disorganized/disoriented" (Type D). These children also displayed other bizarre symptoms in the presence of their caregivers, such as interrupted movements and expressions, freezing and stilling behaviors, and apprehension.

Recent investigations of attachment in maltreated infants and toddlers indicate a preponderance of atypical attachment patterns in maltreated children. Carlson et al. (1989) found that over 80% of the maltreated infants in their study had atypical, disorganized/disoriented attachments compared with less than 20% of a demographically similar nonmaltreated comparison group. Likewise, Crittenden (1988) found that most maltreated children could be classified as having avoidant-resistant (A/C) patterns of attachment. Recently, there have been findings of substantial stability in one of the forms of atypical attachment across the ages of 12, 18, and 24 months. Barnett, Ganiban, and Cicchetti (1992) found that approximately 60% of the infants who were classified as D at 12 months had the same classification at 24 months, whereas over 90% of the infants classified as D at 24 months had previously received the D classification.

As children grow older, the likelihood that they will have one of these atypical patterns of attachment seems to decrease. In an investigation of the attachments of maltreated preschool children of different ages (Cicchetti & Barnett, 1991), 30-month-old children who had been maltreated were significantly more likely to have atypical patterns of attachment (D or A/C) than were nonmaltreated children. However, although approximately one third of the 36- and 48-month-old maltreated children were classified as having either Type D or A/C attachments, this was not significantly greater than the proportion of nonmaltreated children who had such atypical attachment patterns. Along these lines, Lynch and Cicchetti (1991) found that approximately 30% of maltreated children between the ages of 7 and 13 years described "confused" patterns of relatedness to their mothers, in which they reported not feeling close to their mothers despite feeling warm and secure with them. This finding suggests that distortions in maltreated children's relationships with and mental representations of their caregivers may persist at least through the preadolescent years, although at lower rates than found in infancy.

The findings on the prevalence and stability of insecure and atypical attachments in maltreated children point to the extreme risk these children face in achieving adaptive outcomes in other domains of interpersonal relationships. Internal representational models of these insecure and often atypical attachments, with their complementary models of self and other, may generalize to new relationships, leading to negative expectations of how others will behave and how successful the self will be in relation to others. For example, it is believed that the insecurity and disorganization found in many maltreated children's attachments are the result of the inconsistent care and the fear that are common elements of being maltreated (Carlson et al., 1989). If maltreated children's representational models of self and others reflect insecurity and fear, and if these models are generalized to new relationships, then maltreated children may enter relationships with negative expectations that lead to the same type of approach/avoidance conflicts that are seen in their attachment relationships, resulting in maladaptive patterns of relating with their new partners.

It is certainly possible that insecure attachment relationships between caregivers and parents occur during times of war, especially in view of the findings regarding the effects of psychologically unavailable caregivers on the development of insecure attachment relations (Cummings & Cicchetti, 1990). Because parents may be traumatized and overwhelmed, their ability to consistently meet the needs of a young child may be compromised. If, in fact, an insecure attachment does develop, the child is at risk for future relationship failure. Likewise, chronic exposure to the stresses of war, both directly and indirectly (via its impact on parents), may accelerate the development of fear and increase the likelihood that disorganized patterns of attachment will emerge.

3. *The development of an autonomous self.* As issues of body management begin to emerge from the context of the caregiver–infant relationship into the realm of autonomous function, the toddler becomes increasingly invested in self-managing due to new cognitive, emotional, representational, and motor abilities, as well as his or her more sophisticated notions about self and others. The caregiver's sensitivity and ability to tolerate the toddler's strivings for autonomy, as well as the ability to set age-appropriate limits, are integral to the successful resolution of this issue. Caregivers who feel rejected as a result of the toddler's increasing independence, or overwhelmed by their actively initiated demands, may inhibit the emergence of age-appropriate autonomy.

A number of aspects of the self-development of maltreated children have implications for their interpersonal relationships as the result of inner self-organizations being brought forward into new social contexts. Although maltreated infants show no deficits in their ability to recognize their rouge-marked selves in a mirror, they are more likely than nonmaltreated infants to display neutral or negative affect on visual self-recognition

(Schneider-Rosen & Cicchetti, 1984, 1991). In addition, maltreated children talk less about themselves and produce less internal state language than do nonmaltreated children (Cicchetti & Beeghly, 1987). Maltreated children's negative feelings about themselves and their inability to talk about their own activities and feelings may pose one set of obstacles to their being able to engage in successful social interaction. In particular, maltreated children appear to be most resistant to talking about their negative internal states (Cicchetti & Beeghly, 1987). This finding is corroborated by reports that maltreated children may actually inhibit negative affect, especially in the context of the relationship with their caregivers (Crittenden & DiLalla, 1988; Lynch & Cicchetti, 1991). Maltreated children may adopt a strategy of suppressing their own negative feelings to avoid eliciting adverse responses from their caregivers (Cicchetti, 1991). Although this approach may be adaptive in the context of a maltreating relationship, it can become maladaptive in other interpersonal contexts. For example, frustrated and upset children who are not willing or able to communicate what is bothering them can pose a serious challenge to a teacher trying to manage a classroom full of children.

Exposure to the school setting may impact on maltreated children's sense of self in a way that is reflected in their relationships with others. Young maltreated children express an exaggerated sense of self-competence in comparison with non-maltreated children (Vondra, Barnett, & Cicchetti, 1989). By the age of 8–9 years, though, maltreated children perceive themselves as less competent than do nonmaltreated children. Teachers' ratings of the children's competence indicate that these older children's perceptions are more accurate and in accord with their own ratings. Initially, young maltreated children's inflated sense of self may help them to gain feelings of competence in the midst of family relationships that are chaotic and uncontrollable. However, as maltreated children develop and are forced to make social comparisons of themselves to others, they begin to make more negative (and accurate) self-appraisals. These negative appraisals are probably internalized in their self-representations. Feeling less competent in comparison with others again may impact on their ability to interact successfully with others.

Thus, maltreated children display major difficulties in autonomy and self–other differentiation (Cicchetti, 1990b). Moreover, because maltreated children may assume the role of caregiver in their attachment relationships with their parents, they may be more effective at taking care of others than they are of themselves. The data on internal state language also suggest that maltreated children have difficulty recognizing their own needs (Cicchetti & Beeghly, 1987). Consequently, maltreated children may have trouble being alone, thereby exacerbating and contributing to their problems in self–other differentiation (Cicchetti, 1991).

Although the mechanisms through which the interference with autonomy originates are likely to differ for maltreating parents and those struggling with the stress of war, difficulties encouraging toddler autonomy may be present in the latter, as well. This may be due to increased emotional dependency and resulting parent–child enmeshment. Moreover, legitimate concerns about child safety in an unpredictable environment may result in overprotectiveness and discouragement of increased independence. Because the resolution of issues related to separation and individuation is central to future adaptation, the potentially adverse effects of war on this stage-salient task have significant implications for the emergence of future psychopathology.

4. *Peer relations and adaptation to school.* Because of their frequently negative relationship histories, peer relationships and friendships may play an important role in promoting positive adaptation in maltreated children. Unfortunately, maltreated children's relationships with their peers typically mirror maladaptive representational models at home. The inner organization of their models of self and others, which has its origin in the context of atypical relationships with primary caregivers, proves to be dysfunctional when applied to the task of interacting competently with peers. Maltreated children generally exhibit more disturbed patterns of interaction with peers than do nonmaltreated children. On the one hand, maltreated children, especially those who were physically abused, tend to show heightened levels of physical and verbal aggression in their interactions with peers (George & Main, 1979; Kaufman & Cicchetti, 1989). Conversely, one also sees elevated levels of withdrawal from and avoidance of peer interactions in maltreated children, especially in those who have been neglected (George & Main, 1979; Howes & Espinosa, 1985). Consistent with Sroufe and Fleeson's (1988) relationship principles, this profile of avoidance of interaction and increased aggressiveness with peers supports the premise that maltreated children may internalize both sides of their relationship with their caregivers, including the roles of both victim and victimizer (Main & George, 1985; Troy & Sroufe, 1987).

Integration into the peer group, acceptable performance in the classroom, and appropriate motivational orientations for achievement are all part of the task of successful adaptation to school. Once again, however, maltreated children appear to be at risk for an unsuccessful resolution of this issue of development. Eckenrode and Laird (1991) reported that maltreated children perform lower on standardized tests and obtain worse grades than nonmaltreated children do, and receive more referrals and suspensions for discipline problems. Other investigators have found that maltreated children are dependent on their teachers (Egeland, Sroufe, & Erickson, 1983), score lower on tests measuring cognitive maturity (perhaps due to motivational causes; Barahal, Waterman, & Martin, 1981), and are rated by both parents and teachers as less ready to learn in school (Hoffman-Plotkin & Twentyman, 1984).

An especially important factor in resolving the task of adaptation to school may be secure readiness to learn. Aber and Allen (1987) proposed that *effectance motivation*, which is the intrinsic desire to deal competently with one's environment, and successful relations with novel adults (i.e., relations that are characterized by neither dependency nor wariness) are important components of children's ability to adapt to their first major out-of-home environment. Secure readiness to learn is characterized by high effectance motivation and low dependency. Maltreated children consistently score lower than comparison groups of children on a secure readiness to learn factor (Aber & Allen, 1987; Aber, Allen, Carlson, & Cicchetti, 1989). Secure readiness to learn appears to represent a dynamic balance between establishing secure relationships with adults and feeling free to explore the environment in ways that will promote cognitive competence. The findings of Aber and his colleagues are particularly compelling, because they are congruent with prior research on how maltreatment affects infants' and toddlers' development. At both of these developmental stages, maltreatment interferes with the balance between the motivation to establish secure relationships with adults and the motivation to explore the world in competency-promoting ways.

Because war is likely to disrupt the school environment, in extreme war situations, schools may be unavailable. Even in less adverse situations, teachers, individuals who often serve as alternate attachment figures for children, may be less affectively available. Thus, the opportunity for mastery experiences, as well as the possible protective effects available in the establishment of a positive extrafamilial relationship (Masten & Garmezy, 1985), may be adversely affected.

INTERVENTION

Research on the multiple determinants of child maltreatment and its sequelae, as well as the parallels drawn between maltreatment and exposure to war, underscore the need for comprehensive systems of service delivery to parents and children faced with traumatic circumstances. Although we do not believe that all children exposed to war will experience trauma-related difficulties, we do think that the similarities between victims of maltreatment and children exposed to war suggest that these children are at risk for the emergence of difficulties. Interestingly, just as child maltreatment is a heterogenous construct that may vary in consequences as a result of factors such as chronicity, severity, and alternate supports available to the child, so, too, is war likely to span a range of severity. For example, how might an Israeli child, faced with a chronic threat of war, differ from a Kuwaiti child exposed to an intense, but relatively short-term war? Similarly, how might a child whose family fled prior to the outbreak of war differ from a child who remains in a war-torn environment? Questions such as these await empirical investigation. However, based on the paucity of research directly addressing issues such as these, we discuss here intervention strategies that could prove to be useful in the prevention and amelioration of war-related sequelae.

In their discussion of the special needs of children, the task force on war-related stress developed a list of suggestions for helping children to cope effectively with war (Hobfoll et al., 1991). The role of significant adults as supports was emphasized, and the importance of nonjudgmentally listening to children's fears and providing emotional support was stressed. In this regard, caregivers were encouraged to seek help in dealing with their own fears and not burdening their children. Additional suggestions included providing children with accurate, developmentally appropriate information and involving them in helping activities to facilitate their sense of mastery and control over their surroundings (Hobfoll et al., 1991). Suggestions such as these require a comprehensive plan of intervention.

Multiple trauma-related risk factors, rather than any single component of a complex problem network, must be addressed. In fact, the comprehensive intervention systems developed for addressing the needs of multiproblem families (Fraiberg, 1980; Greenspan, 1987; Olds & Henderson, 1989) can also be applied to the needs of those exposed to war. One such model, developed by Greenspan (1987), contains the following elements: (a) responsiveness to basic survival needs, such as clothing, food, and shelter; (b) efforts to meet both parental and child needs for a trusting relationship; (c) clinical techniques sensitive to issues of child development that focus on critical developmental tasks; and (d) single-site provision of child care and parental support services. Conceptualized as a "service pyramid," this mode of service delivery optimally incorporates a whole range of hierarchical intervention services, ranging from attention to basic survival needs to provision of more sophisticated therapeutic services. Because families faced with multiple stressors are likely to experience difficulty utilizing traditional service delivery systems, the provision of multiple services by a single system is of the utmost importance. A consolidation of services decreases the confusion that results when a stressed family is forced to negotiate an array of poorly organized community services and agencies. At the same time, services can be responsive to the broad array of ecological needs and stressors emanating from parents, children, the extrafamilial social system, and economic and cultural factors.

As with prevention and intervention efforts for child maltreatment, addressing the sequelae associated with war requires a complex and comprehensive approach: Remediation efforts must be directed toward the child, as well as the family and the child's broader living situation. A transactional developmental model, which suggests a "Process–Person–Context" mode of intervention (Bronfenbrenner & Crouter, 1983) is applicable. According to the transactional model, attention needs to be directed toward the context in which a child is developing; the constitutional, biological, and psychological characteristics of the child and of the caregiver(s); and the transactional processes through which development is occurring (Cicchetti & Aber, 1986; Cicchetti & Rizley, 1981). The developmental level of the child is a major determining factor in the intervention process, because it helps define the nature of intervention. Interventions must reflect developmental changes, so techniques need to vary in accordance with each child's developmental level. Moreover, multiple domains of development need to be considered. When considering prevention or intervention for children exposed to war, we believe broad-based approaches that attend to multiple domains of individual and family development are necessary.

To apply a transactional model to the development of intervention strategies, one must first consider the specific risk factors present in war. Risk factors can be classified into two basic categories: *potentiating factors*, which increase the probability that maladaptation will occur; and *compensatory factors*, which decrease the probability of maladaptation occurring (Cicchetti & Rizley, 1981). These factors can be either transient or enduring. Within the area of potentiating influences, *vulnerability* factors include relatively enduring characteristics of the child, family, and environment, while *challengers* include more transient factors. Likewise, compensatory influences include relatively stable *protective* factors and more transient *buffers*.

When designing a prevention or intervention program, it is important to assess the status of the elements included in this model in order to identify mechanisms whereby potentiating factors can be decreased and compensatory factors bolstered. Utilization of these naturally occurring resources, in conjunction with recognition of the liabilities that are present, can greatly enhance the effectiveness of intervention efforts (Cicchetti & Toth, 1987). In accordance with the transactional model, potentiating and compensatory factors must be assessed in relation to individual, familial, social, and environmental contexts (Cicchetti & Aber, 1986). Moreover, attention must be directed toward the facilitation of competence on those stage-salient tasks that may be adversely affected in children exposed to war. Because research has shown the deleterious effects of untreated maltreatment, the importance of providing services directed toward the amelioration of possible consequences of war is underscored.

MT. HOPE FAMILY CENTER: A MODEL OF
INTERVENTION

Before moving directly to suggestions for preventing and addressing the sequelae of war, we present a developmentally driven model of prevention designed for maltreated and economically disadvantaged children. This model is utilized at the Mt. Hope Family Center of the University of Rochester, where efforts have been directed toward integrating an ecological/transactional model of the etiology of maltreatment with the development of an intervention model for high-risk and maltreating families.

Intervention with maltreating families in general has proven to be extremely challenging due to the multiple risk factors involved, and service providers have often failed in their efforts to help these families deal with the chaos of their lives. Poverty, intellectual and educational limitations, social isolation, and psychiatric disturbances are but a few of the factors that make these families so difficult to engage in a productive treatment process. Consequently, an ecological and transactional model of intervention that considers multiple risk factors and multiple targets for intervention has been adopted at the Mt. Hope Family Center.

The Mt. Hope Family Center was established in 1979 for the prevention of child maltreatment. More recently, the Center has evolved into a facility that also provides preventive interventions for children considered to be at risk more generally for the occurrence of future emotional disturbances (e.g., children with a depressed parent, extremely disadvantaged children). A multidisciplinary approach, employing the expertise of social workers, special educators, speech therapists, and psychologists, is utilized in the effort to address the complexities associated with child maltreatment. At the Center, therapeutic preschool services are provided for children between the ages of 3 and 5 years. Individual and group psychotherapy are offered to children and parents, and families also participate in a home-based component. Attention to the concrete needs of these families through the provision of transportation, childcare, and facilitation of contacts with agencies providing food, clothing, and shelter, is integral to the success of our intervention program.

Families seen at the Center for issues related to maltreatment often enter into treatment with markedly resistant attitudes. Services have frequently been legally mandated, and parents have been threatened with removal of their children unless they comply with program requirements. Understandably, establishing a therapeutic alliance under these conditions can be extremely difficult. Development of a trusting therapeutic relationship requires persistent outreach efforts tailored to specific family needs. Only then is it possible to promote interpersonal trust and attend to psychotherapeutic issues. Often, however, intervention never progresses beyond an initial supportive function: The therapist assists parents in modifying their caregiving style, provides support in times of crisis, and encourages them in developing supportive social networks. Unfortunately, in these cases, parental improvement persists only as long as this external support is provided, and change is not internalized.

Given these circumstances, efforts are underway to establish the Mt. Hope Family Center as a "Life Center" that can provide ongoing support to families at critical junctures. We consider this to be especially important with multirisk families, who are extremely cautious in developing trust, but also very reluctant to disengage once trust has been established. Because disruptions in the therapeutic process can be devastating to the functioning of these families, we believe that a long-term service orientation and delivery system will improve the efficacy of intervention.

Briefly, the Mt. Hope Family Center seeks to be responsive to the multiple needs of both maltreated children and their families by providing a comprehensive array of interventions within a consolidated service delivery system. Although this goal poses an impressive array of challenges, the maltreatment literature to date suggests that it is the most efficacious approach to use with these multirisk, multiproblem families.

Two programs offered at Mt. Hope Family Center that may be especially relevant to the needs of children exposed to war are the After School and Summer Camp Programs. Both of these programs are designed to reach large numbers of children who face similar challenges and stressors. Although not designed as an intensive model of intervention, the After School Program is a preventive program that builds on peer interaction and sharing, and the facilitation of improved coping and problem-solving skills.

After School and Camp

Approximately 100 children between the ages of 6 and 12 years attend sessions of the After School Program for one afternoon each week throughout the course of the school year. Transportation to and from the Center is provided. Children are organized into groups of 8, and each group is supervised by three adult counselors. Although the orientation of the program revolves around a small-group approach, the high adult-to-child ratio allows for a significant amount of individual attention to be given to the children. The groups remain intact throughout the school year, and they form the basis for a consistent network of relationships. Informed by attachment theory and the knowledge that most maltreated children develop insecure attachments, one of the primary goals of the After School Program is to provide the children with some alternative experiences of positive relationships. Because many of the relationship histories of children attending the program are characterized by inconsistency, unavailability, and lack of warmth, the program strives to provide the children with stable supportive relationships with counselors and peers in the hope of beginning to alter the children's representational models of interpersonal relationships. Much of this relationship building occurs in the context of recreational games and activities supervised by the staff. In addition, each week the groups are given short lessons that comprise an informal curriculum designed to address issues relevant to the social problem-solving needs of this population. Topics for discussion or group projects involve decision making regarding drugs, multicultural awareness, understanding the role of feelings in relationships, and nonviolent conflict resolution.

Parenting groups are provided as a component of the After School Program. Parents of the children attending the program are invited to participate in discussion groups that meet twice each month and are facilitated by a social worker. These groups provide parents with a supportive environment in which to discuss the stresses they experience as parents, while at the same time offering constructive suggestions and feedback. By targeting both children and parents through services that seek to increase coping and problem-solving skills, we have a greater opportunity to improve the quality of parent–child interaction, and thus to avoid some of the negative sequelae for which these children are at risk. This type of parent–child approach may also be applicable to family systems that are experiencing stresses associated with war.

Consistent with our belief in providing ongoing support to children and their families, each summer approximately 250 children participate in a Summer Camp Program. Each child attends one of the week-long session of camp. Several features of the camp are tailored to meet the needs of the families with which we work. Because most of the families involved are on welfare and do not have the financial means to send their children to a summer camp, the camp is free of charge. Additionally, transportation, snacks, and lunch are provided for all children. Children are invited to attend camp annually, thereby promoting a belief in the reliability and consistency of relationships. Although each summer experience is relatively short, many of the participants have formed significant relationships that have become a source of stability and security for children whose interpersonal lives are chaotic and unpredictable. Again, during time of war, the provision of easily attainable services to families that may be materially devastated is an important consideration. A long-term approach, with annual (or more frequent) contacts, may also help to increase the children's sense of predictability and well-being.

Thus, principles of the After School and Summer Camp Programs can be directed toward the development of a preventive program for children exposed to war. Specifically, a small-group format that provides a forum for social support and supplemental caregivers may help alleviate the possible sequelae of war on development. Additionally, providing parents with a support system and with information on how to meet the needs of their children during periods of stress holds promise for minimizing subsequent difficulties.

INTERVENTIONS FOR CHILDREN EXPOSED TO WAR

Prevention

Prevention and early intervention are especially important in dealing with the possible effects associated with exposure to war. Attention must also be directed toward facilitating positive parent–child interactions, and, when possible, the environment must be modified so as to increase the child's perceptions of safety and security.

Ideally, efforts to prevent the adverse effects of war should occur during the conflict itself. Although meeting such needs during periods of war is certainly challenging, mental health providers must be prepared to pool their resources quickly and reach out into the community. The provision of support groups for adults could alleviate stress and serve as a source of stability during an otherwise uncertain time. Increasing the support available for the adult members of the community improves their ability to continue to provide support for and be emotionally available to the children of the community. One valuable avenue of prevention might be the formation of support groups for parents that address issues relevant to caregiving and discussions of how best to address the fears of their children. Helping parents in this way to continue to be responsive to the needs of their children will lessen the potential for insecure attachments in infants and toddlers.

Children exposed to war clearly benefit by efforts that support their parents caregiving roles, but they also benefit from forums developed for them specifically. Both the After School and Summer Camp Programs could serve as models for such forums. Specifically, schools might develop programs where children could express their fears and gain support directly. A small-group format, such as that used in the Mt. Hope Family Center programs, would enable children to establish a peer support network and realize that they are not alone in their experience of fear and trauma.

If efforts such as these are undertaken, failure on the stage-salient issues and the emergence of future dysfunction may be prevented. In accord with the transactional model, the provision of environmental supports to alleviate parental stress is a necessary component of a prevention model. Additionally, the availability of caregiving supplements for children through their participation in community- or school-based support groups provides respite for stressed parents and enables children to establish alternate caregiving models through their interactions with teachers and counselors. This is likely to be especially important if war has resulted in the loss of a parent, or if a parent is too overwhelmed to be able to meet his or her child's needs. Because exposure to nonparental adult attachment figures, such as teachers or counselors, may foster the use of representational models derived from specific positive interactional histories rather than from generalized negative interactional histories, the adverse effects of an overwhelmed or unavailable parent could be minimized (Lynch & Cicchetti, 1992).

Treatment

Even with the availability of supports during war, it is naïve to assume that all adverse effects can be prevented. After the conflict ends, interventions must continue to be made available.

Again, the provision of support groups for adults and children is an ideal outlet for beginning to process and share trauma-related fears. Involving parents in formal or informal "helping networks" that strive to engage them with others in their community is one valuable path to pursue. Along these lines, it is productive to emphasize the social network functions, rather than the remedial and therapeutic functions, of agency-sponsored parent groups. If parents participating in such groups are encouraged to act jointly in planning and participating in community-based activities, they may maintain the social contacts developed, even after the group formally concludes. Due to possible economic difficulties associated with war, helping parents learn about low- or no-cost community activities, assisting them in their business and recreational transportation needs, and encouraging their involvement with others in the community can be major steps toward decreasing isolation and promoting supportive social bonds.

Because the cognitive capacities of children may limit their ability to truly understand that danger has ended, knowledge of their developmental level must be taken into account in the provision of any support or treatment. Because war has been shown to affect family functioning through unresolved family conflict, increased intrafamilial violence, increased dependency, scapegoating, and isolation (Hobfoll et al., 1991), more intensive therapy may be necessary. In cases where significant deficits emerge, individual, as well as family, therapy is indicated.

In this regard, children exposed to war may require therapy due to the emergence of an impaired self-system. This is especially likely if the child has been directly exposed to war-related trauma, has lost a caregiving figure, or has been subjected to intrafamilial conflict. In these cases, therapy may provide a corrective emotional experience for the child and demonstrate that trust and closeness do not inevitably lead to pain. Of course, this cannot be accomplished in a brief therapeutic experience, and the support of the primary caregiver is crucial if the child is to have sufficient time involved in therapy. In view of the child's past experiences, as well as the goals of promoting trust, termination with a child who has experienced war-related trauma is a critical phase in therapy that must be handled sensitively. Minimally, the child must be at a point where he or she has been able to establish a trusting relationship. It is equally important that sufficient time be allotted to prepare the child for the transition out of therapy without causing him or her to feel abandoned. Although these issues will inevitably surface, they must be processed sufficiently within the therapeutic arena.

In contrast to individual therapy, the provision of family therapy may be necessary to help families resolve the dysfunction that may have emerged during wartime. Specifically, efforts need to be directed toward promoting harmony among, and autonomy of, family members. If parental conflict has emerged, the effect of this on overall family functioning will need to be addressed. Also, if any parental figures suffer from PTSD, all family members will require intervention services to help them cope with the effects of the individual dysfunction on the family system.

As the foregoing discussion elucidates, we recommend that a range of preventive and treatment strategies be available for individuals who have been faced with war. We stress the importance of considering not only the effects on the child, but the impact on the family and the broader ecology. Because financial as well as person-power resources may be stressed during a postwar period, we strongly advocate the provision of preventive services during the war.

FUTURE DIRECTIONS

In this chapter, we have presented research on the effects of maltreatment on child and family functioning and have drawn parallels between the effects of maltreatment and war on child adaptation. We also have provided suggestions for prevention and intervention designed to facilitate positive child coping in the aftermath of war-related trauma. Our efforts were limited by the paucity of empirical data on the effects of war on the ontogenetic process.

In considering current needs in the area of war-related trauma and child development, we strongly advocate the pursuit of investigations on the sequelae of war. As is true of most trauma-related occurrences, initial responses are likely to be directed toward helping individual victims rather than toward assessing the immediate and long-term consequences of the trauma. However, if our efforts to prevent and ameliorate war-related maladaptation are to be most effective, we must focus our efforts on understanding the processes affected, as well as the mechanisms that mediate or moderate the adverse sequelae of war on child development.

Our discussion underscores the need for more detailed research on the direct and indirect effects of war on individuals, families, and communities. Research on the etiology, correlates, and consequences of maltreatment offer suggestions that may be important to investigate in determining how war affects family and individual development. The effects of maltreatment on a number of stage-salient issues for families and individuals have been examined. They suggest that early incompetence associated with maltreatment leads to subsequent maladaptation. These far-reaching sequelae of maltreatment are consistent with the scope of the potential symptoms and stress reactions identified by the APA task force as characteristic of families and individuals exposed to war-related trauma (Hobfoll et al., 1991). Moreover, the task force's recommendation that attention be directed toward understanding how war affects children's development is congruent with the approach of researchers in developmental psychopathology, who apply an organizational perspective to investigating adaptation and maladaptation. It is important that investigations of the effects of war on families and children be developed and implemented so that an ecological/transactional understanding of the consequences of war can be formulated. The focus of these investigations needs to be directed toward determining how war influences different levels of the ecology (e.g., individuals, families, communities, societal beliefs, and values; cf. Cicchetti & Lynch, 1993) and how war-related reactions at one level of the ecology affect other levels of the ecology in a transactional manner. Once a more thorough understanding of the effects of war has been developed, it will be possible to apply maximally effective intervention and treatment programs to areas of need.

In accord with this line of thought, one mechanism of development that may be responsible for propagating the effects of war is representational models. These models, which are believed to be shaped by individuals' interactional histories, are extremely vulnerable to the personal and interpersonal stresses brought on by war. In addition to forming models of themselves and others, individuals may form representational models of their families and their communities, as well. Furthermore, families may hold shared models of themselves and their community (Cicchetti & Lynch, 1993; Reiss, 1981, 1989). The organization of these models reflects the attitudes, expectations, and beliefs that individuals and families possess with regard to their environment and their social surroundings. The quality of this inner organization is believed to play a part in an individual's (or family's) unfolding adaptation or maladaptation. However, the specific effects of war-time stress on representational models need to be examined, and research must examine the links between mental representation and stress-related behavior and symptoms. In a related vein, Tomkins (1979) developed the concept of *nuclear scenes* that are created within an individual surrounding major events (e.g., traumatic events connected to war). These nuclear scenes refer to vivid episodic memories that are affectively charged for the individual. They may become integrated with an individual's cognitions to form dominant life themes for that person. These memories, affects, and cognitions are akin to representational models. To the extent that Tomkins' nuclear scenes represent models of how the world operates and establish themes for the individual's life, it is likely that they will influence the individual's ongoing behavior and adaptation.

To further understand how war affects the individual's ability to develop competently, it may be helpful to examine the ways in which persons exposed to war process information. General models of the world and of the interpersonal environment may shape the way in which individuals process incoming information. Just as children's experiences of maltreatment appear to have skewed their information-processing systems to be hypervigilant for signs of aggression (Rieder & Cicchetti, 1989), children who are exposed to the violence and chaos of war may have their ability to process information similarly distorted. Although it may be adaptive within the given environment to attend to particular cues and to be vigilant for signs of threat, outside of this environment it can become maladaptive. This is especially true when individuals begin to interpret ambiguous or nonthreatening stimuli negatively. In this case, the child or adult may make negative attributions about the intentions of another person's actions or the cause of some event, causing that individual to respond in an inappropriate and maladaptive way. For example, maltreated children may perceive that another person's intentions were negative even in situations that are clearly ambiguous or even positive, thus eliciting from the maltreated child an inappropriate social response (e.g., aggression, social withdrawal). It will be important to determine if individuals exposed to war have similar distortions in their ability to process information. Attributions that they are likely to make are that the world is a hostile and unsafe environment, that others can be dangerous, and that they have little control over the events that occur around them. If information processing and attributional biases can be identified in victims, participants, and observers of war, they can be discussed and processed in terms of their usefulness for some settings but not for others. Basic research in this area will have important implications for the tailoring of intervention and treatment services for individuals exposed to war.

Other basic questions must be answered, as well. Researchers need to ask how the timing, duration, and type of exposure to war affect outcomes in individuals. All of these have implications for treatment. For example, the developmental period (or periods) during which an individual is exposed to the stresses of war will determine whether and how that person is able to make sense of the events that are occurring. Furthermore, the quality of adaptation prior to exposure to war may also determine how vulnerable an individual is to the negative consequences of war. For this reason, preventive efforts in areas at high risk for war may be especially important. In addition, the duration of exposure to war may also influence whether an individual experiences acute but relatively short-term deficits in competence that require relatively brief but intense intervention, or chronically pervasive detriments to ongoing adaptation that require long-term treatment. Finally, the type of exposure to war undoubtedly will have an influence on the specific nature of maladaptive outcomes. For example, whether an individual was a combatant in war, had a family member or loved one who was killed in war, witnessed the violence of war, or simply experienced the stress of living in a war-torn region could have specific effects on the individual's representational models, information processing, stress reactions, and ultimate adaptation. The treatment services and programs developed will need to take into consideration the types of experiences of particular groups of individuals. It is also possible that there may be cultural differences in the interpretations of and reactions to war. All of these issues need to be reinvestigated to inform those who are providing care to victims of war.

In terms of service delivery to those who have been exposed to war, there are some general points to consider for the future. In many cases, the family will be the appropriate target for treatment plans. In general, it is critical that we help parents deal with the war-related stress that they experience. It may be the stress of having a partner away or lost at war, or it may be generalized anxiety connected to the ongoing threat of danger. Whatever the case may be, if we can help parents cope with the stressors they experience, whether this is accomplished through support groups or specific treatment programs, they will become more available to their children, who also are undergoing stress. Parents can provide support for their children and become models of how to cope with stress, giving their children the message that the stress is manageable. This knowledge may be critically important in helping children develop feelings of competence and effectance in an environment that does not lend itself to experiences of mastery.

Moreover, parents should be encouraged not to burden their children with difficulties that the parents are experiencing. Maltreating parents are often seen as "parentifying" their children as they look to their children for comfort and support. This creates enormous conflict for maltreated children who, naturally, are looking for reassurance themselves. In times of war, all family members are like to experience significant stress, and the family is definitely an important source of support. However, parents in war areas should be aware that their children do not have the psychological resources to cope with both their own problems and those of their parents.

Parents and nonparental adults should listen to children's thoughts and concerns and encourage them to express themselves. This will foster the children's beliefs that there are havens of safety where they can express their fears without a calamity occurring. Children also need to have war-related events explained to them in a way that is appropriate to their developmental level. This can help children to work through the meaning and significance of the events that they are hearing about, witnessing, and experiencing.

The vast number of children, individuals, and families affected by war requires large-scale treatment services. The example of programmatic service provided at the Mt. Hope Family Center can serve as a model for how to offer treatment to large numbers of war victims. After School programs, where children who have been through similar experiences can deal with important issues in a secure and supportive environment, may be helpful for children who have been exposed to war. Similarly, offering parenting groups to the parents of these children can provide a forum to discuss and understand the difficulties of rearing children in such a strife- ridden environment. However, it may be necessary to provide long-term support for these children and families. Just as maltreatment may exert its effects long after the actual maltreatment incidents have stopped, war and its associated stress may also exert negative influences for a long time after the war is over. For this reason, maintaining regular contacts with children and families who have been exposed to war may be vital. As in the Mt. Hope Family Center's Summer Camp Program, re-establishing contact with children and families on a regular basis can help individuals develop the belief that sources of support are predictably available. The effects of war on all those who are exposed to it are likely to be complex and far reaching. It is the challenge for researchers to delineate these effects and to pass on this information to those who will apply it to the development of effective services.

ACKNOWLEDGMENTS

We acknowledge the support of the William T. Grant Foundation, the Prevention Research Branch of NIMH (1 RO1 MH45027-01A1), the Smith-Richardson Foundation, Inc., and the Spunk Fund, Inc. We also appreciate the cooperation of the Departments of Social Services of Monroe County and of New York State.

REFERENCES

Aber, J. L., & Allen, J. P. (1987). The effects of maltreatment on young children's socio-emotional development: An attachment theory perspective. *Developmental Psychology, 23,* 406–414.

Aber, J. L., Allen, J., Carlson, V., & Cicchetti, D. (1989). The effects of maltreatment on development during early childhood: Recent studies and their theoretical, clinical, and policy implications. In D. Cicchetti & V. Carlson (Eds.), *Child maltreatment: Theory and research on the causes and consequences of child abuse and neglect* (pp. 579-619). New York: Cambridge University Press.

Ainsworth, M. D. S., & Wittig, B. A. (1969). Attachment and the exploratory behavior of one-year-olds in a strange situation. In B. M. Foss (Ed.), *Determinants of infant behavior* (Vol. 4, pp. 113-136). London: Methuen.

Baharal, R., Waterman, J., & Martin, H. (1981). The social-cognitive development of abused children. *Journal of Consulting and Clinical Psychology, 49,* 508-516.

Barnett, D., Ganiban, J., & Cicchetti, D. (1992). *Temperament and behavior of youngsters with disorganized attachments: A longitudinal study.* Unpublished manuscript, Mt. Hope Family Center, University of Rochester, Rochester, NY.

Belsky, J. (1980). Child maltreatment: An ecological integration. *American Psychologist, 35,* 320-335.

Boszormenyi-Nagy, I., & Spark, G. (1973). *Invisible loyalties: Reciprocity in intergenerational family therapy.* New York: Harper & Row.

Bowlby, J. (1982). *Attachment and loss* (Vol. 1). New York: Basic Books. (Original work published 1969)

Bronfenbrenner, U., & Crouter, A. C. (1983). The evolution of environmental models in developmental research. In P. Mussen (Ed.), *Handbook of child psychology* (pp. 357-414). New York: Wiley.

Burgess, R. L., & Conger, R. D. (1978). Family interaction in abusive, neglectful, and normal families. *Child Development, 49,* 1163-1173.

Carlson, V., Cicchetti, D., Barnett, D., & Braunwald, K. (1989). Finding order in disorganization: Lessons from research on maltreated infants' attachments to their caregivers. In D. Cicchetti & V. Carlson (Eds.), *Child maltreatment: Theory and research on the causes and consequences of child abuse and neglect* (pp. 494-528). New York: Cambridge University Press.

Cicchetti, D. (1989). How research on child maltreatment has informed the study of child development: Perspectives from developmental psychopathology. In D. Cicchetti & V. Carlson (Eds.), *Child maltreatment: Theory and research on the causes and consequences of child abuse and neglect* (pp. 377-431). New York: Cambridge University Press.

Cicchetti, D. (1990a). Developmental psychopathology and the prevention of serious mental disorders: Overdue detente and illustrations through the affective disorders. In P. Muehrer (Ed.), *Conceptual research models for prevention of mental disorders* (pp. 215-254). Rockville, MD: NIMH.

Cicchetti, D. (1990b). The organization and coherence of socioemotional, cognitive, and representational development: Illustrations through a developmental psychopathology perspective on Down syndrome and child maltreatment. In R. Thompson (Ed.), *Nebraska symposium on motivation: Vol. 36. Socioemotional development* (pp. 259-366). Lincoln: University of Nebraska Press.

Cicchetti, D. (1991). Fractures in the crystal: Developmental psychopathology and the emergence of self. *Developmental Review, 11,* 271-287.

Cicchetti, D., & Aber, J. L. (1986). Early precursors to later depression: An organizational perspective. In L. Lipsitt & C. Rovee-Collier (Eds.), *Advances in infancy* (Vol. 4, pp. 81-137). Norwood, NJ: Ablex.

Cicchetti, D., & Barnett, D. (1991). Toward the development of a scientific nosology of child maltreatment. In W. Grove & D. Cicchetti (Eds.), *Thinking clearly about psychology: Essays in honor of Paul E. Meehl: Vol. 2. Personality and psychopathology* (pp. 346-377). Minneapolis, MN: University of Minnesota Press.

Cicchetti, D., & Beeghly, M. (1987). Symbolic development in maltreated youngsters: An organizational perspective. *New Directions for Child Development, 36,* 5-29.

Cicchetti, D., & Carlson, V. (Eds.). (1989). *Child maltreatment: Theory and research on the causes and consequences of child abuse and neglect.* New York: Cambridge University Press.

Cicchetti, D., Ganiban, J., & Barnett, D. (1991). Contributions from the study of high risk populations to understanding the development of emotion regulation. In J. Garber & K. Dodge (Eds.), *The development of emotion regulation and dysregulation* (pp. 15–48). New York: Cambridge University Press.

Cicchetti, D., & Lynch, M. (1993). Toward an ecological/transactional model of community violence and child maltreatment: Consequences for children's development. *Psychiatry, 56,* 96–118.

Cicchetti, D., & Rizley, R. (1981). Developmental perspectives on the etiology, intergenerational transmission and sequelae of child maltreatment. *New Directions for Child Development, 11,* 31–56.

Cicchetti, D., & Sroufe, L. A. (1978). An organizational view of affect: Illustration from the study of Down's syndrome infants. In M. Lewis & L. Rosenblum (Eds.), *The development of affect* (pp. 309–350). New York: Plenum.

Cicchetti, D., & Toth, S. (1987). The application of a transactional risk model to intervention with multi-risk maltreating families. *Zero to Three, 7,* 1–8.

Cicchetti, D., & Toth, S. L. (Eds.). (1993). *Child abuse, child development, and social policy.* Norwood, NJ: Ablex.

Colon, F. (1981). The family life cycle of the multi-problem poor family. In E. Carter & M. McGoldrick (Eds.), *The family life cycle: A framework for family therapy* (pp. 432–448). New York: Gardner.

Crittenden, P. M. (1988). Relationships at risk. In J. Belsky & T. Nezworski (Eds.), *Clinical implications of attachment theory* (pp. 136–174). Hillsdale, NJ: Lawrence Erlbaum Associates.

Crittenden, P. M., & DiLalla, D. L. (1988). Compulsive compliance: The development of an inhibitory coping strategy in infancy. *Journal of Abnormal Child Psychology, 16,* 585–599.

Cummings, E. M., & Cicchetti, D. (1990). Attachment, depression, and the transmission of depression. In M. T. Greenberg, D. Cicchetti, & E. M. Cummings (Eds.), *Attachment in the preschool years: Theory, research, and intervention* (pp. 339–372). Chicago: University of Chicago Press.

Cummings, E. M., Hennessy, K. D., Rabideau, G. J., & Cicchetti, D. (1992). *Coping with anger involving a family member in physically abused and non-abused boys.* Unpublished manuscript, Mt. Hope Family Center, University of Rochester, Rochester, NY.

Cummings, E. M., & Zahn-Waxler, C. (in press). Emotions and the socialization of aggression: Adults' angry behavior and children's arousal and aggression. In A. Fraczek & H. Zumkley (Eds.), *Socialization and aggression.* New York: Springer-Verlag.

Damon, W. (1977). *The social world of the child.* San Francisco: Jossey-Bass.

Dubrow, N. F., & Garbarino, J. (1989). Living in the war zone: Mothers and young children in a public housing project. *Child Welfare, 68,* 3–20.

Eckenrode, J., & Laird, M. (1991, April). *Social adjustment of maltreated children in the school setting.* Paper presented at the bi-annual meeting of the Society for Research in Child Development, Seattle, WA.

Egeland, B., & Sroufe, L. A. (1981). Developmental sequelae of maltreatment in infancy. *New Directions for Child Development, 11,* 77–92.

Egeland, B., Sroufe, L. A., & Erickson, M. F. (1983). Developmental consequence of different patterns of maltreatment. *Child Abuse and Neglect, 7,* 459–469.

Erickson, E. H. (1950). *Childhood and society.* New York: Norton.

Fraiberg, S. (Ed.). (1980). *Clinical studies in infant mental health: The first year of life.* New York: Basic Books.

Gaensbauer, T. J. (1980). Anaclitic depression in a three-and-one-half-month-old child. *American Journal of Psychiatry, 137,* 841–842.

Gaensbauer, T. J. (1982). The differentiation of discrete affects. *The Psychoanalytic Study of the Child, 37,* 29–66.

Gaensbauer, T. J., Mrazek, D., & Harmon, R. (1980). Affective behavior patterns in abused and/or neglected infants. In N. Freud (Ed.), *The understanding and prevention of child abuse: Psychological approaches.* London: Concord Press.

Garbarino, J., Kostelny, K., & Dubrow, N. (1991). *No place to be a child: Growing up in a war zone.* Lexington, MA: Lexington Press.

George, C., & Main, M. (1979). Social interactions of young abused children: Approach, avoidance, and aggression. *Child Development, 50,* 306–318.

Greenspan, S. (1987). A model for comprehensive preventive services for infants, young children, and their families. In S. Greenspan, S. Wieder, R. Nover, A. F. Lieberman, R. Lourie, & M. Robinson (Eds.), *Infants in multi-risk families* (pp. 377–390). Madison, CT: International Universities Press.

Hennessy, K. D., Rabideau, G. J., Cicchetti, D., & Cummings, E. M. (1992). *Responses of physically abused children to different forms of interadult anger.* Unpublished manuscript, Mt. Hope Family Center, University of Rochester, Rochester, NY.

Hobfoll, S., Spielberger, C., Breznitz, S., Figley, C., Folkman, S., Lepper-Green, B., Meichenbaum, D., Milgram, N., Sandler, I., Sarason, I., & van der Kolk, B. (1991). War-related stress: Addressing the stress of war and other traumatic events. *American Psychologist, 46,* 848–855.

Hoffman-Plotkin, D., & Twentyman, C. T. (1984). A multimodal assessment of behavioral and cognitive deficits in abused and neglected preschoolers. *Child Development, 55,* 794–802.

Howes, C., & Espinosa, M. P. (1985). The consequences of child abuse for the formation of relationships with peers. *Child Abuse and Neglect, 9,* 397–404.

Kaufman, J., & Cicchetti, D. (1989). The effects of maltreatment on school-aged children's socioemotional development: Assessments in a day camp setting. *Developmental Psychology, 25,* 316–324.

Kazdin, A. E., Moser, J., Colbus, D., & Bell, R. (1985). Depressive symptoms among physically abused and psychiatrically disturbed children. *Journal of Abnormal Psychology, 94,* 298–307.

Lynch, M., & Cicchetti, D. (1991). Patterns of relatedness in maltreated and nonmaltreated children: Connections among multiple representational models. *Development and Psychopathology, 3,* 207–226.

Lynch, M., & Cicchetti, D. (1992). Maltreated children's reports of relatedness to their teachers. *New Directions for Child Development, 57,* 81–107.

Main, M., & George, C. (1985). Response of abused and disadvantaged toddlers to distress in agemates: A study in the day care setting. *Developmental Psychology, 21,* 407–412.

Main, M., & Solomon, J. (1990). Procedures for identifying infants as disorganized/disoriented during the Ainsworth Strange Situation. In M. Greenberg, D. Cicchetti, & E. M. Cummings (Eds.), *Attachment in the preschool years* (pp. 121–160). Chicago: University of Chicago Press.

Marvin, R. S., & Stewart, R. B. (1990). A family systems framework for the study of attachment. In M. Greenberg, D. Cicchetti, & E. M. Cummings (Eds.), *Attachment in the preschool years* (pp. 51–86). Chicago: University of Chicago Press.

Masten, A., & Garmezy, N. (1985). Risk, vulnerability, and protective factors in developmental psychopathology. In B. Lahey & A. Kazdin (Eds.), *Advances in clinical child psychology* (Vol. 8, pp. 1–51). New York: Plenum.

Olds, D. L., & Henderson, C. (1989). The prevention of maltreatment. D. Cicchetti & V. Carlson (Eds.), *Child maltreatment: Theory and research on the causes and consequences of child abuse and neglect* (pp. 722–763). New York: Cambridge University Press.

Reiss, D. (1981). *The family's construction of reality.* Cambridge, MA: Harvard University Press.

Reiss, D. (1989). The represented and practicing family: Contrasting visions of family continuity. In A. J. Sameroff & R. N. Emde (Eds.), *Relationship disturbances in early childhood* (pp. 191–220). New York: Basic Books.

Richters, J. E., & Martinez, P. (1993). The NIMH Community Violence Project: Children as victims and witnesses to violence. *Psychiatry, 56,* 7–21.

Rieder, C., & Cicchetti, D. (1989). Organizational perspective on cognitive control functioning and cognitive–affective balance in maltreated children. *Developmental Psychology, 25,* 382–393.

Sameroff, A. J., & Chandler, M. J. (1975). Reproductive risk and the continuum of caretaking casualty. In F. D. Horowitz (Ed.), *Review of child development research* (Vol. 4, pp. 187–244). Chicago: University of Chicago Press.

Schneider-Rosen, K., Braunwald, K., Carlson, V., & Cicchetti, D. (1985). Current perspectives in attachment theory: Illustration from the study of maltreated infants. *Growing points in attachment theory and research. Monographs of the Society for Research in Child Development, 50*(Serial No. 209), 194–210.

Schneider-Rosen, K., & Cicchetti, D. (1984). The relationship between affect and cognition in maltreated infants: Quality of attachment and the development of visual self-recognition. *Child Development, 55,* 648–658.

Schneider-Rosen, K., & Cicchetti, D. (1991). Early self-knowledge and emotional development: Visual self-recognition and affective reactions to mirror self-image in maltreated and non-maltreated toddlers. *Developmental Psychology, 27,* 471–478.

Selman, R. (1980). *The growth of interpersonal understanding: Developmental and clinical analyses.* New York: Academic Press.

Sroufe, L. A. (1979). Socioemotional development. In J. Osofsky (Ed.), *Handbook of infant development* (1st ed., pp. 462–516). New York: Wiley.

Sroufe, L. A., & Fleeson, J. (1988). The coherence of family relationships. In R. A. Hinde & J. Stevenson-Hinde (Eds.), *Relationships within families* (pp. 27–47). Oxford, England: Clarendon.

Sroufe, L. A., & Rutter, M. (1984). The domain of developmental psychopathology. *Child Development, 54,* 17–29.

Sroufe, L. A., & Waters, E. (1977). Attachment as an organizational construct. *Child Development, 48,* 1184–1199.

Starr, R. A., & Wolfe, D. A. (Eds.). (1991). *The effects of child abuse and neglect.* New York: Guilford.

Stevenson-Hinde, J. (1990). Attachment within family systems: An overview. *Infant Mental Health Journal, 11,* 218–227.

Straus, M. A., Gelles, R. J., & Steinmetz, S. K. (1980). *Behind closed doors: Violence in the American family.* New York: Anchor Press.

Terr, L. M. (1990). *Too scared to cry.* New York: Harper & Row.

Tomkins, S. (1979). Script theory: Differential magnification of affects. In R. A. Dienstbier (Ed.), *Nebraska symposium on motivation: Vol. 26. Human emotion* (pp. 201–236). Lincoln: University of Nebraska Press.

Toth, S. L., Manly, J., & Cicchetti, D. (1992). Child maltreatment and vulnerability to depression. *Development and Psychopathology, 4,* 97–112.

Troy, M., & Sroufe, L. A. (1987). Victimization among preschoolers: The role of attachment relationship history. *Journal of the American Academy of Child Psychiatry, 26,* 166–72.

van der Kolk, B. A. (1987). The separation cry and the trauma response: Developmental issues in the psychobiology of attachment and separation. In B. A. van der Kolk (Ed.), *Psychological trauma* (pp. 31–62). Washington, DC: American Psychiatric Press.

Vondra, J., Barnett, D., & Cicchetti, D. (1989). Perceived and actual competence among maltreated and comparison school children. *Development and Psychopathology, 1,* 237–255.

Wolfe, D. A. (1985). Child abusive parents: An empirical review and analysis. *Psychological Bulletin, 97,* 462–482.

Wynne, L. C. (1984). The epigenesis of relational systems: A model for understanding family development. *Family Process, 23,* 297–318.

II THE MIDDLE EAST CONFLICT: ITS EFFECTS ON CHILDREN

4 The Effect of War on Israeli Children

Avigdor Klingman
Abraham Sagi
University of Haifa

Amiram Raviv
Tel Aviv University

The special needs of children in wartime is a subject of general concern. In some countries, mental health professionals are approached for consultation about the reactions of children to the stress of war (e.g., Klingman, 1992). Hobfoll et al. (1991) recently outlined the typical stress reactions and modes of successful and unsuccessful coping strategies in times of war, giving particular consideration to the needs of children.

Notwithstanding the growing interest in the subject, very little research has been carried out on the effect of war on children (Swenson & Klingman, in press). There are many methodological problems involved in studying the effect of war on children. Moreover, problems related to professional ethics and researchers' personal involvement often get in the way of investigations in this area. For all these difficulties, however, much effort has been invested in studying Israeli children in wartime.

Israel, unfortunately, is a natural laboratory for the study of war stress. When considering war-related anxiety among Israeli children, we should keep in mind that Israeli children are brought up with a continuous awareness of war. Children in Israel know, from a very young age, that they will be called up for military service when they are 18 years old. They also have the experience of their fathers being called up for reserve duty for at least 1 month every year as a matter of routine. They know that in the event of war, he will be required to serve on the front line, remaining there for an indeterminate period of time. Children's fears of their fathers being wounded or killed in action are, therefore, very real. Moreover, given Israel's small population (currently only 4.5 million), nearly everyone in the country knows someone who has either been wounded or died in war. These circumstances distinguish Israeli children from children in other contemporary Western societies.

It is against this background that we review a selection of representative studies that set out the problems and characteristics of Israeli children experiencing war and war-related stress. More specifically, this research focuses on the following issues: (a) expected reactions to war stress, (b) the effects of age and gender on these reactions, (c) the effects of proximity to and intensity of exposure to war stress, (d) the role of social support systems in the appraisal of and reaction to war-related stress, and (e) the role in this of the sense of control. These issues are examined in relation to the various conceptual concerns regarding coping and adaptation in situations of war stress (e.g., short-term vs. long-term adaptation; Breznitz, 1983a, 1983b). We shall deal primarily with the findings of recent studies undertaken during and after the Gulf War.

In the 1991 Gulf War, the Israeli population confronted an armed conflict very different from any that it had experienced in the past. For the first time in the nation's history, the entire civilian population came under threat of a chemical missile attack, so that the danger was no longer limited in its scope nor confined to soldiers at the front. Most of the missiles fell in densely populated areas. Schools remained closed for long intervals. A room was set aside in every home to serve as a shelter, and all its windows and doors were required to be sealed. When the siren sounded, the entire family immediately went into the room, put on gas masks, and completed the work of sealing up the door from the inside. They then had to wait until it was determined which area of the country was hit and if the missiles carried a chemical warhead. Children under the age of 3 years were placed in gas-proof cots, and were, thus, physically isolated from the rest of the family for a time. Additional problems resulted from complications in fastening the gas masks and from the fogging up of lenses on the masks. Many children had to be persuaded or even forced to wear the masks (Klingman, 1992).

A significant number of Gulf War studies have not been published yet, and various data analyses were still incomplete while this chapter was in preparation. We supplement our presentation here with the findings of a number of studies of children's reactions to war and war-like situations in Israel prior to the Gulf War (for an extensive review of investigations predating the Gulf War, see Milgram, 1982; Raviv & Klingman, 1983). Moreover, given the many methodological difficulties associated with war studies, we describe the available data that may shed light on children's responses under conditions of war. Attention is also given to the methodological difficulties of conducting research in wartime, and to the problems of interpreting the results. Finally, we consider the possible directions that war-related research might take in the future.

THE MAJOR VARIABLES

Stress Reactions

It is not surprising that many children express anxiety and fears when confronted by the stressors of war. Various studies have been conducted on fear and anxiety levels in war and war-like situations. Milgram and Milgram (1976) investigated anxiety in 5th- and 6th-grade urban children during the 1973 Yom Kippur War, and found there was a substantial increase in anxiety in wartime as compared to peacetime (the mean scores during the war nearly doubled). The greatest increment in anxiety was noted in those children whose anxiety level had been lowest in peacetime (boys as compared with girls, middle-class children as compared with lower-class children). Their findings also showed that high peacetime anxiety did not necessarily translate into high wartime anxiety; rather, an inverse relationship was found between the two.

Stress reactions of groups of 7th-, 10th-, and 12th-grade students were assessed during the first and fourth weeks of the Gulf War in two high-risk areas of the country that were missile targets (Klingman, 1992a). The stress–response items reported most frequently during the first week of the war were fear of being hit by a missile (69%), frightening images of falling missiles (65%), refraining from taking part in pleasurable activities (59%), and difficulty in falling asleep following a siren warning (58%). Other noted responses included overeating (49%), a feeling of physical weakness (48%), problems in concentration (48%), sleep disturbance (43%), restlessness (35%), and physical pain (31%). Using Spielberger's State–Trait Anxiety Questionnaire, Mintz (1991) found that the physiological symptoms of children ages 12 and 16 were highly correlated with anxiety level. A study of children in the 5th, 7th, and 10th grades, conducted 3 weeks following the cease-fire (Schwarzwald, Weisenberg, Waysman, Solomon, & Klingman, in press) revealed posttraumatic stress rates ranging from 33.5% for the youngest group to 9.1% for the oldest, with an overall rate of 20.4%.

In a telephone survey conducted in August 1991, a representative sample of 1,004 individuals (including 366 parents of children up to the age of 14) were asked to describe the extent of their children's fears, particularly during the beginning of the Gulf War. The distribution of answers was as follows: extremely fearful—17.1%, very fearful—20.9%, moderately fearful—27.8%, mildly fearful—20.6%, and not at all fearful—13.6% (Raviv & Raviv, 1991).

In another study, coping behavior in the sealed rooms during missile attacks was examined in pupils of the 5th, 7th, and 10th grades to whom a battery of questionnaires was administered 3 weeks after the end of the Gulf War (Weisenberg, Schwarzwald, Waysman, Solomon, & Klingman, in press). Common responses from the majority of the respondents consisted of information seeking, checking safety measures, and calming others. The type of coping behaviors was associated with postwar stress reactions and age. Children who reported more severe reactions also reported being less engaged in avoidance and distraction and more inclined to behavior that was directed at the threat (i.e., children relying more on emotion-focused behavior in the sealed room may have coped more effectively).

A study conducted about a week following the cease-fire assessed the nature of 4th- and 5th-grade children's perceived control, social support, psychological defenses, and coping and affective reactions under the threat of missile attack (Zeidner, Klingman, & Itzkovitz, 1993). The children were shown pictures representing significant others in various war-related situations, with an open-ended questionnaire related to these images. Children with lower perceived control and poorer defensive and coping capacities tended to score higher on anxiety. Children who were cognitively more aware of the specific details of the crisis as it unfolded were, on the whole, more expressive and more anxious about the situation.

Most infants and toddlers reacted with significant distress during the Gulf War. Rosenthal and Levy-Shiff (1992) administered semistructured interviews to a sample of 99 mothers of infants and toddlers ages 4–36 months. The respondents reported strong initial negative reactions by their children to the gas- proof cots and gas masks (61.4%), to the parents' gas masks (42.2%), to the sound of sirens (29.8%), and to staying in the sealed room (25%). Although many of the children adjusted to these conditions with the passage of time, some grew more sensitive and tense, especially to being put in gas-proof cots (36.3%) and to the parents' gas masks (25.3%). The responses of those children who had shown strong emotional reactions during the initial stages of the war tended to grow more intense over time. A few mothers reported that their children regressed to less mature patterns of behavior (11.6%), with many displaying a variety of adjustment difficulties, such as prolonged periods of crying, stomachaches, and temper tantrums (57.7%). Many mothers reported changes in their children's habitual routines, such as their sleeping and eating times (53.7%).

The effect of the attacks on children's sleep was studied by Lavie, Amit, Epstein, and Tzischinsky (1992). The sleeping habits and disturbances of sleep among 61 infants were assessed by questionnaires completed by their parents 5 months before and 1–3 weeks after the war. No significant changes were found in sleeping habits and quality of sleep. The only difference that could not be explained by ontogenetically related changes was the tendency of parents to rate their infants as more fatigued during the day in the period following the war. The researchers also monitored the sleep of 55 children by using actigraphs (monitors worn on the wrist at bedtime) during the last 4 weeks of the war. Although all the infants were awakened by the sirens, they went back to sleep immediately after the attack with no observed carryover effects. As for the older population, it was concluded that a "fear to sleep," rather than an actual disturbance of sleep accounted for insomnia (i.e., environmental insomnia). Those who reported sleep difficulties may have been afraid that they would fail to hear the sirens or that they would awaken from sleep in too great a confusion to deal effectively with the complex tasks required by the emergency.

Emotion-focused coping (e.g., avoidance and distraction strategies) was associated with fewer postwar stress reactions than was persistence in direct problem-focused activity (Weisenberg et al., in press). Confinement in a sealed room constrained children to remain relatively passive, a situation that was aggravated by helplessness and unpredictability. In this context, behaviors such as helping and calming others and checking to see if everything was in order, were among the few active types of behavior that remained to complement the high frequency of emotional responses. These data indicate that children who persisted in engaging in activities to change an unchangeable situation may have coped less effectively than those relying on emotion-focused coping.

One would expect various forms of anxiety to be elicited by war conditions, but reductions in stress reactions were reported to have occurred during the war as well. Klingman (1992a) found evidence of a significant decline in the fourth week of the war, to a mean of 3.0, from the first week's mean of 5.8. Rosenbaum and Ronen (1991) assessed the coping of 5th- and 6th-grade pupils and their parents during the fifth week of the war in the vicinity of Tel Aviv, which was the country's worst struck area. They found that both children and parents perceived a significant reduction in their anxiety between the first and fifth weeks of the war. Rosenthal and Levy-Shiff (1992) noted a similar pattern for younger children, with parents reporting that many infants and toddlers gradually became used to exposure to the stress during the state of alarm. The reported reduction in anxiety raises questions not easily resolved, and a number of interpretations have been offered in the literature, including habituation (Rachman, 1990) and denial (Janis, 1983). We return to this issue later in the chapter.

Age Differences

The data under review do not entirely support the claim that children are more vulnerable to stress than adults (Hobfoll et al., 1991). In a telephone survey conducted during the Gulf War (Raviv & Raviv, 1991), a representative sample of 273 parents were asked to identify the age group that was most fearful during the war. Those interviewed perceived that adults were most fearful, followed by the elderly, and only then by children. Young adults and adolescents were perceived as being least fearful. Pynoos and

Eth (1985) suggested that, although the general phenomenology of stress reaction is often similar across age groups, symptom presentation and content of posttraumatic stress reactions vary according to age; thus, children's early efforts to cope with traumatic anxiety and helplessness are dependent on the degree of maturity they have reached. Generally, studies have suggested a significant difference on various measures of reactions to stress as a function of age. Thus, 5th graders were found to be more susceptible to posttraumatic and other stress reactions than were older children (Schwarzwald et al., in press), and state anxiety has been found to be higher in 7th graders than in 10th graders (Mintz, 1991).

In another telephone survey (Raviv and Raviv, 1991), the interviewees were asked about the degree of fear manifested by children below the age of 14 and by adolescents aged 14–18, both during the war and at the time of the survey, which was carried out approximately 4 months after the war. The greatest fears were reported among younger children as compared with those over 14 years of age, and almost a total absence of fear was reported among adolescents. A substantial decrease in fear was also noted at the time of the survey as compared with the situation during the war. Klingman (1992a) found that 7th-grade children reported greater frequency of stress reactions (e.g., physical pain, frightening dreams, and eating less) than did children in the 10th and 12th grades, during both the first and fourth weeks of the war.

The differences identified among children according to age are perhaps explained by the fact that younger children have weaker cognitive resources and less experience in coping with stressful events, circumstances that may cause them to exaggerate the seriousness of their problems and prevent them from anticipating the eventual resolution of difficulties. They may also be developmentally less likely than older children and adults to speak openly of problems or even to know that they are having problems (Hobfoll et al., 1991). Alternatively, they may not have sufficiently developed repressive mechanisms, and may, therefore, respond more openly than do older children to direct questions about their feelings and anxieties.

Gender Differences

The findings concerning gender differences suggest generally higher stress levels among girls than boys. Both Klingman (1992a) and Mintz (1991) found that girls reported a higher frequency of stress reactions during the Gulf War. Zeidner et al. (1993) also found that girls exhibited greater anxiety and emotionality on a semiprojective measure. Moreover, female adolescents reported being more pessimistic and concerned about the threat of unconventional warfare than did males in the same age group (Klingman & Goldstein, 1992).

There are comparable findings unrelated to war which indicate that, irrespective of age, girls tend to report a greater number of fears and anxieties than do boys, and that they also differ from boys in the types of fear and anxiety they experience (Barrios & O'Dell, 1989). One explanation of this relates to modeling and socialization patterns (Maccoby & Jacklin, 1974), which would contend that certain aspects of feminine socialization allow girls to react more openly than boys to traumatic experiences with negative emotions, thereby becoming more aware of their emotions and more likely to rehearse and observe themselves in emotional poses (Ben-Zur & Zeidner, 1988). Alternatively, because of societal expectations, boys tend to use suppression or denial more than girls in order to cope with anxieties concerning physical danger.

Another explanation for the heightened emotional reaction of girls can be derived from recent discussions regarding developmental aspects of gender differences. A recent meta-analysis by Lytton and Romney (1991) of studies regarding parents' differential socialization of boys and girls did not reveal much difference for social behaviors unrelated to stress. The authors proposed that these differences may be inherent in the child rather than being the result of environmental factors. We consider this subject in greater detail further on.

Proximity

The proximity and intensity of a traumatic event have been generally regarded as important factors in stress reactions (Pynoos & Eth, 1985). This is supported by a number of studies of proximity. Klingman and Wiesner (1982) attempted to find a relationship between proximity to areas exposed to war tensions and the level of fear in children ages 11 to 13. As expected, children who were closer to areas of tension reported higher levels of anxiety. Rofe and Lewin (1980, 1981) found a highly significant relationship between scores on the repression-sensitization scale and place of residence. The findings indicated that there is a greater frequency of repressive personality types among populations living in a war environment from early childhood than among comparable populations living in nonwar environments. Moreover, all personality types showed a repressive behavior pattern. Dream analysis revealed that individuals living in war zones had fewer nightmares and fewer sexual, aggressive, and unpleasant dreams. The same was true of daydreams. The authors concluded that living under constant threat of war increases the need for repressive mechanisms both at the level of personality and as a general way of coping with everyday stressors.

Klingman (1992a) found that the situational factors of the intensity and duration of missile attacks were important in influencing stress reactions during the Gulf War. Children in the areas of the country that came under the heaviest missile attacks reported significantly higher frequencies of some symptoms (i.e., avoidance of pleasurable activity, physical weakness, pain, and restlessness). Mintz (1991) found that 12- and 16-year-olds who lived closer to the targeted areas were more anxious than those who lived further away. The findings of Schwarzwald et al. (in press) also revealed that closer proximity to the area of damage was related to higher rates of posttraumatic reaction. Exposure was to two varieties of stress: objective stress, consisting of proximity to missile impact and damage, and of acquaintance with the victims; and subjective stress, consisting of perceived threat to oneself, to relatives, and to acquaintances. In another study of 5th- and 7th-grade pupils (Bat-Zion & Levy-Shiff, this volume, chapter 8), physical proximity was found to be related to greatest distress and negative affect, and to somatic, cognitive, and daily functioning difficulties. However, proximity was not revealed to affect the dynamics of the stress responses: The underlying processes mediating stress responses were similar in children living at a distance from the areas hit by missiles.

Contrary to most findings regarding the role of proximity to the traumatic event, the results obtained by Ziv and Israeli (1973) showed no significant differences in levels of anxiety between children living on kibbutzim exposed to frequent shelling compared to children living on kibbutzim that were never under fire. The adaptation level theory proposed by Helson (1964) furnishes a possible explanation for this discrepancy. According to Helson, adaptation level is a function of the stimulus to which one responds, the context in which the stimulus is represented, and past experiences with similar stimuli. Therefore, as opposed to the effects attested to by studies of children whose war-related experiences were a one-time event, it can be assumed that for the children examined by Ziv and Israeli, constant shelling became a way of life and, consequently, was perceived by them as being less threatening.

Taken together, these studies suggest that, on the whole, stress reactions are to be associated with the degree of proximity to the location of the traumatic event, although there is some indication that physical proximity may not always be the most salient stress factor. For example, personal acquaintance with disaster victims was found to be the most potent contributor to stress reactions following a catastrophic bus accident (Milgram, Toubiana, Klingman, Raviv, & Goldstein, 1988). Thus, it is possible that among children who did not experience the loss of friends or acquaintances during the Gulf War (which resulted in considerable damage to property but few casualties), it was physical proximity to the target area that most influenced stress reactions. Therefore, before venturing any broad generalizations in this regard, we must first undertake further study of the different types of war trauma (Schwarzwald et al., in press). Further more, both objective and subjective stress measures should be used in investigating the intensity of war trauma. Such measures would contribute meaningful information of theoretical and practical value. The objective measures include geographical proximity to the area damaged within the geographical region, and degree of acquaintance and relationship with the victims. The subjective measures of the intensity of trauma include the perceived degree of threat to oneself, to relatives, and to acquaintances and friends (Schwarzwald et al., in press).

Sense of Control

Sense of control, self-control, perceived control and learned resourcefulness are regarded as coping resources available to the individual for use in stressful events (Rosenbaum, 1983, 1990). Several studies have demonstrated the effectiveness of various self-control training programs with children in stressful situations unrelated to war (Melamed, Klingman, & Siegel, 1984). Zeidner et al. (1993) found that children who perceived themselves as strongly in control during the Gulf War also scored high on perceived support, effective defensiveness, and coping. Rosenbaum and Ronen (1991), using a self-report questionnaire to evaluate self-perceived resource skills, found that children scoring high on self-control also believed more strongly in their ability to cope with their anxiety. Highly anxious children believed less in their ability to cope with their anxiety, whereas highly resourceful children with greater self-control skills were more confident in their ability to cope with their anxiety. Parents who reported giving high priority to training their children in self-control methods were more likely to suggest specific methods to their children for coping with war-related fears and to encourage them in the performance of daily routines. These preliminary findings suggest that children's acquisition of self-control skills and parents' teaching their children self-control play an important part in coping with war-produced stress.

These findings indicate that self-control (or learned resourcefulness) may be an important personality variable that promotes coping with war stress, especially during the time of actual warfare. Additional studies are needed to elucidate the relationship between learned resourcefulness and coping in wartime. Also, the meaning of adaptation to repeated exposures to war-related stress remains to be clarified.

Social Support

It has been well documented that a social context that is perceived as supportive can facilitate adjustment and well-being in the face of a wide variety of stressors (Kessler & McLoed, 1985). The possible buffering effect of support systems for children in wartime is highlighted by some of the data. In Bat-Zion and Levy-Shiff's study (this volume, chapter 8), perceived parental behaviors emerged as an important factor in mediating children's stress responses. Zeidner et al. (1993) found that children who perceived their parents to be highly anxious tended to display higher anxiety levels and greater emotionality. They also found that children who viewed their families as communicating better tended to reveal a more complex level of thinking about the situation, greater control, and better coping. In addition, perceived parental behaviors and children's emotionality emerged as significant factors in mediating children's stress responses (Bat-Zion & Levy-Shiff, this volume, chapter 8).

A study of 5th-grade children whose fathers were on active military duty was conducted by Ziv, Kruglanski, and Schulman (1974). The researchers did not find significant differences in the general level of anxiety between father-present and father-absent families. However, they found that children whose fathers were on active duty were more likely to omit their fathers from the pictures they drew of their families, and to include more images of weapons. The researchers suggested that this was a manifestation of a defense mechanism, rather than an expression of anxiety. In another study (Kaffman & Elizur, 1977), a higher frequency of bedwetting was found among children whose fathers' were absent for long periods because of army reserve duty. Elizur and Kaffman (1983), studying 25 children whose fathers were killed in 1973 Yom Kippur war, discovered increased symptoms of pathological bereavement among children who had experienced excessive family conflict before parental loss. They concluded that a family with a prior history of unusual conflict or other maladaptive response would need additional support beyond the acknowledgment and expression of grief. The interactive role of family support was brought out in the work of Rosenthal and Levy-Shiff (1992), who investigated younger children and their parents. Most of the parents (67.4%) derived great emotional support from the closeness, helpfulness, and commitment of their immediate family ("I only now discovered what wonderful children I have," was characteristic of the statements made by mothers).

These data are congruent with the suggestions of Hobfoll et al. (1991) that individual coping efforts may be aided or impeded by the social milieu, and that children's reactions often mirror the reactions of their parents.

METHODOLOGICAL CONSIDERATIONS

Assessment of the extent of fears, scope of anxiety, and feasibility of controlling for relevant variables raised methodological questions for us concerning the proper measuring instruments, research methods, and the time and place of measurement in war-related research with children. A broad range of measures are available for use in such studies. These include interviews, standardized questionnaires, questionnaires designed specifically for the purposes of the study, projective and semiprojective techniques, behavioral observation, physiological measures, content analysis of written material, analysis of children's drawings, and telephone surveys. Subjects can be approached either directly or indirectly (e.g., through evaluations of parents or teachers). Time of measurement may cover different stress points: prior to impact, when war is highly probable, during the impact stage, immediately after a war, and at specific periods following a war. Clearly, each measure has its advantages and disadvantages. The problems and limitations of conducting research during the impact stage of war include technical difficulties (e.g., problems in physically approaching the population); overinvolvement of the researchers; suspension of school, preventing large-scale direct access to children; resistance of both the population and mental health professionals, in the belief that research during wartime is unnecessary and nonfunctional; unavailability of research grants arising from budgetary problems; insufficient time to prepare proposals and to formulate research questions and goals; absence of suitable, situation-specific, research instruments, with the consequent need to develop such tools rapidly; difficulties in gaining permission to enter educational institutions and in obtaining parental consent; questions about the validity of retrospective reports; and other methodological difficulties, such as proper sampling procedures and lack of control groups.

Our own experience during the Gulf War indicates that telephone surveys represent a very effective, and perhaps even the only, methodology available for use in real-time research during emergencies such as war, when the population is in physical danger, schools are closed, and many individuals are homebound. Telephone surveys offer the advantages of giving access to a large part of the population at relatively low cost, and allowing for a representative sampling of most sections of the population (in wartime, most paper-and-pencil measures have been administered to accidental samplings). Also, by employing advanced computer technology that enables rapid data processing, it is possible to compile, during wartime, an accurate picture of the general mood of the population, typical fears, ways of coping, and the needs of children and their families. Orderly gathering and rapid transmission of data to the political leadership, educators, and mental health professionals during war and other situations of mass stress can make real-time intervention possible, and serve as a basis of planned policy and decision making in furnishing assistance and information to the population at large. During times of stress, telephone surveys enable us to gather data bearing directly on children's reactions and functioning, without having to obtain formal permission to enter schools.

Moreover, telephone surveys allow for relatively precise comparisons at different points in time, so that we are able to learn about processes of change in the reactions of the population to stressful situations.

As Dillman (1978) observed, no single method applies equally well to every survey situation, and "until the attributes of each method are considered in relation to the study topic, the population to be surveyed, and the precise survey objectives, the question of which method is best cannot be answered" (p. 39). A major problem in drawing conclusions from research findings about children in war has to do with comparison of results among studies. As demonstrated in our review, studies vary substantially in the nature of the measurement tools employed, the age group investigated, and the time frames for outcome assessment. These factors contribute to the difficulty of comparing study findings and drawing definitive conclusions. Consequently, there is great need of a comprehensive plan designed to ensure comparability and interpretability of findings.

WHAT PRICE HABITUATION?

The anecdotal clinical reports and empirical studies reviewed in this chapter seem to indicate, at least from the perspective of the habituation model (Rachman, 1990), that children have exhibited a high level of adaptation to the war situations under investigation. The results coincide with reports from other areas of the world (especially of London during the Blitz) about adaptation to air raids (Janis, 1951; Rachman, 1990), and tend to support the view that children exhibit wide-ranging habituation, unexpected resilience, and relatively few phobic reactions in war situations. The findings can be understood from a number of perspectives.

Rachman (1990) suggested that fear reactions are subject to a process of habituation that can occur even when fearful stimuli are intense. Moreover, habituation may take place as part of the process or even as a result of decreasing uncertainty. It is common for people initially to overpredict the extent of anxiety they will experience in a novel situation; with repeated disconfirmation of their overpredictions, however, their evaluations become more realistic, so that the situation becomes more predictable and more controllable. In the case of the Gulf War, initially there was no way to predict the number of missiles that Iraq might use, where these would be targeted, or the exact timing of attacks. The possible use of chemical warheads was of major concern, and the warning period prior to an attack was at first no more than 90 seconds. Later, the warning time increased to about 5 minutes, thereby adding significantly more time in which to take cover (i.e., more controllability). In addition, most attacks occurred after dark, so that stress usually decreased in daylight hours, due to the rise in predictability.

These habituation tendencies can also be discussed in terms of what Breznitz (1983a, 1983b) referred to as the *immunization model*. According to this model, people get used to stress even under extreme conditions. Difficult experiences that are successfully concluded strengthen people and make them better prepared for the next difficult experience which is to come. There is an analogy here with the action of antibodies in the biological system: People develop, as it were, psychological antibodies and therefore emerge from their ordeal emotionally stronger.

The reduction in anxiety can also be explained by viewing coping as a cluster of primarily intrapsychic processes by which an individual's emotional functioning is protected from external threat. Thus, when the situation that caused the acute stress cannot be controlled by the individual (as in the case of the Gulf War), high defensiveness may offer a valuable response, allowing the individual more time to recover from the confusion and to assimilate the trauma more rapidly.

In certain cases, denial seems to be a psychologically adaptive state. Folkman (1984) pointed out that, for a situation in which a stressful encounter is realistically appraised as uncontrollable, emotion-focused coping that involves strategies such as devaluing the stakes at risk in a stressful encounter (i.e., defensive appraisal) may be adaptive. For children, war usually presents a situation in which they are placed in a passive and helpless position; problem-focused strategy may serve as a reminder of the uncontrollability of the situation, and consequently lead to higher fears. Given that fear is an unpleasant experience and a threat in its own right (Breznitz, 1984), denial can be interpreted as a coping mechanism used to keep anxiety in check. Denial and avoidance of the situation can, thus, be regarded as attempts to cope effectively with the fear itself, if only in the short run. Although this issue is more understandable at the level of short-term adaptation, the implications for the long term are less clear.

Following Selye's (1966) notion of adaptation energy, Breznitz (1983b) described a model necessary for discussing the long-term effects of stress. According to this model, individuals do not have indefinite quantities of adaptational resources. Energy used is not replaceable, and individuals may, at some point, find themselves short of adequate resources if they are subjected to continuous high levels of stress. This process is the basis for the *exhaustion model*. Obviously, it is difficult to assess the amount of energy available, especially because stresses consist of a combination of the variables of frequency, intensity, and duration. According to Breznitz, the resolution of the issue of immunization versus exhaustion may depend on whether the individual's cognitive appraisal of a situation is subjectively defined as a threat or a challenge. Whatever the subjective interpretation, no one has yet been able to specify the adaptational cost. The exhaustion model implies direct costs. The immunization model may comprehend latent costs, but this possibility needs further clarification. The issue needs further study, especially when we consider children living under enduring stress and examine their transition to adulthood and their entry into society. With this issue in mind, we now summarize the major issues examined in this chapter.

The findings on age differences were expected. Younger children can afford to exhibit their fears more than can adults.

With regard to gender differences, some recent reviews suggest that males may be more vulnerable to stress than are females. Although there is always a great deal of behavioral variation within each gender, there are also a number of domains in which gender differences are evident: Boys are more likely than girls to show virtually all forms of physical, emotional, and cognitive vulnerability to stress (Rutter, 1987). Perhaps because girls can deal with emotions better, they share their concerns and fears more readily, which, in the long run, may involve lower psychological cost resulting from the process of adaptation. On the other hand, boys are more likely to suppress their feelings. Therefore, although they seem to cope on the overt level and in short run, they may eventually pay more dearly in terms of the quality of their future well-being.

In accordance with the exhaustion model, increased social support may work to reduce the need to exhaust available internal psychological resources. The findings regarding social support networks seem to be consistent with most results of research in other areas within the broader field of human development.

Data concerning sense of control are rather complex. The studies reported here follow a cognitive–behavioral approach. A greater sense of control and learned resourcefulness are associated with effective coping strategies, and can therefore be regarded as adaptive. It is not surprising, then, that, in a summary of research surveys, Gal (1991) identified self-control as a major factor associated with coping in adults. However, we have no information about the long-term implications of using increased self-control strategies.

Finally, the extent and consistency with which a decline in anxiety was reported over time would seem to indicate that the process is adaptive. However, it is unclear how adaptive this reduction is in the long run. From our discussion of the methodological issues it is evident that information obtained in wartime mainly through self-reports and telephone surveys is limited in its scope, and cannot provide sufficient insight into the deeper levels of psychological functioning and their adaptive implications. There is some information that may offer a clue in this regard. Immediately following the cease-fire, the Department of Social Services in the Municipality of Tel Aviv encouraged children to write short messages and draw pictures for the American soldiers stationed in the region (Sagi, 1991). The findings, albeit highly tentative, appear to show that verbal motifs tended to be positive (e.g., thanking the U.S. armed forces, emphasizing peace), whereas the pictorial motifs tended to be negative (e.g., killing Saddam Hussein, gas masks, Scud missiles). Thus, deep feelings that were conveyed pictorially may have been repressed or denied at the verbal level. Bat-Zion and Levy-Shiff (1991) suggested that the dreams of children during the Gulf War were filled with strong emotions.

Assessing the cost of habituation with regard to long-term adaptation is a very difficult task. Nevertheless, the endeavor is of crucial importance, even if assessments must remain highly conjectural. We hope, therefore, that researchers and concerned professionals will continue to investigate the subject.

The potential cost of having to live under conditions of stress is discussed on a macrolevel by Moses (1983), who considered the expressions of hostility in Israeli society in reference to a broad range of daily activities (e.g., reckless and inconsiderate driving, externalization of rage toward authority figures). This was further elaborated in a recent assessment of Israeli society by Horowitz and Lissak (1990). In speaking of "Trouble in Utopia," they described a society burned out from continuous exposure to threats to its security, unresolved economic strain, and the need to deal with the complex problems associated with immigration. The consequence has been what Moses (1983) referred to as a "lack of psychological awareness and readiness to see psychological motivations in oneself or others is . . . an integral part of the Israeli way of life" (p. 132–133).

The fact that the Gulf War is no longer discussed in Israel, nor is part of any public agenda, may reflect adaptation in the short term. The Gulf War is perhaps the most profoundly repressed phenomenon that Israelis have ever experienced, despite the serious threat to which the country was exposed at time. It is unclear what the interplay is between the habituation-immunization models, which seem to be in line with the data presented here, and the exhaustion model, for which only some anecdotal and speculative information is available. Thus, the long-term effects that the recent war may have on Israeli children remain to be examined further.

REFERENCES

Barrios, B. A., & O'Dell, S. L. (1989). Fears and anxieties. In E. J. Mash & R. A. Barkley (Eds.), *Treatment of childhood disorders* (pp. 167–221). New York: Guilford.

Bat-Zion, N., & Levy-Shiff, R. (1991, May). *Recent data on the effects of the Gulf War.* Paper presented at the Conference on the Effects of War and Violence on Children, Rockville, MD.

Ben-Zur, H., & Zeidner, M. (1988). Sex differences in anxiety, curiosity, and anger: A cross-cultural study. *Sex Roles, 19,* 335–347.

Breznitz, S. (Ed.). (1983a). *The denial of stress.* New York: International Universities Press.

Breznitz, S. (Ed.). (1983b). The noble challenge of stress. In S. Breznitz (Ed.), *Stress in Israel* (pp. 265–274). New York: Van Nostrand Reinhold.

Breznitz, S. (1984). *Cry wolf: The psychology of false alarms.* Hillsdale, NJ: Lawrence Erlbaum Associates.

Dillman, D. A. (1978). *Mail and telephone surveys: The total design method.* New York: Wiley.

Elizur, E., & Kaffman, M. (1983). Factors influencing the severity of childhood bereavement reactions. *American Journal of Orthopsychiatry, 53,* 668–676.

Folkman, S. (1984). Personal control and stress and coping processes: A theoretical analysis. *Journal of Personality and Social Psychology, 45,* 839–852.

Gal, R. (1991, February). *Emergency survey: Reactions of the Israeli public to the missiles attacks during January 1991.* Unpublished manuscript, Israeli Institute for Military Studies, Zichron Yaakov, Israel.

Helson, H. (1964). *Adaptation level theory: The experimental and systematic approach to behavior.* New York: Harper & Row.

Hobfoll, S. E., Spielberger, C. D., Breznitz, S., Figley, C., Folkman, S., Lepper-Green, B., Meichenbaum, D., Milgram, N., Sandler, I., Sarason, I., & Van der Kolk, B. A. (1991). War-related stress: Addressing the stress of war and other traumatic events. *American Psychologist, 46,* 848–855.

Horowitz, D., & Lissak, M. (1990). *Trouble in utopia: The overburdened polity of Israel.* Tel Aviv, Israel: Am Oved.

Janis, I. L. (1951). *Air war and emotional stress.* New York: McGraw-Hill.

Janis, I. L. (1983). Preventing pathogenic denials by means of stress inoculation. In S. Breznitz (Ed.), *The denial of stress* (pp. 35–77). New York: International Universities Press.

Kaffman, M., & Elizur, E. (1977). Infants who become enuretics: A longitudinal study of 161 kibbutz children. *Monographs of the Society of Research in Child Development, 42*(2, Serial No. 170).

Kessler, R. C., & McLoed, J. D. (1985). Social support and mental health in communities samples. In S. Cohen & S. L. Syire (Eds.), *Social support and health* (pp. 219–240). Orlando, FL: Academic Press.

Klingman, A. (1992a). Stress reactions of Israeli youth during the Gulf War: A quantitative study. *Professional Psychology: Research and Practice, 23,* 521–527.

Klingman, A. (1992b). The effects of parent-implemented crisis-intervention: A real-life emergency involving a child's refusal to use gas mask. *Journal of Clinical Child Psychology, 21,* 70–75.

Klingman, A., & Goldstein, Z. (1992). *Israeli adolescents' response to unconventional war threat: Before and after the Gulf war.* Unpublished manuscript, University of Haifa, Division of Counselling of the Department of Education.

Klingman, A., & Wiesner, E. (1982). The relationship between proximity to tension areas and size of settlement of residence to fear level of Israeli children. *Journal of Behavior Therapy and Experimental Psychology, 13,* 321–323.

Lavie, P., Amit, Y., Epstein, R., & Tzischinsky, O. (1992, June). *Children sleep under the threat of the Scud.* Paper presented at the Annual Meeting of the Association of Sleep Research, Phoenix, AZ.

Lytton, H., & Romney, D. M. (1991). Parents' differential socialization of boys and girls: A meta-analysis. *Psychological Bulletin, 109,* 267–296.

Maccoby, E. E., & Jacklin, C. N. (1974). *The psychology of sex differences.* Stanford, CA.: Stanford University Press.

Melamed, B. G., Klingman, A., & Siegel, L. J. (1984). Childhood stress and anxiety: Individualizing cognitive behavioral strategies in the reduction of medical and dental stress.

In A. W. Meyers & W. E. Craighead (Eds.), *Cognitive behavior theory with children* (pp. 289–313). New York: Plenum.

Milgram, N. A. (1982). War related stress in Israeli children and youth. In L. Goldberg & S. Breznitz (Eds.), *Handbook of stress: Theoretical and clinical aspects* (pp. 656–676). New York: The Free Press.

Milgram, N. A., Toubiana, Y., Klingman, A., Raviv, A., & Goldstein, I. (1988). Situational exposure and personal loss in children's acute and chronic stress reactions to a school disaster. *Journal of Traumatic Stress, 1,* 339–352.

Milgram, R. M., & Milgram, N. A. (1976). The effect of the Yom Kippur War on anxiety level in Israeli children. *The Journal of Psychology, 94,* 107–113.

Mintz, M. (1991). *A comparison between children in two areas following the Gulf War.* Unpublished manuscript, Department of Psychology, Tel Aviv University, Tel Aviv, Israel.

Moses, R. (1982). Emotional responses to stress in Israel: A psychoanalytic perspective. In S. Breznitz (Ed.), *Stress in Israel* (pp.114–137). New York: Van Nostrand Reinhold.

Pynoos, R. S., & Eth, S. (1985). Developmental perspective on psychic trauma in childhood. In C. R. Figley (Ed.), *Trauma and its wake* (Vol. 2, pp. 36–52). New York: Brunner/Mazel.

Rachman, S. J. (1990). *Fear and courage.* New York: W. H. Freeman.

Raviv, A., & Klingman, A. (1983). Children under stress. In S. Breznitz (Ed.), *Stress in Israel* (pp. 138–162). New York: Van Nostrand Reinhold.

Raviv, A., & Raviv, A. (1991). *Telephone surveys during and after the Gulf War.* Unpublished manuscript, Department of Psychology, Tel Aviv University, Tel Aviv, Israel.

Rofe, Y., & Lewin, I. (1980). Attitudes toward an emergency and personality in a war environment. *International Journal of Interventional Relations, 4,* 97–106.

Rofe, Y., & Levin, I. (1981). The effect of war environment on dreams and sleep habits. In N. Milgram, C. D. Spielberger, & I. G. Sarason (Eds.), *Stress and anxiety* (Vol. 8, pp. 67–79). New York: Hemisphere.

Rosenbaum, M. (1983). Learned resourcefulness as a behavioral repertoire for the self-regulation of internal events: Issues and speculations. In M. Rosenbaum, C. M. Franks, & Y. Jaffe (Eds.), *Perspectives on behavior therapy in the eighties* (pp. 54–73). New York: Springer.

Rosenbaum, M. (1990). Role of learned resourcefulness in self-control of health behavior. In M. Rosenbaum (Ed.), *Learned resourcefulness: On coping skills, self-control, and adaptive behavior* (pp. 3–30). New York: Springer.

Rosenbaum, M., & Ronen, T. (1991, November). *How did Israeli children and their parents cope with being daily attacked by Scud missiles during the Gulf War?* Paper presented at the 25th Annual Convention for the Advancement of Behavior Therapy, New York.

Rosenthal, M., & Levy-Shiff, R. (1992). *Stress and coping reactions in Israeli infants and toddlers and their mothers to the threat of chemical warfare.* Unpublished manuscript, School of Social Work, Hebrew University, Jerusalem, Israel.

Rutter, M. (1987). Continuities and discontinuities from infancy. In J.D. Osofsky (Ed.), *Handbook of infant development* (2nd ed., pp. 1256–1296), New York: Wiley.

Sagi, A. (1991, May). *Some initial insights about the Gulf War in Israel.* Paper presented at the Conference on the Effects of War and Violence on Children, Rockville, MD.

Schwarzwald, J., Weisenberg, M., Waysman, M., Solomon, Z., & Klingman, A. (in press). *Stress reactions of school-age children to the bombardment by Scud missiles. Journal of Abnormal Psychology.*

Selye, H. (1966). *The stress of life.* New York: McGraw-Hill.

Swenson, C. C., & Klingman, A. (in press). Children and war. In C. F. Saylor (Ed.), *Children and disasters.* New York: Plenum.

Weisenberg, M., Schwarzwald, J., Waysman, M., Solomon, Z., & Klingman, A. (in press). Coping of school-age children in the sealed room during Scud missile bombardment and postwar stress reactions. *Journal of Personality Assessment.*

Zeidner, M., Klingman, A., & Itzkovitz, R. (1993). Anxiety, control, social support and coping under threat of missile attack: A semi-projective assessment. *Journal of Personality Assessment, 60,* 435–457.

Ziv, A., & Israeli, R. (1973). Effects of bombardment on the manifest of anxiety level of children living in kibbutzim. *Journal of Consulting and Clinical Psychology, 40,* 287–291.

Ziv, A., Kruglanski, A. W., & Schulman, S. (1974). Children's psychological reactions to wartime stress. *Journal of Personality and Social Psychology, 30,* 24–30.

5 Israeli Children Paint War

Nurit Shilo-Cohen
The Israel Museum, Jerusalem

The focus of this chapter is a unique project that took place at the Ruth Youth Wing of the Israel Museum in Jerusalem during the height of the Gulf War. An outline of the background, methods, and ideas behind the project are followed by a discussion of the iconographical motifs, themes, and slogans that involved children in other Israeli museums during the war, and how these visual images compared to the graphics, texts, and images that emerged from advertisements, newspapers, billboards, and so forth.

The Israel Museum remained open during the Gulf War, except for the first few days when people were advised to stay indoors. The busiest department was the Ruth Youth Wing. Scores of children came to the museum, and their first activity entailed decorating their gas mask boxes to disguise the seriousness of the contents and to render the boxes less threatening and more personal (see Fig. 5.1). The children carried their decorated gas mask boxes at all times, even during regular art classes, which began functioning within a few days of the beginning of the war (see Figs. 5.2 and 5.3).

Although the museum was open, a lot of the valuable works of art were stored in the vaults, among them the impressionist and post-impressionist paintings, leaving the gallery looking very empty and gloomy (see Fig. 5.4).

The Youth Wing was asked by the director of the museum to try to fill the empty hall with children's paintings. Because there were a lot of children in the museum daily, among them children of the museum staff because schools were still closed, the Youth Wing staff was confident it could paper the gloomy gallery with children's art and keep the youngsters occupied in an interesting way. This was the background of the project: it was not undertaken with a therapeutic aim.

FIG. 5.1.   Decorating mask boxes in the recycling room.

The children of the Israel Museum's "day camp" consisted of elementary school youngsters aged 6 to 12. Tzipporah Kleiner, an experienced art teacher, organized the project. The children were led into the empty hall and asked to make huge paintings that would cover the walls.

Before the children began their artistic creations, a group discussion took place, in which they were asked to talk about what they saw, heard, felt, and thought about since the beginning of the war. The youngsters opened up and told personal stories about how the cat didn't want to go into the sealed room when the sirens went off, how the house was crowded because relatives from Tel Aviv came, how happy they were that they didn't have to go to school and could watch cartoons on TV all day long, and how they were thirsty in the sealed rooms and Mommy didn't allow them to drink through the mask because it might spill. Some talked about how scared they were, and others said it was great to spend so much time with their parents, who now always came home before dark when the sirens usually sounded.

After the discussion, the children formed groups of about 10 youngsters each. Each team worked on one expansive piece of paper (approximately 9 by 15 ft), using mostly gouache, fingerpaints, oil crayons, pencils, and felt pens. Some groups worked on paper pinned to the wall; others worked around tables.

At first, each child tended to work on a small individual area, but, as the work progressed, an overall interaction emerged: Children moved away

FIG. 5.2.   Art class in the Ruth Youth Wing.

from the domain of their private "territory" and became linked to each other against the common background. Each group worked on its project for about 2 days.

Despite the varying ages of the children, certain common themes occurred in their work: motifs that depict the startling variety of visual images that were thrust into their world overnight. The most common image, of course, was the gas mask (see Figs. 5.5, 5.6, and 5.7). The mask was the closest, most personal, and intimate thing experienced in the war, particularly outside of the Tel Aviv area. The mask was the uncomfortable, malodorous, alien object that Israelis, young and old, wore like suction cups day after day during a war that the rest of the world watched on TV. Along with the images of the masks, there were occasional descriptions of

FIG. 5.3.   Wood class in the Ruth Youth Wing.

mask boxes and their contents, such as the atropine injection against nerve gas and the powder for burns. Sometimes animals—whether pet dogs or elephants—were depicted wearing masks, possibly an expression of the children's wish to save them from the "flood," as in the story of Noah's Ark.

There were some depictions of the sealed room itself (see Fig. 5.8). In this photo, one can see a window sealed with tape. The girl is wearing a mask and a radio sits on the table—another common element and an essential part of the drama of the sealed room. Many of the images that emerged were items from newspaper photos and, even more, from the TV, because the media played such a central role in the Gulf War. Saddam Hussein (see Fig. 5.9) was sometimes even pictured as a demon.

FIG. 5.4. Empty impressionist and post-impressionist hall at the Israel Museum, Jerusalem.

FIG. 5.5. Boy with mask (detail).

FIG. 5.6.   Wearing the mask. Inscription reads, "Fashion today" (detail).

Other images include Israeli, American, and Iraqi flags (Figs. 5.10 and 5.11). In Fig. 5.11, one sees a plane above the American flag, a tank over the Iraqi flag, and the word *shalom* in Hebrew above it all. Additional elements depicted in the paintings are Scud missiles, fighter planes, ruins of homes (see Fig. 5.12), military personnel with dogs looking for survivors, Patriots, sirens, and vipers. *Viper* was the code word sounded on the radio that warned people that the siren was about to go off.

The Hebrew word for *viper* was written repeatedly all over the paintings, graffiti style, as were other expressions and military codes heard regularly during the war. In addition, the paintings depict the map of Israel divided into alphabetically labeled zones (with areas of risk indicated in descending order). Sometimes the map was drawn with targets over various objects (see Fig. 5.13). Less common images are oil spills and cormorants, the large sea birds whose pictures were broadcast all over the world after they became coated with oil on the shores of the Gulf. These last two images were only

FIG. 5.7. Masks (details).

FIG. 5.8. The sealed room (detail).

FIG. 5.9. Entrance panel (Saddam Hussain's portrait lower right).

FIG. 5.10. Panel with Israeli flag.

FIG. 5.11.   American and Iraqi flags (detail).

TV depictions, as far as the Israeli children were concerned, whereas the other images were part of the reality of their everyday lives.

Although the paintings done at the Ruth Youth Wing of the Israel Museum were the result of group efforts, they still strongly reflect the expressions of the feeling and thoughts of individual children. It may have been easier for each child to address such a difficult subject as part of a "chorus" rather than as a solo artist (Shilo-Cohen, 1991).

Two different projects involving children were launched by other museums during the war. The first, Art by Mail, was initiated by Yael Borowich of the Tel Aviv Museum (Borowich, 1992), which was closed throughout the war. The only way to communicate with children, many of whom were out of town, was by mail. Children who were members of the

FIG. 5.12. Panel with mask, ruined house, and soldier with dog.

FIG. 5.13. Israeli map divided into zones with target (detail).

FIG. 5.14.   Masks even for elephants (postcard from the Art by Mail project).

museum received a postcard requesting a return postcard with a drawing. Because the format was small, the results were markedly different from Jerusalem's huge paintings, although some of the motifs were similar. On the whole, the postcards exhibited the characteristics of caricatures or comic strips (see Fig. 5.14).

Another project was organized by the Ramat Gan Museum (Valkstein & Ury, 1991), involving children who were evacuated from their destroyed homes and housed in two hotels. This scheme served primarily a therapeutic purpose, and the technique and the four stages of the project were determined beforehand. In the first meeting, the room was covered with visual images from newspapers. The children were asked to draw their personal stories in comic-strip style with a thin black pen. Pen and ink were used in the second stage and water colors in the third stage. The final result appeared on a large piece of white painted plywood.

The Ramat Gan creations were characterized by fewer masks, but more houses and missiles. Interestingly, some of the missiles were drawn floppy instead of straight, perhaps indicating the children's desire to neutralize the Scuds (see Fig. 5.15). This wish to diminish the power of the Scuds is also reflected in the size of the houses, which tower over the missiles. There were no depictions of animals with masks. Perhaps the children whose houses were destroyed realized the masks did not offer much protection.

FIG. 5.15.   Floppy missiles (from the Ramat Gan project).

FIG. 5.16.   Illustration of Eitan Kedmy, Variation on the flag.

The projects in the three museums were initiated with different purposes in mind. In Jerusalem, the object was to cover the walls of an empty gallery and to keep the children busy; in Tel Aviv, the idea was to keep in touch; and in Ramat Gan, the goal was to help children deal with the psychological stresses of war. Because the museums used different techniques, different

FIG. 5.17.   Illustration by Zeev Engelmayer, *Little Sealed Riding Hood*.

artistic results emerged, but the topics and visual images that were created had much in common.

It is interesting to compare the children's artistic depictions with some of the graphic images that appeared in advertisements, billboards, and newspapers that were assembled in the Tel Aviv Museum's exhibition, "Real Time" (Donner, 1991). In the Tel Aviv exhibition, the emphasis was on textual information. However, visual images were also used: portraits, gas masks, radios, flags, and Saddam Hussein, for example. Patriotism was stressed, and the Israeli flag was depicted often, together with quotes from the Bible. There was mention of borders, such as the "green line," the

FIG. 5.18.   Purim day (February 28, 1991).

border between Israel proper and the territories. The image of borders also refers to the private sealed rooms (see Fig. 5.16). Black humor was also prevalent, as portrayed on the cover of Tzvi Engelmeir's book, *Sealed Little Red Riding Hood,* in which the title of the innocent children's story was changed to incorporate Gulf War terminology. (see Fig. 5.17).

Weeks of stress and uncertainty vanished in an explosion of celebration on the Jewish holiday of Purim, which commemorates an ancient victory over a Persian tyrant who had planned to exterminate the Jews. A traditional day for costumes and masks, Purim, appropriately coincided with the end of the Gulf War, when Israelis joyously untaped their sealed rooms. Jerusalem crowds, dressed in costume, came to the Israel Museum by the thousands, but some still carried their masks one last time, just in case. Figure 5.18 depicts the feelings of that Purim day. The sculpture of the pipe smoker at the entrance to the Youth Wing still carries his gas mask box, but he is already wearing a Purim party hat.

REFERENCES

Borowich, Y. (1992). Art during the Gulf War: The postcard project. *ICOM-CECA, Annual conference, Jerusalem, October 1991: The Museum and the Needs of People* (pp. 141–142).

Donner, B. (1991). *Real time: The Gulf War—Graphic texts.* Tel Aviv: Tel Aviv Museum of Art.

Shilo-Cohen, N. (1991). Children's paintings during the Gulf War. *Ariel, 83,* pp. 40–44.

Valkstein, D., & Ury, N. (1991). *Preservation: Paintings by the children of Ramat Gan.* Ramat Gan: The Museum of Israeli Art.

6 Settler Children and the Gulf War

Charles W. Greenbaum
Chedva Erlich
The Hebrew University of Jerusalem

Yosef H. Toubiana
Tel Aviv University

The various stresses to which human beings are exposed have some common elements and some elements that are unique. The stresses faced by children in the Gulf War have some unique qualities. At the same time, these stresses may have enough general characteristics to allow us to expand our perspective on stress and to contribute to a theory of the effects of stress on children.

The present study attempted to determine whether exposure of Israeli Jewish children to a long-term stress, the Palestinian intifada, affected their response to the short-term, time-limited stress of the Gulf War. Previous research performed on other stresses may not be a good guide for understanding the reactions of children to the stresses of the Gulf War. There is a basic problem with such research involving the identification of the stressor. A child exposed to war may be exposed to a multitude of stressors: physical threat, actual physical or psychological trauma, deprivation, loss, malnutrition, bereavement, abuse, or various other stressors. It is often difficult to understand which of these traumatic events, or which combination of them, has affected the child.

These problems limit the generalizations that can be drawn from previous research on the effects of war on children, because different stresses are involved in each case. This is true, for example, of the studies of Freud and Burlingham (1943), Fraser (1979) and Arroyo and Eth (1985). Although stress is common to each situation studied, each situation is unique. Situations differ with regard to the combination of stressors they include. In fact, much theorizing on the effects of stress, such as the valuable work done by Janis (1958), Lazarus (1991), and Lazarus and Folkman (1984) does not deal with the problem of differences in types of stress situations. Therefore, before presenting our research, we suggest a number of meaningful dimensions along which stress situations can be evaluated. We then locate the Gulf War and the intifada on these dimensions, which leads us to the presentation of our research questions.

Many of these dimensions of stressors have been cited by Benedek (1985), Hobfoll et al., (1991), Eth and Pynoos (1985), Milgram (1989), and Terr (1991), but our categorization is somewhat different. In our view, various dimensions of stressors must be considered in understanding the individual's reactions, because even slight differences in the make-up of the stress situation can affect those reactions.

We suggest that the dimensions of stressors be divided into two major categories: situational or physical sources of stress, including the social conditions and cultural factors in the stress situation; and individual reactions to stressors. The following are the situational aspects of stress that must be considered in the evaluation of any stress situation:

1. Intensity (the most important variable to consider): the degree of trauma inherent in the situation.
2. Time: the duration of the stress situation.
3. Repetition: the number of times that the stress situation is repeated.
4. Threat: the degree to which there is threat to the individual as opposed to actual physical trauma. Threat alone may have strong effects on the well-being of the individual.
5. Predictability (as opposed to uncertainty) in the stress situation.
6. Social and cultural context: including social norms regarding the expression of emotion; which people the person is with before, during and after the stress is experienced; and the relationship between the subject and those people.

Individual difference variables include:

1. Cognitive appraisal (see Lazarus & Folkman, 1984): the perception of stress, which varies widely among individuals.
2. Age and cognitive development, which will affect the degree to which the individual is able to make effective cognitive appraisals of the stress situation.
3. Previous experience with stress.
4. Previous success in coping with stress.
5. Temperament: particularly whether the individual augments or buffers stressful stimuli.
6. Ability to engage in activity, which could overcome the stress or distract the individual's attention from the stressful stimuli.

Let us examine the Gulf War of 1991 and the intifada in the light of some of these dimensions of stress, based on our personal experience and on media accounts at the time. The Gulf War began on January 16, 1991, with the Allied attack on Iraq and Kuwait, and ended on February 25, 1991. For about 6 weeks, the population of Israel and the territories under its control were exposed to the threat of conventional and chemical warfare through missiles sent from Iraq. A number of conventional explosive missiles struck Israel and caused considerable damage, although less than was expected in terms of property damage, loss of life, and injuries. In terms of the dimensions just listed, the Gulf War was a stress of limited length, relatively low intensity, but high threat for much of the population. A small minority of the population, mostly concentrated in the center of the country, experienced missile strikes; for them, the stress situation was of brief but high intensity.

The day-to-day situation during the Gulf War was highly predictable in comparison to other stress situations: The population had warning of almost every strike. Residents could engage in a great deal of cognitive appraisal concerning the threat to them and could take some action to protect themselves, even though it turned out that some of this action directed to self protection against chemical warfare was ineffective. For most of the population, there was limited immediate experience with trauma of this particular kind; however, much of the population had been through previous wars from the time of World War II and the Holocaust to the various wars in which Israel had been engaged.

The children in our sample did not come from areas that had been directly hit in the Gulf War, although missiles fell near some of the places where our subjects lived, away from residential areas, causing no damage. Thus, our subjects did not experience any physical trauma as a result of the war, although they were subjected to the same threats as the rest of the country. There was constant uncertainty each time there was an attack warning, and citizens were ordered to take protective measures against gas attacks. Eventually, the attacks became relatively predictable in space and time (i.e., most attacks occurred at night and in the center of the country, although there were exceptions). As a result, the anxiety level of much of the population was reduced as time went on.

The population in the territories under Israel's control have had experience with a previous and ongoing stressful set of events: the intifada. These territories include the West Bank (officially known in Israel and some other countries as Judea and Samaria) and the Gaza Strip. The West Bank was the locus of our settler sample. This chapter deals, in part, with the reactions of children of Jewish-Israeli settlers to the stress of the Gulf War against the background of the intifada.

The area is populated by approximately 800,000 Palestinians and close to 100,000 Israelis. The Israeli settlements are scattered over a large expanse of territory. Although there are a few relatively large settlements of a few thousand in population, most of the settlements are small, containing up to 1,500 inhabitants; these were the source of our sample.

Intifada is the Arabic word for *uprising* and refers to the sudden outburst of Palestinian resistance to Israeli military occupation that was the outcome of the Six Day War in 1967. The intifada began in December 1987, and has continued in various forms to the present day. We use the term *settlers* to indicate the Jewish-Israeli population that has settled in the territories under Israel's control, claiming historical rights to the land. The term *city children* is used to indicate the group of children whose homes were in Jerusalem or its surroundings. These children were less exposed to the dangers of the intifada than the settler children.

During the intifada, Israeli children of settlers have been subjected to danger in their travels to and from their settlements. For many children, this kind of travel is a daily occurrence, because their schools are in other settlements or, at times, in cities. The dangers to them include road blocks, stone throwing, and occasional Molotov cocktails and gunfire aimed at vehicles.

There has been no systematic psychological research on the effects of the intifada on Jewish-Israeli children. The only previous research on the topic has been on Palestinian children, who have experienced various dangers and stresses (Baker, 1990, 1991). According to Baker, these children reported a higher rate of anxiety-related psychosomatic symptoms than did Arab children whose families were citizens of Israel and who were not living in areas of intifada activity. Masalha (1993; this volume, chapter 7) has described dream content reflecting stress in this population of children.

The dimensions of the intifada are different from those of the Gulf War. The intensity and predictability of the stress of the intifada for Israeli settler children is variable, depending on events. The threat of physical trauma is high, but so is the degree of experience with previous stress. The duration of the experiences has been intermittent, but of long duration. Because the settlements are small, the degree of social support the children receive may be presumed to be high.

The basic question for our research is whether previous experience with stress affects the endurance of the individual in coping with further stress. This question was tested during the Gulf War, when the populations of Israel and the territories under its control were subjected to an additional stress: the threat and actual impact of missiles coming from abroad.

Both the intifada and the Gulf War are relatively new experiences in recent Israeli history. As a result, the conclusions we draw from Israeli stress research prior to the intifada and the Gulf War are limited. The research cited by Breznitz (1983), Rofe and Lewin (1982), Milgram (1986), Milgram, Toubiana, Klingman, Raviv, and Goldstein (1988), and Dreman and Cohen (1990) all dealt with situations in which both the stress stimuli and means of coping were different. These studies reported on children in border settlements undergoing bombardment, children who have undergone trauma in attacks by terrorists on buses, children who have been involved in fatal accidents involving motor vehicles, and children who have been displaced from their homes with their families. All of these situations contain some elements that, using the dimensions outlined earlier, distinguish them from the specific stresses engendered by the intifada and the Gulf War.

Research performed during and immediately after the Gulf War concerning the effects of the war on children and their parents has uncovered some valuable information concerning the effects of stress during the war as a function of age, location in relation to missile hits, and gender of the child. The most striking and consistent result in these studies is the gender difference: Levy-Schiff and Bat-Zion (1993, this volume, chapter 8), Rahav and Ronen (1992), Rosenbaum and Ronen (1992) and Toubiana, Goldstein, and Har-Even (1992) all found that girls had higher stress levels than boys, particularly on self-report measures.

Rosenbaum and Ronen (1992) reported that stress was markedly higher at night, when most of the attacks occurred. They also found that children who were highly anxious to begin with had different coping patterns from less anxious children. Toubiana et al. (1992) did not find strong effects of proximity to missile hits on children's stress reactions. These results are in line with those reported in another context by Rofe and Lewin (1982), who reported that Jewish-Israeli children in a border region under fire actually had fewer anxiety-related reactions than children in no immediate danger.

Rahav and Ronen (1992) found that sixth-grade children (12-year- olds) reported more symptoms during the war than did second-grade children (7-year-olds). They also noted that girls reported more symptoms regarding their state before the war than did boys and that this effect held in both classes. Taken as a whole, these findings show a relatively consistent gender effect, in which girls reported more anxiety than boys in the face of stress stimuli. Other possible factors — such as proximity to a target that has been hit, and the age of the child — were less consistent. These studies did not deal with the effects of cumulative stress.

The present study deals with two major issues, and three minor ones. Of the major ones, the first is the effect of cumulative stress; this was investigated by studying settler children, who had been subjected to the stress of the intifada for approximately 3 years prior to the stress of the Gulf War. The second is the question of delayed effects, which we investigated by studying the children 4–5 months after the end of the Gulf War; this is in contrast to most other studies of the Gulf War, which were carried out during the war itself or shortly thereafter. Given that there were stress reactions during the war, we expected that there would be relatively long-term effects of stress; what we did not know was which groups would have the strongest reactions.

The other issues that concern us have also been addressed in other studies on the Gulf War. One issue common to all the studies is that of gender differences. As we have shown, other studies of the effects of the Gulf War on children have found this to be a strong factor: Girls tended to show more anxiety than boys. Therefore, the issue of gender differences and their interactions with the possible effects of cumulative stress interested us, as well. A second question concerned age. Because age generally reflects cognitive development, we were interested in comparing children between 11 and 14 years of age. This range covers the progression from latency to early adolescence, and so may reflect differences in the way children and adolescents react to stress. The data from other studies concerning the effects of age on reactions to stress, including those concerning the Gulf War that we have already cited, have been inconsistent on this issue. Therefore, our investigation of age must be considered exploratory.

The last issue that we dealt with is one we have in common with some other studies of the Gulf War (e.g., Itzkowitz, Zeidner, & Klingman, 1992; Levy-Schiff & Bat-Zion, this volume, chapter 8): the comparison between self-report and projective measures in dealing with stress. In addition to several self-report measures concerning levels of response to stress and coping with stress, we considered it important to develop situation-specific projective methods to measure the stress that people may feel. Such an approach could supplement the self-report measures. We, therefore, used a word-association technique to uncover responses that might not have been otherwise expressed. Use of both self-report and projective measures allows for a comparison that may enlighten us concerning the most effective ways of measuring responses to stress stimuli.

METHOD

This research was carried out in June and July 1991, about 4 months after the end of the Gulf War. Children were drawn from Grades 5 to 8 (ages 10.5 to 14.5 years) in seven schools; three schools were attended by settler children and four by city children.

Subjects

A total of 428 children participated in the study. There were 200 boys and 225 girls; 3 children did not give information concerning gender.

There were 278 city children, who came from four different schools in Jerusalem, and 150 settler children who studied in three schools, which were located near their homes, about 25 kilometers north of Jerusalem. Two of the four schools in Jerusalem were religious (Jewish-Orthodox), and 198 subjects were drawn from them; an additional 81 children were drawn from two nonreligious schools. Of the settler children, 120 came from two religious schools, and 29 came from nonreligious schools. All the city children were in classes where boys and girls studied together, whereas in the religious schools attended by the settler children, there were separate classes for boys and girls.

Table 6.1 details the allocation of subjects by group (settlers in comparison with city children), gender, and grade. There are relatively few nonreligious subjects among the settler children, reflecting the fact that this group constitutes a minority population among the small settlements from which our sample was drawn. There were few subjects sampled from Grade 8, because we were not able to obtain a large number of subjects from that grade within the time limit set for this study. There were no eighth-grade girls in the settler group.

Questionnaires

The subjects responded to the following sets of questions.

Personal Data. The first page of the first questionnaire contained questions relating to the subject's personal characteristics: age, grade, residence, and country of origin.

Word Associations. The next part of that questionnaire consisted of a set of small-sized pages; on each one, a single word was printed. The

TABLE 6.1
Distribution of Numbers of Subjects by Age, Group, and Gender

	City Children			
Grade	Male	Female	No Info	Total
5	46	50	—	96
6	30	46	2	78
7	24	36	1	61
8	15	28	—	43
Subtotal	115	160	3	278
	Settler Children			
5	28	26	—	54
6	22	14	—	36
7	24	25	—	49
8	11			11
Subtotal	85	65		150
Total	200	225	3	428

subjects were asked by the examiner to write down on each page the words that came into their minds when reading the target word for that page. After giving the children 15 seconds to respond to the first word, the examiner instructed the children to turn the page and do the same for the next word. This procedure was repeated for a total of 13 words.

The words used are shown in Table 6.2, with the results. As indicated, 2 of the words are neutral, 5 are related to the Gulf War (e.g., *siren*, *tape*), 5 are related to the intifada (e.g., *stones*, *tire*; burning tires are often used in demonstrations by Palestinians), and one word, *windowpane*, that is related to both the Gulf War and the intifada.

Issues of Concern.   For these, as for all of the remaining questionnaires, instructions were provided, in writing, on the questionnaires. The subjects were asked to rate, on a 4-point scale, eight issues that were possible sources of stress in their lives, indicating the amount of concern they experienced regarding each. The list is presented in Table 6.3. The two critical items were "missile attack" (relating to the Gulf War) and "intifada."

Proximity to Missile Hits Questionnaire.   This questionnaire consisted of nine items asking the children about their geographical proximity to any place that had been hit by a missile and any family involvement, or involvement by friends or acquaintances with any experience involving the missile hits.

TABLE 6.2
Summary of Differences for Gender and Area in Word Associations Related to the Intifada

		Origin of Difference	
Word	Type of Word	Gender (Boys > Girls)	Group (Settler > City Children)
Blossom	N		
Material	W		
Grenade	I		
Mask	W		
Stones	I		*
Book	N		
Cooperation	I	*	*
Siren	W		
Blocked	I		*
Tape	W		
Room	W		
Tire	I	*	*
Windowpanes	W, I		*

Notes.   Differences were in direction of boys giving more intifada-related associations than girls; and settler children giving more than city children.

N = neutral; W = Gulf War; I = Intifada; * = words for which differences were found.

TABLE 6.3
Mean Concern Ratings for Boys and Girls for Eight Issues

Issues		Boys	Girls	Total Sample
Studies	M	2.43	2.44	2.44
	SD	.90	.78	.84
Problems with siblings	M	1.96	2.13	2.05
	SD	.93	.89	.91
Missile attack	M	2.18	2.64	2.41
	SD	1.02	1.03	1.05
Traffic accidents	M	2.77	2.95	2.86
	SD	.99	.87	.93
Relations with friends	M	2.45	2.57	2.51
	SD	1.06	1.04	1.05
Intifada	M	2.21	2.70	2.47
	SD	1.12	.92	1.05
Illness	M	2.10	2.27	2.19
	SD	.93	.96	.95
Parental demands	M	2.15	2.06	2.10
	SD	1.05	.87	.96

Notes. N boys = 197; N girls = 218.
Ns may differ slightly from cell to cell because of missing information.
1 = low concern; 4 = high concern.

Anxiety Reactions Questionnaire.   This questionnaire asked the subjects to rate, on a 4-point scale, 36 possible reactions that they could be experiencing. The questionnaire contained items from the Child Behavior Checklist (Achenbach & Edelbrock, 1981) concerning psychosomatic symptoms, emotions, behaviors indicating stress, or thoughts reflecting stress. For 8 items that were considered particularly widespread on a pretest, the subjects were also asked to rate, again on a 4-point scale, the degree to which they continued to feel these symptoms after the war was over. They were also asked to indicate the degree to which these phenomena existed before the war.

Coping Questionnaire.   This questionnaire consisted of 18 items, to be ranked on a 4-point scale, reflecting varying coping styles used in dealing with stress. The items were based on observations that we made of children's behavior during the Gulf War; some of the items were similar to those used by Folkman and Lazarus (1985). The items reflect coping through action, hope, relaxation, avoidance, and vigilance.

Worry and Encouragement.   In two open questions, we asked subjects what worried or encouraged them most during the Gulf War.

Sources of Help Questionnaire.   This instrument consisted of eight questions about sources of help (e.g., self, parents, teachers) and the degree to which the subject used them. Subjects responded to each question on a 4-point scale.

Feelings After the War Questionnaire.   Subjects were asked to indicate, on a 4-point scale, the degree to which they experienced each of five emotions (e.g., relief, apprehension) at the end of the war.

Procedure

The study was carried out in school classrooms, with all children in each class participating. The procedure took up one lesson period (i.e., about 45 minutes). In most cases, the class teacher was present when the questionnaires were being administered. Four examiners, all female graduate students in psychology, administered the questionnaires.

The children's parents gave their approval for their children's participation in advance, and the questionnaires were answered anonymously. In our letter requesting permission for their children's participation, we described the research dealing with children's responses to stress situations in the past year. The children were told that the study's topic was behaviors and feelings of school children in various situations. The children were able to read the letter sent to the parents, so we assume that at least some knew that the study dealt with stress. This point is relevant only to the Word Association task, because the subject under study became obvious in the questionnaires administered after this task.

RESULTS

We report on differences when the size of the differences constituted 40% or more of the combined standard deviations of the groups being compared. All such results, as well as some weaker ones, would be considered significant, were such tests appropriate.

Ratings of Stress Situations

Table 6.3 presents the data concerning the subjects' ratings of eight different issues, including "missile attack" and "intifada." The results show that the subjects rated "traffic accidents" as having the highest degree of concern. "Missile attack" and "intifada" were rated high, but still considerably below accidents. These two items dealing with war-related environmental stress showed the strongest gender differences, with girls rating these two situations as being of more concern than did boys. There were no other strong effects on the Issues of Concern ratings.

Ratings of Intifada and Missile Attack

Table 6.4 gives details of the relation between ratings of concern about the intifada and characteristics of the children: gender, grade in school, and area of residence (settlers vs. city children); Table 6.5 does the same for the issue termed *missile attack*. These two concepts are, of course, the two "loaded" topics in the list. These situations were also the only ones for which meaningful effects were found in accordance with our criteria. Table 6.4 shows that, among settler children, girls reported higher concern in response to *intifada* than did boys. These differences did not appear among the city children. Table 6.5 shows that the results for *missile attack* were almost identical to those for *intifada*.

Anxiety Reactions.

Table 6.6 presents the average scores of subjects on the Anxiety Reactions scale used in the study. The results are very similar to those we found for

TABLE 6.4
Mean Concern Ratings for *Intifada* for City and Settler Children

			City		
				Grade	
Gender		5	6	7	8
Boys	M	2.11	2.33	2.75	2.53
	SD	1.18	.96	1.11	1.25
	N	46	30	24	15
Girls	M	2.51	2.44	2.89	2.75
	SD	.77	.92	.85	.80
	N	40	45	36	28

			Settlers		
				Grade	
Gender		5	6	7	8
Boys	M	2.04	1.86	1.92	2.36
	SD	1.26	.99	1.10	.67
	N	28	22	24	11
Girls	M	2.96	2.93	2.83	—
	SD	1.11	1.14	1.01	—
	N	26	14	24	—

Note. 1 = low concern; 4 = high concern.

TABLE 6.5
Mean Concern Ratings for *Missile Attack* for City and Settler Children

City

Gender		Grade 5	Grade 6	Grade 7	Grade 8
		5	*6*	*7*	*8*
Boys	*M*	2.42	2.40	2.54	2.27
	SD	1.07	1.10	1.02	1.16
	N	46	30	24	15
Girls	*M*	2.41	2.59	2.69	2.79
	SD	.93	1.05	1.01	1.07
	N	49	46	36	28

Settlers

Gender		Grade 5	Grade 6	Grade 7	Grade 8
		5	*6*	*7*	*8*
Boys	*M*	1.61	1.86	1.83	2.36
	SD	.92	.89	.82	.51
	N	28	22	24	11
Girls	*M*	2.69	2.85	2.71	—
	SD	1.12	1.07	1.08	—
	N	26	13	24	—

Note.   1 = low concern; 4 = high concern.

ratings of concern for the Gulf War and the intifada. Among Grade 5 settler children, girls showed more anxiety reactions than boys, whereas among the city children there were no gender differences.

The gender difference, showing stronger response among girls who were children of settlers, also showed itself in areas not reported on here. Thus, girls who were children of settlers reported more intense coping responses and gave more intense expressions of relief at the end of the war than did boys who were children of settlers.

Word Associations

The associations given by each child for each stimulus word were classified into those which were intifada-related, Gulf War-related, generally war-related, related to both intifada and Gulf War, and neutral. The classifications were made by graduate students in psychology; interrater agreement was a minimum of 90%.

Subjects gave as many associations as they could in the 15 seconds

TABLE 6.6
Mean Total Anxiety Reactions for City and Settler Children Grades 5–8

				Grade		
Group	Gender		5	6	7	8
City	Boys	M	1.61	1.55	1.57	1.44
		SD	.41	.31	.32	.26
		N	46	30	24	15
	Girls	M	1.60	1.69	1.83	1.83
		SD	.36	.46	.46	.38
		N	50	46	36	28
Settlers	Boys	M	1.33	1.46	1.42	1.39
		SD	.26	.35	.28	.19
		N	28	22	24	11
	Girls	M	1.68	1.96	1.72	—
		SD	.37	.69	.55	—
		N	26	14	24	—

Note. 1 = low concern; 4 = high concern.

allowed for each stimulus word. We present the data for the first association given to each stimulus word, because most subjects gave at least one association for each stimulus word. Table 6.2 summarizes the differences that were found for each stimulus word.

The results show differences between settler and city children in responding to five stimulus words. On all five words, the settler children gave more intifada-related responses than did the city children. For two of the words, *cooperation* and *tire*, boys gave more intifada-related responses than did girls. *Cooperation* is an ambiguous word that could be seen as related to the intifada (cooperation of some Palestinians with the Israeli security Forces) or to the Gulf War (cooperation among the Allies who made up the force sent from abroad). *Tire* is more directly related to the intifada.

An example of the gender difference is presented in Table 6.7, which presents the results for responding to the word *cooperation*. In all age groups, boys gave more intifada-related responses to this word than did girls. In fact, only one girl in the sample gave a response related to the intifada to the word *cooperation*, whereas a relatively large number of boys gave such responses. Most of this effect, however, is due to the responses of boys who were children of settlers. There was no effect of grade. The results for the word *tire*, which are not shown here, are similar.

Thus, the results concerning word association show two strong effects. One is that children who were subjected to the stresses of both the intifada and the Gulf War showed higher levels of intifada-related responses to the stimulus words, particularly those stimulus words that are related to the intifada. This indicates a higher level of concern, given on a relatively involuntary level, by children exposed to the stresses of the intifada. The second effect is that of gender: boys, particularly children of settlers, gave more intifada-related responses to two of the stimulus words, *cooperation* and *tire*. Tables 6.2 and 6.7 show that, in the word association task, which reflects relatively subconscious levels of concern, boys showed more concern than did girls. These findings stand in contrast to the ones we presented earlier, in which boys showed less *conscious* concern than girls. Clearly, these variables are tapping different aspects of the children's concerns.

Our last set of data concerns the use of sources of help by the children; this is presented in Table 6.8. These data reflect the children's perceptions of sources from which they were likely to receive support. The children rated the amount of help that they received from parents and friends relatively high, and made relatively little use of the services provided by schools and hotlines. The highest rating in amount of help was given for self-help. In data not presented here, settler girls made more use of parents and friends as sources of help than did settler boys.

DISCUSSION

The clearest result of the present study was that daughters of settlers expressed a greater concern on a self-report questionnaire when questioned

TABLE 6.7
Percent Distribution of First Word Associations with Gulf War
or Intifada Content to Stimulus Word *Cooperation*

Percent Distribution by Gender and Grade					
			Grade		
Gender	*Association*	*5*	*6*	*7*	*8*
Boys	Gulf War	4	4	5	4
	Intifada	12	10	11	25
	N	73	49	44	24
Girls	Gulf War	5	7	8	0
	Intifada	1	0	0	0
	N	74	60	60	28
Percent Distribution by Group and Grade					
			Grade		
Group	*Association*	*5*	*6*	*7*	*8*
City	Gulf War	8	0	11	2
	Intifada	1	2	2	5
	N	93	76	58	42
Settlers	Gulf War	0	18	2	0
	Intifada	17	11	9	4
	N	54	35	47	10

TABLE 6.8
Mean Ratings of Boys' and Girls' Sources of Help

Source of Help		Boys	Girls	Total
Self	M	2.45	2.51	2.48
	SD	.94	.81	.87
Parent	M	1.93	2.24	2.09
	SD	.91	.95	.94
Relatives	M	1.40	1.51	1.46
	SD	.73	.75	.74
Friends	M	1.51	1.87	1.70
	SD	.79	.88	.85
Teacher	M	1.18	1.25	1.22
	SD	.51	.50	.51
Hot Line	M	1.12	1.12	1.12
	SD	.48	.44	.46

Notes. Boys $N = 197$; Girls $N = 218$. Ns may differ slightly from cell to cell because of missing information.

1 = low use of help; 4 = high use of help.

about the Gulf War and the intifada than did sons of settlers. In the same comparison, settler girls also expressed more anxiety reactions. In data not presented here, girls reported more intense coping and more use of parents and friends as sources of help. These results were not found as strongly for city children, who were not as exposed to the intifada as the settlers, although, in general, girls tended to respond more strongly than did boys. The effect of gender was sharpened for the settler children. We conclude that only situations that had an emotional loading related to the stresses that the children faced elicited a differential response: Girls who faced both sets of stresses responded more strongly than did boys in the same circumstances, whereas in children who did not face both sets of stresses there were no gender differences.

It is worth noting the differences between boys and girls from another standpoint: Settler boys produced the lowest scores reflecting concern caused by the intifada and the missile attacks in comparison with all the other groups, whereas settler girls produced the highest scores. That is, the contrast between the boys and girls who were children of settlers was much greater than that of boys and girls who live in Jerusalem. From this perspective, both the high concern scores of the settler girls and the low concern scores of the settler boys must be explained.

These effects (girls expressing more concern than boys) appear to be reversed in the word association task. Here, boys expressed more concern than did girls in the associations they made to stimulus words. These effects were not influenced by age or religiosity.

One factor that may be involved in the explanation of these findings is the possible difference in degree of social support for children of settlers in comparison to city children. As indicated earlier, settler children live in small, ideologically homogeneous settlements, in which people are more likely to give support to one another and to children. There is a great deal of evidence in the literature concerning the effectiveness of social support in helping people deal with stress (e.g., Dunkel-Schetter & Skokan, 1990; Hobfoll & Lieberman, 1987). Social support does not provide an adequate explanation for our results, however. Although social support may be higher for the children of settlers, not all settler children showed lower levels of concern or anxiety. On the open questionnaire, settler girls showed higher levels of concern and anxiety reactions than city girls; on the word associations, settler boys showed higher levels of concern than boys who lived in the city. Thus, the differences in social support between settler and city children did not prevent many settler children, especially girls, from expressing high levels of concern and anxiety.

The fact that we did not find a gender difference among the city children appears to conflict with other studies conducted during the Gulf War that found such differences. As indicated earlier, the studies by Rosenbaum and Ronen (1992), Toubiana et al. (1992), and Levy-Schiff and Bat-Zion (1992) all found that girls were more likely than boys to report anxiety on self-report questionnaires in the course of the war. All of these studies dealt with populations in the larger cities of Israel. Some of these population centers were not hit by missiles; still, girls reported more anxiety than boys. These findings appear different from ours, where in the urban center of Jerusalem, we found few gender differences in expression of anxiety on self-report measures.

The differences in the findings may be attributed to the different timing of the studies. Our study was conducted 4 to 5 months after the end of the war, whereas the studies we have cited were performed during the war or very soon after. Even during the war, there is evidence (Rosenbaum & Ronen, 1992) that an adaptation process occurred, such that the level of anxiety was reduced the longer the individual was exposed to the threatening stimulus. When the threatening stimulus did not lead to injury, and individuals saw themselves as coping with the threat successfully (Lazarus & Folkman, 1984), adaptation was particularly quick. A further piece of evidence in favor of adaptation was provided by Levinson (1992), who reported on calls to a hotline in the Tel Aviv area. After the first two missile strikes, the calls, most of which came from mothers, were reduced considerably. The anticipation of the threat may have been more anxiety laden than the actual hit of the missile. Once individuals have coped successfully with a threat, the anxiety level associated with it may go down. This may explain why, 4 months after the war, the stress that led to the differences in responses between city boys and city girls may no longer have been present for the children in our sample; the gender difference would then not be expected to appear.

We found a consistent gender difference only for settler children exposed to both the intifada and the Gulf War. Interestingly, Baker (1991) did not find gender differences in symptoms associated with stress among Palestinian children exposed to the intifada. One possible explanation for the discrepancy between the two studies may be different methodology: Baker's data were based on mothers' reports, whereas the present study and the others cited on the Gulf War were based on children's self-reports.

Explanations for Gender Differences

Let us consider four possible explanations for the gender difference in children's reactions to accumulated stress. One emphasizes the display of emotion and assumes that there is no underlying difference in the extent of the emotion in the children. According to this explanation, the difference between boys and girls is that girls express anxiety openly, whereas boys are more likely to deny or repress anxiety. Thus, the level of anxiety in boys and girls is the same; the apparent differences reflect differences in display rules expressing the emotion and its meaning. The gender difference reflects differences in socialization for displaying emotion (Levy, 1984). It has long been recognized that boys and girls are socialized differently on a variety of behaviors related to emotion (Maccoby & Jacklin, 1976).

A second explanation is also based on socialization, but it states that the differences between the emotional expressions of boys and girls reflect real differences in emotion, not merely differences in display. It may be that boys and girls receive different kinds of socialization with regard to the actual *experience* of emotions. This socialization may extend to the actual feeling states themselves and not only to their displays. Again, there is some evidence that socialization of boys and girls with regard to feelings may be different. Boys may be socialized to be less in touch with their feelings and to experience emotions on a shallower level than girls. Our word association results may contradict this explanation. Boys were seen to be concerned, but this concern expressed itself more in projective measures than in self-report measures. There is relatively little evidence concerning socialization for feeling states in stress situations that reflects differences between boys and girls; such research is obviously needed (Maccoby & Jacklin, 1976).

A third explanation, also relevant to the review by Maccoby and Jacklin (1976), is that there are differences in the emotional reactions of boys and girls to stress situations, and that these differences are biological in origin. It would be very difficult to perform research that would prove or disprove this hypothesis clearly, because differential socialization and different biological tendencies may be confounded in the research that is performed. However, given the evidence for biological differences between boys and girls on a range of variables, including differences in cognition, this hypothesis cannot be ruled out.

A fourth possible explanation suggests different defense mechanisms for boys and girls in their reactions to stress, whereby boys would tend to repress their feelings in the service of action, and girls would tend to express them openly. Such mechanisms could be related to the possibly different socialization of boys and girls in their reactions to stress. These differential responses could be associated with different cognitive appraisal (Folkman & Lazarus, 1985) by boys and girls. We know little about such differential appraisal by boys and girls.

We thus have a relatively strong result in our research concerning differences between boys and girls in their reactions to a stress situation. It is a finding in search of an explanation, and one that suggests various directions for research. One problem with much of the research on the effects of stress is that, in most cases, there is very little knowledge of the level of emotional responding before the person entered into the stress situation. This is true of the present study and of most research that has dealt with the effects of wartime stress. Although this kind of research is difficult to perform, it is possible to do so in the context of longitudinal follow-up studies when stress situations happen to occur.

Level of Concern for War-Related Stress

Two other features of our study deserve consideration. One is the level of concern shown by our subjects toward the Gulf War and the intifada. Four months after the end of the Gulf War, in comparison to other issues, the war and the intifada were of considerable concern to the children who participated in the study. However, an issue of greater concern to the children was that of traffic accidents. This is somewhat surprising, because the dangers from the war and from the intifada were more central in the communications media in Israel. However, traffic accidents are a constant concern and the children's ratings reflected this fact. Four months after the end of the Gulf War, then, both the intifada and the Gulf War took their places in the normal course of events concerning children in Israel.

This result is somewhat surprising in the case of the intifada, because this was a stress situation that the subjects were undergoing at the time they participated in our study. The reduction in concern could be due to habituation (i.e., to the near-exposure to a stimulus several times), or to learned ways of coping with that stimulus (Folkman & Lazarus, 1985). By 4 or 5 months after the close of the Gulf War, very little was left of the reaction to it on the part of most subjects. These results reflect a high level of adaptation, but they also reflect the fact that the Gulf War was a relatively brief and only moderately intense set of traumas. The intifada may arouse a relatively low level of anxiety response, because it has been coped with successfully over an extended period of time (Folkman & Lazarus, 1985). Low to moderate levels of anxiety may be achieved by a combination of habituation and successful coping. The relative contribution of each of these factors remains to be established.

Implications for Social Policy Concerning War-Related Stress

A last issue concerns the help received by the children in both the settler and city contexts. All the children in our sample were living with their families and were attending school regularly. None was in special education or had obvious physical or psychological handicaps. The data reported here show that, for this relatively healthy sample, the accumulation of stressors affected girls more than boys.

Two implications are important here. One concerns the possibility of different kinds of communication patterns and social support utilized by girls and boys, which policy planners may have to take into account. For example, girls made more use of parents and friends as sources of psychological help. The question arises of how these sources can be utilized to give such aid effectively.

The second issue concerns the overall importance of the kinds of help children under stress (both boys and girls) reported utilizing the most. The three sources used most from the ones on our list were self, parents, and friends; teachers and hotlines were little used. The use of self suggests the possible mediation of temperament or personality of the individual child as a factor affecting his or her reactions to stress (Wertlieb, Weigel, Springer, & Feldstein, 1990). In addition, children's natural networks have great value in helping children deal with stress due to conflict, a point also documented by Fraser (1979). Hotlines and the educational system, which have been much used in dealing with children's problems in wartime stress situations, may not have as much impact as significant others in a child's life. These "others" could include the child himself or herself.

These results point to the need for developing a social policy that emphasizes the development of family and friendship networks and on teaching children directly how to deal with stress. Such activity would place a great deal of responsibility on parents, and not all parents are up to the task. The recommendations of Hobfoll et al. (1991) emphasized the importance of parents controlling their own emotions and training children to control theirs. Although this may be sound advice generally, this kind of self-control places a great burden on parents. It is also not clear how parents (or teachers) are to learn to help children in stress situations. We suggest that this is a critical topic for future research, which could have a number of applications.

Involvement of parents and paraprofessionals in preparations for stress situations and in dealing with responses of children should be studied systematically and made part of a social policy that teaches people to help children cope with stress.

Last, it should be emphasized that policy must be informed by research that is built on consistent, replicable studies. Despite the large volume of studies in this area, there is a great need for comparability in terms of conceptualization and method. Addressing this task will pay dividends in better research and better informed public policy.

ACKNOWLEDGMENTS

We gratefully acknowledge aid in this study from the following research centers at the Hebrew University of Jerusalem: the Schein Center for the Social Sciences, the Sturman Center for Human Development, and the Levin Center for the Development of the Child and Adolescent. We acknowledge, with many thanks, those who helped on the project: Vardit Arbel, Michal Antman, Adiva Huri, and Yael Landau, who were responsible for the administration of questionnaires and their coding; Yuval Yuval, who managed the computer analysis; and Eda Flaxer and Judith Greenbaum for editorial assistance. We are also grateful to the following at the Ministry of Education: the Pedagogical Center; Office of the Head Scientist; Head Psychologist Dr. Joseph Kolodner; Research Advisor Dr. Avigdor Klingman; and the school principals, teachers, and pupils whose participation made the study possible.

REFERENCES

Achenbach, T., & Edelbrock, C. (1981). Behavioral problems and competencies reported by parents of normal and disturbed children aged four through sixteen. *Monographs of the Society for Research in Child Development, 46* (Serial No. 188).

Arroyo, W., & Eth, S. (1985). Children traumatized by Central American warfare. In S. Eth & R. S. Pynoos (Eds.), *Post-traumatic stress disorder in children* (pp. 101–120). Washington, DC: American Psychiatric Press.

Baker, A. (1990). The psychological impact of the intifada on Palestinian children in the occupied West Bank and Gaza. *American Journal of Orthopsychiatry, 60,* 496–505.

Baker, A. (1991). Psychological response of Palestinian children to environmental stress associated with military occupation. *Journal of Refugee Studies, 4,* 237–247.

Bat-Zion, N., & Levy-Schiff, R. (1993). Children in war: Stress and coping reactions under the threat of scud missile attacks and the effect of proximity. In L. Leavitt & N. Fox (Eds.), *Psychological effects of war and violence on children* (pp. 143–161). Hillsdale, NJ: Lawrence Erlbaum.

Benedek, E. (1985). Children and psychic trauma: A brief review of contemporary thinking. In S. Eth & R. S. Pynoos (Eds.), *Post-traumatic stress disorder in children* (pp. 1–16). Washington, DC: American Psychiatric Press.

Breznitz, S. (1983). Stress in Israel. New York: Van Nostrand/Reinhold.

Dreman, S., & Cohen, E. (1990). Children of the victims of terrorism revisited: Integrating individual and family treatment approaches. *American Journal of Orthopsychiatry, 60,* 204–209.

Dunkel-Schetter, C., & Skokan, L. A. (1990). Determinants of social support provision in personal relationships. *Journal of Social and Personal Relationships, 7,* 437–450.

Eth, S., & Pynoos, R. S. (1985). Developmental perspective on psychic trauma in childhood. In C. R. Figley (Ed.), *Trauma and its wake:The study and treatment of post-traumatic stress disorder* (pp. 36–52). New York: Brunner/Mazel.

Folkman, S., & Lazarus, R. S. (1985). If it changes it must be a process: Study of emotion and coping during three stages of a college examination. *Journal of Personality and Social Psychology, 48,* 150–170.

Fraser, M. (1979). *Children in conflict.* Harmondsworth, Middlesex: Penguin.

Freud, A., & Burlingham, D. T. (1943). *War and children.* London: Medical War Books.

Hobfoll, S. E., Spielberger, C. D., Breznitz, S., Figley, C., Folkman, S., Lepper-Green, B., Meichenbaum, D., Milgram, N. A., Sandler, I., Sarason, I., & van der Kolk, B. (1991). War-related stress: Addressing the stress of war and other traumatic events. *American Psychologist, 46,* 848–855.

Hobfoll, S. E., & Leiberman, Y. (1987). Personality and social resources in immediate and continued stress resistance among women. *Journal of Personality and Social Psychology, 52,* 18–26.

Itzkowitz, R., Zeidner, M., & Klingman, A. (1992, January). *Emotional responses of children to the Gulf War.* Paper presented at Ministry of Education Conference on Stress Reactions of Children in the Gulf War, Ramat Gan, Israel.

Janis, I. L. (1958). *Psychological stress.* New York: Wiley.

Lazarus, R. S. (1991). Progress on a cognitive-motivational- relational theory of emotion. *American Psychologist, 46,* 819–834.

Lazarus, R. S., & Folkman, S. (1984). *Stress, appraisal and coping.* New York: Springer.

Levinson, S. (1992, January). *Calls to a counseling hotline during the Gulf War.* Paper presented at Ministry of Education Conference on Stress Reactions of Children in the Gulf War, Ramat Gan, Israel.

Levy, R. I. (1984). Emotion, knowing and culture. In R. A. Shweder & R. A. LeVine (Eds.), *Culture theory: Essays on mind, self and emotion* (pp. 214–237). Cambridge, England: Cambridge University Press.

Maccoby, E. E., & Jacklin, C. N. (1976). *The psychology of sex differences.* Stanford, CA: Stanford University Press.

Masalha, S. (1993). The effect of prewar conditions on the psychological reactions of Palestinian children to the Gulf War. In L. Leavitt & N. Fox (Eds.), *Psychological effects of war and violence on children* (pp. 131–142). Hillsdale, NJ: Lawrence Erlbaum.

Milgram, N. A. (1989). *Children under stress.* In T. H. Ollendick & M. Hersen (Eds.), *Handbook of child psychopathology* (pp. 399–415). New York: Plenum.

Milgram, N. A., & Hobfoll, S. E. (1986). Generalizations from theory and practice in war-related stress. In N. A. Milgram (Ed.), *Stress and coping in time of war* (pp. 316–352). New York: Brunner/Mazel.

Milgram, N. A., Toubiana, Y. H., Klingman, A., Raviv, A., & Goldstein, I. (1988). Situational exposure and personal loss in children's acute and chronic stress reactions to a school bus disaster. *Journal of Traumatic Stress, 1,* 339–351.

Rahav, G., & Ronen, T. (1992, January). *The prevalence of children's symptoms during the Gulf War and before.* Paper presented at Ministry of Education Conference on Stress Reactions of Children in the Gulf War, Ramat Gan, Israel.

Rofe, Y., & Lewin, I. (1982). The effect of war environment on dreams and sleep habits. In C. Spielberger, I. G. Sarason, & N. A. Milgram (Eds.), *Psychological stress and adjustment in times of war and peace* (pp. 67–79). Washington, DC: Hemisphere.

Rosenbaum, M., & Ronen, T. (1992, January). *How did Israeli children and their parents cope with being threatened by daily attacks of Scud missiles during the Gulf War?* Paper presented at Ministry of Education Conference on Stress Reactions of Children in the Gulf War, Ramat Gan, Israel.

Terr, L. (1991). Childhood traumas: An outline and overview. *American Journal of Psychiatry, 148,* 10–20.

Toubiana, Y. H., Goldstein, I., & Har-Even, D. (1992, January). *Schoolchildren during the Gulf War and its aftermath: Assessment of anxiety level, stress responses and need for help among schoolchildren in various danger zones.* Paper presented at Ministry of Education Conference on Stress Reactions of Children in the Gulf War, Ramat Gan, Israel.

Wertlieb, D., Weigel, C., Springer, T., & Feldstein, M. (1990). Temperament as a moderator of children's stressful experiences. *American Journal of Orthopsychiatry, 57,* 234–245.

7 The Effect of Prewar Conditions on the Psychological Reactions of Palestinian Children to the Gulf War

Shafiq Masalha
Birzeit University

The effect of war is commonly measured by the physical damage inflicted on people and property. The psychological effect of war on those directly or indirectly involved has been overlooked. Milgram (1985) pointed out that studying war-related stress is emotionally difficult because during war enormous suffering is inflicted on man by his fellow man. This difficulty is even greater, I believe, when the direct victims of war are children.

Although the pioneering study of the psychological effects of war on children was done during World War II (Freud & Burlingham, 1943), it is only in recent years that this area has begun to receive the attention it warrants. Several recent developments have drawn our attention to the impact of war on children. One is that sophisticated military technology has proven that war can easily, and quickly, reach beyond the battlefield and literally hit home. Another is that, in general, more attention is being given to the well-being of children, including an awareness of child abuse and posttraumatic stress disorders. Third, in several areas of conflict, such as South Africa, Central America, and the Israeli-occupied territories (the West Bank and Gaza Strip), children have taken an active role in political struggles.

Studies of veterans of World War II have consistently demonstrated the existence of long-term disabling stress following combat. Archibald and Tuddenham (1965) described symptoms in World War II American veterans 20 years after their war experience. The syndrome they described resembles the clinical picture of what became known as *posttraumatic stress disorder* (PTSD). Current studies make it abundantly clear that war-related traumas adversely affect the psychology of children and interrupt their development.

Terr (1991) stated that childhood psychic traumas are a prominent etiological factor in serious disorders of childhood and adulthood. Arroyo and Eth (1985), working with children and adolescents in Central America, concluded that children are heavily influenced by war traumas. Punamaki (1987) reported that psychological symptoms among Palestinian children in the West Bank and Gaza correlated with the level of the trauma they had experienced. Studies of Palestinian children after the start of the intifada reported an increase in children's complaints, in sleep disturbance, and in depression (Baker, 1990). South African children who were exposed to politically related traumas showed symptoms of PTSD (Straker & Moosa, 1988).

In trying to trace the factors that influence an individual's reaction to stress, including war-related stress, several hypotheses have been raised. Archibald and Tuddenham (1965) suggested that disabling conditions following a war experience are determined by pre-existing personality; the nature and severity of the stress; and the type, intensity and timing of the treatment provided after the trauma. Benedek (1985) emphasized the following factors: type of trauma (natural or manmade), its intensity and duration, the age at which the trauma took place, and the familial and social support provided. In studying the impact of war on children, it is important to examine the social, political, cultural, and psychological circumstances existing prior to the onset of war, and to evaluate their impact on reactions to war-related stress. Studying pre-existing circumstances adds another dimension that is not addressed by studying the qualities of the war itself or the postwar interventions.

Although neither Israelis nor Palestinians in the West Bank and Gaza were active combatants in the Gulf War, both peoples, for different reasons, experienced severe psychological stress. Prior to the Gulf War, which broke out in January 1991, Palestinians in the occupied territories had been involved in the intifada for some 3 years. This chapter discusses the psychological characteristics and the sociopolitical circumstances of the Palestinian children during the intifada. It also examines the effect of those circumstances on the children's reaction to the Gulf War.

THE PSYCHOLOGICAL STATE OF THE PALESTINIAN CHILDREN DURING THE INTIFADA PRIOR TO THE GULF WAR

Palestinian children in the West Bank and Gaza have been going through a very unique experience characterized by violent confrontation with the Israeli army. In their information sheet of November 1990, B'Tselem (The Israel Information Center for Human Rights in the Occupied Territories) reported that between December 1987 (the onset of the intifada) and October 1990 (3 months prior to the Gulf War), 712 Palestinian residents of the occupied territories had been killed by the Israeli forces, among whom were 45 children ages 12 and under, and 116 children ages 13–16. The prevalence of killings, injuries, and detentions among Palestinian children during the 3 years prior to the Gulf War indicates the violent atmosphere that dominated their daily lives.

The findings that are discussed here, on the psychological state of Palestinian children during the intifada and prior to the Gulf War, are taken from a larger study on children's dreams. Due to the space limitations, the methodology of the research is briefly presented and only relevant findings are discussed. The part of the study that is concerned with children's dreams may be considered a follow-up to an earlier study conducted by Nashif (1984). Although the methodology and the theoretical premise in the two studies are similar, certain changes were made to fit the new circumstances of the intifada.

The participants were 10- to 11-year-old Palestinian boys and girls from two refugee camps in the West Bank and the Gaza Strip. The children were asked to write down three dreams within a 2-week period in a special dream booklet, using their native language (Arabic). Table 7.1 shows the number of dreamers who participated in the study and the number of dreams analyzed.

In keeping with the theoretical orientation of Hall (1966), dreams are viewed as expressions of not only personal conflicts, but of concerns on the macro level (i.e., as reflecting political and social processes that children experience). A recent empirical validation of Hall's hypothesis was demonstrated by Bilu (1989), who studied over 2,000 dreams of Arab and Jewish children living in the West Bank and Israel. Bilu's data on Palestinian children were collected in 1984 (prior to the intifada), and the data for this study were collected in 1989 (a year after the intifada started), so a comparison of the findings of the two studies could indicate the changes that Palestinian children underwent. The dream analysis method used in this study was similar to that used by Hall and Van de Castle (1966) and by Bilu (1989). The manifest content of the dreams was classified into categories and analyzed.

The following are the categories of dreams used in the present study. The

TABLE 7.1
Number of Dreamers and Dreams According to Gender

Variable	Males	Females	Total
Dreamers	39	66	105
Dreams	121	202	323

findings are used as a basis for understanding the reactions of Palestinian children to the Gulf War.

The Involvement of Children in the Political Conflict

The results of the present study indicate that the prevalence of dreams reported by Palestinian children in which they violently encounter the Israeli army has increased since 1984. Nashif (1984) reported that 56% of the dreamers reported violent encounters with Israelis in general, and 28% of the dreams were characterized by violent confrontation between the children and the Israeli army specifically. None of the dreamers reported friendly encounters with Israelis. In the present study, 75% of the dreamers reported violent encounters with Israelis in general, and 53% of the dreams had aggressive interactive elements between children and the Israeli army. Similar to Bilu's findings, no friendly encounter dreams occurred. All of this suggests the continuation, and increase, in the preoccupation of Palestinian children with the Israeli–Palestinian conflict.

Although the quality of the encounters between the Palestinian children and Israelis remains aggressive, the role of the children in such encounters has changed. In most encounter dreams collected prior to the intifada, the Palestinian child was a passive victim. The following is a typical dream:

> I dreamed that the Israeli soldiers attacked our home when we were asleep. They took my brother to jail. After two days, he was released and rearrested and badly beaten.

Dreams collected during the intifada more often portrayed the child as active and initiating:

> I dreamed that a march took place in the camp. Soldiers came and threw bombs. Youngsters (shabaab) went away but three of them were arrested.

In fact, this dream reflects the mixed passive–active qualities of children. In the dream, children initiated the act. Some of them were arrested, and others were able to escape. Some dreams showed the children as inflicting harm on the Israeli soldiers. The active role that Palestinian children have taken in confronting the Israeli army has drawn special attention by the media and has been described by researchers (Baker 1990, Punamaki 1987).

Children in Their Community

Home and school usually provide a sense of protection and confidence for children. During the intifada, there has been an alteration in the status of both institutions.

Fathers appeared in only 10% of the reported dreams. In half of these cases, when the children saw themselves being beaten by the army, the fathers were not able to rescue them. However, mothers appeared more frequently, and were present in 21% of the dreams. This finding is consistent with the impression one has in observing the circumstances of Palestinian families during the intifada. In violent confrontation, women have a better chance than men of protecting the children without being hurt by the soldiers. Fathers, who had been the symbol of authority and protection, have become unable to protect their children.

The home has also become an unsafe place for children. This feeling of insecurity at home is illustrated in this dream:

> One night when I was sleeping, I saw in my dream the Israeli soldiers taking children out of their homes and killing them along with their mothers and fathers. I screamed loudly. The soldiers went after me, but I escaped.

School is another place where children usually feel protected and safe. Teachers, as authority figures, provide safety for the children. Since the intifada started, the educational system has been seriously disrupted. B'Tselem (September–October 1990) reported that during the first 3 years of the intifada, schools in the West Bank were shut down for lengthy periods, and the educational system was severely affected. This has registered in the children's dreams. A 10-year-old child reported the following:

> I dreamed that schools reopened. When I went to school, I was surprised that it was quiet. I asked my sister, 'Why are there no demonstrations?' She said, 'Because the school and the camp are surrounded by soldiers.'

Dreamers' peers appeared in 62% of the dreams, far exceeding the number of dreams in which parents appeared. This may indicate that the prominent figures in children's lives are no longer their parents, but their peers (shabaab). Because data on this aspect were not reported in previous research, it is difficult to determine whether substituting peers for families is a normal developmental phenomenon among 10-year-old children, or whether it is an outcome of the sociopolitical circumstances that the children are experiencing.

The role of peers is illustrated in the following dream:

> I dreamed that on my way to school, I saw shabaab demonstrating. Immediately I went back home, threw away my school bag, and joined the demonstration. While I was throwing stones at soldiers, a bullet hit my arm. Then I woke up.

All of these findings raise some serious questions regarding social changes that may be occurring in Palestinian society. These social changes involve: family dynamics, the changing roles of men and women, the role of fathers as authority figures, the role of schools, and the role of peer groups. If such social changes are occurring, they are likely to impact on child development.

Attitudes Toward the Future

Among the questions that one might pose is how children who live in a traumatic reality view the future. More specifically, what do they see as an outlet from their harsh circumstances? How do they envision the resolution to the conflict? Some children had dreams ("outlet dreams") that conveyed a way out of the conflict. The following are some examples:

> Last night, I dreamed that an earthquake hit the Israeli settlements, like the one that hit Armenia. The whole country was shattered. Only then the Israelis turned toward us and asked to make peace. I woke up with tears in my eyes.

> I dreamed that I was walking on a distant road. Wherever I went, I saw the Israeli soldiers in front of me. I kept walking. The road had no end, and the soldiers kept chasing me. Finally, I went into a mosque which was at the end of that road. I prayed and asked God to bring peace to our land and return happiness to our hearts.

> While I was walking with my friend Manal, we met an Israeli soldier. He was regretting the fact that he was not a Palestinian.

Dreams are rich material that, when analyzed, may take on different meanings. One commonality in these three dreams, however, is the unrealistic manner of resolving the conflict. In the first dream, an earthquake is required to obtain peace. In the second, God's intervention is sought. In the third, converting Israelis into Palestinians is seen as the solution.

In other outlet dreams, aggressive action is seen as the solution:

> Last night, I dreamed that shabaab did a violent act. They blew up five houses and killed 10 soldiers. Afterwards we started a demonstration, a violent one. Only then, victory was achieved — the victory that everyone wished for.

In light of these dreams, it appears that Palestinian children, during the intifada and prior to the Gulf War, had no hope that peace could be achieved via peaceful negotiations between the parties to the conflict. The despair had reached the point where they felt that only a supernatural power could help. Furthermore, because this option did not seem possible, a turn to greater violence became likely, as reflected in the last dream. Such, it seems, was the spirit of the children when the Gulf War began.

REACTION OF PALESTINIAN CHILDREN TO THE GULF WAR

Reactions to war are more genuine during the war itself than afterward, but it is difficult to conduct a study during wartime. Reactions recorded after a war often have lost something of their poignancy. People usually are not enthusiastic about reliving horrible times. They find it difficult to re-experience their emotional reactions. A new threat that caused concern during the Gulf War was the possible use of chemical weapons. Gas masks were distributed to all citizens in Israel, but those in the West Bank and Gaza were unable to get gas masks. In certain areas, only parents were able to get masks. The fact that the war was relatively short and considered an unconventional one increased difficulties for conducting systematic studies.

Palestinian reactions to the Gulf War were especially difficult to obtain. All Palestinians in the occupied territories (except East Jerusalem) were put under curfew during the war. They remained under a strict curfew for 42 days.

When psychological stress was felt among Palestinians during the war, a number of Palestinian mental health professionals based in Bethlehem University and at the Palestinian Counseling Center in East Jerusalem established a "hot line" telephone service through which people were able to receive counseling. Because the service was established only during the second half of the war, and because of advertising limitations and unavailability of television and radio services, very few of calls were received concerning psychological health. These calls came mostly from Jerusalem, Ramallah, and Hebron.

The calls were registered and analyzed. As illustrated in Table 2, complaints were classified into four major categories: children's anxiety, men's concerns, practical issues, and rumors. Intense fear of the siren — often expressed through panic attacks and enuresis in children — and fear of wearing the gas masks accounted for 31% of the total number of calls. It was Shouval's (1991) impression that symptoms of fear and distress among Israeli children appeared when parents became tense and when there was no clear parental authority. Whether this causative factor applied in the case of Palestinian children is unknown. Research limitations are inherent in the circumstances of the war, and applying the same measures to both populations for a comparative study was almost impossible.

During the war, Palestinian men expressed major concerns regarding

TABLE 7.2
Major Categories of Complaints

Children's Anxiety (17)	Men's Concerns (9)	Practical Issues (21)	Rumors (22)
Fear of siren	Bothered by feelings of helplessness	Disconnected from home because of the curfew.	Mass graves prepared by the Israelis for the Palestinians
Panic attacks when the siren is on	Being unable to protect the children	Lack of gas masks	Mass expulsion of the Palestinians by the Israelis
Enuresis especially when the siren is heard	Managing the children	Child management	
Fear of wearing gas masks	Unemployment and family financial support	Seeking health services	

The overall number of complaints was 69 which means of course that there was more than one complaint in some telephone calls.

family protection and child management, and were bothered by feelings of helplessness. These feelings may have been intensified by such circumstances as the lack of gas masks, and shortages of food (in some areas) and medical care. (Defense for Children International-Israel [DCI] and the Association for Civil Rights in Israel [ACRI] jointly petitioned the High Court of Justice to distribute gas masks to all the people in the territories. Although the Court ordered the gas masks to be distributed, the war ended soon after the decision, so it was of little practical value.)

Dreams of Palestinian children, as already presented, point to a shift in family dynamics during the intifada and prior to the Gulf War. Fathers seemed to be absent from their children's lives. Protection of children came not from the usual authority figures, fathers and teachers, but from peers. Mothers appeared to be even more protective than fathers. During the 42 days and nights of curfew, fathers and their children found themselves unexpectedly together under the same roof. It is assumed that the interactions between the fathers and the children were quite stressful at that time. It is well known that, prior to the intifada, fathers had no trouble disciplining their children. In other words, the curfew during the Gulf War seems to have caused fathers and sons to face the new dynamics in their relationships that had developed during the 3 years prior to the War. This hypothesis might find support in the fact that almost half of the telephone calls received during the war that involved calls for help came from males (see Table 7.3). What makes this finding all the more surprising is that in Arab society, males, more than females, find it difficult to complain of psychological problems, and avoid admitting their vulnerability.

I also surmise that Palestinian children, having actively confronted the

TABLE 7.3
Number of Calls Received According to Gender and District

Gender Jerusalem	Ramallah	Hebron	Total	
Male	20	5	0	25
Female	22	4	3	29
Total	42	9	3	54

Israeli army during the intifada, found it very difficult to be locked at home for the long period of the curfew. In addition, Arab homes, especially in villages and camps, were ill-equipped with games and/or other diversions to occupy the children. They could not even relate to television programs on Israeli TV, which neither reflected their feelings and thoughts nor used their language. It is worth noting that Israeli TV intensively broadcast programs to help children calm down and help parents manage their own anxieties and those of the children.

Israeli fathers also faced an unfamiliar situation during the Gulf War. In a conference held on February 26, 1991, immediately after the war ended, under the auspices of the DCI, Israeli psychologists discussed the experiences of Israeli fathers. For the first time, they were in the same room with their children, rather than on the battlefield, while the country was being attacked. However, they apparently experienced no threat to their authority as fathers.

Another area of interest, as reflected in the content of the telephone calls received on the hot line, is the matter of rumors and their effect on the Palestinian population in the territories. One widespread rumor, for instance, was that the Israeli authorities were digging mass graves for Palestinians. It was believed that bulldozers and tractors had been drafted for that purpose. Another rumor that was widely believed was that Israeli forces had planned a mass expulsion of Palestinians. These rumors were so widespread, in fact, that a committee of Palestinian health experts in Jerusalem was formed to adequately cope with them. Theoretically, the groundwork had already been laid for these rumors to start and spread. Allport and Postman (1965) pointed out that rumors travel when current events have importance in the lives of the individuals, and when the news is either lacking or ambiguous. There is no question regarding the importance of these events that went to the heart of every Palestinian. With regard to ambiguity, although there were round-the-clock news broadcasts, people felt that they knew very little about the war. At the same time that Israeli families feared the threat of Iraqi missiles, Palestinian families were realistically under a similar threat. In addition, they feared retaliation by Israeli forces. It is believed that such fear necessarily touched the Palestinian children as well.

During the Gulf War, many Israelis were deeply upset about the

Palestinian reaction to the Iraqi missiles fired at Israel. The Israeli media stated that Palestinians were welcoming the Scuds fired at Israel and even celebrating their arrival. It is understandable that such news would cause tremendous anger among Israelis. Psychologically, the Palestinian reactions may be viewed as an expression of the despair that Palestinians felt during the intifada and prior to the war. The dreams reflecting the children's view of the future, as described earlier, demonstrate that they were unable to envision any peaceful solution to the conflict. They saw no realistic outlet from the harsh reality they were facing daily. Therefore, it is possible that they developed unrealistic hopes that Saddam Hussein would rescue them. In fact, many religious speculations connecting Saddam with historic religious legends gained credence among Palestinians during the war period.

SUMMARY AND CONCLUSIONS

The impact of war on children has been given increased attention recently by psychologists and social scientists. Researchers have invested greater effort in studying both the pathological symptoms caused by war-related stress and the effects of postwar psychological intervention. This chapter adds still another dimension to the study of the war's impact on children, in discussing the importance of psychological and sociopolitical circumstances affecting children's reactions to war. The experience of Palestinian children during the intifada and the Gulf War provided the focus of this study.

The psychological state of Palestinian children during the intifada and prior to the Gulf War was evaluated by means of dream analysis. I found that, prior to the war, Palestinian children were already actively involved in violent confrontation with the Israeli army. The two major protective institutions, family and school, were seen by children as offering less protection than their peer group. In addition, the attitude of children toward the future was characterized by hopelessness; they did not envision a peaceful resolution to the conflict between Palestinians and Israelis.

The major concerns that Palestinians experienced during the Gulf War were explored through an evaluation of the content of telephone calls received at a counseling service in East Jerusalem. These concerns were better understood in light of the psychological and sociopolitical state of the Palestinians, in general, and the Palestinian children, in particular, prior to the war. Among the major concerns expressed in the telephone calls were fathers' feelings of helplessness and their difficulties in managing their children. This phenomenon already existed since the beginning of the intifada. When the war broke out, Palestinian fathers and sons confronted each other during the long hours that they were forced to spend together during the curfew. Thus, the fathers suffered from the loss of control over their children who, for some time, had been actively involved in the intifada. The long curfew during the war exacerbated the pre-existing conflict over authority between fathers and their children. At the same time, a different phenomenon worked in the direction of splitting families: Family members—usually fathers—who worked far from home and were unable to return home from work during the curfew period were sometimes cut off from their families for days at a time.

Another major concern raised during the war was the children's anxiety. I hypothesize that their anxiety increased because they became passive after having been active participants in the struggle for the 3 years prior to the war. The anxiety in the Palestinian population, in general, and the children, in particular, was expressed through widespread rumors (e.g., of mass killings and expulsion). Anxiety of Palestinians during the War was generated not only by unrealistic fears, but also by realistic circumstances. Many of the complaints during the war addressed the lack of gas masks, the lack of health services, and the curfew conditions that separated members of families from one another.

In conclusion, to better understand the impact of war on children, one needs to know about their psychological state and the sociopolitical conditions that existed prior to the outbreak of war.

REFERENCES

Archibald, N. E., & Tuddenham, R. D. (1965). Persistent stress reaction following combat: A twenty year follow-up. *Archives of General Psychiatry, 12,* 475–481.

Allport, G., & Postman, L. (1965). *The psychology of rumor.* New York: Russell & Russell.

Arroyo, W., & Eth, S. (1985). Children traumatized by general American warfare. In S. Eth & R. Pynoos (Eds.), *Post-traumatic stress disorders in children* (pp. 101–120). Washington, DC: American Psychiatric Press.

Baker, A. (1990). The psychological impact of the intifada on Palestinian children in the occupied West Bank and Gaza: An exploratory study. *American Journal of Orthopsychiatry, 60,* 496–505.

Barry, H., Bacon, M., & Child, I. (1957). A cross-cultural survey of some sex differences in socialization. *Journal of Abnormal Social Psychology, 55,* 327–332.

Benedek, E. (1985). Children and psychic trauma: A brief review of contemporary thinking. In S. Eth & R. Pynoos (Eds.) *Post-traumatic stress disorders in children* (pp. 1–17). Washington, DC: American Psychiatric Press.

Bilu, Y. (1989). The other as a nightmare: The Israeli–Arab encounter as reflected in children's dreams in Israel and the West Bank. *Political Psychology, 10,* 365–389.

B'Tselem (1990, September–October). Information sheet update [English version]. The Israeli Center for Human Rights in the Occupied Territories.

B'Tselem (1990, November). Information sheet update [English version]. The Israeli Center for Human Rights in the Occupied Territories.

Freud, A., & Burlingham, D. (1943). *War and children.* London: Medical War Books.

Hall, C. S. (1966). *The meaning of dreams.* New York: McGraw-Hill.

Hall, C. S., & Van de Castle, R. L. (1966). *The content analysis of dreams.* New York: Appleton-Century-Crofts.

Milgram, N. (Ed.). (1985). *Stress and coping in time of war: Generalizations from the Israeli experience.* New York: Brunner/Mazel.

Nashif, Y. (1984). *On either side of the Green Line: A comparison of the dreams of refugee children in a camp on the West Bank and children of an Arab village in Israel.* Unpublished masters thesis. Hebrew University of Jerusalem, Jerusalem, Israel.

Punamaki, R. (1987). Psychological stress responses of Palestinian mothers and children in conditions of military occupation and political violence. *Quarterly Newsletter of the Laboratory of Comparative Human Cognition, 9,* 76–84.

Shouval, M. (1991). The effect of the Gulf War on children. Paper presented at a conference sponsored by the Israel section of Defense for Children International (DCI), Jerusalem, Israel.

Straker, G., & Moosa, F. (1988). Post-traumatic stress disorder: A reaction to state-supported child abuse and neglect. *Child Abuse and Neglect, 12,* 383–395.

Terr, L. (1991). Childhood traumas: An outline and overview. *American Journal of Psychiatry, 148,* 10–20.

8 Children in War: Stress and Coping Reactions Under the Threat of Scud Missile Attacks and the Effect of Proximity

Naomi Bat-Zion
Rachel Levy-Shiff
Bar-Ilan University, Israel

War is unique among sources of extreme psychic stress. Children are exposed to the terrors of wars and armed conflicts worldwide, yet relatively few attempts have been made to study, empirically, war-related stress and coping reactions and the underlying psychological processes operating in children's efforts to adapt in these situations. The aim of the present study was to explore the dynamics of Israeli children's stress responses under the threat of missile attacks during the Gulf War, and the relationship between the degree of exposure to the war-induced threatening events and these stress responses.

Theorists such as Lazarus and Folkman (1984), Haan (1983), and Pearlin and Schooler (1978) have converged on conceptualizing stress responses in terms of the relations between the person's resources and the demands of the environment perceived as relevant to his or her well-being, for which the person's resources may be taxed or exceeded. This view implies the use of various processes, such as cognitive appraisal, emotional arousal, and coping efforts, which are crucial to stress-related responses.

Cognitive appraisal refers to evaluative processes that imbue a situational encounter with meaning. They involve evaluations and judgments, such as whether the encounter is relevant, benign or positive in its implication, or stressful (i.e., implying threats and potential for harm and loss; Lazarus & Folkman, 1984). One reason the process of cognitive appraisal is central to stress responses is that appraisal serves as a final common pathway through which diverse personal and environmental variables influence the outcomes of a stressful encounter. Emotion is the experience of the occurrence of stress. Theoretically, a distinction is made between pleasant or positively toned emotions and unpleasant or negatively toned emotions. In war-related situations, the latter dominate. Emotion has been considered to motivate behavioral responses that are invoked to reduce or manage anxiety and other distressing emotional states (e.g., Cox, 1978; Vaillant, 1977). These responses, often called *coping mechanisms*, may be of a physiological nature and/or of a psychological nature.

At the most general level, coping has been considered to include all responses to stressful events or external life strains that serve to prevent, avoid, or control emotional distress (Pearlin & Schooler, 1978; Silver & Wortman, 1980). However, theorists from a variety of perspectives have argued that this definition is too broad. They have emphasized the importance of distinguishing coping, as an effortful or purposeful reaction to stress, from other, reflexive or automatic, responses. A broad array of taxonomical attempts has sprung up to identify and categorize adult coping efforts. Lazarus and Folkman's (1984) seminal distinction of problem-solving–focused versus emotion-focused types of coping has served as one important point in the field. Moos and Billing (1983), synthesizing this and other systems, have presented a widened, three-part typology, distinguishing among: (a) cognitively oriented efforts, alterating or minimizing appraisals of threat or misfortune; (b) emotionally oriented efforts, dampening, venting, or directly counteracting negative feeling states; and (c) practically oriented efforts, resolving or circumventing problems or threats. Similar typological distinctions have appeared in attempts to type coping in childhood and adolescence (Band & Weisz, 1988; Compas, 1987; Curry & Russ, 1985; Dise-Lewis, 1988). Children in middle childhood are at least partially aware of their own coping efforts, and are able to report on them in a reliable fashion (Altshuler & Ruble, 1989), but their coping efforts are of a somewhat non-differentiated nature and of limited efficacy (Hoffman, Levy-Shiff, Sohlberg, & Zarizki, 1992).

Stress responses may also include various functional difficulties and inadequacies, disorganization or intrusion of thoughts of a distressing nature, somatic manifestations that reflect activation of altered autonomic and neuroendocrine patterns, and other inadequate or inappropriate behaviors that are associated with psychological distress (Hourani, Armenian, Zurayk, & Afifi, 1986).

The application of general models of stress responses in adults to children requires some alterations and additions. The basic features of child cognitive and socioemotional development are likely to affect stress responses (e.g., Eth & Pynoos, 1985; Maccoby, 1983). Most importantly, children's dependence on adults, and on parents in particular, emphasizes the need to include children's social context in understanding their stress responses. Parental reactions during war are assumed to be a critical factor in mediating children's stress responses, exacerbating or buffering the children's stress. Children's success in achieving new levels of stability following disruption depends, at least in part, on the skill with which their parents respond; the younger the children, the greater the reliance on parental figures to provide interpretation of the stressful event, emotional security, and structural stability (i.e., presence of familiar routines and predictable, understandable, physical, and social environment). In a stressful situation, a distressed, disorganized child imposes additional stress on caregivers. If parents can control their own stress responses and engage in their own forms of problem solving, seeking ways to help the child reorganize, progressive rather than regressive solutions may be fostered. Yet, diminished parenting may occur under the impact of stressors that are external to the parent–child relationship (Bryce, Walker, Ghorayeb, & Kanj, 1989). Hence, the first task in the present study was to explore the dynamics of children's stress responses based on a model (see Fig. 8.1) that takes into consideration general stress notions, the cognitive and socioemotional characteristics of child development stage, and the specific characteristics of the stressor.

Despite the commonalities of wars that all populations share, all wars are not alike, and, therefore, the induced stress responses may differ. War events vary considerably (e.g., bombardment, death in the family, evacuation; Tsoi, Yu, & Lieh-Mak, 1986), are embedded in different geopolitical and socioeconomic situations (e.g., immigration, poverty) that affect the outcome of the specific experience significantly (Arroyo & Eth, 1984), and may be associated with either chronic or acute danger (Bryce et al., 1989; Garbarino, Kostelny, & Dubrow, 1991). Chronic danger, particularly when that danger comes from violent day-to-day social reality, requires developmental accommodation that is likely to include persistent posttraumatic stress disorders (PTSD), alterations of personality, and major changes in patterns of behavior (Kinzie, Sack, Angell, Manson, & Ratah, 1986; Mazor, Gampel, Enright, & Orenstein, 1988). Acute incidents of danger often require situational adjustment by normal children leading normal lives through measures of objective change in the conditions of life or subjective alteration of one's stance toward life events, or both. If the traumatic stress is intense enough, it may leave permanent psychological scars (Dreman & Cohen, 1990).

The war-induced event of missile attacks on Israel can be considered as a relatively short-term, time-limited, uncontrolled stressor with acute but repetitive occurrence of life-threatening danger. This was the first time that an entire civilian population was under threat of conventional and chemical missiles, so the stressor was totally unfamiliar. Prior coping strategies could not exist in the individual or in the community repertoire. All parts of Israel were exposed to the threat. Thirty-seven missiles hit various areas, some of which were inhabited civilian neighborhoods, and caused substantial de-

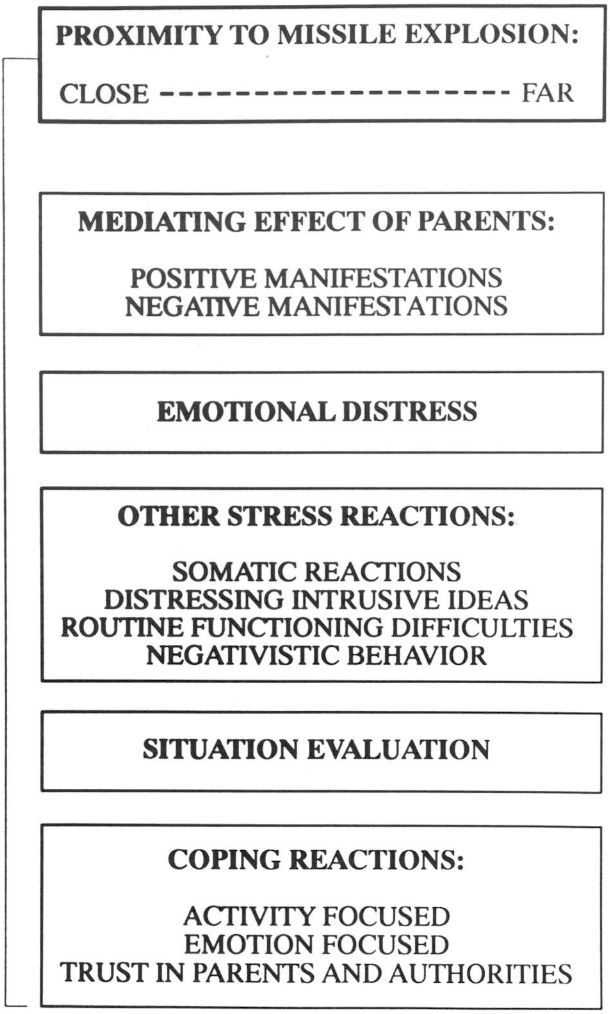

PROXIMITY TO MISSILE EXPLOSION:

CLOSE ------------------- FAR

MEDIATING EFFECT OF PARENTS:

POSITIVE MANIFESTATIONS
NEGATIVE MANIFESTATIONS

EMOTIONAL DISTRESS

OTHER STRESS REACTIONS:

SOMATIC REACTIONS
DISTRESSING INTRUSIVE IDEAS
ROUTINE FUNCTIONING DIFFICULTIES
NEGATIVISTIC BEHAVIOR

SITUATION EVALUATION

COPING REACTIONS:

ACTIVITY FOCUSED
EMOTION FOCUSED
TRUST IN PARENTS AND AUTHORITIES

FIG 8.1.   Theoretical model for children's stress responses.

struction. The Israeli population was advised to take defensive measures, because it was impossible to predict where the next missile would hit: At the sound of the alarm signal, people were to wear gas masks, enter a room fast, and seal it. There were about 4 to 5 minutes between a given alarm signal and the falling of a missile. The war lasted 6 weeks that were characterized by the disruption of the infrastructure of life and major disturbances of daily routine.

The second issue addressed in the present study explores the effect of proximity, or degree of exposure, to the war-related stressful experiences on children's stress responses. Clinical studies of psychic trauma have demonstrated a relationship between the degree of exposure to a disaster or life-threatening event and subsequent levels of symptoms or degrees of impairment in adults (Shore, Tatum, & Vollmer, 1986; Wright, Ursano, Bartone, & Ingraham, 1990). Studies have suggested a similar relationship for children (Ayalon, 1983; Newman, 1976). In particular, Pynoos et al. (1987) elucidated the initial posttraumatic responses of children to an isolated, life-threatening, violent event. Their results provided evidence that acute PTSD symptoms occur in school-age children, with notable correlation between proximity to the violence and type and number of PTSD symptoms. The findings regarding the effect of proximity to warfare on children were not conclusive, however, especially with regard to a normal population.

METHOD

Subjects

The sample was composed of 571 Israeli school-age children from the fifth and seventh grades, 48.5% boys and 51.5% girls. Of the children, 33.6% were first-born, 27.4% were last-born, and 39% were of some middle position. With regard to family structure, 93% came from intact families, and 7% came from one-parent families. Parental education reflected the substantial heterogeneity of the sample (for maternal education: up to 12 years, 32.6%, 12 years and maturity, 36%; academic, 30.9%; for paternal education: up to 12 years, 33.4%, 12 years & maturity, 31.2%; more than 12 years, 35.4%).

The sample consisted of two groups. The near-proximity group included 341 children drawn from three schools located in an area within 200–500 m of a missile hit in the center of Israel. These schools suffered damage, mainly broken windows from air pressure. The children resided in the neighborhood in which many houses were also damaged or completely destroyed and people were hurt, and from which many families were evacuated. The far-proximity group included 229 children who were drawn from two schools. These schools were located in areas that were relatively far from any missile hit (25–30 miles).

Measures and Procedure

A multidimensional self-report questionnaire was administered to all children in the schools. The students filled this questionnaire out in class. Data collection started on the first day that classes had resumed (the fifth week after the outbreak of the war) and were completed shortly thereafter. The measures were as follows:

1. Background information about the child: gender, number of siblings, birth order, structure of the family, and paternal and maternal education.

2. War-related measures of stressful experiences: (a) proximity to a missile explosion, (b) compliance with the instructions of the civil defense authorities (e.g., wearing gas masks, staying in a sealed room at the sound of an alarm signal), (c) hearing explosions, (d) knowing people who were hurt or whose homes were damaged, (e) having suffered damage (oneself or one's close relatives), and (f) leaving town and staying in an area considered to be less dangerous during the war. Answers were rated on a 4-point scale.

3. War-related emotions: 17 items denoting mainly distressing and negative feelings (e.g., fear, worry, anger, confusion, frustration). Answers were rated on a 4-point scale. The Cronbach alpha coefficient was .83.

4. Stress reactions, a 25-item part of the questionnaire designed to assess four areas most commonly characterizing involuntary stress reactions and disturbed functioning: (a) somatic reactions (e.g., heart palpitation, hand shaking, knee trembling, heavy breathing, headache, stomachache, nausea, loss of appetite, dry mouth, sleep disturbances); (b) intrusive, distressing ideas, thoughts, and daydreams (e.g., bad dreams and daydreams, frightening thoughts, sleep disturbances); (c) difficulties relating to practical and daily functioning (e.g., inability to perform school tasks, getting up late, inability to perform regular duties); (d) negativistic attitudes (e.g., being quarrelsome, refusing to fulfill routine tasks). Answers were rated on a 4-point scale. Cronbach alpha coefficients were .79, .72, .64, and .44, respectively.

5. Ways of coping, a 29-item part of the questionnaire designed to assess various coping efforts and behaviors: (a) activity-focused coping (e.g., keeping oneself occupied by doing unnecessary things, helping smaller children, seeking information by reading newspapers, playing, coloring, talking to friends, praying); (b) emotion-focused coping relating to more passive efforts, such as wishful thinking, emotional distancing, denial, and cognitive reframing (e.g., accepting the situation, convincing oneself that it will soon be over or that it's best to wait until it's over, trying to understand the situation better, trying to see the positive aspect); and (c) trusting parents or authorities (e.g., trusting parents, trusting military or civilian defence authorities, believing that school authorities will do anything possible to help, trusting God will help). Answers were rated on a 4-point scale. Cronbach alpha coefficients were .73, .61, and .78, respectively.

6. Children's perception of parental emotional manifestations, seven items, designed to assess two dimensions of parents' behaviors and attitudes as perceived by the child: (a) parents' positive emotional manifestations

(e.g., parents holding, parents soothing); and (b) parents' negative emotional manifestations and exhaustion (e.g., to what extent parents were confused, tired, and angry). Answers were rated on a 4-point scale. Cronbach alpha coefficients were .69 and .68, respectively.

7. Cognitive appraisal of the situation, a 1-item question related to how stressful the child evaluated the war situation on a 5-point scale (1 = *not at all*, 5 = *very much*).

8. Child self-perception of war-induced changes, a 5-item section designed to assess the child's subjective perceptions of personal changes that occurred during the war (e.g., behaviors, feelings, thoughts, and dreams). Answers were rated on a 5-point scale. The Cronbach alpha coefficient was .66.

RESULTS

Children's War-Related Stressful Experiences

Table 8.1 presents the frequencies of the war-related measures of stressful experiences. Inspection of the table indicates that during the missiles attacks, all children, in both the near-proximity area and the far-proximity area, were likely to enter a sealed room (about 99%). Yet, those who lived in the near-proximity area were significantly more likely than those in the far-proximity area to wear gas masks during the missile attacks, $X^2 (3) = 64.80$, $p < .000$; to hear missile explosions, $X^2 (3) = 335.66$, $p < .000$; to know people whose houses had been damaged or destroyed by the missiles, $X^2 (3) = 303.86$, $p < .000$; to know people who had been hurt by the missiles, $X^2 (3) = 145.23$, $p < .000$; to be hurt and suffer damage themselves, $X^2 (1) = 96.02$, $p < .000$; and to leave town for a supposedly more secure area, $X^2 (4) = 104.74$, $p < .000$.

The Effect of Proximity on Children's Stress Responses

To examine the effect of proximity on the children's stress responses, a series of one-way analyses of variance (ANOVA) and one-way multiple analyses of variance (MANOVA) with one factorial (proximity: near, far) were carried out (see Table 8.2).

The results of the ANOVA on emotional reactions indicated that children in the near-proximity area reported more distress and negative emotions than did children in the far-proximity area, $F(1, 569) = 76.13$, $p < .001$. Furthermore, the results of the MANOVA on stress reactions indicated a significant main effect for proximity, $F(4, 566) = 7.19$, $p < .001$. The follow-up univariate analyses revealed a significant main effect for proximity on the children's somatic reactions, frightening and intrusive

TABLE 8.1
Frequencies of War-Related Measures of Stressful Experiences

Measures	Near Proximity	Far Proximity	X^2
Entering sealed room or shelter			
Yes	99.1	99.1	.00
No	.9	.9	
Wearing gas masks			
No	1.5	4.5	64.80*
Sometimes	6.2	20.1	
Most of the alarms	15.0	30.8	
Always	77.3	44.6	
Hearing missiles explosion			
No	3.0	54.1	335.66*
Weak	3.9	25.2	
Strong	26.4	18.5	
Very strong	66.7	2.3	
Knowing people whose houses were damaged			
No	5.9	70.8	303.86*
One	6.2	13.0	
Several	44.4	11.2	
Many	43.5	4.9	
Knowing people hurt by missiles			
No	31.9	82.1	145.22*
One	8.7	7.1	
Several	37.0	;8.0	
Many	22.3	2.7	
Oneself (or close relatives) hurt or suffered damage			
Yes	33.7	.4	96.02*
No	66.3	99.6	
Left town during war			
Never	23.7	50.2	104.74*
One day	14.6	30.5	
Several days	31.9	16.0	
Most of the time	26.1	1.4	
All the war period	3.6	1.9	

Note. Frequencies are given in percentages.
*$p < .001$.

thoughts, and difficulties in performing routine tasks, $F(1, 569) = 17.44$, $p < .001$; $F(1, 569) = 22.74$, $p < .001$; and $F(1, 569) = 9.77$, $p < .003$, respectively, but not on negativistic attitudes. That is, children who lived in the near-proximity area reported more somatic reactions, more intrusive thoughts, and more daily routine difficulties. Likewise, the results of the ANOVA on the child situation evaluation indicated that children in the near-proximity area evaluated the situation as more stressful than did children in the far-proximity area, $F(1, 569) = 32.16$, $p < .001$.

TABLE 8.2
Means and Standard Deviations of Children's Stress Responses Measures by
Proximity and the Results of the ANOVAs

| | Proximity | | | | |
| | Near Proximity | | Far Proximity | | |
Measures	M	SD	M	SD	F
Emotions	2.50	.60	2.04	.61	76.13***
Stress reactions					
Somatic	1.92	.48	1.74	.50	17.44***
Intrusive thoughts	2.27	.75	1.97	.69	22.74***
Daily functioning difficulties	2.06	.62	1.89	.62	9.77**
Negative attitudes	1.90	.57	1.84	.54	1.94
Situation evaluation	3.55	1.21	2.97	1.24	32.16***
Ways of coping					
Activity focused	2.64	.52	2.41	.51	26.30***
Emotion focused	2.83	.60	2.72	.65	3.84*
Trusting parents and authorities	3.12	.60	2.84	.61	30.35***
Perceived changes					
Behaviors	1.74	.82	1.75	.99	.00
Feelings	2.09	.79	2.05	.94	.31
Thoughts	2.18	.83	2.14	.91	.23
Dreams	1.76	.99	1.86	1.14	1.14
Parental emotional manifestations					
Positive	2.37	.87	1.98	.82	30.13***
Negative	2.15	.64	1.94	.99	15.28***

*$p < .05$.
**$p < .01$.
***$p < .001$.

The MANOVA on the children's coping efforts also indicated a significant main effect for proximity, $F(3, 567) = 14.94, p < .001$. The follow-up univariate analyses revealed a significant main effect of proximity on coping behaviors: activity-focused, $F(1, 569) = 26.38, p < .001$; emotion-focused, $F(1, 569) = 3.84, p < .05$; and trusting parents and authorities, $F(1, 569) = 30.35, p < .001$. That is, children who lived in the near-proximity area used more coping behaviors.

The MANOVA on the self-reported, war-induced changes did not indicate a significant main effect for proximity. Children in the near-proximity area did not perceive any more changes in behaviors, feelings, thoughts, or dreams during the war than did children who lived in the far-proximity areas.

Finally, the MANOVA on the perceived parents' behavior variables indicated a significant main effect for proximity, $F(2, 568) = 21.01, p < .001$. The follow-up univariate analyses showed higher levels of parental positive emotional expression as well as parental negative manifestations and exhaustion, $F(1, 569) = 30.13$, $p < .001$, and $F(1, 569) = 15.28$, $p < .001$, respectively.

Empirical Model for Testing the Dynamics of Children's Stress Responses and the Effect of Proximity

Using the theoretical model of the structure of children's stress and coping responses during the war and the effect of proximity on them as the basic empirical model (Fig. 8.1), we analyzed the correlation matrix (Table 8.3) for the whole sample, using the statistical package of Linear Structural Relationships (LISREL VI program; Joreskog & Sorbom, 1984). Proximity was presented in the path model as an exogenous variable, that is, one unexplained by any of the other variables in the model, but explaining them (i.e., the variability was assumed to be determined by causes outside the model). The endogenous variables, whose variability was explained by the model, were parental positive emotional manifestations and parental negative manifestations and exhaustion, child emotions, child stress reactions (i.e., somatic; intrusive and frightening thoughts; difficulties in daily routine functioning; and negativistic attitudes), and situation evaluation. The outcome of the model was child coping behaviors (activity focused, emotion focused, and trusting parents and authorities). Table 8.4 presents a summary of the LISREL estimates (maximum likelihood) for direct and indirect effects for the whole sample. It displays the significant coefficients for the revised model that were above .17 ($p < .001$), given the sample size. Figure 8.2 displays only the significant path coefficients (betas for the

TABLE 8.3
Correlations Matrix of Children's Stress Responses Measures

Measure	2	3	4	5	6	7	8	9	10	11	12
Proximity	.24	.16	.34	.18	.20	.13	.06	.22	.21	.08	.23
Parental positive		.14	.49	.40	.44	.29	.20	.25	.39	.27	.52
Parental negative			.35	.32	.27	.26	.33	.22	.24	.18	.20
Emotion				.62	.76	.54	.26	.41	.46	.28	.50
Somatic reactions					.51	.52	.35	.29	.35	.19	.34
Instrusive thoughts						.52	.30	.36	.37	.23	.36
Routine difficulties							.28	.24	.28	.17	.28
Negative attitudes								.07	.11	.07	.12
Situation evaluation									.26	.25	.32
Activity-focused coping										.53	.55
Emotion-focused coping											.43
Trusting parents and authorities											

Note. r = .13, p < .001.

TABLE 8.4
Significant Direct and Indirect Effects of Children's Stress Responses Model

| | Coping | | | | | |
| | Activity-focused | | Emotion-focused | | Trusting Parents & Authorities | |
Indicator	Direct	Indirect	Direct	Indirect	Direct	Indirect
Proximity		.18				
Parental positive emotional manifestations	.25		.18		.36	
Parental negative emotional manifestations						
Emotion	.29				.25	
Situation evaluation				.17		

| | Situation Evaluation | |
Indicator	Direct	Indirect
Proximity		
Parental positive emotional manifestations		
Parental negative emotional manifestations		
Emotion	.18	
Situation evaluation		

| | Stress Reactions | | | | | | | |
| | Somatic Reactions | | Intrusive Thoughts | | Daily Difficulties | | Negative Attitudes | |
Indicator	Direct	Indirect	Direct	Indirect	Direct	Indirect	Direct	Indirect
Proximity		.23		.29		.22		
Parental positive				.28		.20		
Parental negative				.20			.28	
Emotion	.48		.74		.53			
Situation evaluation								

| | Emotion | | Parental Emotional Manifestations | | | |
| | Emotion | | Positive | | Negative | |
Indicator	Direct	Indirect	Direct	Indirect	Direct	Indirect
Proximity	.23		.23		.17	
Parental positive	.38					
Parental negative	.27					
Emotion						
Situation evaluation						

Note. The values for direct and indirect effects are unstandardized coefficients.

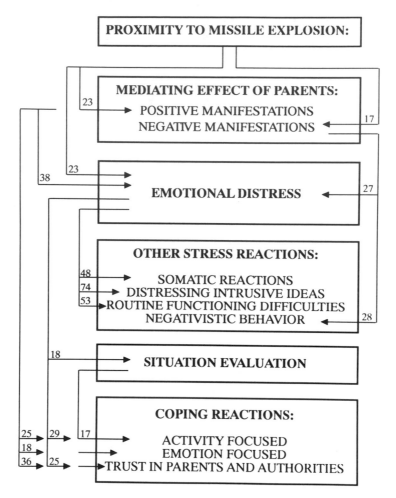

FIG 8.2. Revised empirical model for children's stress responses.

endogenous variables and gammas for the exogenous variable) for the revised model.

On the whole, the model explained 33.3% of the variance. The goodness-of-fit index of the model was .98, X^2 (14, N = 571), p = .96. This suggests a good fit of the model to the data, and the model can therefore be considered validated. With regard to the children's coping efforts, over 27% of the variance in their activity-focused behaviors, over 14% of the variance in their emotion-focused behaviors, and over 37% of the variance in their trusting parents and authorities behaviors were explained by the measures of the model. Children's active coping behaviors were directly predicted by parents' emotional expression and by the measure of child emotion, and indirectly predicted by proximity (betas were .25, .29, and .18, respectively). The more positive emotional manifestations the parents showed, the more distress the children felt, and, in near-proximity areas, the more activity-focused coping behaviors they reported. Children's emotion-focused behaviors were directly predicted by the situation evaluation and parental positive emotional manifestations (betas were .17 and .18, respectively). The more intense parents' positive emotional manifestations were, and the more the children evaluated the situation as stressful, the more they used emotion-focused coping behaviors. Children's coping focused on trusting parents and authorities was directly predicted by parents' positive emotional manifestations and by child emotion (betas were .36 and .25, respectively). The more the parents expressed emotion and the more distressed and negative emotions the children felt, the more they reported trusting parents and authorities.

In addition, over 22% of the variance in children's situation evaluation was explained by the measures of the model, mainly by child emotion (beta was .18). The higher the distressing emotions level, the more stressful the evaluation of the situation.

With regard to stress reactions, over 44% of the variance in children's somatic reactions, over 60% of the variance in children's intrusive and disturbing thoughts, over 31% of the variance in children's difficulties in routine functioning, and over 15% of the variance of negative attitudes were explained by the measures of the model. Children's somatic reactions were directly explained by emotion and indirectly explained by proximity (betas were .48 and .23, respectively). Children's intrusive and frightening thoughts were directly predicted by child emotion, and indirectly by proximity and by parents' positive and negative emotional manifestations (betas were .74, .29, .28, and .20, respectively). Children's daily routine difficulties were directly predicted by child emotion, and indirectly by proximity and by positive parental emotional manifestations (betas were .53, .22, and .20, respectively). Finally, children's negative attitudes were explained directly by negative parental manifestations and exhaustion (beta was .28).

Furthermore, over 41% of the variance in children's distressing emotions was explained by the measures of the model, directly by proximity and by positive and negative parental emotional manifestations (betas were .23, .38, and .27, respectively).

Finally, only 8% of the variance of parents' positive emotional manifestations and 3% of the variance of parents' negative emotional manifestations and exhaustion were explained in the model, mainly by proximity (beta were .23 and .17, respectively).

To explore whether the dynamics of children's stress responses in the near-proximity and the far-proximity areas differed, the correlation matrices were reanalyzed separately for the two groups, using the LISREL method and the aforementioned theoretical model. The results were very similar for the two groups, indicating identical structure of children's stress responses in the near-proximity and the far-proximity areas (they were, therefore, not reported).

DISCUSSION

Proximity to missile hit areas was found to affect the intensity of the children's stress responses, directly and indirectly, via parental behaviors and attitudes. The children who lived in the near-proximity areas, as compared with the children who lived in the far-proximity areas, reported more distress and negative emotions, and more somatic, cognitive, and daily routine difficulties; they appraised the situation as more stressful, and used greater coping efforts. In part, this is explained by these children's greater exposure to the war-related stressful experiences and traumatic stimuli (e.g., the terrifying sounds of sirens, the earth-shattering thuds of missile explosions, the sight of house destruction). Proximity also affected parental behaviors and attitudes: Parents in the near-proximity area were reported to display higher levels of agitation than those in the far-proximity area, reflecting negative and positive behaviors, which, in turn, were associated with children's increased stress responses.

The findings of the present study regarding the deleterious effect of proximity are in line with those of Pynoos et al. (1987) on the effect of exposure to a single life-threatening event (i.e., a sniper attack on the school playground). The findings in the literature regarding the effect of exposure to stressful warfare events on children seem to be intricate. For example, Klingman and Wiesner (1981) found higher levels of anxiety in children who were closer to areas of tension and who were exposed to shelling. Ziv and Israeli (1973) compared the anxiety levels of children in kibbutzim that were frequently shelled and children in kibbutzim that were not under fire. Contrary to their hypothesis, they found that shelling did not cause a higher level of anxiety. The authors explained their finding by postulating continuous adaptation and habituation to a stress, making it less threatening, and relating it to social support, which may be higher in a kibbutz that is directly subjected to danger. Likewise, comparing Israeli high school children from a township near the border with those living in the center of the country, Rofe and Lewin (1981) found that the former were more repressive, and that they had fewer daydreams and fewer nocturnal dreams as well. Content analysis of their dreams revealed that they contained fewer elements of aggression and anxiety. The authors believed that living under the constant threat of war increases the need to use repressive mechanisms, both on the personality level and as a general method of coping with everyday life stressors. These disparate findings suggest that the mechanisms underlying the effect of exposure to warfare stressors on children's adaptation are complex and depend on a host of conditions, such as the characteristics of the war-related stressors, the type of reactions measured, and the forces in the child's environment.

Proximity, however, did not affect the dynamics of the stress responses. The underlying processes mediating the stress responses were similar in the children who lived in the near-proximity areas and those who lived in the far-proximity areas. Although it validates the model, a possible explanation for this similarity is that all areas were under the life threat of the missile attacks, and the whole population was immobilized with extensive disruption of daily life, although the exposure to the threat was more intense in the near-proximity areas; hence, the difference was in the intensity of the stress responses, but not in their dynamics.

Parents emerged as a central mediating factor. Both parental negative emotional expressions and parental positive emotional expressions were found to be directly associated with increased levels of distress feelings and emotions, and indirectly with other manifestations of somatic, cognitive, and daily routine difficulties. Parental emotional expressions, negative or positive, probably reflected aroused parental states of agitation and distress that were an important signal for their children to decipher the threat. This would be similar to the social referencing phenomenon in infants: When young children feel threatened or experience uncertainty, they turn quickly to the mother, father, or other attachment figure, to seek information about the degree of safety or danger in a particular situation, and then act accordingly (Klinnert, Campos, Source, Emde, & Svejda, 1983). Parents serve as filters through which children process the essence or the meaning of the threatening situation.

Whereas parental negative emotional manifestations were associated more particularly with negative attitudes in the children, parental positive emotional manifestations were associated with increased coping efforts. This is consonant with the adult literature on the use of social support in coping processes across a variety of stressors in an individual's life. Social support is viewed as a form of coping or as a factor that facilitates coping (Barrera, 1981).

Previous studies on children in war have also indicated that children's responses are based, to a large extent, on the behavior of their parents or other significant adults. In World War II, Freud and Burlingham (1943) observed that young children in the care of their own mothers or a familiar mother substitute were not psychologically devastated by wartime experiences, mainly because the parents could maintain day-to-day care routines and project high morale. Other authors who conducted studies on how children met the stress of displacement and evacuation noted that the children who were evacuated from the great cities of England then under air attack to rural areas manifested distress symptoms far above the rate among the children who remained in the cities close to their families during the Blitz. They suggested that the security engendered by parents compensated for the traumatic effects of the air raids (Garmezy, 1983; Papanek, 1942). In addition, they found that if a parent exhibited psychiatric symptoms secondary to the warfare, the child often assumed a very similar symptom picture. Burt (1943) concluded that, for physically uninjured children, "the mental shock of being bombed is in itself far less serious and persistent than the effect of having been in the company of an adult who has flown into a panic — possibly the child's own parent" (p. 324).

More recent studies have reported similar findings. In her study of Israeli and West Bank Palestinian children, Punamaki (1987) found that the best predictor of increased mental disorders among children during periods of intense stress caused by military actions was maternal depression. Likewise, Bryce et al. (1989) found that in West Beirut, mothers who perceived the events in their lives as affecting them negatively, mothers who were exposed to more war-related events, and mothers who reported a tendency to respond to these events emotionally were found to have the highest levels of depressive symptomatology, which, in turn, were associated with increased morbidity among their children.

The crucial role of parents in the lives of their children in general, and in mediating children's stress responses in cases of traumatic events more specifically, explain why children who are involved in traumatic events in which they witness harm done to their parents (Pynoos & Eth, 1985), or in war situations where parents are not physically or emotionally available (Arroyo & Eth, 1984), react with acute psychic trauma.

Emotional arousal has emerged as the other important factor in explaining children's reactions. This supports the theoretical contention of the centrality of emotion in mediating stress responses (Vaillant, 1977), especially in an uncontrollable situation. The less in control an individual feels in the face of a threat, the higher the distress and negative emotions he or she experiences, and the greater centrality the events maintain in the individual's system (for a review, see Silver & Wortman, 1980). Much of the research on the relationship between emotion and stress responses has focused on the way emotion motivates coping and the ways in which emotion, and in particular anxiety, can interfere with functioning. Two mechanisms of interference have been emphasized: a motivational one, in which attention is redirected from a task at hand to a more pressing emergency; and a cognitive one, in which anxiety-related thoughts that are irrelevant to performance impede functioning.

The emotional arousal experienced by the children in this study was accompanied by substantial somatic, cognitive, and routine functioning difficulties. The difficulties were explained by parental reactions and by the children's emotion, but were not found to affect other stress responses, such as coping efforts or cognitive appraisal of the situation. These difficulties are probably part of the general arousal response; they do not necessarily have to persist or have severe consequences for the majority of the children. Children may develop various forms of stress responses: maladjustment (e.g., PTSD; Arroyo & Eth, 1984; Lyons, 1989), resilience (Garmezy, 1985), or adjustment, but adjustment for which the child pays a high price in terms of his or her mental health (Garmezy, 1983).

Cognitive appraisal of the situation was found to be of relatively marginal importance in the present study. This is in sharp contrast to the theoretical formulation (Lazarus & Folkman, 1984) that cognitive appraisal plays a major role in the transaction between the person and the potentially stressful environment, and that individual differences are relevant to the cognitive appraisal of stressors. One possible explanation is that, in the present study, this factor, a one-item variable, and other forms of cognitive appraisal (primary and secondary) were not assessed. Another possible explanation is that cognitive processes related to coping with stress may be more limited in children, because of their relatively undeveloped cognitive capacities (Inhelder & Piaget, 1958), and because of the uncontrolled and life-threatening nature of the stressor, as opposed, for example, to other routine stressors with which the children have to cope (Band & Weisz, 1988). The metacognitive literature and the literature directly relevant to children's awareness of coping strategies also suggest that there are limits in individuals' ability to cope by means of mental activities (Altshuler & Ruble, 1989). For example, children have considerably more difficulty than adults in employing cognitive forms of coping designed to alter their cognitive state or to manipulate mental states (Brown, Bransford, Ferrara, & Campione, 1983). If this explanation is valid, it also explains why children rely so heavily on parents' cues in interpreting and translating threatening situations, and in determining the range of appropriate strategies to use.

From a theoretical point of view, the findings of the present study — emphasizing the important role of parental behaviors and child emotion in mediating children's stress responses and the marginal role of the cognitive processes — should be understood in terms of the developmental phase of the children and in terms of the nature of the stressor. It is plausible that the dynamics of stress responses would vary in older or younger children, or in different stressful situations. At the very least, the theoretical implications of these findings to the general theory of stress and coping is that models adequate for adults cannot be applied to children without modifications.

REFERENCES

Altshuler, J. L., & Ruble, D. N. (1989). Developmental changes in children's awareness of strategies for coping with uncontrollable stress. *Child Development, 60,* 1337–1349.

Arroyo, W., & Eth, S. (1984). Studied children traumatized by Central American warfare. In S. Eth & R. S. Pynoos (Eds.), *Post traumatic stress disorders in children* (pp. 101–121). Washington, DC: American Psychiatric Press.

Ayalon, O. (1983). Coping with terrorism: The Israeli case. In D. Meichenbaum & M. E. Jaremko (Eds.), *Stress reduction and prevention* (pp. 293–339). New York: Plenum.

Band, E. B., & Weisz, J. R. (1988). How to feel better when it feels bad: Children's perspectives on coping with everyday stress. *Developmental Psychology, 24,* 247–253.

Barrera, M. (1981). Social support in the adjustment of pregnant adolescents: Assessment issues. In B. H. Gottlieb (Ed.), *Social networks and social support* (pp. 69–96). Beverly Hills, CA: Sage.

Brown, A., Bransford, J., Ferrara, R., & Campione, J. (1983). Learning, remembering, understanding. In P. H. Mussen (Series Ed.), J. Flavell & E. Markman (Eds.), *Handbook of child psychology: Vol. 3. Cognitive development* (pp. 76–166). New York: Wiley.

Bryce, J. W., Walker, N., Ghorayeb, F., & Kanj, M. (1989). Life experiences, response styles and mental health among mothers and children in Beirut, Lebanon. *Social Science and Medicine, 28,* 685–695.

Burt, C. (1943). War neuroses in British children. *Nervous Child, 2,* 324–337.

Compas, B. E. (1987). Coping with stress during childhood and adolescence. *Psychological Bulletin, 101,* 393–403.

Cox, T. (1978). *Stress.* London: Macmillan.

Curry, S. L., & Russ, S. W. (1985). Identifying coping strategies in children. *Journal of Clinical Child Psychology, 14,* 61–69.

Dise-Lewis, J. E. (1988). The life events and coping inventory: An assessment of stress in children. *Psychosomatic Medicine, 50,* 484–499.

Dreman, S., & Cohen, E. (1990). Children of victims of terrorism revisited: Integrating individual and family treatment approaches. *American Journal of Orthopsychiatry, 12,* 204–209.

Eth, S., & Pynoos, R. (1985). Developmental perspectives on psychic trauma in childhood. In C. R. Figley (Ed.), *Trauma and its wake* (pp. 36–520). New York: Brunner/Mazel.

Freud, A., & Burlingham, D. T. (1943). *War and children.* London: Medical War Books.

Garbarino, J., Kostelny, K., & Dubrow, N. (1991). What children can tell us about living in danger. *American Psychologist, 46,* 376–383.

Garmezy, N. (1983). Stressors of childhood. In N. Garmezy & M. Rutter (Eds.), *Stress, coping, and development in children* (pp. 43–84). New York: McGraw-Hill.

Garmezy, N (1985). Stress-resistant children: The search for protective factors. In J. E. Stevenson (Ed.), *Recent research in developmental psychopathology* (pp. 213–233). Oxford: Pergamon.

Haan, N. (1983). *Coping and defending: Process of self-environment organization.* New York: Academic Press.

Hoffman, M. A., Levy-Shiff, R., Sohlberg, S., & Zarizki, J. (1992). Impact of stress and coping: Developmental changes in the transition to adolescence. *Journal of Youth and Adolescence, 21,*451–470.

Hourani, L. L., Armenian, H., Zurayk, H., & Afifi, L. (1986). A population-based survey of loss and psychological distress during war. *Social Science and Medicine, 23,* 269–275.

Inhelder, B., & Piaget, J. (1958). *The growth of logical thinking: From childhood to adolescence.* New York: Basic Books.

Joreskog, K. G., & Sorbom, D. (1984). *LISREL VI: Analysis of linear structural relationships by the method of maximum likelihood* (3rd ed.). Mooresville, IN: Scientific Software.

Kinzie, D., Sack, W. H., Angell, R. H., Manson, S., & Ratah, B. (1986). The psychiatric effects of massive trauma on Cambodian children: 1. The children. *Journal of the American Academy of Child Psychiatry, 25,* 370–376.

Klingman, A., & Wiesner, E. (1981). *The relationship of proximity to tension areas and size of settlement or residence to fear level of Israeli children* (Unpublished research report). Jerusalem: Psychological and Counseling Service, Ministry of Education.

Klinnert, M. D., Campos, J., Source, J. F., Emde, R. N., & Svejda, M. J. (1983). Social referencing. In P. Plutchik & H. Kellerman (Eds.), *The emotions in early development* (pp. 123–134). New York: Academic Press.

Lazarus, R. S., & Folkman, S. (1984). *Stress, appraisal and coping.* New York: Springer.

Lyons, J. A. (1989). Posttraumatic stress disorder in children and adolescents: A review of the literature. In S. Chess, A. Thomas, & M. E. Hertzig (Eds.), *Annual progress in child psychiatry and development* (pp. 451–467). New York: Brunner/Mazel.

Maccoby, E. E. (1983). Social-emotional development and response to stressors. In N. Garmezy & M. Rutter (Eds.), *Stress, coping, and development in children* (pp. 217–234). New York: McGraw-Hill.

Mazor, A., Gampel, Y., Enright, R. D., & Orenstein, R. (1988). Holocaust survivors: Coping with post-traumatic memories in childhood and 40 years later. *Journal of Traumatic Stress, 3,* 1–36.

Moos, R. H., & Billing, A. G. (1983). Conceptualization and measuring coping resources and processes. In L. Goldberg & S. Breznitz (Eds.), *Handbook of stress: Theoretical and clinical aspects* (pp. 210–230). NY: The Free Press.

Newman, C. J. (1976). Children of disaster: Clinical observations at Buffalo Creek. *American Journal of Psychiatry, 133,* 306–312.

Papanek, E. (1942). My experiences with fugitive children in Europe. *Nervous Child, 2,* 301–307.

Pearlin, L. I., & Schooler, C. (1978). The structure of coping. *Journal of Health and Social Behavior, 22,* 337–356.

Punamaki, R. L. (1987). Psychological stress response of Palestinian mothers and their children in conditions of military occupation and political violence. *The Quarterly Newsletter of the Laboratory of Comparative Human Cognition, 9,* 76–79.

Pynoos, R. S., & Eth, S. (1985). Children traumatized by witnessing acts of personal violence: Homicide, rape, or suicide behavior. In S. Eth & R. S. Pynoos (Eds.), *Post traumatic stress disorders in children* (pp. 17–44). Washington, DC: American Psychiatric Press.

Pynoos, R. S., Frederick, C., Nader, K., Arroyo, W., Steinberg, A., Eth, S., Nunez, F., & Fairbanks, L. (1987). Life threat and posttraumatic stress in school-age children. *Archives of General Psychiatry, 44,* 1057–1063.

Rofe, Y., & Lewin, I. (1981). The effect of war environment on dreams and sleep habits. In N. Milgram, C. D. Spielberger, & I. G. Sarason (Eds.), *Stress and anxiety* (Vol. 8., pp. 231239). New York: Hemisphere Publishing.

Shore, J., Tatum, E., & Vollmer, W. (1986). Psychiatric reactions to disaster: The Mount St. Helens experience. *American Journal of Psychiatry, 143,* 590–595.

Silver, R. L., & Wortman, C. B. (1980). Coping with undesirable life events. In J. Garber & M. E. P. Seligman (Eds.), *Human helplessness: Theory and applications* (pp. 279–340). New York: Academic Press.

Tsoi, M. M., Yu, G. K. K., & Lieh-Mak, F. (1986). Vietnamese refugee children in camps in Hong Kong. *Social Science and Medicine, 23,* 1147–1150.

Vaillant, G. E. (1977). *Adaptation to life.* Boston: Little, Brown.

Wright, K., Ursano, R. J., Bartone, L. H., & Ingraham, M. (1990). The shared experience of catastrophe: An expanded classification of the disaster community. *American Journal of Orthopsychiatry, 60,* 35–42.

Ziv, A., & Israeli, R. (1973). Effects of bombardment on the manifest anxiety level of children living in kibbutzim. *Journal of Consulting and Clinical Psychology, 40,* 287–291.

9

On The Value of a Psychoanalytic Perspective in Research on Children in War: Group Interviews of Israeli and Palestinian Children During the Gulf War and 1 Year Later

Roberta J. Apfel
Bennett Simon
Harvard University

The core problem in understanding the experience of children in war situations is that we ask them to speak of things that are so often unspeakable, to describe emotions and states that are so often unbearable for the child and unbearable for the listener. Accordingly, research methods have been developed to record and capture the trauma, while containing its impact for the child and for the adult trying to gather this information.

Research on children in highly traumatic situations has clearly entered the developmental stage of relying heavily on standardized instruments for systematically assessing the effects of such traumas on children. These instruments are typically developed by adapting already existing instruments and, optimally, modifying them using information and insights made available through more open-ended interviewing of children, parents, and teachers. Ideally, information from research conducted with systematic instruments can then feed back into more informed interventions, including clinical interviews that are enriched by the availability of the systematic knowledge. Tortorici (1988), for example, has explored the relative values of open-ended and systematic interviewing and assessment in the Central American context.

Psychoanalytic exploration of children in traumatic situations of war and separation began with the pioneering work of Anna Freud during World War II (1973) and then John Bowlby (1951), investigations foreshadowed by the work of Hug-Hellmuth (1915/1991). Freud's work in her Hampstead Heath nursery was marked by careful observation and recording of as much detail as the war-time circumstances of London allowed. Bowlby's naturalistic observations of infants in hospitals and child-care settings, conducted in post-war Europe, was simultaneously of a survey nature and somewhat systematized. Such work considerably stimulated and enriched a large number of more systematic studies of infants in such situations.

The data in Freud's (1973) work were largely observational in origin, gathered by psychoanalytically trained or informed observers. Relevant data can also be gathered by formal psychoanalytic treatment, in both adults and children. In general, there is little psychoanalytic data from children directly in war zones or collected in times of war, and of that small amount, little has been published. What there is principally comes from Israel and from Britain during the London Blitz. There is much more extensive data, although not much that is systematized, from psychoanalytic treatment of adults who survived war or persecution situations, principally Jewish survivors of the Holocaust (e.g., Bergmann & Jucovy, 1982), and adults who were children during the London Blitz.

There is a great wealth of data in a large-scale psychodynamic interview study of adults who were children in Europe during World War II, principally Jewish children, but also other children, including those of Nazis and Nazi collaborators. This is the Jerome Riker Study of the Organized Persecution of Children, headed by Dr. Judith Kestenberg, a study in which we participated as interviewers. The interviewees volunteered and did not represent a clinical population per se, although many of them either had been in some form of psychological or psychiatric treatment, or had never been in treatment but clearly seemed to be suffering greatly at the time of the interview. These interviews have been mined qualitatively, and a number of reports have been published (e.g., Kestenberg, 1988). Currently, a group at Tel Aviv University is undertaking more systematic research based on these interviews plus other postinterview studies (Y. Gampel).

In other places in the world, where there has been active conflict and/or refugee populations who were exposed to active conflict, plus the availability of psychodynamically trained therapists and/or researchers, anecdotal and some systematic information has been accumulated from evaluation, educational, and treatment settings. Again, much of this is unsystematized.

Psychodynamic and psychoanalytic orientations have informed and helped shape a variety of other interventions and investigative modes, principally those now categorized as studies of posttraumatic stress disorders (PTSD). The integration of psychoanalytically derived knowledge with knowledge derived from studies of children with severe stress syndromes is in an early stage, and much work remains to be done in this regard.

What characterizes the psychoanalytic approach that is the common denominator in these domains? First, the approach assumes that a dialogue must be established between two people, that a relationship and connection of some significant sort must be established if the data that emerge are to be credible and useful. Second, it assumes that the nature of the current relationship will, sooner or later, be shaped by past significant relationships and, further, that as the current investigative or treatment relationship proceeds, that the connection between the past and present relationships will become clearer to both the therapist-investigator and the subject. Broadly speaking, this is what is referred to as *transference*. Third, it assumes that affects are extremely important, both as motivators of the relational process and as sources of data about what the subject has experienced and how those experiences have been processed. A subsidiary assumption is that the investigator-therapist can tap into his or her own emotional reactions to the interview as a potential source of information about what the subject is experiencing. The modes, methods, and ground rules for the investigator-therapist utilizing his or her affective states constitutes a large portion of the training of the psychoanalyst or psychodynamic therapist.

There is also the core assumption that it is possible and desirable to investigate the inner life of the subject from the perspective of conflict. In fact, one plausible definition of *psychoanalysis* is the study of the mind from the perspective of conflict. The corollary assumption is that the evidence of the conflict is often disguised, transformed, or symbolically represented, and that the person must continuously utilize modes of keeping certain conflicts out of awareness. The motive for keeping conflict out of conscious awareness is avoidance of painful affect — anxiety, guilt, shame, dread of annihilation; the awkward term *mechanisms of defense* has often been used to describe a number of such ways of protecting the self. There is, thus, both the possibility that painful and conflicted experience is encoded in disguised forms and the potential, using the appropriate setting and methods, for the therapist, working with the subject, to help the subject bear the pain of this decoding and re-experiencing of affective distress.

There are other assumptions, as well, such as that memory of painful or potentially painful events is encoded in symbolically disguised and transformed modes. These disguises and transformations constitute a part of normal development and maturation of the person. In some sense, nothing is forgotten, but rather, the form in which it is remembered is continually reshaped over the course of development. A methodological consequence of these considerations — about the nature of memory processing and the nature of symbolic connections among seemingly disparate domains — is the idea of free association. Although free association was originally defined in the clinical psychoanalytic setting, its utility in an appropriately modified form in other settings is impressive. More than any other single feature of a psychoanalytic approach, free association is the best method of tying together past, present, and the relationship to the interviewer.

A detailed discussion of the uniqueness of psychoanalytic approaches compared to other modes of studying child development, or the overlap of psychoanalytic methods with other methods, or the validity of psychoanalytic methods, is obviously beyond the scope of this report. Rather, at various points in the presentation and discussion, we suggest some of the especially important aspects of a psychoanalytic orientation.

We report here on a particular kind of interviewing that we believe provides a rich source of insights and information about the interior life of children in war, data that might, in turn, be utilized in improving standardized instruments, and as an adjunct to those instruments. We believe this way of listening can uniquely capture children's ordinary, age-appropriate worries and their affective responses.

We are primarily psychiatric and psychoanalytic clinicians. We came to the study of children in war in the past 4 years, and have approached the field primarily through interviewing and taking narrative life histories. Work with the Jerome Riker Study of the Organized Persecution of Children has made us aware of the rich inner life of the child in war, even as filtered through and remembered by the adult many decades later. In particular, these interview experiences have given us clues as to the intensity, modes of experiencing, and ways in which both traumatic and pleasurable memories have been processed. The intense sensory quality of the small child's way of experiencing the world is conveyed by the adult interviewees, as they recall the sights, sounds, textures, smells, colors, and bodily sensations that go into the matrix of memory and recollection. We also have learned about the role of certain pivotal internalized models and ideals, such as early beloved and admired parental figures, that helped sustain children through extraordinarily difficult situations.

By reading a number of autobiographies and fictionalized autobiographies describing childhoods in traumatic war situations, we have come to appreciate the complexities and conflicted nature of the mind and heart of the young child. The astonishing altruism of the children described in these autobiographies is consistent with accounts we and others have noted in interviews with adult survivors. The role of altruistic deeds by adults toward children in allowing the children themselves to become altruistic is yet another awe-inspiring finding that emerges from these personal narratives.

Overall, as we have immersed ourselves in the various writings and research on children in war, we have been continually impressed with the power of the personal story to inform, to influence, and to articulate for both teller and audience events and feelings that are so often unbearable and unspeakable.

THE STUDY

During the Gulf War in February 1991, we went to Israel with a set of questions that had been generated by a class of 8-year-olds in our suburban public school system. These questions ranged from the more concrete third-grade concerns ("Is your gas mask next to your bed?", "Can you have a birthday party during a Scud attack?") to the terrors of war and abandonment ("Are you afraid about coming home [from school] and finding your house wrecked?"; see Appendix for the list of questions we actually used, with some modification). We met with two groups of children to discuss these questions, and to get answers and reactions to bring back to the children at home. Because of the realities of school bureaucracies, compounded by the stress of the war situation, we made informal arrangements through personal contacts. We do not begin to believe that our sample was randomly or carefully selected.

The Palestinian children we studied were developmentally around 8 years, although many of them were actually 9 or 10. They attended an Arabic-speaking public school for mildly handicapped children in Jerusalem, run by the Israeli government. Our contact and primary translator was the physical therapist at the school, who was very devoted to the school, the children, and their families. The Israeli Jewish children were 8-year-olds on a religious kibbutz who were chosen to speak with us by their art teacher, a woman with a longstanding shared interest in children in war. Sessions were tape recorded and later transcribed.

Meetings with these two groups were held twice, once during the war and once a year later. We visited the local U.S. third-graders who supplied the original questions and so, were able to get their responses and carry questions back and forth.

INTERVIEW WITH THE ISRAELI CHILDREN

These interviews took place when the war had been on for about 3 weeks, and the frequency of Scud attacks had subsided somewhat. In retrospect, the peak had passed, but of course no one was sure at that juncture. The kibbutz was quite a distance from the coastal area, where most of the Scuds had landed and done their damage, but parts of a Scud missile and/or Patriot had fallen on a kibbutz only a few kilometers away. As was true for all Israeli children, their fathers and older brothers had been or were currently in the regular army or on reserve duty; their older sisters also had been, were then, or would be in the army. Although this kibbutz had not seen any of its members killed or seriously wounded in the intifada or in the current fighting in Lebanon, everyone knew someone—often a family member—who had been killed or injured in some war, and they were very attuned to news of anyone from the nearby area or who had been at some time connected with the kibbutz being killed or injured. Similarly, although there had been no terrorist or guerrilla raids on the kibbutz for many years, the area was not free of infiltrators from Jordan. Further, this kibbutz had, at one time, been an area of very active shelling from Jordan and infiltration of guerrillas. In short, although there were no current losses, years of warfare, armed conflict, a history of losses, and the attendant fears and defenses against those fears formed the background of the current war. For example, several Torah scroll covers that were seen every week by the children bore the names of children of the kibbutz who had died in wars.

For the interview, 10 children and their art teacher sat in the children's art studio on the kibbutz. The children were all about 8 years old and in the third grade; half were boys and half were girls. The place was a familiar and comfortable one; in fact, the children had spent more time there than usual, because the district school had been closed during the early days of the war. The group was lively, only a bit shy and reserved at first, which was eased by their beloved teacher's introduction and some snacks she had brought. They quickly and enthusiastically began to respond to the questions we brought from the children in the United States. At various points during the interview, the children volunteered to sing songs they and their teacher had written about the war, especially about Saddam Hussein. They interspersed their replies to our questions with age-appropriate jokes about Iraq and Saddam Hussein (in some ways quite similar to jokes we recalled from our childhood years during World War II about Hitler, Mussolini, and Hiro-hito) and jokes that placed this current villain in the context of Jewish history, especially with the upcoming holiday of Purim and its villain, Haman.

They reported, in varying degrees of detail, on how they first learned of the war, and on their first Scud attack: where they were and who helped them with their masks. They were proud of themselves, and focused much more on whom they helped with the masks, rather than on their own needs to be instructed. For most of the interview, their replies were lively, charming, age-appropriate, and very upbeat. Even when describing fear or sleep disturbances, they did so almost in unison, shouting "yes" when we asked them if they had trouble sleeping.

At one point in the interview, we asked them a question from our list that we thought was a pedestrian: "What do you see on television?" To our surprise, their collective affect changed quite dramatically. They became sad and reflective, and several spoke of seeing the children of Baghdad wandering around the streets, looking forlorn, dirty, and very sad, and commenting, for example, that they had to bathe in the river because there was no water or electricity. One child added that he had seen the birds covered with oil, struggling to fly and, in fact, to live. Here, too, the affect of sadness was most prominent and was contagious within the group.

Another place where sadness or mildly distressed affect appeared, although not as dramatically, was in the words of some of the songs about

Saddam Hussein and the war, especially lyrics addressed to Saddam Hussein: "Why are you so intent on destroying the world and the children in Israel?" Overall, they were very aware of the political situation and of the need to endure, and had faith in their government and the U.S. Patriot missiles.

FOLLOW-UP INTERVIEW

The group for the second interview was almost the same group we had previously interviewed. Our follow-up interview, in February 1992, showed how much the children remembered about the war, and how the stories had become magnified and transformed during the year's time. The war had ended shortly after we left in 1991, but a year later many families had not yet put their gas masks away. The children were eager to talk; in fact, children who had not been in the group the previous year begged to be included in the follow-up (they were not, however). The affect and bravado were similar, as was the relationship to the art teacher, but there was more disorganization around the snowy weather (more than there had been during the war).

Despite discussions in the news about the questionable effectiveness of the masks — of which the children were quite aware, and which one girl brought up — they dismissed the criticism of a particular government official (Miriam Ben-Porat, a very outspoken inspector general), and remained trusting in the government and the ability of adults to protect them. Each had some detailed and specific memory of one or another Scud attack: where he or she was, with whom, what each one was eating or doing. All the children recalled the special times of eating in the dining room, and of being together with families in sealed rooms. Again, they remembered images from television, this time images of black rain in Kuwait (one boy who was particularly attuned to bird migrations in the area, had a theory that the reason cormorants appeared on the kibbutz that year was to escape Iraq and come to a place with lots of good fish), the children, and the Iraqi soldiers surrendering and begging for food. For themselves, as long as no one got hurt, they added, they had wanted the war to last longer, so that they could stay out of school more. They were annoyed that the cancellation of school caused by the war had to be made up, and that their summer vacation was commensurately shortened.

The most interesting and unexpected response was to our question of what they would tell their children about the Gulf war. One boy said, "If they ask or if they don't ask?" He expressed resentment that his parents had not told him fully about other wars when he had inquired. This was followed by a very intense, serious, and sophisticated discussion about what parents tell their children and when and how. An analogy was made to adoption, a relevant topic for this community, which had adopted one of the girls in the group and had incorporated some recent Russian emigré families. One girl proclaimed, "I want to hear everything!"

The children ended the session with three questions for us (and for the children in the United States): "Did you see the snow in Jerusalem?" "Are there gas masks in the United States?" "Are you afraid Russia will send missiles against the United States?"

These questions suggested to us a merging of the fear and excitement of the war and of snow, both very unusual events in their lives. Their teacher pointed out to us that the parents' affective response to the snow was much more open and unrestrained than had been their response to the war. In the case of the war, the parents felt a need to shield the children from their own fears; in the case of the snow the parents felt they could freely share their own excitement.

INTERVIEW WITH THE PALESTINIAN CHILDREN

The setting for these interviews was an Israeli government urban school. We were introduced to the school by a physical therapist who made the arrangement with the principal, a woman who lived in a nearby village. She had to go up two levels in school administration to get permission. All of the staff—the principal and the teachers—were Israeli Palestinians, and school was taught in Arabic. The atmosphere of the school was orderly, but quite relaxed and comfortable, with parents, teachers, and children somehow mingling and yet gradually going to their regular places.

On the way to our meeting place, one of the teachers said jokingly, "Talk to me first. I'm a child of war!" This same teacher participated actively in the discussion as if she were one of the children. Ten children (with several moving in and out) met with one of us (B.S.) who understood a few Arabic words; our contact person and the teachers translated. There was a melange of Arabic, Hebrew, and English, but the overall thrust was to maximize communication, rather than to use language difficulties to disguise it.

At first, the children were quite shy, but within several minutes, they warmed to the discussion and became lively and engaged. Some of their teachers were amazed at how much the children said and how much they knew about the war and the political situation. Questions elicited anecdotes about the gas masks and the sealed rooms, especially emphasizing the role of children in helping adults in the family to prepare things at home. (Teachers later said they thought the children had exaggerated their own abilities, because they had required considerable instruction with gas mask alarm drills at school to prepare themselves.) The children talked excitedly about Scuds and drew them, but never mentioned the Patriot missiles, which were more the focus of the kibbutz children's drawings. Asked when the war would be over, three children responded with similar, yet different, answers, indicating three different views on who had the power: "When Saddam Hussein is dead," "When Shamir is dead," and "When King Fahd is dead."

Several of the children had relatives in Kuwait and one had relatives in Iraq, but questions about these people in the war zone did not elicit any more affect. Exuberance was high in response to the question about sleep troubles. When asked about dreams, the children hesitated at first, and it was the teacher who said, "I've had scary dreams."

The greatest affect was generated around the question about what they saw on television. Sadness and pain were conveyed in their descriptions of the children of Baghdad. (These urban children showed no particular interest in the birds.) Needless to say, we were quite struck with the similarity and spontaneity of the response by both the Israeli and Palestinian children to what we thought was a relatively bland question.

In a debriefing with the principal afterward, we were reminded that part of the political consciousness of this population is not to talk to casual strangers about personal beliefs. This meant that we definitely had not heard the whole story of what these children thought and believed, but we had heard quite a bit, given all the possibilities for caution in their speech. The principal interpreted some of what we observed as a kind of imitative contagion within the group (e.g., in indicating when the war would end, all the responses used the formula, "When so-and-so is dead").

We later saw the drawings that the children had made at our request: We had asked them to draw whatever they wished about war or peace while we were talking with the principal. Almost all of them were about Scuds, often showing them on route from Baghdad to Tel Aviv. Many had Palestinian nationalistic emblems, such as flags or inscriptions. Only one, by a girl, had a more pastoral scene.

FOLLOW-UP INTERVIEW

A year later, we returned, again making arrangements with the principal through the Israeli physical therapist. The structure for reinterviewing this group was not ideal: The physical therapist was not as heavily involved in school in terms of time, spending most of her time working at another school, for somewhat older handicapped children. It was also the day after a huge snow storm for which school was cancelled, so everything was disrupted, and many of the children were only slowly returning to school.

Of the 9 or 10 children present during the interview at any one time, only 3 had been in the group interviewed the previous year.

Our interview with the children was preceded by a long meeting between the principal and her teachers about the allocation of duties for the day, with several teachers being assigned to tasks other than working with the children. She apologized for the delay and for the day not being ideal, and we proceeded with children from two classes, with the teacher of one of them, who was a recent graduate and a new teacher. He spoke Hebrew well and acted as the main translator, with some assistance from the physical therapist. The teacher introduced us briefly; it was not clear if any of the 3 children who had been present at the previous meeting remembered us or not. We then introduced ourselves, told the children of the previous year's meeting, and explained how we had brought their answers back to children in the United States. Some new questions we introduced were: "What do you remember of the war?" "What will you tell your children?" "How old will you be when peace comes?" "Do you have any relatives now in Iraq, Kuwait, and Jordan, and what do you hear from them?"

Among the interesting differences between 1991 and 1992 was in their versions of the war: In 1991, there were many references to the Scuds, but none to the Patriots, neither in words nor in drawings. In 1992, the children said, "Saddam sent missiles [Scuds] against Israel, and Shamir sent missiles back." The name "Patriot" was familiar to them when we mentioned it, but it did not arise spontaneously.

In response to our question, "What will you tell your children about the war?," the answers were varied. Some said, "God will take care us"; others said they would describe how they watched television and wore masks, and how they put the masks on. They would also describe how, when the sirens blew, they sealed their houses with "nylon" (i.e., plastic sheets).

A few had relatives in other Arab countries: one an uncle in Iraq, and one an uncle in Amman. The uncle in Iraq was said to have sent some clothes after the war was over. There were no particular responses or connected associations to questions about the children of Baghdad; they did not connect with the question on the second interview. "When will there be peace?" and "How old will you be when there will be peace?" were not questions that elicited much interest or response. Overall, what emerged was a rather confusing and concrete series of personalized anecdotes that were not closely or obviously closely related to topics of war and peace, and were difficult to understand literally, let alone symbolically.

Toward the end of the meeting, there was much talk about the snow. They were very excited and involved in talking about the snow and about making snowpeople and snowballs. We commented to them that they seem to like the snow better than the war. Only one child directly responded, saying that he liked both—that both were exciting.

At that point, various anecdotes, stories, and fantasies emerged that indicated considerable tension and anxiety: Someone told a story of a woman who was left with a scar on her right cheek from the gas mask; another child showed, with a gesture, that the scar was bigger than that; and then a third child said, "No, her whole face was scarred." We took that as emblematic of the "scars" left on their faces by the experiences of the war, and our surmise was made more credible as we heard anecdotes of the intifada, which they proceeded to describe, that involved more references to faces: Masked youths threw gasoline on a store near one girl's grandfather's house (soldiers chased them); a boy told of soldiers coming knocking on his door—he ran up to the roof, and looked down, and they somehow found him and slapped his face. We interpret these responses as collectively revealing more of the anxiety and discomfort in thinking about war, the intifada, and the current political Israeli–Arab tensions, than did the miscellany of stories and literal responses to our questions earlier in the session.

MEETING WITH THE THIRD-GRADERS IN THE UNITED STATES

We report only briefly on the interchange with the U.S. third-graders, which took place shortly before the war ended. The children were quite enthusiastic about having us report back to them about the children in Israel and the territories, and remembered the questions they had made up with their teacher. In addition, several of the children had corresponded with children in Israel and had their own sources of data. On the whole, they mostly wanted to know details about the gas masks, the sirens, and how and when life was disrupted by the threat and actuality of Scud attacks and/or gas attacks. Several of the children came from families that were strongly pro-Israel and, in the discussion, voiced strong political opinions about the situation.

One incident near the end of the meeting suggests how much children need to assimilate terrible events around them to their own emotional and cognitive scale of understanding. One little boy named Noah said that he had heard that there were people getting married during Scud attacks, and that they had worn gas masks during the ceremony. He could not understand this, because, in order to get married, you have to kiss! How could they kiss with gas masks on? One of us replied that somehow they had managed—perhaps they had merely rubbed the snouts of the gas masks together to suggest a kiss. At this, one little girl raised her hand and said, "This is not a question for Dr. Apfel, but a comment to Noah. Noah, you don't have to kiss to get married—you can just hold hands!"

DISCUSSION

Overview of the Answers and of the Group Comments

Although we made no attempt to code and count responses systematically, we were able to categorize the responses of the children to our questions as follows:

1. Fairly literal and factual answers, with little expressed emotion. In general, these replies did not permit much further discussion and seemed to signal either lack of interest in the topic, or, occasionally, that the question had literally simply not been well understood and needed rephrasing, or contextualizing in the appropriate, culturally sensitive language.

2. Factual answers, with a good deal of affect and/or a great deal of factual detail. Either of these signaled much greater involvement of the children in the interview process and pointed to important areas for further exploration and elaboration. Detailed political information in the answers, for example, suggested how much cognitive mastery and/or identification with informed parents and teachers, were part of the overall pattern of the children's coping.

3. Answers that seemed tangential or irrelevant at first, but were associated with significant affect, and turned out to be symbolic or displaced modes of representing issues that stirred up considerable anxiety and/or more depressive affect.

4. Answers that seemed to make no sense. These sometimes represented the children's wandering attention (particularly among the Palestinian children) but sometimes, in retrospect, appeared defensive, as more charged material often emerged shortly thereafter.

What is especially valuable and important in this kind of interviewing from a research point of view? First, surprising and unexpected events can always occur. The prime examples in this study were the answers to the question, "What do you see on television?", answers conveying great sadness and distress about the children of Baghdad. Other examples were the associations among the Israeli children for the question, "What will you tell your children?" and the emergence of concerns about adoption, and the associations among the Palestinian children of the "woman with the scar on her face made by the gas mask" to other issues of "face."

Second, the overall affective involvement of the children in the interview provides important data about how children were thinking, feeling, and coping. The high level of excitement and enthusiasm in both groups during the actual period of the war reminds us that, inter alia, war can be very exciting for children, and that the excitement may be one major means of coping with fear and depression. The intrusion at occasional points of those distressing affects suggests the defensive role of the excitement.

Needless to say, other hypotheses about the role of excited affect may be applied to the data: such as that the children included in the interview are gratified by being the center of attention, that the war situation made them special in the eyes of adults, especially adults coming from the outside; or that the opportunity to tell what they were feeling and thinking was itself gratifying and relieved, at least temporarily, some of their anxiety.

Third, these interviews are reminders that, at a time of war, war is not the only stress and distress in children's lives. Rather, war accentuates and potentiates children's concerns about separation, loss, abandonment, mutilation, fairness, and unfairness in the world, as well as concerns for the plight of other children. Some years ago, Anna Freud (1973) made the point that for children at various stages of development attempting to master their issues about aggression — its expression, containment, and channeling — war makes mastery much more difficult. Although we did not see material relevant to this issue in these interviews, interview material, if it were also correlated with some behavioral observations (e.g. schoolyard play), could tell us much about individual and group issues in regard to aggression. The response of the third-grade girl that you don't need to kiss to get married but you can just hold hands, suggests that the potential stress of war interacts with the age-appropriate sexual concerns of children as well (a point made most poignantly in the French World War II film, *Forbidden Games*).

Fourth, such interviews, when done with follow-up, give an opportunity to see how children remember, affectively as well as cognitively, the events of war and its impact. Thus, in the two interviews of the Israeli children, we posit a continuity in the theme of how war affects children. In the first interview, manifest concern for the Iraqi children popped up unexpectedly. However, the material the next year (also unexpected) about comparing telling about war to telling about adoption suggests the affective residue of the war is an ongoing concern about how war can lead to loss and abandonment by parents. Although the data we have are not adequate to confirm or refute this surmise, we suggest that we are seeing, in formation, the way war sensitizes children, long term, to further losses, even if the cause of the loss is independent of war. Similarly, our second interview with the Palestinian children suggests that one form in which they remember the war, and one form in which the Gulf War may sensitize them to subsequent traumas, is around the issue of face, shame, humiliation, and pride.

An alternative hypothesis about the response of the Israeli children to the question, "What will you tell your children about the war?" was suggested by the children's teacher. She argued that their associations to what and when you tell children about adoption was more immediately germane to issues of honesty in parental responsiveness and the gratification of legitimate curiosity than with loss and abandonment. In this view, one of the burdens that war presents to children is whether or not they can trust their parents to be honest with them. This concern, in turn, may overlap with other ongoing concerns of many children that their parents and other adults are withholding or lying about the truth, especially in regard to questions of their origins. This line of reasoning is compatible with our hypothesis about the war stirring up concerns about loss and abandonment.

Finally, the political awareness of the children we interviewed emerged in interesting and surprising ways during the interviews. In retrospect, of course, we should not have been surprised at their level of awareness of the larger events taking place around them, but adults are often surprised when they realize how much of the unpleasant political world around them children actually absorb. These interviews are consonant with the findings of investigators who have questioned children more explicitly about their political attitudes and knowledge, as in Coles (1986).

Overall, these five aspects of the interviews can lead to a richer design of research protocols, whether in questionnaires, semi-structured interviews, open-ended interviews, or expressive therapies, such as drawing and drama. Moreover, it is possible to systematize the analysis of the interview material itself, and we have suggested one method of categorization that might be used in future interviewing as a basis for more systematic and comparative treatment of the children's responses.

In and of themselves, our data do not answer questions about how children feel, think, and cope, but they do raise important issues to consider before one lays down definitive judgments about what is going on with children (especially those that claim the absence of any residual effects from war).

Didactic and Therapeutic Aspects of the Interviews

The interviews set a model for the teachers and the children for discussion of charged topics, a model that could be used after the interviewers had gone. Of course, the fact that teachers and school officials agreed to and were interested in the interviews suggested a readiness on their part to deal openly with the children about the impact of the war (or of war, in general). Still, they may have needed some help and reinforcement in their own conflicts about whether it was better for the school, the teachers, and the children to discuss these issues in a school setting. We do not have much data on this issue with regard to these children and their school settings, but we have the impression that the experience was a very important and helpful one. In our experience, most adults need help in seeing and tolerating the ways in which children attempting to cope with severe external stress. Sometimes the poignancy and immediacy of a child's response is overwhelming for the adult, and sometimes the indirectness of the child's response allows the adult to deny and minimize how much the child is hurting. Studies done on children's processes of mourning (e.g., over a parent who has just died), indicate how much adults' inability to experience the child's pain plays a role in discouraging the child from communicating his or her distress more directly (e.g., Furman, 1974; Wolfenstein, 1965).

The interview itself was a form of enhanced connection and attachment for the children, for whom the war stirred up fears of abandonment, separation, and loss. For a short time, it brought together the children, the adults in their school, and interviewers from the outside. In addition, the interviewers brought with them a connection to children outside of their community — the children in the United States. Similarly, the interviews and the steps leading up to and following them brought about a new connection for the American children with children in situations very different from their own.

For us as interviewers, the experience was also one of establishing and deepening connections around experiences of anxiety and dread of separation and loss that adults experience in war settings. Especially with the opportunity for follow-up (we plan annual visits to these settings), we become more involved and more immersed, and our anxieties become contained, channeled, and used in ways that help both ourselves and, hopefully, others.

Ayalon (1979, 1982) and the Kiryat Shmonah (Lahad & Cohen, 1988) experience with Community Stress Reduction Programs have demonstrated the value of secondary preventive intervention around war trauma in children. Storytelling and opportunities to communicate and acknowledge fearful experiences is one way to reduce stress over time and free developmental energy for other tasks. Studies of the effects of trauma on children show how much trauma fractures, disintegrates, and breaks apart the soul and sometimes the body of the child. The process of open-ended talking with the child — allowing the expression of distress and inner turmoil in a safe setting — is holistic, integrative, and restorative.

APPENDIX

Questions from Third Graders in the United States for the Children in Israel, and modified for use with the Palestinian children.

1. What do you think of Saddam Hussein?
2. Have you had Scud missile drills?

3. Is it scary? Rate it on a scale of 1-10.
4. Are some of your relatives in the army fighting?
5. How do you feel being so close to the fighting?
6. How did you feel when you first heard air-raid sirens?
7. What do you do when you get out of school?
8. How did you feel when you first heard about the war?
9. Has a Scud missile hit your neighborhood?
10. Is it hard to concentrate on your work?
11. How long do you think the war will last?
12. How does it feel to have a gas mask on?
13. Are you worried about coming home and finding your house wrecked?
14. Do you worry about anything happening to your parents?
15. Are many shops open? Are you able to get food?
16. Is your sleep interrupted? Are you getting many hours (of sleep)?
17. Have you even been separated during an air raid? If so, how did you feel?
18. Is your gas mask next to your bed?
19. Do you ever forget about the war?
20. How long does a gas mask last? Does it wear out?
21. If you wear glasses, is it hard to wear a gas mask?
22. Are you nervous as you walk along the street?
23. If a gas mask breaks, do you have a replacement?
24. Do you have any questions about the war? If so, what?
25. What games do you play? Dreams?
26. What do you see on television?

REFERENCES

Ayalon, O. (1979). Community oriented preparation for emergency: COPE. *Death Education, 3*, 227–244.

Ayalon, O. (1982). Teaching children strategies for coping with stress. *Bereavement Care, 2*, 2–3.

Bergmann, M. S., & Jucovy, M. E. (Eds.). (1982). *Generations of the Holocaust*. New York: Basic Books.

Bowlby, J. (1951). *Maternal care and mental health*. Geneva: World Health Organization.

Coles, R. (1986). *The political life of children*. Boston: Houghton Mifflin.

Freud, A. (1973). Reports on the Hampstead nurseries 1939–1945. In A. Freud (Ed.), *The writings of Anna Freud: Vol. III. 1939–1945* (pp. 3–540). New York: International Universities Press.

Furman, E. (1974). *A child's parent dies: Studies in childhood bereavement*. New Haven: Yale University Press.

Hug-Hellmuth, H. (1991). War neurosis and children. In G. MacLean & U. Rappen (Eds.), *Hermine Hug-Hellmuth: Her life and work* (pp. 129–134). London and New York: Routledge. (Original work published 1915)

Kestenberg, J. (1988). Child survivors of the Holocaust. *Psychoanalytic Review, 75*(4).

Lahad, M., & Cohen, A. (1988). *Community stress prevention.* Kiryat Shmonah, Israel: Community Stress Prevention Centre.

Tortorici, P. J. (1988). *The war in El Salvador: The child as witness, participant, casualty, survivor: A phenomenological study.* Unpublished doctoral dissertation, University of Southern California, Los Angeles.

Wolfenstein, M. (1965). Death of a parent and death of a president: Children's reactions to two kinds of loss. In M. Wolfenstein & G. Kliman (Eds.), *Children and the death of a president* (pp. 62–79). Garden City, NY: Doubleday.

10 The Children of Kuwait After the Gulf Crisis

Kathi Nader
Robert S. Pynoos
University of California, Los Angeles;
Neuropsychiatric Institute and Hospital;
Center for the Health Sciences, Los Angeles

Among the most serious long-term sequelae of war for children is the psychological trauma resulting from seeing and experiencing life threat, violence, and torture (Garbarino, Kostelny, & Dubrow, 1991; Kinzie, Sack, & Angell, 1986). Children exposed to extreme violence have been reported to exhibit the full range of posttraumatic stress and grief reactions reported for adults (Nader, Pynoos, Fairbanks, & Frederick, 1990; Pynoos et al., 1987). Such reactions can seriously interfere with normal childhood development, including the capacity to learn, the development of creativity and conscience, the acquisition of socially appropriate behaviors, the ability to control impulses and tolerate negative emotions, the capacity to be productive, and the courage to resolve problems (Pynoos, Nader, & March, 1991). After violent exposures, both increased aggressive and antisocial behaviors, and increased inhibition and reticence to act have been noted. Dangerous reenactment behaviors have also been observed. These manifestations of posttraumatic stress disorder (PTSD) and associated psychological disturbances may be ameliorated by early and appropriate mental health intervention (Pynoos & Nader, 1993).

This chapter describes the screening and intervention components of a program conducted in consultation with the UCLA Program in Trauma, Violence, and Sudden Bereavement. It reports on the findings of a pilot screening of 54 Kuwaiti children, which was conducted 4 months after the liberation of Kuwait from Iraqi occupation in 1991. It also outlines a more comprehensive epidemiological survey of a representative sample of Kuwaiti children conducted from October to December 1991. Analysis of this latter survey is on-going and will be used in implementing an intervention program.

The program was carried out in two segments: In June 1991, four psychologists from the Ministry of Health of Kuwait completed training in the methods of screening children for postcrisis responses; then from October to December, the four psychologists joined Dr. Nader in the initial phases of training approximately 75 psychologists and social workers to systematically screen children in the schools of Kuwait. In June, a pilot sample of children was screened in order to collect preliminary information and to test the translated and adapted screening instrument. In November and December, over 2,000 children were evaluated using two final versions of the screening instrument. In addition, during both the summer and the fall, a group of clinicians underwent the first phase of training in the treatment of children with posttraumatic stress and grief reactions. The authors wish to acknowledge Manal Al Ajeel and Dr. Jasem Hajia of Kuwait for their assistance with the June training and screening.

SCREENING OF CHILDREN FOR POST-CRISIS REACTIONS

Phase I: June 1991

In both the June and the fall screenings, the Childhood Posttraumatic Stress Disorder Reaction Index (CPTSD-RI; copyrighted by Frederick, Pynoos, & Nader in 1992), the Grief Inventory, and the Exposure Questionnaire were used. There were several translations into Arabic prior to the trip to Kuwait, followed, in June, by revised translations and adaptations for Kuwait. This process included forward and backward translations, as recommended by Karno, Burnam, Escobar, Hough, and Eaton (1983). The June versions of the instruments were tested for use with Kuwaiti children during the training phase. Assessment of other anxiety disorders and comparisons of parent, teacher, and child ratings of distress will be completed in the future on a subsample of subjects included in the large epidemiological survey.

The June screening provided useful information in the further adaptation and streamlining of the Arabic translation of the CPTSD-RI and its additional questions. The adaptation process itself (summer and fall) provided an opportunity to learn about cultural issues relevant to the screening. The June screening was extremely useful for planning the extended screening of children after the schools had reopened in the fall. We learned, for example, that separate questionnaires would be needed for 7- to 10-year-olds and 11- to 17-year-olds because of the differences in the younger children's cognitive and verbal abilities. Also, we changed the question on startle response because of its association with fear in Arabic.

Rewording permitted the measurement of a physiological startle response, rather than appraising general fear, which was referred to in other questions.

The June training included didactic and experiential components. The June household survey of children ages 7–17 provided experience in the administration of the instruments, as well as preliminary testing. A team of five screeners completed a June school survey ($N = 54$). Because of language differences and the nature and prolongation of children's experiences during the crisis (exposure to multiple horrors, both human and material losses and prolonged fear), children's interviews took approximately 2 hours each during training and 1 hour with experience, a greater length of time than had been required in previous studies in the United States following more circumscribed disasters or violent occurrences.

Kuwaiti children were out of school for a full year as a result of the crisis. A supplemental summer school session was organized for voluntary participation in an attempt to help the children to regain some of the skills lost during the crisis. There were only about 8 schools open for the optional session, compared to the usual 400 schools. Children from these schools were randomly selected for participation.

The fall sample was planned so that it would be representative of Kuwaiti children by age, gender, and demographic and geographical region; the children surveyed in the summer schools were not a representative sample. The June sample included children with middle-range exposure to the war atrocities; the fall sample included children both more and less severely exposed than the June sample. Although tortured and other severely affected children were interviewed in June for the purposes of the clinical and screening training, these more severely traumatized children were not well-represented in the summer school. Very few of the children in the June pilot study were exposed to the most severe life threat, and only two were injured during more frightening circumstances than a slap, a cut, or a fall. Nevertheless, more than 70% of the children interviewed reported moderate to severe posttraumatic stress reactions. The June pilot study was analyzed for the following: (a) the intensity of exposure, (b) casual and risk factors for postcrisis reactions, (c) patterns of response.

Phase II: Fall, October–December 1991

Approximately 3 months after schools reopened on August 24, screening for PTSD and grief reactions began in the schools. A randomly selected group of children from each of three groups were interviewed: primary, middle, and secondary school children. The three groups ranged from 7 to 17 years of age. Percentages of each age group sampled were based on their percentage in the population of Kuwait.

Sampling Criteria

Random Sampling and Distribution of Screeners. According to the Kuwait Ministry of Education's Director of Research, there are cultural differences between the five districts of Kuwait. Within each school in any given district, however, the demographic distribution is comparable. Therefore, schools were randomly selected from each district, classrooms were randomly selected from each school and children were randomly selected from each classroom list. Selection of males and females and of age groups was based on respective representation in the greater population of Kuwait. Each screener interviewed both boys and girls from each age group and from each district.

Obtaining a Representative Sample. All five geographical regions were sampled so as to include all populations of Kuwait. Schools were selected randomly from each district to ensure the inclusion of each demographic constellation. Individual children were chosen from randomly selected schools in each district to provide a variety of crisis experiences. These included: (a) children who were in Kuwait during the crisis, and those who were out of the country: (b) children who were captured and/or tortured, and those who remained at home; (c) children who only heard of, those who witnessed, and those who experienced atrocities: (d) children who experienced concern for others or experienced the loss of significant others, and those who did not; and (e) children from a few private schools, to ensure that all ethnic groups were screened.

Training in Research Methodology and Use of the Instruments. Screeners underwent extensive training in administration of the screening instruments. It was necessary, in postcrisis Kuwait, to train screeners for a period of 5½ weeks prior to the beginning of screening. Specific attention was given to addressing prejudgments that might jeopardize accurate results. In order to achieve acceptable interrater reliability standards, screening was monitored, and additional training and feedback sessions occurred periodically.

Absences and Nonenrollment. Because absences may be greater for children who are traumatized, children included in the screening were randomly selected from the class rolls rather than from those who showed up for school on the day of screening. Every attempt was made to screen children on the selected list who were absent; this group screening was conducted as close as possible to the time the rest of the class was screened.

It was possible that children who were severely traumatized or injured might not have re-enrolled in school. It was hoped that these children would be identified and a group of them screened separately. Thus far, this separate screening has not been conducted. However, there were tortured and severely exposed children among those screened in the fall sample. The goals of the screening were:

1. To assess the PTSD responses of children ages 7–17.
2. To identify specific children with PTSD and grief reactions, and make referrals for treatment.
3. To identify risk factors for posttraumatic response.
4. To provide an estimate of the percentages of children with PTSD reactions.
5. To assess personnel needs for the treatment of children with moderate to severe reactions.
6. To identify important public health issues that could improve the postwar recovery environment.

CLINICAL TRAINING: THERAPEUTIC INTERVENTIONS FOR CHILDREN

Six psychiatrists and four psychologists from the Ministry of Health joined the June treatment team. Three weeks of training included two to three didactic sessions, and at least two observations of Dr. Nader conducting the specialized initial interview. For some of the trainees, this was their first experience in the treatment of children. It was advised that between this initial and subsequent training, the trainees read the clinical articles provided, which helped to explain the treatment methods. These trainees also conducted interviews with children.

In the fall, an additional eight clinicians were identified from among the Ministry of Education screening trainees to undergo initial training in the methods of treatment for childhood PTSD and grief. Two didactic sessions were scheduled at intervals during 2½ weeks. Between these sessions, therapists were scheduled to observe Dr. Nader conducting clinical interviews with children. Treatment sessions were scheduled at 2-hour intervals to allow time between sessions for brief feedback to be given to parents and a short period of discussion between Dr. Nader and the trainees. The goals of the training included:

1. To begin training in the use of the initial diagnostic and therapeutic interview elaborated by us (Drs. Nader and Pynoos).
2. To demonstrate treatment methods by conducting these clinical interviews in the presence of trainees.

3. To elaborate the basic principles of treating PTSD and trauma-related grief in children.
4. To identify additional professionals with appropriate clinical experience and education to be trained in these treatment methods on a later occasion when this group undergoes its second training period.
5. To prepare and provide future periods of the clinical training.

The plan was to offer this training at 4-month intervals, followed by the trainees conducting clinical interviews with children. During the June visit, one parent meeting was held and was observed by three Kuwaiti psychologists. The fall sampling required 16-hour workdays to complete, so additional training, through parent, teacher or administrator group meetings, was not possible at that time.

THE JUNE PILOT SAMPLE

Methods

The Sample

The 54 Kuwaiti children evaluated were randomly selected from randomly selected classrooms in two of the approximately eight schools open for the summer session. The group was comprised of 8- to 10-year-olds (26%), 11- to 17-year-olds (70%) and 20- to 21-year-olds (4%); it included 32% males and 68% females. Ninety-six percent of the children were Kuwaiti, and 4% were Egyptian. Thirty-three percent of the children were in Grades 2–4; 22% were in Grades 6–8; and 45% were in Grades 9–12.

Results

PTSD Levels

The children interviewed were distributed primarily across mild, moderate, and severe levels of posttraumatic stress reactions. Because only 4% of the children interviewed had no posttraumatic stress response, the categories of *none* and *mild* were combined for the purposes of further analysis. Thus, 29% of the children had *none–mild* reactions, 40% had *moderate* reactions, and 31% had *severe* reactions. There were no cases of *very severe* reactions in this particular group of Kuwaiti children (see Table 10.1).

TABLE 10.1
Pilot Study: June 1991
Distribution of Symptoms by Severity of Posttraumatic Stress

Number of Symptoms Severity	%	
0–11	Doubtful	4
12–24	Mild	25
25–39	Moderate	40
40–59	Severe	31
> 59	Very Severe	0

Children's Experiences

The following brief descriptions, given by children, elaborate some of their experiences during the occupation. Amla described how she would lie awake at night next to her siblings worrying about soldiers coming into the house or bombs hitting them. She could hear the bombs and the gunfire. Everyone else was asleep. She was very scared but had no one to tell. One night, her father forgot to put the pillows in the window. Windows were sometimes blown out by the bombs or bullets. She tried to put the pillows in herself, but was especially scared when doing so.

Foaziah also described unrelenting fear. At night, the family would listen to the radio in the living room. She would stand while the others sat and listened. She could not be still, and her stomach hurt all the time. When someone knocked at the door, she was most afraid because it could be the Iraqi soldiers, who often came into the house to search it. Foaziah had heard that sometimes they would take the father or brothers away, rape the women, inject people with lcthal fluids or something that made them sterile, or shoot the young men in front of their families. When the soldiers did come, she was very scared because her grandmother yelled at them. She wanted to hit her grandmother and hide her father. She followed her father and the soldiers around the house during the search to somehow protect him. They almost looked into the bag with her father's army clothes. When her father offered to get them a chair to help them look, they decided not to bother. All Kuwaiti soldiers, when identified, were taken away or killed.

Mohammed, a 15-year-old, trembled and chewed on his fingers while he described a scene at the grocery store where the Iraqi soldiers beat another teenage boy into unconsciousness. He was unable to intervene without risking his own life. He anxiously described feeling emotionally torn: wanting to help, wanting to hurt the soldiers, and wanting to run for safety. He ran and later described tremendous guilt feelings.

Jasem, a 16-year-old boy, described seeing a girl his age naked in the street. She was red and scratched all over her body after being raped. He was horrified and angry. He wanted to marry the girl and reject all of the girls who had left Kuwait during the crisis. He was also quite distressed about having stood by silently as the Iraqis threatened another boy for the graffiti Jasem had written on a wall insulting Saddam Hussein. Even 6-year-old boys were sometimes executed for such graffiti. Luckily, the boy was released.

Fatim, a 12-year-old girl, described being at home throughout the crisis and hearing the bombs and bullets. A window blew out on the other side of her house. She heard all of the rumors about young boys being shot or tortured in front of their mothers. She saw the mutilation on television. Throughout the crisis, she was angry and felt helpless to do anything. Once she went on top of the water tanks on her roof to shout bad words at the Iraqis. She helped to write and distribute pamphlets denouncing the Iraqis. She said that her parents did not want to listen to her distress. Once, after the crisis, she went up on the roof top to jump off. Her sister stopped her. Another time she went to jump out her second-story window. Again, her sister arrived in time to stop her.

Noura, a 17-year-old girl, had a live-in cousin who had been like a beloved brother. He was riddled with bullets in a skirmish with the Iraqis. He was taken to a makeshift hospital in a hotel where the Iraqi sergeant told medical personnel to let him die. He was not worth the energy to save him. Noura had cried every day since his death during the crisis. She did not want to live.

Case Example. When Abdul, age 10, entered the room for his clinical interview, he said that he had seen a child on television whose leg had been exploded by a mine. It upset him to see the child on television. He was asked to draw a picture and tell a story. His picture was of a woman with a blackened, broken leg. He said an Iraqi hit her leg with a hammer. His story was of hunger, danger, and harm to a couple on the sea.

Abdul said that Iraqis ate the meat, the rice, and all of Kuwait. There were bombs and scary noises. Abdul asked, "Didn't Saddam's head explode?" He wished to send a missile to explode his head. He saw his brother kill six Iraqis. When Iraqis came, the family hid his brother's gun and soldier clothes.

Abdul was inside the house when the Iraqis broke the door down. He thought they were coming to take the family because he and his brother had killed Iraqis. He was adamant that he had killed one Iraqi. When the Iraqis came into their house, Abdul pulled a knife. An Iraqi took it and slapped Abdul's face. Then they put the family in prison in Iraq. Abdul became very agitated on several occasions while describing his experiences during the occupation. He would leave the room briefly to see his friends, who waited in the hallway. When he became upset, he would say "God is generous."

Abdul became very agitated when he described an Iraqi opening fire on Kuwaitis. The Iraqis burned him and scratched his hand when he was captured. He pulled up his sleeves to show the large cigarette burns on his arms. He said he could not talk about being burned because it would scare Dr. Nader too much. His family was released from prison when the Americans came. Abdul had to walk home across the desert after he was released.

Summary of Exposures

Most of the children, 78% or more, worried about one or more individuals, knew one or more who had been injured, and knew captured persons. In this sample, 60%–70% of children saw mutilation on television, saw dead or injured bodies, or knew someone who died during the crisis.

Only two of the children were hurt under adverse circumstances. One was cut by blown-out window glass while he was imprisoned by the Iraqis, and the other was tortured with electric shock. They reported correspondingly moderate and severe post-traumatic stress reactions. Only one adolescent had killed someone. He reported a severe reaction (see Table 10.2).

Trauma and CPTSD-TI Scores

This pilot study provided a preliminary examination of what might increase traumatic response. Our conclusions were restricted by the limitations of this nonrepresentative sample. Not surprisingly, the most severely affected children were not well represented in the temporary schools.

TABLE 10.2
Pilot Study: June 1991
Exposure to Trauma

Event	n	Number of Yes	% Exposed
Worried about someone	51	46	90
Knew captured persons	51	44	86
Knew injured	49	38	78
Saw mutilation on TV	48	33	69
Saw bodies, injured, or dead	51	33	65
Knew a deceased person	48	30	63
Felt threat of death	51	29	57
Felt threat of injury	51	21	41
Witnessed death or injury	51	18	35
Had previous trauma	49	12	25
Was injured	50	12	24
Hurt someone else	51	8	16

Although we did see a few tortured children in the summer clinical training, there were very few in the summer sampling.

The following specific events were examined for their effect on severity level: knowing persons who were injured, knowing persons who were captured, knowing persons who were killed, directly witnessing injury or death, seeing dead or injured bodies, seeing tortured or mutilated bodies on television, experiencing the threat of death, experiencing the threat of injury, being injured, injuring someone else, worrying about a significant other, and experiencing a previous trauma.

These children witnessed death by shooting, beating, hanging, strangulation, and torture. Witnessing a killing increased CPTSD-RI scores (pooled $t = 2.65, p < .01$) and increased severity of ratings of PTS reaction (Pearson $X^2, p = .02$; linear trend, $p = .01$; see Table 10.3).

During and after the crisis, images of dead and mutilated martyrs and enemy soldiers were repeatedly displayed on television. During Dr. Nader's second trip to Kuwait between October and December 1991, adults and children continued to view these images on videotape; in magazines, books, and photos; and in a special room holding the instruments of torture. In June, Dr. Nader was taken to this room. Its walls displayed pictures of martyrs, and there were mannequins cut and colored to depict the tortures. It was important to the Kuwaitis that the investigator see and understand what the Iraqis had done to them.

The children reported being a combination of proud, angry, sad, and helpless at the sight of their badly mutilated countrymen. The most significant effect for this sample of children was the witnessing of these burned, mangled, or mutilated bodies on television. This television witnessing increased CPTSD-RI scores (pooled $t = -3.19, p = .003$) and increased the severity of posttraumatic stress (Pearson $X^2, p = .01$; linear trend, $p = .003$; see Table 10.4).

A stepwise regression was performed to determine which exposures and other factors influenced traumatic response. At Step 0, witnessing mutilated bodies on television was the strongest predictor of CPTSD-RI score ($F = 11.2$). Witnessing a killing was next ($F = 4.2$), and knowing someone who

TABLE 10.3
Stress Reactions of Those Who Witnessed an Injury or Death While Occurring
($n = 51$)

Witnessed	Stress Reaction		
	None–Mild	Moderate	Severe
Yes	1 (5%)	9 (50%)	8 (44%)
No	14 (42%)	11 (33%)	8 (24%)

Note. Pearson $\chi^2, p = .02$; linear trend, $p = .01$.

TABLE 10.4
Pilot Study: June 1991
Stress Reactions of Those Who Saw Mutilated Bodies on TV ($n = 48$)

During Crisis	Stress Reaction		
	None–Mild	Moderate	Severe
Seeing TV mutilation	6 (18%)	12 (36%)	15 (46%)
Did not see TV bodies	8 (53%)	6 (40%)	1 (7%)

Note. Pearson χ^2, $p = .01$; linear trend, $p = .003$.

died was third ($F = 3.23$). After removing instances of seeing bodies on television, all coefficients fell below 3.

Knowing someone who died significantly increased CPTSD-RI scores (pooled $t = 2.13$, $p = .04$), and there was a borderline effect of knowing someone who died on severity level. The highest CPTSD-RI scores were for hurting someone else, witnessing death, and seeing mutilation on television.

Other Variables

In previous studies (Nader et al., 1990; Pynoos et al., 1987), we found a correlation between amount of exposure and CPTSD-RI scores, independent of loss. We also found that grief increased CPTSD-RI scores for children with less severe exposures (Nader et al., 1990). In the Kuwait sample, grief and PTSD were significantly correlated with each other. Children had high PTSD scores without high Grief, but did not have high Grief scores without high levels of PTSD ($n = 48$, $r = 33$, $p = .02$).

Previous studies have found that guilt significantly increased CPTSD-RI scores in children exposed to violence. In this study, too, guilt was significantly associated with severity of stress reaction. The effect of a previous trauma on severity level was borderline ($p = .07$)

Combined Indices

We grouped the types of traumatic exposure and looked at the correlation between the level of this cumulative exposure with CPTSD-RI and Grief scores. *Life-threat* scores were composed of (a) experiencing the threat of death, (b) experiencing the threat of injury, and (c) being in some way injured. *Witnessing* scores were a combination of (a) seeing dead or injured bodies after the fact, (b) seeing someone being killed, and (c) seeing mutilation on television. *Worry* scores combined (a) worry about a significant other, (b) knowing someone who was captured, (c) knowing someone who was injured, and (d) knowing someone who died. Each category in a cumulative score was rated 0, 1, or 2, for *none, mild,* or *severe* experience, respectively; worry about another was 0 or 1, no or yes.

This sample of 54 children was not large enough to determine the interrelationships between the variables. Viewed independently, the effect of life threat on CPTSD-RI score approached significance ($r = .25$, $p = .08$). The effect may be more measurable and pronounced in the larger, more representative sample, because this pilot sample did not include a significant number of children with the greatest degree of life threat. There were no children with high life-threat scores who had low CPTSD-RI scores; this suggests that both other factors and life threat increased scores. Life threat did not affect the measure of grief.

Witnessing significantly affected CPTSD-RI scores ($r = .37$, $p = .007$) and Grief scores ($r = .48$, $p = .001$). Worry scores had a borderline effect on CPTSD-RI scores ($p = .07$) and no effect on measured grief. Again, there were high CPTSD-RI scores for children with low worry scores, but there were no low CPTSD-RI scores for children with high worry scores.

We also combined life threat and witnessing scores with knowing someone who died. The combined effect of these factors on CPTSD-RI scores correlated at .40 and was significant at the .003 level. Its correlation with Grief was .42 and was significant at .003. Therefore, this particular combination of experiences had the most significant effect on PTSD for this group of children.

CPTSD-RI: Other Effects

Several other effects on severity level were examined. Severity of Posttraumatic reaction also significantly affected play and activities. According to the children's own reports, severity of posttraumatic stress reaction did not significantly affect interpersonal relationships or fears. Reports of increased fear, at the various severity levels, ranged between 40% and 55% (*ns*). There was no significant effect of severity level on changes in future orientation including general expectations, plans to marry, or plans to have children. However, in this country where children are highly valued and it is common to desire a large family, the greater the severity of traumatic response the greater likelihood that the child said he or she did not wish to have children.

We examined the effect of severity of posttraumatic stress response on television watching habits. There were changes in watching comedy (Pearson $X^2 = .07$; linear trend $= .02$) and drama (Pearson $X^2 = .08$; linear trend $= .05$), but no changes were reported for adventures, scary movies, or cartoons. There was a borderline linear effect on watching violence ($p = .07$).

Age

Older children tended to have greater levels of exposure to traumatic events ($r = .27$, $p = .053$). For this sample, there was an effect of age on

CPTSD-RI ($r = .41$, $p < .01$), arousal symptoms ($r = .36$, $p < .01$), avoidance symptoms ($r = .28$, $p < .05$) and on the individual symptoms of intrusive imagery and sounds, guilt, and impulse control. Other symptoms and symptom complexes may show a difference by age for the larger, more representative sample. Following the classroom screening, discussions were held with the children regarding their experiences and concerns and addressing common traumatic responses. There were age differences in children's expressed concerns, preoccupations, and symptoms. One area of concern was a posttraumatic stress related disregulation of aggression. For example, school-age children noted that it was harder to keep themselves from saying bad words. Preadolescents were worried about tendencies to be more irritable with younger siblings. Adolescents expressed concerns about peers engaging in overly aggressive or reckless behaviors. Analysis of the fall sample will determine if these age differences are statistically significant.

Children Who Remained out of Kuwait (n = 2)

Not all Kuwaitis had returned by June of 1991. Those children who had been away had generally been able to continue their schooling, in contrast to their peers who remained in Kuwait. Therefore, in sampling in the temporary schools, we saw only two children who had been out of the country and one who left the country during the crisis. The two children who had been out of the country during the crisis had followed events on television, and one of them had seen the horrible images of the dead and mutilated on television. The two children expressed extreme concern about relatives who had remained behind. They described bothersome images of feared deaths and mutilations of the close relatives with whom they were unable to maintain contact. These two children reported moderate and severe levels of posttraumatic stress reactions. The postwar atmosphere was influenced by the dichotomy (and dissension) between those who were in Kuwait during the crisis and those were not. We frequently heard both children and adults say, "The people who were not here during the crisis do not understand what we went through." There were also issues regarding participation in the resistance, martyrdom, and accusations of disloyalty for remaining in a country occupied by an enemy. These two traumatized children demonstrated that it was essential, for the purposes of an accurate study, to dispel the idea that being out of the country guaranteed an absence of symptoms.

DISCUSSION

This preliminary study confirms the significant impact of exposure to war atrocities on children. The pilot sampling provided evidence that: (a) many children who remained in Kuwait during the occupation had multiple exposure to atrocities, (b) more than 70% of the children with midrange exposure reported moderate to severe posttraumatic stress reactions, and (c) the viewing of graphic images of mutilation on television and in public posters had a measurable influence on severity of reaction. Many things cannot be prevented during war. This study emphasizes the importance of protecting children, insofar as is possible, from witnessing bloody injury, mutilation, or grotesque death directly, via television, in pictures, and through other media presentation.

This study was completed as a prelude to analyzing the more extensive data from the fall sampling. In terms of posttraumatic stress response, we anticipate an increased effect of exposure to life threat and the continued influence of witnessing. Although the viewing of mutilation on television may not maintain a primary role in the prediction of traumatic response, its impact with this group of children suggests that in the absence of the ability to maintain a psychological distance, seeing horrible real death, blood, and mutilation on television can increase the symptoms and severity of post-traumatic stress reactions. One public health recommendation to emerge from this pilot study is to control the media exposure, through television and posters, of continued sights of mutilation and atrocities so as to limit the unnecessary increase in postoccupation traumatic stress reactions of children and adolescents. This study and our experiences in Kuwait make clear that, in addition to the efforts to educate families and teachers, there is a significant need for increased medical and psychological services for children following hostile occupations.

ACKNOWLEDGMENTS

This work was supported by UCLA, UNICEF and the Kuwait Ministries of Health and Education. The writing of this chapter was supported, in part, by the UCLA Program in Trauma, Violence and Sudden Bereavement, the Bing Fund, and David Hockney.

REFERENCES

Garbarino, J., Kostelny, K., & Dubrow, N. (1991). What children can tell us about living in danger. *American Psychologist, 46,* 376–383.

Karno, M., Burnam, A., Escobar, J. I., Hough, R. L., & Eaton, W. W. (1983). Development of the Spanish-language version of the National Institute of Mental Health Diagnostic Interview Schedule. *Archives of General Psychiatry, 40,* 1183–1188.

Kinzie, J.D., Sack, W.H., & Angell, R.H.. (1986). The psychiatric effects of massive trauma on Cambodian children: I. The children. *Journal of the American Academy of Child*

Psychiatry, 25, 370–376.

Nader, K., Pynoos, R. S., Fairbanks, L., & Frederick, C. (1990). Childhood PTSD reactions one year after a sniper attack. *American Journal of Psychiatry, 147,* 1526–1530.

Pynoos, R. S., Frederick, C., Nader, K., Arroyo, W., Steinberg, A., Eth, S., Nunez, F., & Fairbanks, L. (1987). Life threat and posttraumatic stress in school-age children. *Archives of General Psychiatry, 44,* 1057–1063.

Pynoos, R. S., & Nader, K. (1993). Issues in the treatment of post-traumatic stress in children and adolescents. In J. P. Wilson & B. Raphael (Eds.), *The international handbook of traumatic stress syndromes* (pp. 535–549). New York: Plenum.

Pynoos, R. S., Nader, K., & March, J. (1991). Childhood post-traumatic stress disorder. In J. Weiner (Ed.), *The textbook of child and adolescent psychiatry* (pp. 955–984). Washington, DC: American Psychiatric Press.

III INTERNATIONAL PERSPECTIVES ON CHILDREN AND VIOLENCE

11 The Young Lions: South African Children and Youth in Political Struggle

Christine Liddell
University of Ulster, Northern Ireland

Jennifer Kemp
Molly Moema
Human Sciences Research Council, Pretoria, South Africa

> And you—the Young Lions who carried on the struggle while we were in prison—we salute you. (Mandela, 1990, p. 2).

It is estimated that 20 million people worldwide have been killed in armed conflict since the end of World War II (Kanji, 1990). Women and children have comprised three quarters of the victims (UNICEF, 1989). Concern about the impact of war on children is relatively recent, however, beginning in the 1970s. The upsurge of interest probably reflects the increasingly popular belief amongst Western postindustrial nations that childhood constitutes a period of special privilege and need (Straker, 1991).

Research on armed conflicts and their effects on children has focused principally on relatively well-developed countries such as Northern Ireland and Israel. Yet the majority of armed conflicts since the 1970s have taken place in the Third World (Kanji, 1990). In Africa alone, there have been large-scale armed struggles in Nigeria, Angola, Zimbabwe, Kenya, Sudan, South Africa, Ethiopia, and Somalia (Dodge & Raundalen, 1987). In most of these, the effects on children have never been documented. In 1984, 63 people died as a result of political violence in Northern Ireland (Cairns & Wilson, 1989a); in the same year, 17,000 civilians are estimated to have died in Uganda's civil war (Dodge & Raundalen, 1987). Studies of the effects of armed struggle in Africa are rare, despite the vast numbers of people whose lives are affected by it.

The seriousness of this is exacerbated by the fact that armed conflict in Africa can rarely be equated with armed conflict in the developed world. Sophisticated warfare and military occupation appear to have little in common with the chronic civil strife, high civilian involvement, and plethora of social and economic hardships experienced by most African people immersed in conflict. The effects of armed conflict in many African countries, therefore, may be substantively different from those in more intensively researched regions of the world.

In South Africa, children and youth have found themselves in the front line of armed struggle perhaps more than in any other nation (UNICEF, 1989). This chapter examines the historical roots of this phenomenon, the scale of children's involvement, and the possible consequences for the children and their country.

DEFINING CHILDHOOD AND YOUTH IN CULTURAL CONTEXT

It is important to clarify what is meant by the words *children* and *youth* in the context of this chapter. In South Africa, *childhood* is generally defined as spanning the period from birth to 10 years old. Between 10 and 18 years old, the term *youth* is commonly used (Straker, 1989). A cutoff at about 10 years is seen as justified by the fact that most Black South African children begin to assume significant domestic responsibilities at around this age, contributing in important ways to their families' subsistence by selling newspapers, herding cattle, digging vegetable gardens, and so on. In fact, by as early as age 5, it has been reported that such children spend 6% of their day in household and subsistence-related chores (Liddell, Kvalsvig, Strydom, Qotyana, & Shabalala, in press). The early assignation of the term *youth* is, therefore, considered a meaningful reflection of young people's experiences in South Africa.

THE HISTORICAL ROOTS OF CHILD AND YOUTH INVOLVEMENT IN SOUTH AFRICA'S ARMED STRUGGLE

Dissolute town boys . . . of 20 years and under . . . have grown up since the Zulu War of 1879 with no conception of our justice or our might. (Hausse, 1990, p. 89).

This magistrate's statement of 1907, referring to the Amalaita gangs at the turn of the century, was to prove bitterly prophetic 80 years later. There are an estimated 12 million Black South African children under 18 years of age (Ennew & Milne, 1989). Between 1984 and 1986, as we document further on, more than 200,000 of them were arrested and detained for trial after clashes with security personnel. This amounts to almost 2% of the population under 18.

The involvement of young South Africans in armed conflict is not a recent phenomenon. Its roots can be traced at least as far back as the Amalaita gangs that emerged around the turn of the century (Minnaar, 1990). At that time, an increasing number of youth aged 14 to 20 years were migrating from their rural homesteads into large towns like Durban in search of employment as domestic workers, rickshaw pullers, and gardeners. By 1904, it is estimated that some 6,000 youth had migrated along the routes from the Natal hinterland into Durban—one third of the migrant work force (Hausse, 1990). Deprived of their traditional rites of passage into adulthood, they began to form gangs that would reinforce group identity. Physical strength was virtually their only asset, and violence became an inevitable instrument for enforcing group interests. These Amalaita gangs soon came to the attention of their employers, but they usually defied all attempts at control by curfew (Hausse, 1990).

The second precedent emerged during the 1920s, with the prison- and workers'-compound gangs known as the Isithozi. These were reputed to be extremely violent in maintaining clan divisions (Breckenridge, 1990). The Isithozi warlords actively recruited youth, not only for their physical strength and malleability, but because of their potential as "wives" for warlords who were denied access to their spouses under the migrant labor system. The social and political dynamics of many Isithozi gangs appears to have revolved principally around the adolescent boys who were enrolled as members (Breckenridge, 1990).

Neither of these organizations appear to have expressed any large-scale political aspirations. Their activities and the violence they perpetrated revolved almost exclusively around between-gang disputes and internal struggles for power. Nevertheless, the principle of young people being recruited into violent activity—either as leaders in the case of the Amalaita, or as followers in the case of the Isithozi—has clear historical precedents in South Africa.

The emergence of children and youth as significant players in *political* struggle can be dated very specifically: June 16, 1976 (Chikane, 1986; Dawes, 1987). This date is marked each year as a day of mourning in South Africa, and tens of thousands of workers and students remain at home. On that day in 1976, 15,000 young people gathered in Soweto to launch a peaceful protest against the Education Department's ruling that half of their schooling should be conducted in Afrikaans, the language of the ruling government.

The protest march met with a brutal reaction from armed security personnel. The number killed has never been established. The official toll was 25, but unofficial estimates are closer to 100 (Hirson, 1979). Over the ensuing months, the violent reactions of the state led to children and youth becoming increasingly desperate to find effective means of changing the educational system (UNICEF, 1989), and the country embarked on a wave of political violence that has abated only rarely over the past 15 years.

Despite the carnage, there was a growing realization among children and youth that they could wield power. They did not appear to consider violence a particularly effective strategy, but it nevertheless secured some benefits occasionally (Booth, 1987). As Straker (1991) described, it was a time of euphoria *and* terror for young people. Woods (1989) reported that a group of youths representing less than 5% of a community could impose a political identity on communities unchallenged. This realization of power encouraged many young people to look beyond the Afrikaans-in-education debate, to look more broadly at the apartheid system itself (Chikane 1986). In widening their scope, they began to embrace the demands of other mass democratic movements in the country and, in so doing, developed important cooperative links with participants in the broader struggle.

However, these cooperative links developed slowly (Hirson, 1979). At first, the children's protest movement alienated their parents' generation, both because of their violence and militancy after the June 16th uprising (Hermer, 1980), and because of the criticism young people were voicing of their parents' long submission to apartheid (Gibson, 1989). Intergenerational conflict predominated from 1976 to the early 1980s (Straker, 1987).

With the emergence of the United Democratic Front (UDF) in 1983, a new cooperation developed between young people's militant groups and workers' organizations. The UDF actively encouraged workers to assist the children and youth in their struggle (Chikane, 1986). This lent substantial weight to the children's resistance movement. By 1986, the government had banned the Council of South African Students (COSAS)—one of the principal children's liberation movements—and 2 years later, half of the 32 anti-apartheid organizations that were restricted under the State of Emergency were concerned with young people's issues (International Defence and Aid Fund, 1989).

All this does not necessarily imply a high level of political knowledge on the part of children and youth. Woods (1989) reported that most of the youth who are active in political struggles have only sketchy notions of ideology or general political movements in the country. Dawes (1987) noted that this is unremarkable considering the emotional and intellectual immaturity of most children and youth.

The predominantly active role young people have played in the process of political protest underlines the manner in which young people have affected South African society (Burman, 1986). In this regard, children and youth must not only be seen as victims of political struggle, but also as active social agents in the mass democratic movement. In this they are probably unlike the children involved in the majority of African conflicts (Dodge & Raundalen, 1987), and bear more resemblance to the children involved in the Palestinian struggle for liberation (Punamaki, 1988).

The zealous commitment of children and youth to the struggle following the June 16th uprising is reflected in one of the most popular slogans to emerge from the children's anti-apartheid movement: "Freedom or Death — Victory is Certain." This symbolizes active and sacrificial commitment to struggle, and stands in sharp contrast to the images of vulnerability and special need that many international organizations, such as UNICEF, are promoting in reports dealing with South Africa (Straker, 1989).

HOW MANY YOUNG PEOPLE? THE SCALE OF SOUTH AFRICAN CHILDREN'S INVOLVEMENT IN ARMED CONFLICT

The South African government has decided that, in order to break the spirit of protest, you have to break the spirit of youth, which means a repression felt by young people who may not even be activists. (Ennew & Milne, 1989, p. 135)

Unlike most other countries in the world, South African law has long permitted the arrest and detention of children and youth (Dawes, 1987). Although some improvements in the law were effected by the new Child Care Act of 1983, South Africans have spent most of the past 5 years under a state of emergency. This contains no special provisions with regard to children and overrules the regulations prescribed by the Child Care Act (McLachlan, 1986). Even today, with the national state of emergency lifted, and a new Child Care Act in place, it remains legally possible for a child to be arrested, detained, tried, and sentenced from the age of 7 years. This procedure may take place without the child's family being notified of events (McLachlan, 1986).

How prevalent is the arrest and detention of children and youth in South Africa? What is their fate once they are in police custody? The state of emergency imposed powerful restrictions on the dissemination of information regarding political activities, so exact figures are hard to establish. However, between 1984 and 1986, 312 people under the age of 18 were killed by police (Thomas & Mabusela, 1991), with an estimated 25% of these being under 10 (UNICEF, 1989).

Collated official statistics reveal that in this same period, 1,000 children and youth were wounded by police, and an additional 202,000 were awaiting trial, the majority being held in police cells (Straker, 1991). Between 1986 and 1988 another 10,000 children under 18 were held in police custody (*The Lancet*, 1988). It appears that only 7% of these young people have ever been charged, and less than 1% have been convicted (UNICEF, 1989).

The time spent in police detention before trial varies widely, but can amount to more than a year. A group of seven youngsters were sentenced to 1–2 years imprisonment in 1987 for having thrown stones at a demonstration in 1985. They had been detained without trial during the intervening period (Dawes, 1987).

Evidence of police brutality against young people being held in custody has been documented by Ennew and Milne (1989) and *The Lancet* (1988). In the former study, 24 of 40 people under the age of 18 (60%) who were detained reported being assaulted; in the latter, 53 of 83 (64%). After examining statistics such as these, the North American Lawyers Committee for Human Rights concluded that South Africa was involved in "a war against children" (UNICEF, 1989).

It is not only children and youth arrested by security forces who experience first hand the effects of South Africa's armed struggle. Bluen and Odesnik (1988) found that 22% of township homes in the Johannesburg area had been raided by the police or army; Dawes and Tredoux (1989) reported this to be the most frequently cited fear among Black children, suggesting that such raids are carried out with scant regard for civilian rights. Twelve percent of homes contained a family member who had been arrested for political offenses, and 36% contained children who had been harassed at school by security personnel. In some of the most violent community clashes, as many as 70,000 people have been left homeless in the space of 3 months (Dawes & Tredoux, 1989).

What these figures illustrate is the extent to which political violence impinges on the everyday lives of ordinary people, children and youth included. Beyond the direct experiences of arrest, torture, and detention, many thousands more young people are directly affected by the anti-apartheid struggle in South Africa.

POLITICAL VIOLENCE IN THE BROADER PERSPECTIVE OF COMMUNITY VIOLENCE

In South Africa, areas of high political unrest also tend to be areas of high criminal activity (Dawes, 1990). A general culture of violence has grown up alongside violent forms of state control (Straker, 1991). Inevitably, the involvement of young people in politically motivated violence leads to an increased likelihood of their becoming involved in other forms of violent activity and conventional crimes. For example, in the Pietermaritzburg area, where Minnaar (1990) reported 625 deaths for 1989 in a region covering 400 square kilometers, 90% of all violence was perpetrated by youth (Woods, 1989).

Murder, assault, and rape are also common occurrences in many areas of political disturbance. The per capita murder rate in Soweto, where over 2 million people live (Thomas & Mabusela, 1991), is 120 times greater than it is in the United Kingdom (Hicks, 1987).

It is, of course, extremely difficult to separate the political and nonpolitical antecedents of violence in South Africa, and studies of this issue have produced divergent findings. A study by Schoeman (1985) suggested that 25% of respondents in an opinion poll attributed violence in their area primarily to education-related grievances, but as we have illustrated, these are grievances with deep roots in the apartheid system.

Further to this issue, a study by Turton, Straker, and Moosa (1991) compared 1985 and 1987 cohorts of youth in Alexandra township in terms of their exposure to and interpretation of violence. The 1985 cohort had been in the front line of major political upheavals, whereas the 1987 cohort was predominantly exposed to street and domestic violence. The two groups did not differ in their responses to questionnaire items on violence, its effects, or their interpretation of violent incidents, suggesting that the level of overt political violence made little difference to how youth viewed violent experiences.

However, Alexandra township is exceptional in some respects, having been a deeply politicized community for many years (Jochelson, 1990). Even in times of relative peace, this is a township characterized by an unusually high level of political activity. In a nationwide sample interviewed by Schlemmer (1983), the level of dissatisfaction with specifically political and legal circumstances was considerably higher than dissatisfaction with nonpolitical aspects of life in South Africa.

The combined prevalence of violent crime and political unrest has resulted in violence being considered an inevitability for many communities in South Africa. Violence passes as normal, as indeed it is in statistical terms. Thus, during a 12-month period, 83% of youth respondents in Alexandra township had either been assaulted or observed an assault, and 72% had observed a killing (Turton et al., 1991).

Chronic levels of community violence are far more difficult to document in terms of their effects on children and youth, than are discrete and traumatic clashes (Ennew & Milne, 1989). Yet living in a day-to-day environment characterized by criminal violence may be as, if not more, deleterious for young people, than their relatively infrequent exposure to political unrest.

POLITICAL VIOLENCE IN THE BROADER PERSPECTIVE OF OPPRESSION

We started with problems in the yard: only one line for washing, no drains, the bucket system (for sewerage), night soil spilling in the yard and kids getting sick. People tended to blame themselves or their neighbors instead of seeing it as the state's problem. People had to unite and direct their grievances at apartheid. (Jochelson, 1990, p. 7)

The focus on young people's role in political activities has directed attention away from the more general suffering most of them experience under apartheid (UNICEF, 1989). It would be a mistake to construe detention, torture, and large-scale political flashpoints as the main events impinging on South African children and youth (Swartz & Levett, 1990). More pressing are factors such as malnutrition, poverty, and poor education.

In 1978, South Africa was rated as having the highest inequality ratio among the 57 countries for which data were available (UNICEF, 1989). Almost 15 years later, the levels of inequality remain remarkable. Poverty impinges on almost every Black child, with the average annual per capita income being $542 (Liddell & Kemp, in press).

The effects of chronic poverty on young people are reflected in numerous statistics: An estimated one third of Black South African children are malnourished (Hansen, 1984). Infant mortality rates in 1985 were almost nine times higher for Black children than for White children (Thomas & Mabusela, 1991).

The more general hardships faced by young South Africans are also reflected in the high levels of child labor in the country: Some 60,000 children are currently employed as farm laborers, and the majority are paid extremely low wages (Swartz & Levett, 1990).

There is also a tendency for families to keep children at home if they fail a grade at school, so that they can play a full-time role in the domestic unit's subsistence—as herd boys or caregivers to younger siblings, for example. Some of these children may be as young as 7 years old when they are withdrawn from formal education (Liddell & Kvalsvig, 1991). The number of children thus affected remains unknown, although it seems particularly common in families whose financial status makes it impossible for them to sponsor the education of all children in the family.

With respect to education, the state expends four times more on each White child than it does for each Black child (Liddell & Kemp, in press), and the majority of schools serving black communities are without electricity (de Villiers, 1990).

Although these factors are at least partially the result of the apartheid system of government, to understand the impact of political struggle per se on the lives of children and youth, it is imperative that this broader background of oppression be considered. The average young Black South African is probably more deeply affected by poverty, substandard education, and poor physical health than by the specific concomitants of resistance, although all of these have their roots in an unjust political system.

These other factors undoubtedly place at risk young people's potential for achievement, and possibly their cognitive status, too. However, there is no evidence that poverty, malnutrition, and poor education are associated with the social or emotional disorders commonly reported for children exposed to political violence (Liddell, Kvalsvig, Qotyana, & Shabalala, in press; UNICEF, 1989). Thus, the effects of poverty, malnutrition, and poor education appear to be of a different order than those imposed by political unrest. As in other regions of the world, the two sets of risk factors probably interact to increase children's vulnerability (Punamaki, 1988); in South Africa, they undoubtedly act as a double-edged sword.

THE EFFECTS OF POLITICAL VIOLENCE ON CHILDREN AND YOUTH

When my two-year-old daughter sees a military vehicle passing, she looks for a stone.(Chikane, 1986, p. 343)

There are relatively few theoretical frameworks and scant empirical evidence regarding the processes by which political events influence the mental health of children. The effects of the state and the macrodynamics of society are rarely examined by developmental psychologists (Cairns & Wilson, 1989b; Punamaki, 1989).

In the South African context, some case studies have been published since the late 1980s (e.g., Foster, 1987; Straker, 1987). However, the first study focusing on the impact of political violence on substantial samples of families and young people did not appear until 1989.

There are also a variety of methodological difficulties in assessing the effects of political violence on South African children and youth. Not least among these is the so-called "code of silence" that prevails in most communities (Dawes & Tredoux, 1989; Gibson, 1989), which makes it difficult to assess the extent to which individuals have been exposed to political activities.

Studies are also hampered by the difficulty of following up on families that have been exposed to political violence. The destruction of houses and the displacement of large numbers of people hamper efforts to follow up on individuals (Dawes, 1990). In addition, many communities erase street names and house numbers in an effort to prevent individuals being traced (Thomas & Mabusela, 1991).

The credibility of researchers also seems to affect the results obtained in studies, with government-sponsored investigators reporting substantially lower levels of exposure and fewer effects than independent researchers (Dawes, 1990; Swartz & Levett, 1990). Indeed, to undertake investigations on the effects of political violence, it has recently become almost mandatory for researchers to share the ideological commitment of the communities in which they work (Swartz, Gibson, & Swartz, 1990). When using parental report measures or even child interviews (the most common instruments used so far), affirmations of ideology must be expressed before data are collected, which may result in a priming effect, encouraging respondents to report adverse effects at the hands of oppressive forces. These methodological difficulties, coupled with the scarcity of data, make the assessment of effects somewhat problematic.

Research that has been successfully completed can be divided into two categories: studies of direct exposure to political violence that impinges on some young people's lives, and studies of the more general effects of politicization on children and youth.

The Effects of Direct Exposure to Political Violence

It is difficult to talk of political violence in terms of discrete events, because, in many cases, political violence in a community is composed of a prolonged series of flashpoints. For` this reason, Straker (1987) recommended changing the conventional term, *posttraumatic stress disorder* (PTSD), to *continuous traumatic stress syndrome* for case studies in South Africa. It is generally accepted that this sort of ongoing political unrest is associated with higher frequencies of disorder among children than are discrete events (Dawes & Tredoux, 1989).

It is also difficult to separate out the effects of political and criminal violence on children and youth. As indicated earlier, areas of high political unrest are usually areas of high crime, too. In a study of 5-year-olds growing up at home in the year before school, not only were children in areas experiencing frequent political unrest exposed to more political violence; what most distinguished them from children in low-unrest areas was their higher exposure to criminal activities (e.g., assault, theft, and violent domestic arguments). Although children living in high-violence areas were much more likely to express aggression in their day-to-day activities, this could not justifiably be attributed to political violence per se (Liddell, Kvalsvig, Qotyana, & Shabalala, in press).

In studies throughout the world, the most severe stressors generally affect only 50% of the populations exposed to them (Rutter, 1985). South Africa follows this pattern. Thus, 40% of the young people whose homes had been destroyed and whose families were forced to relocate following 6 weeks in refugee camps showed symptoms of emotional disorder when evaluated by parent interviews (Dawes & Tredoux, 1989). As with Palestinian children (Punamaki, 1987), boys were most susceptible in early childhood, and girls were most susceptible in adolescence. This is thought to be attributable to the greater politicization of boys in later childhood, when active involvement in the struggle leads to the development of more effective coping strategies. Straker (1991) reported similar findings: 50% of Leandra youth, studied following a long period of particularly violent township unrest, were symptomatic.

The effects of exposure to political violence in South Africa also tend to be very similar to those reported for children in other countries experiencing conflict: nightmares, clinginess, anxiety, crying bouts, and so on.

That half of those exposed appear to cope well with the experience illustrates clearly that it is not the *event* which is critically important, but the child's *interpretation* of the event (Gibson, 1987). As with children in other areas of conflict (e.g., the Middle East and Northern Ireland; Gibson, 1989; Punamaki, 1989), children's interpretations seem, in turn, to be mediated by the interpretations offered by significant others in the environment, even for adolescents (Straker, 1991). Mothers seem especially important in this regard, at least for younger children (Dawes & Tredoux, 1989). Strong political beliefs in the family also appear to assist young people in coping (Dawes, 1990; Straker, 1991).

Thus, family support structures appear to exert a positive influence on a young victim's interpretation of political violence, and may well account for many of the cases where children and youth seem to escape major trauma. However, it is also possible that communities suffering from oppression may simply be socialized into the expectation of abuse (Swartz et al., 1990a), and, thus, may interpret it as normal and unremarkable. This form of passive resilience must also be taken into consideration as a protective factor, although its etiology and long-term effects on children's outlook are, of course, more worrisome.

There seems to be little evidence in South Africa that young people's exposure to political violence results in them being more likely to condone the use of violence (Dawes, 1990; Rabinowitz, 1988), a finding also reported for children in Northern Ireland (Lorenc & Branthwaite, 1986) and Uganda (Dodge & Raundelen, 1987). On the contrary, researchers have suggested that young South Africans are more negative about violence following exposure (Dawes & Tredoux, 1989).

There is contradictory evidence regarding the degree to which children sublimate their experiences of political violence in fantasy games. Parents report the prevalence of police raid games and violent mock-aggression in exposed children, as do the caregivers of children with one or both parents in detention (Swartz & Levett, 1990). However, Liddell, Kvalsvig, Strydom, Qotyana, & Shabalala (in press) found this to be a relatively rare form of fantasy play when taken in the context of all fantasy that children engaged in, even in areas of high violence. This disagreement probably stems from the different methodologies used. The first study was based on caregiver ratings, and may reflect the anxiety adults felt when children used sublimi-nated fantasy in this manner.

For this reason they may have been particularly sensitive to the occasions on which it was observed.

Less direct effects of political violence may be very important, too. During periods of high unrest, it is common for schools to be closed, often for long periods (Straker, 1991), which disrupts children's education. There is also some concern that the predictable occurrence of violent reactions to community problems may lead to young people being incapable of developing more flexible and cooperative strategies for solving problems (Chikane, 1986; Dawes, 1990).

The Effects of Politicization on Children and Youth

Like adults elsewhere, adults in war-torn countries view children as their society's hope of the future. Ugandans see children as symbolizing "hope for a better world" (Dodge & Raundalen, 1987). The late Samora Machel referred to Mozambique's children as the "flowers that never wither" (Ennew & Milne, 1989). The next generation is often a focus for optimism, even in countries where conflict has been a long and cruel experience. This is not entirely true of South Africa, though, where the politicization of young people has led some to question the potential of today's children to participate in peaceful negotiations for a settlement (Chikane, 1986).

Press reports in South Africa amplify the dangers of politicization among children so much that many South Africans perceive children as the "villains of apartheid rather than the victims." Hence, reports describing them as the "Khmer-Rouge Generation," "Frankenstein's Monsters," and "Psychopathic Teen-agers" (Straker, 1989).

On a more realistic level, one of the main concerns regarding the effects of politicization is that children and youth may be unwilling to surrender power to their elders in the event of a peaceful settlement in South Africa (Straker, 1991). Having forfeited their childhoods in the interests of liberation, and having wielded substantial power, the devolution of power to older political leaders may prove difficult for many young people to accept.

This was a concern in Zimbabwe as well, following the termination of civil war in the 1980s. However, as Reynolds (1986) described, the transfer of power to adults was undertaken relatively successfully in Zimbabwe, with one of the most important factors being the ready acknowledgment of the role children had played in liberation. For South Africa, Nelson Mandela's description of children as "The Young Lions"—people who kept up the struggle when their elders were incarcerated—seems an important part of this process of acknowledgment of children's role in the South African context (Mandela, 1990). Portrayal of South African children in the international press as innocent and helpless victims undermines their role and the sacrifices they have been willing to accept. This may not be constructive in the process of devolution of power.

CONCLUSIONS

What emerges from this review is that children, families, and communities exhibit a remarkable resilience in the face of violence and poverty, but this may only sometimes reflect positive coping strategies. In at least some instances, it may be described more accurately as a passive acceptance, particularly of violence, as a normal or acceptable way of life. In these cases, the absence of marked effects on children, families, and communities cannot be considered lightly.

We also know that violence engendered by political struggle is strongly associated with criminal violence in many South African communities, and, in this sense, violence is begetting violence at least at community level. At the *individual* level, too, children living in more violent communities seem to express aggression more readily at a very young age, although there is little to suggest that young people's exposure to violence results in their construing it as an acceptable form of social expression. This, in itself, gives some grounds for optimism.

Throughout this chapter, we have referred to children and youth from Black communities in South Africa. There is also, of course, a minority group of White South African children, to which this chapter has not given attention. However, very few of these children have experienced political violence directly (Drew 1988), and very few suffer extreme poverty, malnutrition, and inadequate education. For these reasons, the effects of political unrest and apartheid do not impinge on these children's lives with the same force. Nevertheless, one should not overlook the fact that living in a highly militarized country probably affects some of these children adversely, too (Ennew & Milne, 1989).

The civil war being waged in South Africa has had effects on many young people, but the situation is considerably worse in neighboring states. For example, in Mozambique it is estimated that war and destabilization cost the lives of 84,000 children in 1986. Children died being caught in the crossfire, due to starvation brought on by untended or destroyed harvests, and due to diseases that could not be treated because clinics had been destroyed or damaged (Kanji, 1990). Very little is known about the thousands of casualties that must accompany this mortality rate. The scale of problem facing South Africa's children may be far larger than it is for children in, say, Northern Ireland, but is not of such epic proportions as that facing children in countries like Mozambique.

Violence is always context bound. Consider, for example, the content of traditional nursery rhymes and lullabies. These are much loved by children, yet many depict scenes of alarming violence and misfortune: a ladybird entreated to fly home because her house is destroyed and her children have fled, Humpty Dumpty who falls off a wall and is irreparably broken. Traditional South African rhymes sung by preschool children also reflect this:

Jo ndenze njani kulomhlaba?
Oh, ndenze ntoni. Kumnyama
pambi kwam?
(How can I live in this world?
Oh, what can I do? It is so dark
ahead of me). (Reynolds, 1989, p. 73)

These simple illustrations highlight the fact that children interpret the content of violence in terms of socialized expectations and cultural context.

Punamaki's (1989) research on children in Beirut and the West Bank suggested that children living in areas where there is some hope of liberation are significantly less affected by living with conflict. Perhaps young people in South Africa may cope better as the 1990s unfold, as hope increases for a negotiated and just settlement. This more positive aspect must, however, be offset against the potential effects of young people having been involved in South Africa's political struggle—and in the criminal violence that has grown alongside this—over the past 15 years.

ACKNOWLEDGMENTS

The financial assistance of the Anglo American Chairman's Fund, JCI, and First National Bank are gratefully acknowledged.

REFERENCES

Bluen, S. D., & Odesnik, J. (1988). Township unrest: Development of the township life events scale. *South African Journal of Psychology, 18,* 50–59.

Booth, D. G. (1987). *An interpretation of political violence in Lamontville and Kwa Mashu.* Unpublished masters thesis, University of Natal, Durban, South Africa.

Breckenridge, K. (1990). Migrancy, crime and faction fighting: The role of the Isithozi in the development of ethnic organisations in the compounds. *Journal of Southern African Studies, 16,* 55–78.

Burman, S. (1986). The contexts of childhood in South Africa. In S. Burman & P. Reynolds (Eds.), *Growing up in a divided society* (pp. 1–15). Johannesburg, South Africa: Ravan Press.

Cairns, E., & Wilson, R. (1989a). Coping with political violence in Northern Ireland. *Social Science and Medicine, 28,* 621–624.

Cairns, E., & Wilson, R. (1989b). Mental health aspects of political violence in Northern Ireland. *International Journal of Mental Health, 18,* 38–56.

Chikane, F. (1986). Children in turmoil: The effects of township unrest on township children. In S. Burman & P. Reynolds (Eds.), *Growing up in a divided society: The context of childhood in South Africa* (pp. 333–344). Johannesburg, South Africa: Ravan Press.

Dawes, A. (1987). Security laws and children in prison: The issue of psychological impact. *Psychology in Society, 8,* 27–47.

Dawes, A. (1990). The effects of political violence on children: A consideration of South African and related studies. *International Journal of Psychology, 25,* 13–31.

Dawes, A., & Tredoux, C. (1989). Emotional status of children exposed to political violence in the Crossroads squatter area during 1986–1987. *Psychology in Society, 12,* 33–47.

dc Villiers, E. (1990). *Walking the tightrope.* Cape Town, South Africa: Jonathan Ball.

Detention of schoolchildren in South Africa [Editorial]. (1988. March). *The Lancet,* pp. 623–624.

Dodge, C. P., & Raundalen, M. (1987). *War, violence, and children in Uganda.* Oslo: Norwegian University Press.

Drew, M. L. (1988). *A developmental analysis of children's understanding of war and conflict in South Africa.* Unpublished masters thesis: University of Durban, Westville, South Africa.

Ennew, J., & Milne, B. (1989). *The next generation: Lives of Third World children.* London: Zed Books.

Foster, D. (1987). *Detention and torture in South Africa: Psychological, legal, and historical studies.* Cape Town, South Africa: David Philip.

Gibson, K. (1987). Civil conflict, stress and children. *Psychology in Society, 8,* 4–26.

Gibson, K. (1989). Children in political violence. *Social Science and Medicine, 28,* 659–667.

Hansen, J. (1984). Food and nutrition policy with relation to poverty. *Second Carnegie Enquiry into Poverty and Development in Southern Africa.* Paper No. 205.

Hausse, P. L. A. (1990). The cows of Nongoloza: Youth, crime and Amalaita gangs in Durban, 1900–1936. *Journal of Southern African Studies, 16,* 79–109.

Hermer, C. (1980). *The diary of Maria Tholo.* Johannesburg, South Africa: Ravan Press.

Hicks, G. R. (1987). *Aggressiveness, assertiveness and submission among black adolescents.* Unpublished masters thesis, Rand Afrikaans University, South Africa.

Hirson, B. (1979). *Year of fire, year of ash. The Soweto revolt: Roots of a revolution?* London: Zed Press.

International Defense and Aid Fund. (1989). *Review of 1988: Repression and resistance in South Africa and Namibia. Fact paper on Southern Africa, No. 16.* London: Author.

Jochelson, K. (1990). Reform, repression and resistance in South Africa: A case study of Alexandra township, 1979–1989. *Journal of Southern African Studies, 16,* 1–31.

Kanji, N. (1990). War and children in Mozambique: Is international aid strengthening or eroding community-based policies? *Community Development Journal, 25,* 102–112.

Liddell, C., & Kemp, J. (in press). Providing services for young children in South Africa: An economic perspective. *International Journal of Educational Development.*

Liddell, C. & Kvalsvig, J. (1991). *Early school failure—getting to the bottom of being bottom of the class.* Unpublished client report. Human Sciences Research Council, Pretoria, South Africa.

Liddell, C., Kvalsvig, J., Qotyana, P., & Shabalala, A. (in press). *Community violence and levels of aggression in young South African children. International Journal of Behavioral Development.*

Liddell, C., Kvalsvig, J., Strydom, N., Qotyana, P., & Shabalala, A. (in press). An observational study of 5-year-old black South African children in the year before school. *International Journal of Behavioral Development.*

Lorenc, L., & Branthwaite, A. (1986). Evaluations of political violence by English and Northern Irish schoolchildren. *British Journal of Social Psychology, 25,* 349–352.

McLachlan, F. (1986). Children in prison. In S. Burman & P. Reynolds (Eds.), *Growing up in a divided society: The context of childhood in South Africa* (pp. 345–359). Johannesburg, South Africa: Ravan Press.

Mandela, N. (1990, February 11). [Speech delivered at the Cape Town City Hall]. Cape Town, South Africa.

Minnaar, A. de V. (1990). *Conflict and violence in Natal/KwaZulu: Historical perspectives.* Pretoria, South Africa: Human Sciences Research Council.

Punamaki, R. L. (1986). Stress among Palestinian women under military occupation: Women's appraisal of stressors, their coping modes, and their mental health. *International Journal of Psychology, 21,* 445–462.

Punamaki, R. L. (1987). Content of and factors affecting coping modes among Palestinian children. *Scandinavian Journal of Development Alternatives, 6,* 86–98.

Punamaki, R. L. (1988). Historical-political and individualistic determinants of coping modes and fears among Palestinian children. *International Journal of Psychology, 23,* 721–739.

Punamaki, R. L. (1989). Factors affecting the mental health of Palestinian children exposed to political violence. *International Journal of Mental Health, 18,* 63–97.

Rabinowitz, S. R. (1988). *The impact of exposure to civil "unrest" on children's evaluation of violence.* Unpublished masters thesis. University of Cape Town, South Africa.

Reynolds, P. (1986). Concepts of childhood drawn from ideas and practices of traditional healers in Musami. *Zambezia, 13,* 1–10.

Reynolds, P. (1989). *Childhood in crossroads.* Cape Town, South Africa: David Philip.

Rutter, M. (1985). Resilience in the face of adversity: Protective factors and resistance disorder. *British Journal of Psychiatry, 147,* 598–611.

Schlemmer, L. (1983, March). Conflict in South Africa: Build-up to revolution or "impasse"? In *Violence and conflict management in divided societies.* Workshop conducted at the Arnold Bergstraesser Institute: Freiburg, Germany.

Schoeman, S. (1985). Unrest and violence in South Africa: Symptoms of social disorder. *Bulletin, 25,* 11–12.

Straker, G. (1987). The continuous traumatic stress syndrome: The single therapeutic interview. *Psychology in Society, 8,* 48–79.

Straker, G. (1989). From victim to villain: A "slight" of speech? Media representations of township youth. *South African Journal of Psychology, 19,* 20–27.

Straker, G. (1991). Faces in the revolution: The psychological effects of violence on township youth in South Africa. Cape Town, South Africa: David Philip.

Swartz, L., Gibson, K., & Swartz, S. (1990). State violence in South Africa and the development of a progressive psychology. In N. C. Manganyi & A. Du Toit (Eds.), *Political violence and the struggle in South Africa* (pp. 234–264). Johannesburg, South Africa: Southern Book Publishers.

Swartz, L., & Levett, A. (1990). State violence in South Africa and the development of a progressive psychology. In N. C. Manganyi & A. Du Toit (Eds.) *Political violence and struggle in South Africa* (pp. 265–286). Johannesburg, South Africa: Southern Book Publishers.

Thomas, A., & Mabusela, S. (1991). Foster care in Soweto, South Africa: Under assault from a politically hostile environment. *Child Welfare, 70,* 121–130.

Turton, R. W., Straker, G., & Moosa, F. (1991). Experiences of violence in the lives of township youths in "unrest" and "normal" conditions. *South African Journal of Psychology, 21,* 77–84.

UNICEF. (1989). *Children on the front line.* Paris: Author.

Woods, G. (1989) Rebels with a cause: The discontent of black youth. *Indicator SA, 7,*(1), 63–65.

12 Children and Political Violence in Northern Ireland: From Riots to Reconciliation

Ed Cairns
University of Ulster at Coleraine, Northern Ireland

Ignatius J. Toner
University of North Carolina at Charlotte

To understand the challenges that the ongoing conflict in Northern Ireland presents to developmental psychology, it is necessary to spell out a few basic facts about Northern Irish society and to place the political violence in its proper perspective.

First, although Northern Ireland is a small country (just 5,500 square miles) with a population of only 1.5 million, a large proportion are children and young people, compared to other Western countries. For example, about 25% of the population of Northern Ireland is aged 14 years or less.

Second, it is important to understand that political violence is not the major problem that children in Northern Ireland have to contend with. The major problem, many would claim, is that Northern Ireland is one of the least affluent regions of Western Europe, with substantially lower average income, higher levels of unemployment, and larger families than the rest of the United Kingdom. Further, these economic problems predate the onset of the current political violence (Simpson, 1983).

What most people in the rest of the world know about Northern Ireland, of course, relates to the political violence. To many people, it must have appeared that the political conflict in Northern Ireland suddenly appeared from nowhere on their television screens in 1968. The reality is that conflict in Ireland dates back at least 300 years. In the 20th century alone, violence has broken out in at least four decades, beginning in the 1920s, when Ireland was partitioned to create an independent state—the Republic of Ireland—leaving Northern Ireland to remain as part of the United Kingdom, along with England, Scotland, and Wales.

Put very simply, the conflict today can be seen as a struggle between those who wish to see Northern Ireland continue to be part of the United Kingdom and those who wish to see it reunited with the rest of Ireland. The former, the Protestants or Loyalists, make up some 62% of the population; the latter, the Catholics or Nationalists, are in the minority in Northern Ireland (38%), but not on the whole island of Ireland. Indeed, surveys suggest that the majority of Catholics prefer to label themselves as Irish, and the majority of Protestants see themselves as British (Waddell & Cairns, 1991).

These two communities live relatively socially segregated lives, although not necessarily in residentially segregated housing. In particular, the two groups have separate churches, an important factor in a society in which almost everyone claims church membership and some 62% attend church at least weekly (Cairns, 1991). The major impact that this has on children is that there are two separate school systems: a Catholic-run system and a state-run (but, de facto, Protestant) system, which provide separate athletic, social, and cultural activities.

In Northern Ireland, there has been ongoing political violence since 1968. In those 25 years, the world's media have tended to present the conflict as a homogeneous entity. The truth, as ever, is rather more complicated. During this period, the violence has varied in at least three important ways. First, the intensity has varied from year to year. Second, there have been geographical variations (Poole, 1983), with some areas experiencing high levels of violence and others remaining virtually unscathed over the whole period since 1968. Finally, the violence has varied qualitatively. For example, much of the early violence took the form of street rioting, but this has since been replaced by bombings and, more recently, assassinations.

Taken together, although many children have been directly involved in the political violence (and, indeed, children have become both psychological and physical victims), not all children in Northern Ireland have been exposed to equal levels of political violence, or even to violence of the same kind. Nevertheless, most children are exposed to the socialization that accompanies living in a divided society; this provides developmental psychologists with a range of phenomena of interest, from the acute stress of riots to the more subtle effects of intergroup conflict.

CHRONOLOGICAL OVERVIEW OF RESEARCH ON THE CHILDREN OF "THE TROUBLES"

The protracted nature of "the Troubles" in Northern Ireland has provided those with interests in child development a setting in which to examine both the reactions of children to exceedingly unfortunate conditions and the changing role of developmental research in a society under stress. Civil unrest has been a recurring feature of life in parts of Northern Ireland for centuries, but only since the outbreak of violence in 1968 have we had significant objective data about how the children of Northern Ireland were coping with their situation. There are scarce data (McCauley & Troy, 1983) on the pre-1969 cohort to which we can compare recent generations. What has been learned about the reactions of the children in this conflict has been influenced by the changing nature of the involvement of developmental researchers since 1969.

Some of the first observations came from H. A. Lyons, a Belfast psychiatrist, who recorded the reactions of his patients after rioting on August 14 and August 15, 1969, and during the weeks following, during which looting, rioting, arson, and intimidation occurred. Noting that few children were referred to him, Lyons (1973) observed that the children seemed to enjoy the excitement, often playing on the barricades with toy guns. He contended that this younger generation might be lost, despite apparent short-term resiliency, and warned that the children could display more disturbing reactions in later years, becoming so accepting of violence that "when peace returns to Northern Ireland there will be a continuing epidemic of violent and antisocial behavior amongst teenagers" (p. 236). Morris Fraser (1973), another Belfast psychiatrist who treated disturbed children in the areas of worst conflict, contended that there were short-term disturbances as well. He described the reaction most commonly found in teenage boys, wherein the youth became hostile and violent not only toward the security forces, but toward their parents, as well. The more common reaction among girls was intense anxiety. While these two Belfast psychiatrists were writing about their impressions of the children of "the Troubles," there were, apparently, no ongoing programs of study of the situation by resident research psychologists who, according to some, maintained the pretense of normality. This was not necessarily a successful coping strategy, according to Lockwood (1982), who wrote, "Indeed the very attempt to preserve the traditional view of the academic world may produce abnormalities of vision within that world; until eventually, neither are traditions maintained, nor does a new realism replace them" (p. 222).

Initially, the role of resident researchers initially was taken by psychologists from Great Britain. The first major study was carried out by a researcher from outside Northern Ireland, when Russell (1973) of Strathclyde University in Glasgow, Scotland, surveyed 3,000 schoolboys from throughout Northern Ireland. He found that a majority approved of violence to some degree. He also noted that a sizeable minority of the boys said they wanted to leave their country when they were older. In 1975, Jahoda, also of Strathclyde University, and Harrison, of the University of London, reported data on the social perceptions of children in Northern Ireland during the violent year of 1973. These investigators found that most children from the more troubled areas displayed unfavorable attitudes toward police officers, soldiers, and religious outgroup figures (ministers or priests), and perceived cigarette packets, letters, milk bottles, or packages lying in the street as bombs. Jahoda and Harrison concluded that "the findings were so striking and internally consistent that they leave little room for doubt concerning the damaging impact of the Ulster [Northern Ireland] situation on Belfast children of both creeds in the worst affected areas" (p. 18). Although sporadic research by British psychologists on the effects of "the Troubles" on the children of Northern Ireland continues (e.g., Houston, Crozier, & Walker, 1990; Lorenc & Branthwaite, 1986), interest from Britain, and, for that matter, from researchers in the Republic of Ireland, remains minimal.

Instead, the greater part of the vacuum left by Northern Ireland's research psychologists was initially filled by visitors from the United States. Some wrote evocative pieces that were not intended to be carefully databased (e.g., Coles 1980), whereas others attempted to collect data more systematically. Perhaps most notable of these latter investigators was Rona Fields of Clark University, the author of *A Society on the Run: A Psychology of Northern Ireland* (1973). (In 1977, Temple University Press in the United States published a reworking of the book.) Fields offered a most pessimistic outlook on the short- and long-range consequences of growing up among "the Troubles." However, Fields openly rejected objectivity, noting her anger and desire to "hit back at those who bullied and abused me " (1973, p. xii), and she acknowledged that she walked "a methodological tightrope" (p. 25).

In the early 1970s, local psychologists began to make sporadic contributions (e.g., Cairns & Duriez, 1976). Their systematic involvement, however, dates from September 1978, when the Northern Ireland Regional Office of the British Psychological Society sponsored a 2-day conference to encourage research psychologists from within Northern Ireland to study the impact of contemporary Northern Ireland on children and young people. Several papers presented at that meeting were collected in a book edited by Harbison and Harbison (1980), entitled *A Society Under Stress: Children and Young People in Northern Ireland*. This conference and text represented a partial reassertion by resident researchers of the legitimacy of their own perspective on the problems of Northern Ireland.

In that book, Heskin (1980) presented a comprehensive review of the research on the children and young people of Northern Ireland. In 14 pages, he was able to devote considerable space to every relevant published research report. Heskin cautioned researchers that the nature of "the Troubles" varied considerably over time and location. In particular, he noted that many outsiders failed to recognize the significance of the fact that, since "the Troubles" began, the entire subject population of children had changed. It is necessary, wrote Heskin, "to move on from the 1969 Belfast conception of Northern Irish society which probably is held by all too many international observers" (p. 21), advice many Northern Irish psychologists feel still has not been assimilated by all visiting researchers.

Hella Beloff (1980), of the University of Edinburgh, Scotland, offered the final word at the 1978 conference and in the text. She was most encouraging in her charge to research psychologist in Northern Ireland and praised their courage. She contended that investigations conducted in contemporary Northern Ireland might never conform to the "niceties" expected from other developmental research, and that problems of ethics, diplomacy, and even physical danger should not deter investigators. She concluded on a most optimistic note: "Even under conditions of deprivation, disorder and stress where options may be narrowed (to put it technically), young people are still out there making rational strategies, having flexible ideas, and setting themselves goals which are as idealistic as those of other young people" (p. 168).

Two books followed the publication of the 1980 text, reaffirming the perspective of resident researchers and broadening the research base: *Children of the Troubles: Children in Northern Ireland* (Harbison, 1983) and *Growing Up in Northern Ireland* (Harbison, 1989). These volumes focused on economic (Bush & Marshall, 1983; Osborne & Cormack, 1989), educational (Fee, 1983; Wilson, 1989), and clinical and health care issues (Blease, 1983; Jones & McCoy, 1989), and all the chapters were written by investigators who lived and worked in Northern Ireland. A major facilitator of internal investigation, and a clear demonstration of the willingness of resident researchers to study the situation in their own country, was the initiation of ambitious, systematic research programs on the effects of "the Troubles" on children and youth by investigators at both the Queen's University in Belfast and the Centre for the Study of Conflict at the University of Ulster in Coleraine.

A relatively optimistic viewpoint was advanced by the researchers at the Queen's University, and several conclusions were forwarded by these investigators. First, the violence of "the Troubles" is not a prominent part of the children's world and, thus, has had less of an effect on the young people of Northern Ireland than outsiders might believe. They supported this conclusion with evidence that the children of Northern Ireland did not restrict themselves to "the Troubles" when they wrote about violence (McWhirter, 1982), and that, although the children made distinctions between Protestants and Catholics, allusions to intergroup hostility and negative intergroup evaluations were infrequent (McWhirter & Gamble, 1982). Second, it is the fact that Northern Ireland is one of the poorest and most socially disadvantaged areas in Europe that is having a most profound impact on generations of children. Doubts were expressed about whether integrated education would significantly reduce Protestant–Catholic friction in Northern Ireland (McWhirter, 1983a), although this position was revised (McWhirter 1983b). Finally, there was no evidence, they contended, that today's youth in Northern Ireland represents "a lost generation" (McWhirter & Trew, 1982), or that investigators from within Northern Ireland failed to bring as valid a perspective to the issues as that provided by outsiders.

The Centre for the Study of Conflict at the University of Ulster was established in 1977. Research carried out at the Centre on the effects of "the Troubles" on children, plus other related work, has been comprehensively reviewed in *Caught in Crossfire: Children and the Northern Ireland Conflict* (Cairns, 1987). Several of the earlier studies (e.g., Cairns, 1980, 1982) focused on the development of religious discrimination in the children of Northern Ireland in the context of Tajfel's theory of intergroup conflict, Social Identity theory. He contended that the distinction between Catholic and Protestant was an important one for most of the children: By age 11, they were able and willing to classify themselves and others. In particular, this program of research asserted that "the Troubles" were dominant in the minds of the children, whether in terms of the violence or in terms of the classification system that underlies the conflict. The children of Northern Ireland, therefore, are affected by the violent turmoil around them, especially because it is exacerbated by economic and social hardship (Cairns, 1989; Cairns & Wilson, 1989). Further, Cairns (1983, 1987) warned of the implications of large-scale emigration from Northern Ireland of the most tolerant of its youth. More recently, these researchers argued that the stressful social contexts associated with relatively high levels of violence may interact with other chronic sources of stress to foster psychological processes that lead to the perpetuation of violence (Wilson & Cairns, 1992).

The research on children in Northern Ireland illustrates how, over a period of 20 years, the emphases moved from an interest in the simple, short-term effects of political violence—in particular, stress—to a multidimensional approach, focusing on the influence of more subtle, long-term variables, such as education or economics, which may be seen as both causes and effects. In part, these changes reflect the changing nature of the actual conflict, as already noted. They also reflect the slow realization of the complexity of the problem.

This approach has served to illustrate how the main protagonists in the area have changed from local psychiatrists, to outside researchers, to mainly local psychologists. This latter change has led to a view from the "inside" that is more complicated and more optimistic in some ways than the view from the "outside". There is little doubt that, in stressful times and places, most children have proved remarkably resilient in the face of "the Troubles". However, there is also little doubt that "the Troubles" have been a recurring feature, on some level, in the day-to-day life of several generations of children in Northern Ireland. Simplistic answers to the vexing questions regarding the impact of the political turmoil on children are properly elusive, and there seems to be a problem for every solution.

PROGRAMS FOSTERING CONTACT BETWEEN CHILDREN ACROSS THE DIVIDE

As Northern Irish society searches for ways to prevent the next generation becoming enmeshed in conflict, psychologists, working in cooperation with educationalists, have again found a role, this time in contributing to the theoretical bases underlying attempts at remediation (Cairns 1987), and, in particular, in evaluating the various attempts at reconciliation that are now being undertaken.

Most of the schemes include, as a rationale, the simple belief that relations between members of conflicting groups can be improved by equal-status contact (Amir, 1969). This is seen to be important in Northern Ireland, because the educational system is still largely segregated along religious lines.

Evidence that such an approach might be fruitful came from an early study by Lockhart and Elliott (1980), which described the changes in attitude by young offenders brought together with youths of the other religious community in an integrated setting. Careful observations revealed that sectarian hostility was reduced by such admittedly brief contact, and that such attitudinal modification seemed to be remarkably enduring.

Even before this study was reported, since at least 1974, organizers in Europe and North America had set up programs designed to bring Catholic and Protestant children from Northern Ireland together for short periods, usually in the summer, in a setting often far removed from the unrest of their homeland. So far, attempts to evaluate such programs have been limited, but they suggest that, often, few attitudinal changes occur. One possible explanation may be that in many summer programs there are few actual attempts to bring all the children together, and perhaps as a result, the children often do not know that there are children from the other religious community in the program (Trew, McWhirter, Maguire, & Hinds, 1985). As Trew (1989) noted in a recent review, there is surprisingly little work in this area, and there is a particular need for more systematic, longitudinal research. An example of such an approach is an ongoing evaluation of an American-based project, the Irish Summer Program of Charlotte, North Carolina. Two cohorts of working-class Belfast children who were placed in pairs in Charlotte in the summers of 1987 and 1988 have been the focus of several investigations focusing on the way in which these children are perceived and the way they perceive the other children in their traveling group.

One study (Toner, Stanley Hagan, Copses, & Lincourt, 1990) described an attempt to evaluate the impact of the cohabitation intervention on the self-perceptions and social perceptions of the children in the Charlotte program.

In this program, each child in the program were asked, twice, to rank the relative attractiveness of the first name of the children who were in the program. Initial testing was done in the children's Belfast homes, just after the children had met the members of their traveling group; the second assessment took place immediately after departure from the United States, 6 weeks later. The study focused upon where children placed their own names in the rank ordering, which provided a subtle index of each child's self-evaluation. An analysis of where the children ranked their roommates' names and the names of the other children in the traveling group provided an index of the children's social perceptions.

Before and after the summer experience, boys of both religions ranked their own names more favorably than did girls. Both Catholic girls and Protestant boys ranked their own names more favorably following the intervention than they had before the experience. The self-ranking of the Catholic boys and Protestant girls did not change significantly. Thus, the cohabitation intervention appeared effective in improving some children's perceptions of themselves, but not their perceptions of their roommates. The rankings of roommates' names became less favorable following the cohabitation. Both Protestant girls and Catholic girls were somewhat less favorable in their rankings of roommates' names after the intervention. The Protestant boys' rankings of their Catholic roommates declined most dramatically, whereas the Catholic boys' rankings of their Protestant roommates changed little. An examination of the children's rankings of the names of the other children in their traveling group indicated that distinctions among children who were not in very close contact were unaffected by the intervention, and were more likely to be based on the target child's gender than on the target child's religion.

If temporary cohabitation programs for children from different sides of a divide have a positive impact on the children's self-perceptions but not on their social perceptions, programs that promote such contact may be less successful in achieving future harmony and understanding between children than in improving individual children's self-esteem.

Family variables may interact with the conflictual environment of Northern Ireland to produce differential levels of vulnerability to stress among the young (Vannan, 1989). In a further investigation, Toner and Hagan (1990) found that, although paternal employment status did not affect children's self-rankings, maternal employment was found to affect girls' pre-intervention self-rankings. In Protestant families, girls whose mothers did not work outside the home ranked themselves more favorably prior to the intervention than did girls whose mothers did work outside the home. The opposite was the case in Catholic families, where the girls had higher initial self-perceptions when their mothers were employed. Further, living in a single-mother home was found to be an impact on the changes in children's self-rankings due to the intervention, whereas there was virtually no change in children from two-parent households. The self-rankings of Protestant children, especially girls, from single-mother homes improved following the intervention, whereas the self-rankings of corresponding Catholic children, especially girls, declined. The results of this investigation reinforced the importance of considering the interactive effects of simultaneously occurring stressors on the effectiveness of interventional programs.

Recently two further ideas that (among other things) foster contact, have begun to attract government funding and support. These are the movement to set up integrated schools as a counter to the religiously segregated schools attended by most children in Northern Ireland, and a curriculum-based approach, known as Education for Mutual Understanding, which has become compulsory in all schools (including the segregated schools).

The integrated school movement began in the 1970s, when a group of parents campaigned, initially, to bring children together in existing school settings (Dunn, 1986). Eventually, this led to the founding of Northern Ireland's first planned integrated school in 1981. As of 1993, some 14 such schools existed, all but 2 at the elementary level. All aim to have roughly equal numbers of Catholic and Protestant students.

Surveys carried out in Northern Ireland have indicated that the idea of integrated education receives wide support in the general population. However, the one study that focused more closely on measuring the intentions of parents with preschool children (Cairns, Dunn, Morgan, & Giles, 1989) suggested that, although future planned integrated schools will be supported by parental action, in practice, the proportion who actually send a child to a planned integrated school is likely to fall well short of the 70%–80% who offer verbal support when questioned as part of a public opinion exercise.

Serious researchers have been anxious to allow the planned integrated schools time to establish themselves before attempting to evaluate their impact on children. For this reason, research in this area is only now getting underway, and is, as yet, mostly unpublished. Irwin (1991), an anthropologist, carried out an intensive study of one planned integrated secondary-level school in Northern Ireland. This study produced firm evidence that the school was successful in establishing positive intercommunity friendships among those attending the integrated school. In addition, the study compared a very small number of children from the integrated school to somewhat younger children from similar backgrounds attending totally segregated schools. The results of this exercise suggested that the integrated secondary school was having little effect on national identity. In other words, as in the adult community, most Catholics thought of themselves as Irish, whereas most Protestants thought of themselves as British. Finally, the report claimed that there was preliminary evidence that children attending the integrated school were beginning to develop a better understanding, and possibly even a less confrontational acceptance, of the politics of the children from the other community.

Recently, a more ambitious program of research was undertaken, aimed at understanding integrated education in Northern Ireland and evaluating its impact on children. The research consisted of three linked projects. The first (Dunn, Morgan, Cairns, & Bowring-Carr, 1990) looked at curriculum issues in relation to integrated education. The second (Morgan, Dunn, Cairns, & Fraser, 1991) examined the role of parents and teachers in relation to integration. The final project (Cairns, Dunn, Morgan, & McClenehan, 1992) targeted the impact of integration on children. To do this, the final study compared Catholic and Protestant children attending a planned integrated school (that had approximately equal numbers of children from the two groups) with children attending other (nonplanned integrated) schools, where there was a predominance of either Catholics or Protestants (but some children from the other community) and with children from schools that were totally segregated, attended by only Catholic children or only Protestant children. Children in years 1 and 4 took part; the children in the planned and nonplanned integrated schools were seen at the beginning of the school year and again at the end.

At the time of this writing, only preliminary data were available. However, already there is evidence that children in both the planned and nonplanned integrated schools are making friends on a cross-community basis. This replicates Irwin's (1991) results obtained in a planned integrated school and those of Davies and Turner (1984) in a nonplanned integrated school. Sociopolitical identity was also measured in a series of questions. For example, children were asked to name their country (Northern Ireland is more common among Protestants, Ireland among Catholics) and their national capital (Belfast for Protestants, Dublin for Catholics), and to choose where in the British Isles they would most like to live when they leave home (after Northern Ireland, Catholics were more likely to choose the Republic of Ireland, which Protestants placed last, after Scotland or England and Wales). Preliminary results suggest neither planned nor unplanned integration is having a major impact on responses to these questions.

Education for Mutual Understanding (EMU) is the most recent attempt in Northern Ireland to use education to influence community relations. This scheme is sponsored by the government; the aim is to make EMU a compulsory part of the curriculum. Smith and Dunn (1990) carried out the first evaluation of the impact of such a program on secondary school children in one town in Northern Ireland. Because not all children in the five schools involved were part of the EMU program, they were able to compare contact with noncontact children. They reported finding no evidence that the program eroded Catholic or Protestant children's sociopolitical identities. Where awareness of the other community was concerned, they found that this was related to the majority–minority balance in the group, with the minority developing a greater awareness of the majority. Finally, they hinted at attitude change in the emergence of "uncertainty" where, previously, issues had seemed simple and clear cut.

At present, only very limited evidence is available concerning the impact of the various reconciliation schemes on children in Northern Ireland. However, what this evidence is beginning to indicate is that short-term contact schemes may be of limited value if their sole objective is the improvement of cross-community relations, although such programs may help to improve children's self-esteem. More long-term contact in integrated school settings is at least likely to promote cross-community friendships. Still, it appears that such contact may not radically alter children's sociopolitical identities. This can be regarded as a positive outcome, if one sees the aim of such programs as achieving a pluralistic society in Northern Ireland, with individuals able to tolerate differences. On the other hand, if one sees the aim as building a middle ground between the two warring factions, then this result must be seen as failure.

OVERVIEW AND CONCLUSIONS

We have reviewed briefly the existing research relating to children and political violence in Northern Ireland to illustrate both the content of the research and the course that this research has taken since the late 1960s. We believe that such a chronological approach is important, because, in the unsettled world we live in, at any one time other societies throughout the world may be setting off down the same dark road as Northern Ireland. It may, therefore, be helpful for researchers in these areas to benefit from the hindsight that an historical analysis of research in Northern Ireland can offer.

In particular, the whole question of the roles of outsiders versus insiders is one that should be given more prominence. Too often, it would appear that outsiders attracted to Northern Ireland, no doubt for the best of motives, have failed to make use of the knowledge of local researchers. As a result, outside researchers have often been perceived as arrogant by local researchers, and both groups have failed to gain from the cross-fertilization that could have been beneficial to both.

Also, an examination of psychological research in Northern Ireland makes it clear that carrying out research with children in a society where political violence is prevalent provides some special challenges: in particular, the need for sensitivity, ethical concerns, and, of course, personal courage. Such research highlights two particular weaknesses in the general field of developmental psychology. There is the need for both more longitudinal research and more cross-cultural data. Only cross-cultural studies, such as those of Hosin and Cairns (1984), will allow researchers to decide what is unique to their particular society and what can be thought of as a more generalized phenomenon.

Examination of the actual content of the research in Northern Ireland reveals that, since "the Troubles" began in 1968–1969, researchers have moved from concern with the short-term consequences of political violence to look at more long-term consequences. This has been accompanied by a shift from a unidimensional approach to a more multidimensional approach, as a recognition of the complexities of the situation has developed. An interesting example of this is the investigation of a possible link between psychosocial stress and aggressive motivations in the context of the Northern Ireland conflict (Wilson & Cairns, 1992). This is an area that deserves further attention, because of its implications for other societies where children are exposed to stress as a result of the combination of adverse economic conditions and violence.

Therefore, there is now much less research in Northern Ireland on stress and the immediate consequences of violent events. Instead, as we have shown, a predominant theme is a concern with the need to implement ways of reconciling the two conflicting groups. Unfortunately, the early reliance on simple-minded research designs, plus an undue emphasis on the effect of stress, means that knowledge about such things as how children are socialized into conflict is not always available. As a result, reconciliation work has had to begin in the absence of such basic data.

Finally, the experience of working as a research psychologist in a society embroiled in political conflict leads one inevitably to the understanding that a multidisciplinary approach, to what may at first seem purely psychological problems, is essential. Psychologists must embrace knowledge from other disciplines. They must also help to bring psychological knowledge to the attention of those researchers who espouse a nonpsychological approach — and, even more so, to policymakers — if they are to make a lasting impact in their attempts to improve life for children caught up in political violence.

REFERENCES

Amir, Y. (1969). Contact hypothesis in ethnic relations. *Psychological Bulletin, 71,* 319–342.
Beloff, H. (1980). A place not so far apart: Conclusions of an outsider. In J. Harbison & J.

Harbison (Eds.), *A society under stress: Children and young people in Northern Ireland* (pp. 167-176). London: Open Books.

Blease, M. (1983). Maladjusted school children in a Belfast centre. In J. Harbison (Ed.), *Children of the troubles: Children in Northern Ireland*. Belfast, Northern Ireland: Learning Resources Unit, Stranmillis College.

Bush, L., & Marshall, P. (1983). The social and economic circumstances of disadvantaged children in the community. In J. Harbison (Ed.), *Children of the troubles: Children in Northern Ireland* (pp. 12-20). Belfast, Northern Ireland: Learning Resources Unit, Stranmillis College.

Cairns, E. (1980). The development of ethnic discrimination in young children in Northern Ireland. In J. Harbison & J. Harbison (Eds.), *A society under stress: Children and young people in Northern Ireland* (pp. 115-127). London: Open Books.

Cairns, E. (1982). Intergroup conflict in Northern Ireland. In H. Tajfel (Ed.), *Social identity and intergroup relations* (pp. 277-297). London: Cambridge University Press.

Cairns, E. (1983). The political socialisation of tomorrow's parents: Violence, politics and the media. In J. Harbison (Ed.), *Children of the troubles: Children in Northern Ireland* (pp. 120-126). Belfast, Northern Ireland: Learning Resources Unit, Stranmillis College.

Cairns, E. (1987). *Caught in crossfire: Children and the Northern Ireland conflict*. Belfast, Northern Ireland: Appletree Press; and New York: Syracuse University Press.

Cairns, E. (1989). Society as child abuser: Northern Ireland. In W. S. Rogers, D. Hevey, & E. Ash (Eds.), *Child abuse and neglect: Facing the challenge* (pp. 119-126). London: Batsford and the Open University Press.

Cairns, E. (1991). Is Northern Ireland a conservative society? In P. Stringer & G. Robinson (Eds.), *Social attitudes in Northern Ireland*. Belfast, Northern Ireland: Blackstaff Press.

Cairns, E., Dunn, S., Morgan, V., & Giles, M. (1989). Attitudes toward integrated education in Northern Ireland: The impact of real choice. *Education North, 1*(2), 20-23.

Cairns, E., Dunn, S., Morgan, V., & McClenehan, C. (1992). *The impact of integrated schools in Northern Ireland on cultural values and social identity*. Final Report to the Economic and Social Research Council (UK).

Cairns, E., & Duriez, B. (1976). The influence of accent on the recall of Catholic and Protestant children in Northern Ireland. *British Journal of Social and Clinical Psychology, 15*, 441-442.

Cairns, E., & Wilson, R. (1989). Mental health aspects of political violence in Northern Ireland. *International Journal of Mental Health, 18*, 38-56.

Coles, R. (1980, December). Ulster's children: Waiting for the Prince of Peace. *The Atlantic*, pp. 33-34.

Davies, J., & Turner, I. F. (1984). Friendship choices in an integrated primary school in Northern Ireland. *British Journal of Social Psychology, 23*, 285-286.

Dunn, S. (1986). The role of education in the Northern Ireland conflict. *Oxford Review of Education, 12*, 233-242.

Dunn, S., Morgan, V., Cairns, E., & Bowring-Carr, C. (1990). *Curriculum and culture in integrated schools in Northern Ireland*. Final report to the Leverhulme Trust.

Fee, F. (1983). Educational change in Belfast school children 1975-1981. In J. Harbison (Ed.), *Children of the troubles: Children in Northern Ireland* (pp. 44-58). Belfast, Northern Ireland: Learning Resources Unit, Stranmillis College.

Fields, R. (1973). *A society on the run: A psychology of Northern Ireland*. Harmondsworth, England: Penguin.

Fields, R. (1977). *Society under siege: A psychology of Northern Ireland*. Philadelphia: Temple University Press.

Fraser, M. (1973). *Children in conflict*. New York: Basic Books.

Harbison, J. (Ed.). (1983). *Children of the troubles: Children in Northern Ireland*. Belfast, Northern Ireland: Learning Resources Unit, Stranmillis College.

Harbison, J. (Ed.). (1989). *Growing up in Northern Ireland*. Belfast, Northern Ireland: Learning Resources Unit, Stranmillis College.

Harbison, J., & Harbison, J. (Eds.). (1980). *A society under stress: Children and young people in Northern Ireland*. London: Open Books.

Heskin, K. (1980). Children and young people in Northern Ireland: A research review. In J. Harbison & J. Harbison (Eds.), *A society under stress: Children and young people in Northern Ireland* (pp. 8–21). London: Open Books.

Hosin, A., & Cairns, E. (1984). The impact of conflict on children's ideas about their country. *Journal of Psychology, 118,* 161–168.

Houston, J. E., Crozier, W. R., & Walker, P. (1990). The assessment of ethnic sensitivity among Northern Ireland schoolchildren. *British Journal of Developmental Psychology, 8,* 419–422.

Irwin, C. (1991). *Education and the development of social integration in divided societies*. Belfast, Northern Ireland: Unpublished report Queen's University Belfast.

Jahoda, G., & Harrison, S. (1975). Belfast children: Some effects of a conflict environment. *Irish Journal of Psychology, 3,* 1–19.

Jones, D. R., & McCoy, D. B. (1989). Indicators of health in Northern Ireland. In J. Harbison (Ed.), *Growing up in Northern Ireland* (pp. 2–27). Belfast, Northern Ireland: Learning Resources Unit, Stranmillis College.

Lockhart, W., & Elliott, R. (1980). Changes in the attitudes of young offenders in an integrated assessment centre. In J. Harbison & J. Harbison (Eds.), *A society under stress: Children and young people in Northern Ireland* (pp. 100–112). London: Open Books.

Lockwood, J. (1982). Conducting research in Northern Ireland: A personal view. In P. Stringer (Ed.), *Confronting social issues: Some applications of social psychology* (pp. 215–228). London: Academic Press.

Lorenc, L., & Branthwaite, A. (1986). Evaluations of political violence by English and Northern Irish schoolchildren. *British Journal of Social Psychology, 25,* 349–352.

Lyons, H. A. (1973). Violence in Belfast: A review of the psychological effects. *Public Health, 87,* 231–238.

McCauley, R., & Troy, M. (1983). The impact of urban conflict and violence on children referred to a child psychiatry clinic. In J. Harbison (Ed.), *Children of the troubles: Children in Northern Ireland* (pp. 33–43). Belfast, Northern Ireland: Learning Resources Unit, Stranmillis College.

McWhirter, L. (1982). Northern Irish children's conceptions of violent crime. *The Howard Journal, 21,* 167–177.

McWhirter, L. (1983a). Contact and conflict: The question of integrated education. *Irish Journal of Psychology, 6,* 13–27.

McWhirter, L. (1983b, August). *The Northern Ireland conflict: Could integrated education have an impact?* Paper presented at the Biennial Meetings of the Society for the study of Behavioral Development, Munich, Germany.

McWhirter, L., & Gamble, R. (1982). Development of ethnic awareness in the absense of physical clues. *Irish Journal of Psychology, 5,* 109–127.

McWhirter, L., & Trew, K. (1982). Children in Northern Ireland: A lost generation? In E. J. Anthony & C. Chiland (Eds.), *The child in his family. Children in turmoil: Tomorrow's parents. Yearbook of the International Association for Child Psychiatry and Allied Professions* (pp. 69–82). New York: Wiley.

Morgan, V., Dunn, S., Cairns, E., & Fraser, G. (1991). *Parents and teachers in integrated schools in Northern Ireland*. Final report to the Economic and Social Research Council (UK).

Osborne, R. D., & Cormack, R. J. (1989). Gender and religion as issues in education, training and entry to work. In J. Harbison (Ed.), *Growing up in Northern Ireland* (pp. 42–65). Belfast, Northern Ireland: Learning Resources Unit, Stranmillis College.

Poole, M. (1983). The demography of violence. In J. Darby (Ed.), *Northern Ireland: The background to the conflict*. Belfast, Northern Ireland: Appletree Press.

Russell, J. (1973, July). Violence and the Ulster schoolboy. *New Society*, pp. 204–206.

Simpson, J. (1983). Economic development: Cause or effect in the Northern Ireland conflict? In J. Darby (Ed.), *Northern Ireland: The background to the conflict* (pp. 79–109). Belfast, Northern Ireland: Appletree Press.

Smith, A., & Dunn, S. (1990). *Extending inter-school links*. Coleraine, Northern Ireland: Centre for the Study of Conflict.

Tajfel, H., & Turner, J. C. (1986). The social identity theory of intergroup behaviour. In S. Worchel & W. G. Austin (Eds.), *Psychology of intergroup relations* (2nd ed., pp. 33–54). Chicago: Nelson-Hall.

Toner, I. J., & Stanley Hagan, M. (1990, August). *Factors mediating the effect of temporary residential cohabitation on the self-perceptions of children from Northern Ireland*. Paper presented at the European Conference on Developmental Psychology, Stirling, Scotland.

Toner, I. J., Stanley Hagan, M., Copses, K., & Lincourt, A. (1990, March). *The effect of temporary intervention on the self- and social perceptions of children experiencing ongoing stress*. Paper presented at the Biennial Conference on Human Development, Richmond, VA.

Trew, K. (1989). Evaluating the impact of contact schemes for Catholic and Protestant children. In J. Harbison (Ed.), *Growing up in Northern Ireland* (pp. 131–159). Belfast, Northern Ireland: Learning Resources Unit, Stranmillis College.

Trew, K., McWhirter, L., Maguire, L., & Hinds, J. (1985). *Irish children's summer program in Greensboro (NC): Evaluation 1984–1985*. Unpublished report.

Vannan, E. J. (1989). Community differences in vulnerability to stress. In J. Harbison (Ed.), *Growing up in Northern Ireland* (pp. 107–114). Belfast, Northern Ireland: Learning Resources Unit, Stranmillis College.

Waddell, N., & Cairns, E. (1991). Identity preference in Northern Ireland. *Political Psychology, 12*, 205–213.

Wilson, J. (1989). Educational performance: A decade of evidence. In J. Harbison (Ed.), *Growing up in Northern Ireland* (pp. 28–41). Belfast, Northern Ireland: Learning Resources Unit, Stranmillis College.

Wilson, R., & Cairns, E. (1992). Psychosocial stress and the Northern Ireland troubles. *The Psychologist, 5*, 347–350.

13 Violence at a Distance: Thinking About the Nuclear Threat

Susan Goldberg
The Hospital for Sick Children
Toronto, Ontario, Canada

There was a time when war was close to a "spectator sport," and civilians could observe battles without fear of harm. Those days, needless to say, are long past. At the time of World War I, only 5% of the victims of war were civilians. By World War II, the comparable figure was 50%; in the Vietnam War, civilian casualties were estimated at 80–90%, and upward of 95% of the victims of current wars are civilians. Thus, earlier conventions which protected civilians, including children, no longer exist. This change has been accompanied by a shift from direct soldier-to-soldier confrontation to release of weapons from a distance: The push of a button can now send weapons many miles away to unseen targets and wreak "collateral damage" rather than "kill people." Distance no longer protects us. Knowledge of this allows the possibility of war and concern over becoming a war casualty to pervade the everyday lives of those who are geographically distant from war and conflict.

The vulnerability of children to this psychological invasion is further enhanced by extensive communication networks and the exposure given to war and conflict by the popular media. The war in the Persian Gulf was broadcast continuously and invaded our living rooms as it happened, so that many children absorbed confused pictures of ongoing events. One child in Metropolitan Toronto thought that the war was happening on the golf course near his home. Another thought it was in the nearby city of Guelph. In one pediatric hospital, hundreds of patients saw the early stages of the war on their bedside television sets while most staff were unaware of their exposure and others were frantically trying to figure out how to turn off the ubiquitous hospital television network.

Although no one would claim that the psychological casualties of this "violence at a distance" are in any way comparable to those of children with direct experience of war, one of the horrors of modern-day warfare is its pernicious insertion into the daily lives of those who are seemingly safe. A dramatic documentation of this is found in the research on children's concerns about nuclear war.

NUCLEAR FEARS: HISTORICAL PERSPECTIVE

During the 1980s, both the popular press and professional publications were filled with stories about children's nuclear fears. In many cases, there was the suggestion that worry about world tensions and possible nuclear war were responsible for major mental health problems. Often, these assertions rested on the simple documentation that children were more aware of the threat of nuclear war than most adults wanted to believe.

The study of children's fears has a long history, but it is only recently that fears of war have been investigated. In a review of the literature on children's fears, Croake (1969) noted that from the 1930s to the 1950s, fears of war were rarely mentioned, but by the mid-1960s, 14%–20% of sixth graders mentioned international conflicts among their fears, and such fears were among the most prevalent type mentioned.

In 1965, 350 youngsters were asked how they thought the world might be different in 10 years. Although nuclear war was not mentioned explicitly, 70% spontaneously mentioned "the bomb," nuclear war, or a destroyed world in their replies (Escalona, 1965). Much more recently, at what is now perceived to have been the peak of optimism about the end of the Cold War, a colleague and I conducted a pilot survey of 100 youngsters between 10 and 18 years of age and asked the same question. Although most of them thought that they personally would be better off 10 years hence, the majority saw the world's future as gloomy. Shortly thereafter, events in the Persian Gulf confirmed the realism of these youngsters. We never conducted the larger study for which this was the pilot.

Between Escalona's survey and our orphaned pilot lies an era of expansion of studies in the area of children's awareness of the threat of nuclear war. During the mid-1980s, my colleagues and I contributed to this burgeoning literature. The focus of this chapter is on that work.

PRIOR STUDIES

The classic work in this field is a survey conducted by Beardslee and Mack (1982) as part of a task force report for the American Psychiatric

Association. In this study, 1,151 students in Grades 5–12 were surveyed in urban and suburban areas of Los Angeles, Boston, and Baltimore between 1978 and 1980. Ten questions were asked, beginning with, "What does the word *nuclear* bring to mind?," and including some very direct questions about how the students would feel in a threatened nuclear attack. Descriptive statistics suggested that about half the sample was aware of nuclear issues by age 12; a majority of students in all age groups felt that the development of nuclear weapons and power affected their lives; and 50% or more felt that radiation from power plants and nuclear waste would shorten their lives.

Two subsequent studies placed worries about nuclear war in a broader context and used indirect methods that laid the groundwork for the work I did, as well as research done in other countries. In the first study, open-ended questions about nuclear war were inserted in a Finnish survey of general health administered to over 6,800 youngsters, 12 to 18 years old. In addition, a subset of over 2,100 students responded to eight structured questions about thoughts of nuclear war (Solantaus, Rimpela, & Taipale, 1984). In one of the open-ended questions, students were asked to list their three greatest worries. Seventy-nine percent of 12-year-olds mentioned nuclear war first. This percentage dropped with increasing age, but 45% of 18-year-olds mentioned nuclear war first, and overall fear about war and nuclear war was the most frequently mentioned worry.

These open-ended questions have now been used in other surveys (sometimes with minor modifications), and, throughout the 1980s, war or nuclear war continued to hold first place in the worry/fear list, although the exact percentage of students raising the issue varied by country and by age group (Eisenbud, van Hoorn, & Berger-Gould, 1986). In the surveys I was involved with, we also incorporated modifications of the structured questions.

The second study was conducted in California, where 913 high school seniors rated 20 possible worries on a 4-point scale to indicate how much they worried about each item (Goldenring & Doctor, 1983). In this survey, the highest scores were given to worry about parents dying (74% of respondents gave one of the two higher ratings). Nuclear war was rated as a worry by 58% of the students and ranked fourth, after bad grades and violent crime. However, when asked to identify "my greatest worry," nuclear war ranked second, following parental death.

This questionnaire form was also widely used in subsequent studies. In one of these (Chivian et al., 1985), new data from California, including 201 youngsters 9 to 17 years old, were explicitly compared to responses from 293 Soviet children of the same age attending Young Pioneer camps. In the U.S. sample, parent death was, again, the highest ranked item; in the Soviet sample, nuclear war was given the highest ranking.

When my colleagues and I began doing surveys, this was the extent of the systematic work. Other projects similar to ours were underway, but anecdotal reports dominated both the professional and popular literature. To a large extent, especially in the popular media, the demonstration that a substantial number of children were aware of nuclear issues, and were worried about the threat of nuclear war, was used as the basis for speculating about a major impact of this concern on personality develop-ment (Escalona, 1982; Verdon-Roe, 1983). In some cases, far-reaching consequences, including major social problems (e.g., dropping out of school, drug abuse), were blamed on the psychological effects of nuclear fears. These sweeping and undocumented charges also gave rise to a "backlash," in which the phenomenon of nuclear fear was attributed to only a small group of middle-class children or to children of peace activists. Researchers and peace activists were accused of instigating these fears (e.g., Adelson & Finn, 1985; Coles, 1985, 1986).

SETTING FOR THE CANADIAN NATIONAL SURVEY

It was in this context that my colleagues and I undertook our first survey. We realized that there was no way to document an association between an increase in nuclear fears and major social changes in children's lives, and, therefore, restricted ourselves to more limited questions: (a) How pervasive and influential are nuclear fears relative to other future-oriented worries and concerns? and (b) How do children who worry about nuclear war frequently differ from those who worry very little or not at all?

Our first survey was conducted in three school districts in metropolitan Toronto in the spring of 1984. A second was conducted several weeks later in Hamilton, a smaller urban center within commuting distance of Toronto. The first sample included 1,011 students in Grades 7–13; the second included 1,020 students in Grades 7–12. Both of these samples were found to be representative of their local populations with respect to gender, social class, and ethnic origins. The following year, the survey was expanded to national dimensions. The total group surveyed included students from 20 communities across Canada in eight provinces and the Northwest Territo-ries. (Data from Quebec were not available at the time of these analyses, because translation of the questionnaire delayed data collection. We also lacked data from Saskatchewan, largely because we did not identify a local contact to coordinate the survey.) The timing of these surveys was important. We were concerned that unless all locations were surveyed on the same day, new and unforeseeable events could bias individual samples toward more or less concern with the threat of war. Of course, this ideal design was not feasible. As far as we could determine, there were no specific events that occurred that would have heightened interest in the topics surveyed. However, this was a period during which cruise missile tests were begun in Western Canada and the breakdown of disarmament talks in Geneva was widely discussed.

Following the first set of surveys we were asked by a school board that participated in the adolescent study to conduct a similar study with younger children. Below Grade 5, pencil-and- paper questionnaires were inappropriate, and individual interviews were indicated. In addition, we were not sure at what age children were likely to first encounter the concept of nuclear war, and thus felt that we should not ask any direct questions without a set of pilot interviews.

In 1987, we interviewed 60 students in Grades 2, 4, and 6 in an inner city school in Toronto. The interviewer asked the open-ended questions about hopes and worries and engaged the children in topics that provided opportunities to mention issues of war and peace (e.g., Did the watch the news on television?, Could they remember something reported in this week's news?), but did not ask any direct questions on the topic. We did, however, ask the classic "three wishes" questions often used in psychological assessments: "If you had three wishes and could change anything in your life, what would you wish for?" This was followed by, "Now imagine that you were in charge of the whole world and had three wishes to change anything in the world, what would you wish for?" It was in response to this last question that children were most likely to mention global issues such as war and peace, widespread poverty, and degradation of the environment.

Finally, in the summer of 1989, when we felt that the concerns of the Cold War had dissipated, we began to prepare for another large survey. We used the open-ended questions from the prior studies with a small convenience sample to determine which current issues to compare with nuclear war. For this purpose, we had 100 volunteers between 10 and 18 years of age who were visiting the Ontario Science Centre answer the open-ended questions about hopes and fears and write two discursive paragraphs: one about "what you think your life will be like 10 years from now" and one about "what you think the world will be like 10 years from now."

Most of the subsequent material in this chapter draws on the larger surveys from which two reports have already been published (Goldberg et al., 1985; Lewis, Goldberg, & Parker, 1989). I occasionally refer to the smaller pilot studies, whose data have not, heretofore, been published.

SURVEY FORMAT

In the main survey, we relied primarily on indirect questions in a paper-and-pencil format. In the first section, we adapted the open-ended question from the Finnish survey (Solantaus et al., 1984) and asked, "When you think about the future, what are the three things you look forward to the most?" and "When you think about the future, what are the three things that worry you the most?" In the second section, we adapted the list used by Goldenring and Doctor (1983) and asked the students to rank 10 hopes and 10 worries on a 4-point scale. In the third part, we asked parallel questions about three areas: (a) national unemployment, (b) personal job/career plans, and (c) nuclear war (in that order). Specific questions about nuclear war were deliberately placed last and followed the pattern of the other areas. In these three sections, we adapted questions from the Finnish survey to ask about three aspects of student worries: (a) preoccupation (how much did they talk about or think about an issue), (b) knowledge (how much did they feel they had learned about the issue from a list of different sources), and (c) control (how much did they think they and others could affect the course of events).

RESULTS

In the main survey, in response to the open-ended questions, with only minimal geographical variation, over half of the students (52%) mentioned nuclear war as one of their three main worries, and it was the most common worry. It was generally followed by job/career-oriented concerns (mentioned by 41%–51% of the students). In the 1989 pilot study, nuclear war remained the most frequently mentioned worry, although only 33% of the youngsters listed it.

When it came to frequency of worries, however, those about nuclear war were not more frequent than those in the other two domains we surveyed. For example, in 1984–1985, 64% of youngsters said they felt fearful and anxious about job/career plans at least once in the previous month, compared with 60% who worried about unemployment and 58% who worried about nuclear war. In this group, 7% said they had felt fearful and anxious about nuclear war almost every day in the previous month (Lewis et al., 1989), which was similar to the percentage that worried daily about unemployment and job/career plans. The percentage reporting daily fear was comparable to the 8% reported in Finland (Solantaus et al., 1984).

Worries about nuclear war differed from those in the other two domains with respect to the students' source of knowledge and sense of control. In our survey, as in most others, the primary source of information about nuclear war was television. School and family were not ranked highly, and students reported little discussion with adults on the topic (Goldberg et al., 1985). In addition, among the three domains, students felt (appropriately) they had least control over the threat of nuclear war. Thus, although worries about nuclear war were not more prevalent or frequent than other future-oriented concerns in students' lives, they may have been qualitatively different because they were not discussed with significant adults, and students perceived themselves to have little ability to improve the situation.

Our second question concerned differences between those who worried about nuclear war a great deal (almost daily) and those who worried little or not at all (the rest of the sample). We reasoned that if nuclear worries had a negative effect on mental health, this should be most obvious among those who worried the most. The children in the daily-fear group did not differ from the others with respect to gender, ethnic origin, or whether they reported their parents as having taken any action against the arms race. In some subsamples, the daily-fear group was more likely to have taken action themselves, in others not. This was also true of social class differences: They appeared in some local samples but not others. However, where social class differences did appear, it was often lower class students who expressed more worry. (These data are discussed in more detail further on.)

Of greatest interest to us were responses to questions reflecting future job/career plans and feelings of control. If worries about nuclear war lead youngsters to give up on their futures, then the daily-fear group would be expected to report less concern with future job/career plans. This was not our finding. Those who worried about nuclear war "almost every day" were also those who reported the highest frequency of worry about job/career plans. Those who said they had not worried about nuclear war at all in the last month also reported the lowest frequency of concern with job/career plans, X^2 (2) = 15.41, $p <$. 01) A similar pattern was found with respect to worries about national unemployment: Those with daily fears about nuclear war also had more frequent worries about unemployment. They were also more likely to discuss the threat of nuclear war at home, $\chi^2(3df)$ = 132.2, $p < .001$); at school, $\chi^2(3df) = 47.3, p < .001$); and with friends, $\chi^2(3df) = 75.3, p < .001$). Thus, the data suggest that the daily-fear group was more concerned than others with all three issues and more likely to discuss all three of these areas.

We already knew that the students felt little control over the threat of nuclear war. The specific questions about control asked: (a) "How much do you feel that you personally can influence . . . "; (b) "How much do you think your parents and other adults can influence . . . "; and (c) "How much do you think Canada as a nation can influence . . . "? The choices were *none, some, a lot*, and *total control*. Among those who said they had not worried about nuclear war at all in the last month, 77%–80% said they could have no influence over the threat of nuclear war; of those who worried almost daily, only 35%–57% reported they could have no influence. In this latter group, 28%–45% felt they could have some influence, compared with 16%–18% of those who had not worried at all in the previous month, $\chi^2(2df) = 24.74, p < .01$). A similar pattern was found for the perceived influence of other adults, $\chi^2(2df) = 26.2, p < .001$); and for Canada as a nation $\chi^2(2df) = 28.7, p < .001$). Those in the daily-fear group also felt they and others had more influence over national unemployment and personal job/career plans. This led us to conclude that the daily-fear group had a greater sense of social efficacy than the others, which we considered a positive attribute.

MENTAL HEALTH AND NUCLEAR FEARS

A more recent report by Tudge, Chivian, Robinson, Andreyenkov, and Popov (1990) based on responses of U.S. and Soviet students in 1986 and 1988, also indicated that realistic awareness of the threat of nuclear war was not associated with pessimism. In fact, those who were most worried were more likely to indicate optimism about the future rather than pessimism. However, among those who believed that a nuclear war was likely to occur, there was increased pessimism about the future. In addition, although Soviet adolescents were more worried about nuclear war than their American peers, they were more convinced that it would not occur. The authors attributed these national differences to different national postures reflected in the popular media in the two countries and to the greater number of children and adolescents, as well as people of all ages, in the Soviet Union actively engaged at the time in political activities for peace, such as writing to world leaders, designing peace posters, and participating in demonstrations. Such activities may or may not influence the political situation, but they do have beneficial psychological consequences of enhanced feelings of social efficacy.

This position contrasts sharply with those who argue that it is researchers who ask children questions about nuclear war and peace activist parents who create such fears (Abelson & Finn, 1985; Coles, 1985, 1986) in a small group of middle-class children. The existing data are in sharp disagreement with such assertions, which appear to be popular North American myths. The remainder of this chapter scrutinizes these myths.

Myth 1. Fears about nuclear war are limited to a small group of children.

Facts. In our sample, worries about nuclear war were reported by a majority of adolescents. This finding was consistent with the earlier Finnish and California surveys (Goldenring & Doctor, 1983; Solantaus et al., 1984), as well as many subsequent studies in the U.S., eastern and western Europe, and Australia (Eisenbud et al., 1986). When surveys have examined differences within national samples, there has been little geographic difference (Lewis et al., 1989).

Although many studies have reported greater worry among girls than boys, this has not consistently been the case (e.g., Tudge & Chivian, 1989). In our own work, we specifically examined gender differences in response to direct and indirect questions about the threat of nuclear war. Males were actually somewhat more likely than females to include nuclear war as one of their three worries (53% of males vs. 50% of females), and there were no gender differences in the frequency of thinking about or talking about nuclear war. However, in response to the single question concerning the frequency of feeling fearful and anxious about the threat of nuclear war, females reported more frequent anxious feelings than did males. We concluded that males and females differed little in their concern and preoccupation with the threat of nuclear war, but, consistent with the social norms that allow females to express a greater range of emotions, females were more likely to express emotional distress in connection with their concerns.

Myth 2.   Only middle-class children have nuclear fears.

Facts.   Few social class differences have been reported, even in studies specifically designed to explore influences of social class (e.g., Tudge & Chivian, 1989). In our study (Goldberg et al., 1985), we found social class differences in some of the communities surveyed, but not in all. Although there were some class differences in the national study, they were not systematic and could not be explained a as greater concern among middle-class children (Lewis et al., 1989). When we examined social class differences by considering responses to specific questions as a function of fathers' and mothers' occupations (18 comparisons), only 1 comparison showed a social class effect. Students who reported lower social class occupations for their fathers also reported more frequent discussion of nuclear war at home, $\chi^2 = 22.3, p < .05$. In large-scale surveys conducted in the United States, lower class students reported worrying about the threat of war more than others (Bachman, 1983).

Our grade-school interviews were conducted in a school located in a large housing project, and included predominantly lower class immigrant children. One quarter of second graders, half of fourth graders and 80% of sixth graders spontaneously mentioned concerns about world war. One boy in Grade 4, when asked for the three wishes he would make if he were in charge of the world said he wished for "no more war" and "that my parents could pay all the bills."

Thus, the data generally show that concern about the threat of nuclear war is not restricted to any specific social class, but is widespread. Because most of the surveys were conducted with children over 10 years of age, and primarily adolescents, broad conclusions about younger children cannot be drawn.

Myth 3.   Parents who are engaged in peace activism are the main source of children's worries.

Facts.   From the data cited, it is clear that child worriers far outnumber parents who are peace activists. In our sample, only 7%–10% reported that their parents had taken any action against the arms race, whereas over 50% of the children mentioned nuclear war as a worry. We did not inquire in detail about the nature of such activity, so it could presumably range from one signing of a petition or financial contribution to a life committed to civil disobedience.

We compared children who reported parent activism with the remainder of the sample with respect to their frequency of worry and sense of control. Those who reported parent activism reported both more worry, $\chi^2(1df) = 14.53$, $p <. 005$, and a greater sense of control, $\chi^2(1df) = 42.7$, $p < .00001$). Among those who said they had discussed the threat of nuclear war at home, there was also both increased worry, $\chi^2(3df) = 127.6$, $p < .00001$, and an increased sense of control, $\chi^2(3df) = 627.4$, $p < .00001$. Thus, for the small proportion who did report parent activism, this was associated with increased worry, but it was also associated with increased social efficacy. Thus, those who wish to blame parents for increasing nuclear worries must also credit parents with enhancing their children's social efficacy.

However, these findings must be tempered with the reminder that, in general, parents are not a primary source of information on this topic. In our survey, and others that haves asked the question, the leading source of information is television. On a national basis, 74% of Canadian students mentioned television, 60% newspapers and magazines, 32% books, followed by 29% family. School was even further down the list. Thus, the data clearly indicate that parents, activist or otherwise, do not play a major role in children's ideas and information gathering about the threat of nuclear war.

If these popular myths are abandoned, the data suggest that a less popular myth — one shared by many of the early researchers — must also be abandoned.

Myth 4.   Children's mental health is negatively affected by thoughts of nuclear war.

Facts.   The bulk of the relevant research, including ours, indicates that there is little association between concerns about nuclear war and mental health problems. Anecdotal evidence from therapists indicates that children referred for other problems may have worries about nuclear war as a more fundamental anxiety. At the same time, a small number of children presenting with extreme fear of nuclear war as the major symptom may have other fundamental problems. Only a systematic review of such cases can illuminate the process by which nuclear fears can play a role in clinically significant behavior problems.

Surveys of nonclinical populations, such as those described here, can tell us little about serious mental health problems. However, the available data do indicate that those who worry about the threat of nuclear war most frequently are equally (if not more) preoccupied with their personal career plans and are more optimistic than other students, in that they believe they and others can have some influence in affecting the situation. This was true not only in our survey (Goldberg et al., 1985) but in U.S. and Soviet surveys (Tudge et al., 1990), as well.

The fact that children are able to cope with worries about war does not mean that such concerns are harmless. Clearly, they consume effort and energy more profitably spent in other activities. At the World Summit for Children in September 1990, 71 world leaders signed a declaration promising to protect children from war, preserve the environment, enhance children's health, mount a global attack on poverty, and increase educational opportunities. This declaration echoed commitments made earlier at the United Nations Convention on the Rights of the Child. UNICEF estimated the cost of meeting these commitments to be $20 billion annually. This sounds expensive, but the Gulf War cost over twice this amount in considerably less time. The loss in life and health to children directly exposed to this war is shocking. The impact on children at a distance is yet to be measured.

During the weeks of active conflict, there was great concern about the psychological well-being of children. Every television station was interviewing psychologists and psychiatrists about what to tell children. When guidelines developed by the Toronto Board of Education were published in a nationally distributed newspaper, requests to duplicate the material flooded in from across Canada. Once the cease-fire seemed imminent, however, these concerns disappeared. A public meeting held at my hospital in response to these numerous requests took place several days after the cease-fire. The auditorium was almost empty.

Why are people no longer concerned? In the 1980s, while conducting the research described here, my colleagues and I came to the conclusion that children's fear of nuclear war per se was not a problem. What was a problem was the inability or unwillingness of adults to listen to and discuss children's concerns (see, e.g., Zeitlin, 1984). The war in the Persian Gulf has not changed this. The attention given to children's concerns was a temporary interest forced on the public by the media at a time when people could not ignore children's awareness. Everyone was quick to return to the false security of "not knowing," because it was more comfortable that way. We must all ask ourselves whether adult comfort justifies the potential costs to our children.

REFERENCES

Adelson, J., & Finn, C. E. (1985). Terrorizing children. *Commentary, 79*, 29–36.

Bachman, J. (1983). American high school seniors view the military: 1976–1982. *Armed Forces and Society, 10*, 86–94.

Beardslee, W., & Mack, J. (1982). The impact on children and adolescents of nuclear developments. In R. Rogers (Ed.), *Psychosocial aspects of nuclear developments: Task force report No. 20* (pp. 64–93). Washington, DC: American Psychiatric Association.

Chivian, E., Mack, J., Waletzky, J., Lazaroff, C., Doctor, R., & Goldenring, J. (1985). Soviet children and the threat of nuclear war: A preliminary study. *American Journal of Orthopsychiatry, 55*, 484–502.

Coles, R. (1985, December 8). Children and the bomb. *The New York Times Magazine*, pp. 44, 62.

Coles, R. (1986). *The political life of children*. Boston: Atlantic Monthly Press.

Croake, J. (1969). Fears of children. *Human Development, 12*, 239–247.

Eisenbud, M.B., van Hoorn, J., & Berger-Gould, B. (1986). Children, adolescents, and the threat of nuclear war: An international perspective. In D. Jeliffe (Ed.), *Advances in international maternal and child health* (Vol. 6, pp. 1–24). Fairlawn, NJ: Oxford University Press.

Escalona, S. (1965). Children and the threat of nuclear war. In M. Schwebel (Ed.), *Behavioral science and human survival* (pp. 201–209). Palo Alto, CA: Science and Behavior Books.

Escalona, S. (1982). Growing up with the threat of nuclear war: Some indirect effects on personality development. *American Journal of Orthopsychiatry, 52*, 600–607.

Goldberg, S., LaCombe, S., Levinson, D., Parker, K.R., Ross, C., & Sommers, F. (1985). Thinking about the threat of nuclear war: Relevance to mental health. *American Journal of Orthopsychiatry, 55*, 503–512.

Goldenring, J. M., & Doctor, R. M. (1983, September 20). *Adolescents' concerns about the threat of nuclear war*. Testimony for the House of Representatives Select Committee on Children, Youth, and Families, Washington, DC.

Lewis, C., Goldberg, S., & Parker, K.R. (1989). Canadian youth and the nuclear threat: Replication and extension. *American Journal of Orthopsychiatry, 59*, 520–527.

Solantaus, T., Rimpela, M., & Taipale, V. (1984). The threat of war in the minds of 12–18-year-olds in Finland. *The Lancet, 8380*, 784–785.

Tudge, J., & Chivian, E. (1989). Nuclear war in the minds of youth: The influences of class, age, and gender. In K. Boehnke, M. McPherson, & F. Schmidt (Eds.), *Leben unter atomarer Bedrohung: Ergebnisse internationaler psychologischer forschung* (pp. 179–194). Heidelberg: Asanger.

Tudge, J., Chivian, E., Robinson, J., Andreyenkov, V., & Popov, V. (1990). American and Soviet adolescents' attitudes toward the future: The relationship between worry about nuclear war and optimism. *International Journal of Mental Health, 19*(4), 55–84.

Verdon-Roe, V. (1983, January). Growing up in the nuclear age: What children can tell us. *East West Journal*, pp. 24–30.

Zeitlin, S. (1984, March–April). What do we tell Mom and Dad? *Networker*, p. 31.

14

Children as Victims of and Witnesses to Violence in a Washington, D.C. Neighborhood

John E. Richters
Pedro Martinez
National Institute of Mental Health

The United States is the most violent country in the industrialized world, particularly for young people. Homicide in the United States ranks as the second leading cause of death among those between 15 and 24 years of age (Earls et al., 1991). Males, especially, are at high risk. As indicated in Fig. 14.1, during 1986–1987, those between 15 and 24 years of age were more likely to be murdered than their counterparts in all 22 other developed countries for which comparable homicide statistics were available (Fingerhut & Kleinman, 1990). Young males were 4 times more likely to be murdered than their counterparts in the next highest ranking country, Scotland; 7 times more likely than young males in Canada; 21 times more likely than those in West Germany; and 40 times more likely than same-age

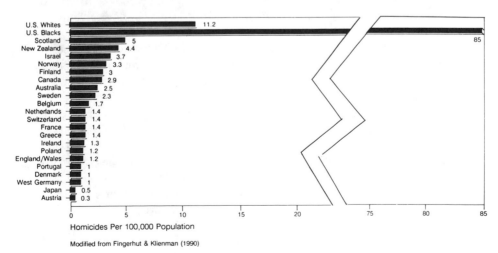

Modified from Fingerhut & Klienman (1990)

FIG. 14.1.   International comparison of homicide rates for males between the ages of 15 and 24 years.

243

males in Japan. Moreover, the U.S. homicide rate for Black males (between 15 and 24 years) was more than 7 times the homicide rate for White males in this age range. These figures are even more alarming in light of the fact that homicide rates in major U.S. cities have increased steadily since these data were recorded.

The 1980s witnessed an extraordinary increase in community violence in most major cities across the United States. In 1990, the homicide rate in Boston increased by 45% over the previous year; in Denver, it increased by 29%; in Chicago, Dallas, and New Orleans, by more than 20%; in Los Angeles, by 16%; and in New York, by 11%. In Washington, DC, which has the highest per capita homicide rate in the country, the 1990 murder rate set an all-time record in the District's history (Escobar, 1991). Across the country, 1 out of 5 teenage and young adult deaths was gun related in 1988—the first year in which firearm death rates for both Black and White teenagers exceeded the total for all natural causes of death combined. Also in 1988, the firearm homicide rate for young Black males increased by 35%, and Black male teens were 11 times more likely than their White counterparts to be killed by guns (Christoffel, 1990). Firearms account for the majority of homicides among teens and young adults (Centers for Disease Control, 1988; Christoffel & Christoffel, 1986). Since the mid-1980s, firearms have accounted for 96% of the increase in U.S. homicide rates (Centers for Disease Control, 1990), and have become a staple of childhood and teenage life in many American cities. In a few short years, the widespread availability and use of handguns has transformed childhood into something quite foreign to what most adults can recall of their own childhoods. In urban school districts around the country, school dress codes have given way to metal detectors, hall monitors have given way to armed security patrols, and schoolyard spats over minor injustices have given way to murders and drive-by shootings.

Although the murder rate has received nationwide attention and concern, it represents only a crude index of the day-to-day community violence that characterizes many neighborhoods throughout American cities. Increasingly, children have been involved both as victims of and eyewitnesses to episodes of community violence. In Washington, DC, for example, even school-based violence has become so common that many school principals in the District have banned students from wearing coats or carrying bookbags during class hours, for fear that they may be carrying weapons (R. Sanchez & Horwitz, 1989). Between September 1988 and January 1989, 20 area students were wounded by gunshots or knives on or near their school grounds. In December 1988, 2 students were wounded by gunfire from a passing car as they left a DC high school; in January 1989, 4 students were wounded when two gunmen sprayed bullets into a crowd of several hundred students leaving another District high school, an incident sparked by a lunchtime argument in the cafeteria (R. Sanchez & Horwitz, 1989); in March 1989, 4 children were wounded when two youths approached and sprayed shots at them without saying a word (C. Sanchez, 1989). These are not isolated incidents. During the first 8 months of 1988, an estimated 220 children and teenagers were wounded or killed by shootings in Washington, DC (C. Sanchez, 1989). Shootings have become so commonplace that schools throughout Washington, DC, and in major cities across the country, have found it necessary to install metal detectors to prevent students from bringing weapons to class. Despite the alarming portrait of community violence depicted by police statistics and media coverage, there has been little systematic research into the nature and consequences of children's exposure to violence in urban communities.

This rising tide of violence in American cities has placed its causes and consequences squarely on the public health agenda. The U.S. government's *Year 2000 National Health Promotion and Disease Prevention Objectives* includes a full chapter devoted to violence issues, and delineates a number of goals and programs aimed at reducing the number of deaths and injuries associated with violence (Public Health Service, 1990). Notably absent from these objectives, however, has been attention to the possible adverse psychological consequences of exposure to acute or chronic violence. Nonetheless, in light of numerous media reports of children's exposure to community violence and recent reports documenting high levels of exposure even among very young children, it is reasonable to question whether the risks of exposure extend beyond death and physical injury to psychological well-being.

RELATED RESEARCH ON CHILDHOOD STRESSORS

Unfortunately, there has been no systematic research to date concerning the psychological consequences for children of being raised in chronically violent neighborhoods. Mainstream studies of stress and children's adjustment have focused on a variety of childhood stressors both within and outside the family. Prominent within-family stressors have been bereavement (Brown, Harris, & Bifulco, 1986), divorce (Emery, 1982), parent psychopathology (Watt, Anthony, Wynne, & Rolf, 1984), child abuse (Cicchetti & Rizley, 1981), life stress (Compas, 1987), and the like. There also have been less frequent reports over the decades concerning children's symptoms in the wake of natural disasters, such as floods (Burke, Borus, Burns, Milstein, & Beasley, 1982; Gleser, Green, & Winget, 1981), tornadoes (Silber, Perry, & Bloch, 1958), earthquakes (Galante & Foa, 1982), landslides (Lacy, 1972), nuclear power plant accidents (Handford et al., 1986), and transportation accidents (Tuckman, 1973), as well as their symptoms following kidnappings (Terr, 1979, 1981, 1983), concentration camp experiences (Kinzie, Sack, Angell, Manson, & Rath, 1986; Sack, Angell, Kinzie, & Rath, 1986), familicide (Lebovici, 1974; Malmquist, 1984), and a range of other violent and traumatic experiences (Garmezy & Rutter, 1985). Perhaps most germane to the issue of community violence are the clinical literatures concerning the effects on children of exposure to the chronically violent circumstances of war (McWhirter, 1982, 1983; Rosenblatt, 1983).[1]

CHILDREN'S REACTIONS TO WARTIME STRESS

Clinical-descriptive reports of children's reactions to wartime stress date back to World War II (Bodman, 1941; Freud & Burlingham, 1943; Glover, 1942), with more systematic studies appearing in the wake of the Yom Kippur War in Israel (Breznitz, 1983; Kristal, 1975; Milgram, 1982; Milgram & Milgram, 1976; Ziv & Israel, 1973), and during the ongoing conflict in Northern Ireland (Lyons, 1973, 1979; McAuley & Troy, 1983; McWhirter, 1982, 1983; McWhirter & Trew, 1981). Reports of children's symptom patterns have varied considerably across studies as a function of the domains of adjustment targeted, stressors involved, age and gender of children, and other background characteristics of the samples studied. Generally, however, children's reactions associated with exposure to war-related violence have included intrusive thoughts, fear of recurrence, anxieties, difficulty concentrating, depression, psychosomatic disturbances, sleep disturbances, and other symptoms that, in the extreme, have come to be associated with posttraumatic stress.

As Garmezy and Rutter (1985) observed in their excellent review of these and related studies, point estimates of psychiatric risk among children exposed to wartime stressors are difficult to judge due to the clinical-descriptive nature of many reports and inattention to methodological detail. Important information concerning children's baseline or prestressor symptom levels, the full range of stressors involved, and mediating conditions is often not reported, rendering comparisons across studies difficult. Consequently, there is little basis for reconciling the highly variable estimates of significant psychiatric symptoms in children; prevalence estimates have ranged from 10% to 50%. Nonetheless, it is clear that some children exposed to wartime stress do suffer socially handicapping emotional problems. Typically, however, it is impossible to determine from

---

[1]There is, of course, an enormous research literature concerning the effects on children of exposure to media violence. In contract to living in chronically violent circumstances, however, violence on television is a vicarious source of stimulation that children characteristically seek out, enjoy, and can easily escape. This literature, therefore, may have limited relevance to the present focus, despite its potential as a source of influence on children.

empirical reports whether their symptoms are reactions to particular stressors, such as bombings (Ziv & Israel, 1973), evacuations (John, 1941), or the death/absence of a parent (Kinzie et al., 1986), or to the more generalized chronic violence and unpredictability of wartime conditions, or, more generally, to characteristics of the children's environments that are unrelated to war violence. Hence, the cumulative literature on children in wartime highlights an important problem, but yields few systematic conclusions about the immediate and long-term consequences for children who live in chronically violent circumstances, or about factors that mediate their reactions.

CHILDREN'S REACTIONS TO ACUTE VIOLENCE IN THE COMMUNITY

In perhaps the most systematic study of the effects of children's exposure to community violence, Pynoos et al. (1987) recently reported on the distress symptoms of children (grades K–6) 1 month following a fatal schoolyard sniper incident in Los Angeles. Their report supported several conclusions. First, a host of children's distress symptoms covaried significantly with their levels of actual proximity to the shooting incident. Second, children who knew the deceased child reported more severe symptoms. Third, children who had experienced other traumatic events during the previous year reported having renewed thoughts and images of those events, and many of their distress symptoms were related to both events. Finally, these effects held equally for children as young as 6 years old.

Pynoos et al.'s study provides compelling evidence for children's post-traumatic symptoms following exposure to an acute episode of urban violence, but the authors specifically set out to examine children's symptoms in response to a single, particularly traumatic violent incident. Therefore, their report does not address important questions concerning (a) the long-term sequelae of exposure to *chronic* violence; (b) family, neighborhood, and the children's own characteristics that may mediate their reactions—immediate and long-term, adaptive and maladaptive—to violence; or (c) the impact of violence exposure on characteristics of children's social and emotional functioning beyond those associated with distress.

Notwithstanding the limitations of earlier reports concerning children and violence, two common themes have emerged that are worthy of note. First, children who are exposed to violent incidents are significantly more likely than those not exposed to suffer from a wide range of social and emotional problems. Prevalence rates are not always as high as one might expect a priori, but they are certainly high enough to warrant concern about violence as a risk factor for children's adjustment. Second, characteristics of children's families and family relationships seem to be major mediators of both their short- and long-term adaptation in the wake of violence. This theme emerges strongly from reports concerning British children following bombing-related evacuations in Britain in World War II (Freud & Burlingham, 1943), and more recently concerning traumatized Cambodian children who were relocated to the United States following their concentration camp experiences (Kinzie et al., 1986; Sack et al., 1986). It is not yet clear, however, whether similar exposure–distress reactions are also characteristic of children living in chronically violent urban neighborhoods, nor is it clear to what extent distress reactions are associated, more broadly, with emotional and behavioral problems in children.

The need for research concerning children's exposure to violence in the community is clear. It is only by identifying children most at risk for exposure and its consequences, including psychopathology, physical injury, and death, that public health agencies and services delivery systems can target their scarce resources. It is only on the basis of such risk–exposure information that preventive intervention programs aimed at reducing exposure and its consequences can be designed, implemented, and evaluated effectively. Beyond these immediate needs lie a host of equally pressing theoretical questions concerning the consequences of being raised in violent environments on shaping various dimensions of personality development and the emergence of psychopathology.

The study described here was an initial effort to (a) describe the extent to which young children living in a moderately violent inner-city community in Washington, DC had been exposed, both directly (as victims) and indirectly (as witnesses), to various forms of violence, and (b) examine links between those exposure patterns and symptoms of distress.

METHOD

Subjects

The primary sample included 165 children, ages 6 to 10 years, living in a low-income, moderately violent neighborhood in Southeast Washington, DC. All children attended the same elementary school (Grades K–6); 111 children were in the first and second grades, and the remaining 54 children were in the fifth and sixth grades. Information concerning children's violence exposure was elicited independently from the children and their parents (typically, their mothers). In addition, teachers rated the stability and violence levels of homes of all children in their classes, including those who did not participate in the study. Thus, teacher-informant data were collected on all children attending Grades 1 and 2 ($n = 152$), and 5 and 6

(n = 88); parent-informant and/or child-informant data were collected from 111 (73%) of the first and second graders, and 54 (61%) of the fifth and sixth graders.

Procedures

Recruitment letters describing the study were sent home to the parent(s) of all children attending Grades 1, 2, 5, and 6. The letters were printed on school letterhead and were cosigned by the school principal and the investigators. The study was described as an effort to document the extent to which the children had been exposed, directly and indirectly, to different forms of violence in the community. Teachers then contacted parents directly to answer questions about the study, encourage participation, and schedule appointments for visits to the school for interviews. On their arrival at school, parents were greeted by the investigators, who explained the study in detail and secured informed consent. In light of the literature on experimenter/interviewer effects on respondents, particularly those associated with race (Sattler, 1970), parents were told explicitly to neither exaggerate nor conceal instances of violence to which their children had been exposed; they were told that the success of the study depended on total honesty from respondents. Then, depending on their reading skills, parents either completed the assessment battery with minimal assistance from, or responded to an oral administration of the assessment battery by, one of the investigators. All parents were paid $20 for their participation.

Children were then interviewed by the investigators in small groups during school hours in a reserved classroom. Teachers completed their measures following parent and child participation. Children and teachers were also told explicitly to neither exaggerate nor conceal instances of violence to which the children had been exposed, and that the success of the study depended on total honesty.

Parent-Completed Measures. All parents completed the parent report version of the Survey of Children's Exposure to Community Violence (Richters & Saltzman, 1990), which assesses the frequency with which an index child has been victimized by, has witnessed, or has heard about 20 forms of violence and violence-related activities in the community (explicitly not including media exposure; see Table 14.1). For each positive response, the questionnaire includes context questions about (a) where the violence took place (in or near school vs. home); (b) who perpetrated the violence (ranging from stranger to family member); (c) who, if not the child, was victimized (ranging from stranger to family member); and (d) when the incident occurred (ranging from 1 week ago to more than 5 years ago). Parents also completed the Conflict Tactics Scales (CTS; Straus, 1979), a widely used

TABLE 14.1
Parents' Reports of Their Children's Community Violence Exposure

	Prevalence Rates			
	Grades 1 and 2 (n = 77)		Grades 5 and 6 (n = 51)	
Violence Category	Victim (%)	Witness (%)	Victim (%)	Witness (%)
Shooting	3	9	6	14
Stabbing	1	13	4	4
Sexual assault	0	1	2	4
Mugging	9	25	8	43
Physical threat	5	17	14	18
Approached: Drug trade	4	5	6	12
Approached: Drug use	1	53	4	61
Arrest*	—	37	—	20
Punch/hit/slap*	—	39	—	38
Illegal weapon*	—	18	20	—
Forced entry: Other	3	5	6	10
Forced entry: Own*	—	5	—	0
Dead body outside*	—	16	—	16
Murder*	—	3	—	4
Suicide*	—	0	—	3

*Victimization question not asked and/or not logically possible.

questionnaire for assessing within-family violence between adults. In addition, parents completed a questionnaire concerning a variety of characteristics of family history, composition, and demographics.

Finally, parents completed the parent report version of the Checklist of Child Distress Symptoms (CCDS; Richters & Martinez, 1990a), which was developed for this study from diagnostic criteria described in the DSM-III-R (American Psychiatric Association, 1987). The CCDS questionnaire includes 28 symptom descriptions, each with a Likert scale response format for rating symptom presence ranging from *never* (1) to *a lot of the time* (4). Parents also completed the Child Behavior Checklist (CBCL), a widely used checklist of children's behavior problems for which a considerable body of reliability and validity data have been published (Achenbach & Edelbrock, 1983).

Child-Completed Measures (First and Second Grade).   First- and second-grade children were assembled in small groups to participate in two age-appropriate interviews. The first was a cartoon-based interview of children's distress symptoms (*Levonn*; Richters, Martinez, & Valla, 1990), based on the original work of Valla (1989), and modified to (a) depict the central character (Dominique) as an urban child (Levonn), (b) include depictions of symptoms associated with posttraumatic stress disorder not included in the original interview, (c) include a two- to three-sentence script with each carton, and (d) include a new response format for indicating frequency, consisting of thermometers filled with varying degrees of mercury (Fig. 14.2).

Above each cartoon was a picture of three thermometers, each filled with a different level of mercury, labeled *never, some of the time,* and *a lot of the time.* Prior to administration, children were taught how to use the thermometer response format correctly to indicate frequency. Next, each child was given a numbered set of the cartoon depictions. Each cartoon was described orally from a script. Following each cartoon description, children were asked to circle a thermometer indicating how often they felt like

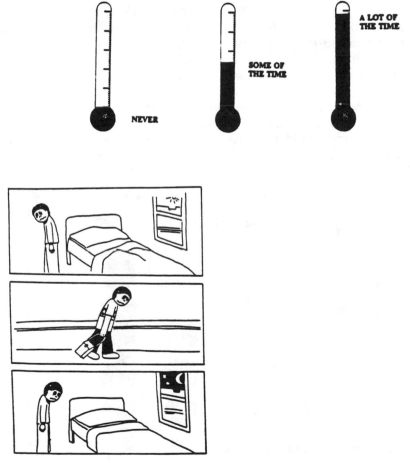

FIG. 14.2.   Sample cartoon from *Levonn: A Cartoon-Based Structured Interview for Assessing Young Children's Distress Symptoms* by J. E. Richters and P. Martinez, 1990a.

Levonn. One week test–rest data based on *Levonn* were collected from a random subsample of younger children. Reliability for the composite distress rating, computed by summing across all symptom scores, was high and significant ($r[22] = .81, p < .001$). Across the full sample of younger children, the composite symptom score based on *Levonn* was significantly related to parent-rated CBCL scores ($r[76] = .30, p < .01$) and to parent ratings of children's distress on the CCDS ($r[76] = .32, p < .01$).

The younger children also completed *Things I Have Seen and Heard* (Richters & Martinez, 1990b), a 15-question structured interview that probes young children's exposure to violence and violence-related themes in an age-appropriate format (Fig. 14.3). The interview consists of 15 pages, each describing a different form of violence or violence theme. As shown in Fig. 14.3, five stacks of balls are depicted below each description of violence, each with a different number of balls, ranging from 0 to 4; the columns are labeled sequentially from *never* to *many times*. Prior to test administration, children were taught how to circle the stacks to indicate frequency of exposure. As each violence description was read aloud, children were asked to circle a stack of balls indicating how often they had either witnessed or been victimized by that form or theme of violence. The 1-week test–retest reliability of the composite variable reflecting the sum of all instances of child reported exposure was $r = .81$ for a random subsample of 21 children, with a small, nonsignificant attenuation in the absolute levels of exposure reported at Time 2, $t(20) = 1.34$, *(ns)*.

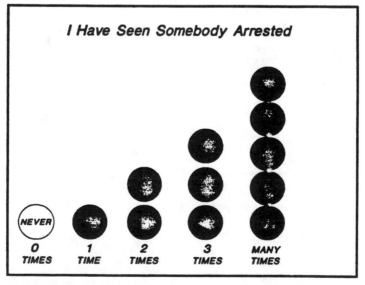

FIG. 14.3.   Sample drawing of violence exposure questions from "Things I Have Seen and Heard" asked of younger children (first and second grade).

Child-Completed Measures (Fifth and Sixth Grade).   Fifth and sixth grade children were assembled in small groups to complete several measures of violence exposure and distress symptoms. Initially, they completed the self-report version of the CCDS completed earlier by their parents about them, and the Child Depression Inventory (CDI), a widely used measure of children's self-reported depressive symptoms (Kovaks, 1985). The children's composite symptom scores based on the CCDS were significantly related to their CDI scores ($r[37] = .49, p < .01$).

Finally, the older children completed the self-report version of the Survey of Children's Exposure to Community Violence (Richters & Saltzman, 1990), completed earlier by their parents about them. Again, depending on their reading and comprehension skills, children either completed the assessment battery with minimal assistance, or responded to an oral administration of the assessment battery by an investigator.

Teacher-Completed Measure.   Teachers completed the Teacher Observation of Classroom Adaptation (TOCA-R; Werthamer-Larsson, Kellam, Dolan, Brown, & Wheeler, 1990). The TOCA-R includes 43 classroom problems of children, including internalizing and externalizing behaviors. Each behavior is rated on a 6-point Likert scale, reflecting the frequency with which it is manifested by the child. In addition, teachers were asked to what extent each child's home was characterized by stability and by violence. Both additional questions were also rated on 6-point Likert scales. Analyses of the TOCA-R ratings of classroom adaptation are not included in this report.

RESULTS

Sample Characteristics

As indicated in Table 14.2, the families of the younger and older children did not differ significantly on any of the major demographic characteristics assessed. The majority of participating parents had not completed high school. Fifty-four percent of the parents in both the younger and the older samples were employed full time; the median family income was less than $19,000, and one quarter of the families were receiving some form of public assistance. The majority of parents were not currently married, and almost 50% had never been married. As a consequence, more than 50% of the children had rarely or never lived with their biological fathers.

Comparison of Participating and Non-Participating Families.   The availability of teacher ratings of nonparticipating as well as participating children and families provided a basis for estimating the extent to which

TABLE 14.2
Sample Characteristics

Focus	Prevalence Rates		
	Grades 1 and 2 %	Grades 5 and 6 %	p
Respondent			
Relationship to child			
Biological mother	79	80	ns
Biological father	9	10	ns
Other relative	12	10	ns
High school graduate/GED	36	26	ns
Employed full time	54	54	ns
Marital status			
Currently married	17	16	ns
Never married	46	43	ns
Race: Black	97	96	ns
Family			
Income < $19,000	57	49	ns
Receiving some public assistance	26	27	ns
Living in apartment	67	64	ns
Child			
Male	51	52	ns
Female	49	48	ns

Note. All demographic differences between families of young and older children were nonsignificant.

participation in the study was systematically associated with characteristics of either the children or their families. The results of these comparisons are presented in Table 14.3. As indicated, there were no significant differences in teacher-rated family violence or family stability between participating and nonparticipating families for either age group. Moreover, children of participating and nonparticipating families did not differ significantly on teacher ratings of classroom-based behavior problems or overall student progress. There was, however, a nonsignificant trend toward higher levels of teacher-rated behavior problems among children of nonparticipating families in the younger sample, but this trend did not hold for children in the older sample.

Neighborhood Violence Level. Data concerning the prevalence, frequency, and correlates of children's exposure to violence are most interpretable in the context of figures concerning actual levels of neighborhood violence. Such data allow for comparisons across studies, and support the computation of violence exposure–risk estimates for prevention, intervention, and policy- planning initiatives. Figure 14.4 reflects the levels of

TABLE 14.3

Comparison of Participating and Nonparticipating Famlies Based on Teacher Ratings of Families and Children

Teacher-rated Characteristic	Younger Children					
	Participating (n = 78)		Nonparticipating (n = 35)			
	Mean	SD	Mean	SD	t	p
Family stability	3.13	(1.75)	2.66	(1.63)	1.35	.18
Family violence	2.40	(1.60)	2.17	(1.27)	.74	.46
Child behavior problems	102	(25.97)	110	(25.00)	1.70	.09
Student progress	2.78	(1.46)	2.69	(1.43)	.33	.74

Teacher-rated Characteristic	Older Children					
	Participating (n = 52)		Nonparticipating (n = 35)			
	Mean	SD	Mean	SD	t	p
Family stability	4.22	(1.47)	4.10	(1.78)	.32	.75
Family violence	3.24	(1.83)	3.24	(2.04)	.01	.99
Child behavior problems	128	;(33.65)	127	(35.36)	.03	.97
Student progress	2.76	(1.15)	3.03	(1.46)	.93	.36

reported violent crimes for each of the seven wards[2] in Washington, DC during 1989, the year immediately preceding that in which the study was conducted.[3] As indicated, the study school was located in a moderately violent ward (Ward 7) in comparison with other areas of the District; violence in Ward 7 was just below the median level of reported violence across all seven District wards. Thus, the results reported are not a consequence of sampling in an unusually violent community within the District, although community violence levels in Ward 7 were high by conventional (i.e., middle-class, suburban) standards.

Patterns of Community Violence Exposure

Parents' Reports

The parents' reports of the prevalence rates of children being victimized by and witnessing each form of community violence are presented in Table

---

[2]The wards represent multicensus-track geographical areas of the District with approximately equal population densities.

[3]Data were supplied by the District of Columbia Criminal Justice Plans and Analysis Unit, 1990.

Reported Violence In Washington, D.C.
1989

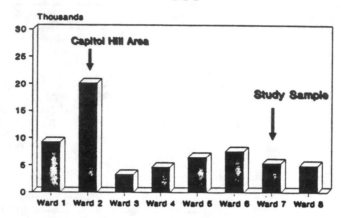

FIG. 14.4.   Reported violence in Washington, DC: Comparison of study Ward 7 with
other Wards in District. Data supplied by the Washington, DC Criminal Justice Plans
and Analysis Unit.

14.1; prevalence rates are reported separately for younger and older children.
For initial comparison purposes, all categories of violence exposure were
collapsed into two categories, representing direct victimization by violence
and witnessing violence to others. The resulting variables reflect the proportion of children who had been victimized by or had witnessed at least one
instance of violence in the community. Across all forms of violence, parents'
reports indicated that children were significantly more likely to report having
witnessed violence to someone else than to have been victimized themselves.
These significantly higher rates of witnessing than victimization held for
children in both the younger (84% vs. 21%, $p < .001$) and older (90% vs.
35%, $p < .001$) groups. As indicated in Table 14.1, however, there are more
ways to witness violence to others than to be victimized oneself (e.g., witnessing a dead body, witnessing a killing, witnessing someone carrying an
illegal weapon). Therefore, the data presented next examine differences
between the prevalence rates for victimization and witnessing across a standard set of violence categories: namely, those for which it is logically possible
to be victimized directly and to witness violence to someone else, including
shootings, stabbings, muggings, sexual assaults, threats of serious physical
harm, being approached about illegal drug use, being approached about drug
dealing, and forced entries. Therefore, the following data underestimate the
actual prevalence rates for witnessing violence.

Victimization Versus Witnessing.   Both younger and older children
were significantly more likely to have witnessed violence directed at

someone else than to have been victimized themselves. Whereas 19% of the younger children had been victimized by some form of violence in the restricted set of categories, 61% had witnessed violence to someone else, $X^2(1) = 30.41, p < .001$. This difference was accounted for by higher rates of witnessing stabbings (13% vs. 1%, $p < .01$), muggings (25% vs. 9%, $p = .01$), threats of physical harm (17% vs. 5%, $p = .02$), and illegal drug use (53% vs. 1%, $p < .001$). Similarly, whereas 32% of the older children had been victimized by some form of violence, 72% had witnessed violence to someone else ($p < .001$). This difference was accounted for among older children by a significantly higher rate of witnessing muggings (43% vs. 8%, $p < .001$) and illegal drug use (61% vs. 4%, $p < .001$).

Between-Age Differences. Across the restricted set of violence categories, older children were somewhat, although not significantly, more likely than younger children to be victimized by (32% vs. 19%, $X^2[1] = 2.34$, *ns*) and to witness (72% vs. 61%, $X^2[1] = 1.27$, *ns*) community violence. Nonetheless, individual comparisons reveal that older children were significantly more likely than younger children to have witnessed both muggings (43% vs. 25%, $X^2[1] = 4.80$, $p < .05$) and arrests (70% vs. 37%, $X^2[1] = 14.37$, $p < .001$).

Across all forms of violence, there was a nonsignificant tendency for parents to report a higher prevalence of victimization by violence among older compared with younger children (35% vs. 21%, $X^2[1] = 3.31$, $p = .07$). Thus, although older children suffered rates of victimization in particular violence categories that were sometimes double the rate for younger children, the absolute rates in each group were sufficiently low to fall well short of statistical significance.

Within-Family Violence. The parents' responses on the CTS (Straus, 1979) indicated that a significant number of the children's homes were characterized by relatively high levels of violence between adults. The proportions of families in which adults used each form of physical violence in the home during the previous year are shown in Fig. 14.5. As indicated, the prevalence rates for both minor and severe violence in the study sample were between 5 and 6 times the national average, based on population survey data collected in 1985 (Straus & Gelles, 1990).

Younger children were not probed about violence exposure within the family. Older children, however, were asked a single question about how often they had been victimized by and had witnessed slapping, hitting, and punching within the family. We compared these responses with a summary variable reflecting the highest level of family violence reported by parents. Across all families, the older children's reports of victimization and witnessing violence in the family were not significantly related to maternal

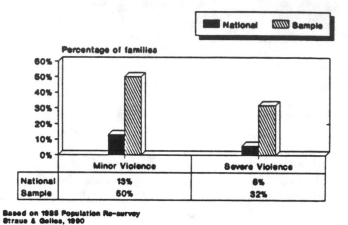

FIG. 14.5.   Prevalence rates of within-family violence reported by parents.

reports of family violence level. This lack of association is influenced strongly by two factors. First, a subset of parents ($n = 5$) reported that they never engaged in any of the conflict resolution strategies described in the CTS, including discussing issues calmly; their failure to endorse any resolution tactics may, therefore, reflect an unwillingness to disclose any information about conflict resolution within the family. Second, 51% of the children reported never having experienced or witnessed slapping, hitting, or punching within the family. For the subset of families in which the children reported any violence and the parents endorsed some method of conflict resolution, their agreement on the relative level of family violence was strong and significant, $r(14) = .67, p < .01$.

Teachers responded to two single-item questions concerning the violence level and stability of the children's homes. Across all families of younger children, teachers' reports of family violence and stability were not significantly related to parents' reports. For the subset of families in which parents endorsed some form of conflict resolution, however, agreement between teachers and parents was low but significant, $r(60) = .32, p = .01$.

Older Children's Reports

The prevalence rates for victimization and witnessing community violence based on the older children's reports are presented in Table 14.4 according to type of violence. Consistent with parents' reports, significantly more older children reported having witnessed violence to others than having

TABLE 14.4
Older Children's Reports of Community Violence Exposure

Community Violence Categories	Victim (%)	Witness (%)
Shootings	11	31
Stabbings	0	17
Muggings	22	43
Sexual assaults	6	3
Physical threats	47	22
Drug trade	9	67
Drug use	0	22
Arrests	11	74
Punch/hit*	—	44
Weapon*	—	58
Chased by gang	37	39
Forced entry	3	14
Dead bodies*	—	23
Woundings*	—	29
Murders*	—	9
Suicides*	—	3

* Denotes victimization question not asked and/or not logically possible.

been victimized themselves (97% vs. 59%, X2[1] = 14.45, $p < .01$). Moreover, among the subset of families for which both parent and child reports were available, significantly more older children reported having been victimized by some form of violence than was indicated by their parents' reports (69% vs. 44%, $X^2[1] = 4.59, p < .05$). Follow-up analyses, however, revealed that boys reported significantly higher rates of victimization than girls (88% vs. 25%, $X^2[1] = 14.44, p < .01$), accounting entirely for the higher rates of victimization reported by children compared with parents. In contrast, the prevalence of witnessing community violence based on the older children's reports was identical to the rate reported by their parents (75%). These prevalence estimates, however, were based on group-level comparisons of parents' and children's reports. Pairwise agreement between parents and their children is examined next.

Parent–Child Agreement About Exposure. Composite violence exposure variables were created separately for parents' and children's reports by summing across all reports of victimization by, and all reports of, witnessing community violence. Pairwise comparisons of parents' and children's reports based on these summary variables revealed gender-related differences in parent–child agreement about violence exposure. Moderately high agreement held between boys and their parents for both victimization ($r[18] = .39, p = 11$) and witnessing ($r[18] = .51, p < .03$) violence, although agreement reached significance only for witnessing violence, due to the small sample size. In contrast, agreement between girls and their parents was poor for both victimization ($r[17] = .16$, ns) and witnessing violence ($r = .08$, ns). Inspection of the bivariate scatterplots revealed that these gender differences in parent–child agreement are not attributable to gender-related range differences. Finally, children and parents were about equally likely to report having heard the sound of gunfire in their neighborhoods (74% vs. 61%). Pairwise agreement between parents and children about how often they had heard gunfire in their neighborhoods was moderately high and significant, $r(35) = .51$, $p < .01$. Again, agreement was substantially lower for girls ($r = .27$) than boys ($r = .47$), but neither of these separate estimates reached significance, due to sample size ($n = 24$).

Location of Violence Exposure.   For each instance of violence exposure, older children were asked whether the event took place in the home, near home, in school, or near school. According to children's reports, none of the victimization events took place in their homes, although 48% of the reported victimizations took place somewhere near their homes. In contrast, 22% of the victimizations, according to children's reports, took place in school, and the remaining 30% took place near school. Thus, the older children were slightly more likely to be victimized by violence in or near school (55%) than near their homes (48%), although the difference was small and nonsignificant.

The majority of violence witnessed by the older children took place near their homes (68%), with 22% of the incidents taking place in school. A relatively small proportion of the violence witnessed by the older children took place in their homes (7%) or in school (9%).

Involvement of Family and Friends.   Older children were asked, also, whether each instance of victimization and witnessing violence involved family members, friends, acquaintances, and/or strangers. According to the children's reports, a relatively small proportion of victimization events were perpetrated by family members (13%). The majority were committed by those familiar to the children (friends 50%, acquaintances 12%), whereas only 25% of the events were perpetrated by strangers. Similarly, the majority of violence witnessed by the children was committed by those familiar to them (family 21%, friends 25%, acquaintances 16%); in contrast, 38% of the violence witnessed was committed by strangers. Victims of violence witnessed by older children were distributed similarly. The majority of victims were known to the children (family 13%, friends 38%, acquaintances 16%), whereas 38% of the victims were strangers.

Frequency of Exposure.   Table 14.5 presents the distributions of exposure frequency for each category of violence according to the older children's reports. Consistent with the prevalence rates for exposure,

TABLE 14.5
Frequency of Victimization by and Witnessing Different Forms
of Community Violence

Violence Categories	Vic/Witn Never	One Time	Two Times	Three or Four Times	Five or Six Times	Seven or Eight Times	At Least Once a Month	At Least Once a Week	Almost Every Day
Shootings	89/70	8/8	/5	/8	3/3	/5			
Stabbings	100/84	/8	/5	/3					
Muggings	78/58	11/19	5/6	5/3		/6	/3	/3	/3
Sexual assaults	95/97	/3				5			
Physical threats	54/78	16/8	5/3	11/8		8			5
Drug use	92/35	5/8	/14	/5		/8	3/	/8	/22
Drug trade	100	/3	/3	/5		/3	/3		/5
Arrests*	−/28	−/17	−/8	−/8	/14	−/3	/3	/6	/14
Punch/hit*	−/57		−/16	−/8	/3	/3	/5		/3
Weapon*	−/43	−/19	−/14	−/11	/3	/5			/5
Chased by gang	64/62	6/19	6/11	14/5		/3	3/	6/	3/
Forced entry	97/91	/9	3/						
Dead bodies*	−/75		/14		/6	/3			/3
Woundings*	−/72	−/11	−/17						
Murders*		−/91	−/3		−/3	−/3			
Suicides*	/97	/3							

Note. All numbers represent proportions of children responding positively to each frequency. Numbers before each slash represent the proportions for victimization; numbers following the slash represent proportions for witnessing.

*Denotes victimization not asked and/or not logically possible.

witnessing violence to others was generally more common than direct victimization. For example, 22% of the older children reported witnessing illegal drug use almost every day, whereas being approached about drug use was a relatively uncommon event, occurring as often as once a month for only 3% of the children. Similarly, 15% of the children reported having witnessed a mugging or beating seven or eight times, whereas none reported having been victimized by a mugging or beating more than three or four times. These data are most useful in underscoring the fact that the prevalence rates reported earlier do not, for most categories of violence, reflect exposure to single, isolated events. Finally, composite variables reflecting the total frequency of both victimization and witnessing violence were significantly associated for boys ($r[18] = .52$, $p < .05$), but not for girls ($r[17] = .11$, *ns*).

Younger Children's Reports

The reports of first- and second-grade children about their violence exposure are more difficult to compare with their parents' reports than those of the older children; younger children were probed about exposure to only a limited set of violence categories, using an age-appropriate response format that differed substantially from the one used by their parents. Among the categories probed, six were directly comparable with parents' reports, including the witnessing of arrests, drug deals, muggings, shootings, and stabbings, and the encountering of dead bodies outside.

As indicated in Table 14.6, younger children were significantly more likely than their parents to report that they had witnessed six out of the seven types of violence. For more than half of these categories (shootings, muggings, stabbings, and serious accidents) the children were between 2 and 6 times more likely than their parents to report their having been witnesses to violence. These child-reported prevalence rates, particularly for witnessing muggings (45%), shootings (47%), stabbings (31%) and dead bodies (37%), seem unusually high for 6- and 7-year-old children. Most of these rates, however, did not differ significantly from the rates reported by their older fifth- and sixth-grade schoolmates (muggings 40%, shootings 31%, dead bodies 26%). The exception to this pattern was the number of younger children who reported having witnessed a stabbing (37% vs. 17% for the older children, $X^2[1] = 7.63, p < .01$).

Despite the sizable absolute discrepancies between parents' and younger children's reports of community violence exposure, their pairwise agreement concerning relative levels of exposure parallels the agreement patterns between older children and their parents. Separate summary variables were created for parents' and children's ratings of both victimization and witnessing by summing across all categories of violence. Agreement between boys and their parents, based on these summary indices, was moderate for both victimization ($r[26] = .38, p = .05$) and witnessing community violence ($r[26] = .42, p < .05$). In contrast, agreement between girls and their parents was poor for both victimization ($r[23] = .09, ns$) and witnessing ($r[23] = -.24, ns$).

TABLE 14.6
Prevalence Rates for Younger Children's Community Violence Exposure:
Comparison of Parent and Child Reports About Witnessing Violence

| | Prevalence Rates | | | |
| | Parents' | Children's | | |
Violence Categories	Reports	Reports	χ^2	p
Shootings	9%	47%	25.30	< .001
Stabbings	13%	31%	3.88	.05
Muggings	8%	45%	23.54	< .001
Arrests	57%	88%	17.40	< .001
Drug deals	53%	69%	3.54	.06
Dead body	16%	37%	7.63	< .001
Serious accidents	11%	74%	58.48	< .001

Mediators of Community Violence Exposure

Several demographic family characteristics were examined as possible mediators of risk for violence exposure, including respondent's education, income level, marital status, and living arrangements. Both younger and older children's reports of total violence exposure were significantly associated only with family living arrangements. For example, younger children who reported higher levels of victimization by violence in the community were more likely to live in houses rather than apartments ($r[62] = .29, p < .05$) and to have lived for a longer period of time in their current dwellings ($r[62] = 25, p = .05$). Similarly, younger children who reported higher levels of witnessing violence in the community were more likely to live in houses rather than apartments ($r[62] = .34, p < .01$). Those who lived in houses also had moved less often during the previous 5 years ($r[62] = -.26, p < .05$) and tended to have lived longer at their current addresses ($r[62] = .43, p < .01$).

The exposure context information provided by older children allowed for separate examinations of risk factors associated with violence involving those familiar to them versus those involving strangers. Results indicated a trend toward higher levels of exposure involving familiar persons among the children of less educated parents ($r[33] = .33, p = .06$); this trend did not hold for exposure to violence involving strangers ($r[33] = .03$, ns). Conversely, exposure to violence involving strangers was significantly higher among children living in houses compared with those living in apartments ($r[36] = .39, p < .05$); this association did not hold for exposure to violence involving those familiar to the children ($r[36] = -.03$, ns).

Distress Symptoms in Younger Children

First- and second-graders' responses to the cartoon-based symptom interview were reduced initially to four scales, representing depression (10 items, Chronbach's alpha $= .78$), anxiety/intrusive thoughts (14 items, Chronbach's alpha $= .84$), and sleep problems (7 items, Chronbach's alpha $= .71$). Girls reported significantly higher levels of depression ($t[75] = 1.66, p = .05$), anxiety/intrusive thoughts ($t[75] = 1.72, p < .05$), and sleep problems ($t[75] = 1.84, p < .05$) than boys. In contrast, boys reported slightly higher levels of impulsiveness than girls, although the difference was nonsignificant. Correlations among the scales (rs: .64–.85) were sufficiently high to justify combining them into a single index of children's distress symptoms.

The age-appropriate wording and response format of the young children's symptom interviews differed substantially from the symptom checklist completed by their parents, precluding direct comparisons of parents' and children's reports of absolute symptom levels. Parent–child agreement about the relative levels of children's symptoms was modest but significant across all children ($r[76] = .32, p < .01$). Although parent–child agreement was significant for boys ($r[38] = .41, p < .01$), it did not reach significance for girls ($r[38] = .19, ns$). This prompted us to examine differences between characteristics of the girls' and boys' families that might account for the absence of parent–daughter agreement. As expected, families of boys and girls did not differ significantly on any of the major demographic characteristics assessed. There was, however, a sizable and significant overall difference in the levels of severe within-family violence reported by parents of boys ($M = 1.63,$) and girls ($M = 4.92$), $t(70) = 2.43, p < .05$. Moreover, this difference was associated with a significantly wider range of within-family violence scores for families of boys (0–14) and girls (0–26). We, therefore, reexamined mother–daughter agreement about the daughters' distress symptoms within the more restricted range of the within-family severe violence scores defined by the boys' families. Parent–daughter agreement for this subset of families was moderate and significant ($r[31] = .34, p < .05$) and did not differ significantly from agreement between boys and their parents. Given the relatively small number of families at the highest end of the severe within-family violence range, it was not possible to explore alternative models to account for the absence of parent–daughter agreement in the most violent families.

Violence Exposure and Distress Symptoms.   The associations between child-reported violence exposure and both child- and parent-reported symptoms are presented in Table 14.7. As indicated, children's reports of their victimization by violence in the community were significantly related to their overall self-ratings of distress symptoms ($r[81] = .28, p < .01$), and significantly more strongly to their specific ratings of fear while in school ($r[81] = .50, p < .01$) and at home ($r[81] = .43, p < .01$).

Children's reports of witnessing violence in the community were also associated with higher self-ratings of overall distress ($r[81] = .30, p < .01$), but not to fear at school ($r[81] = .07, ns$) or at home ($r[81] = .09, ns$). Similarly, children's ratings of how often they had seen guns or drugs in their homes were significantly associated with overall distress ($r[81] = 30, p < .01$), fear while at school ($r[81] = .36, p < .01$), and fear at home ($r[81] = .25, p < .01$). The relative contributions of the three forms of violence exposure to a composite index (a sum of the z scores for each measure) of children's distress symptoms were examined using a forward stepwise regression model. After controlling for the contribution of child-reported victimization to the prediction of children's distress symptoms ($r = .54, F[1, 77] = 31.09, p < .001, adj\ r^2 = .28$), neither of the other exposure variables entered the equation. Similar results were obtained when other predictors were entered into the equation first: The remaining variables and their

TABLE 14.7
Symptom Correlates of Children's Violence Exposure

	Children's Symptoms			
Categories	Mother CBCL (n = 36)	Mother-Rated Distress (n = 35)	Child-Rated Distress (n = 37)	Child-Rated CDI (n = 37)
Older Children's Violence Exposure[a]				
Community violence victimization[b]	.13/.09	.06/.05	.37*/.08	.42**/.01
Community violence witnessed[c]	.03/ − .20	.01/ − .22	.39*/ − .05	.35*/.01
Home violence witnessed[d]	.04	.11	.33*	.24

	Mother CBCL (n = 77)	Mother-Rated Distress (n = 76)	Child-Rated Distress (n = 84)	Child-Rated Fear at School (n = 82)	Child-rated Fear at Home (n = 81)
Younger Children's Violence Exposure					
Community violence victimization[b]	.10	.12	.28**	.50**	.43**
Community violence witnessed[c]	− .04	− .02	.30**	.07	.09
Witnessed guns/drugs in home[e]	.13	.13	.30**	.36**	.25*

*p < .05.
**p < .01.
[a]Correlations based on violence involving family, friends, and acquaintances appear before the slash; those based on violence involving strangers appear after the slash.
[b]Frequency of exposure across all forms of victimization.
[c]Frequency of exposure across all forms of witnessing.
[d]Frequency of witnessing slapping, hitting, and/or punching in the home.
[e]Sum of frequency of witnessing guns and/or drugs in the home.

interactions failed to make a significant incremental contribution to variance in children's distress symptoms beyond the variance accounted for by the initial exposure variable. None of the children's reports of exposure to violence were related significantly to parent-completed CBCL ratings.

To isolate the violence exposure variables most associated with high levels of distress symptoms, we compared children with the highest levels of self-reported distress (above the 75th percentile) with the remaining children on each of the child-reported violence exposure variables. Children experiencing the highest levels of distress were more likely to report having been threatened with a knife ($t[82] = 2.59$, $p = .01$), having witnessed someone being stabbed ($t[82] = 2.30$, $p < .01$), drugs in the home ($t[82] = 2.60$, $p < .01$), and guns in the home ($t[82] = 2.38$, $p < .01$).

Mediators of Exposure–Distress.   In a series of exploratory analyses, we tested for demographic mediators of the link between children's violence exposure and distress symptoms. Most demographic factors were unrelated to the exposure–distress association. There was one exception: The exposure–distress link was significantly stronger for children of parents who had not graduated high school ($r[15] = .65$, $p < .01$) than for children of parents who had graduated high school ($r[60] = .37$, $p < .01$).[4] Although there was also a trend for girls to come from homes with less educated parents ($X^2(1) = 2.80$, $p = .09$), their reports of violence exposure were no more likely to be associated with distress symptoms than those of boys ($r[38] = .39$ vs. $r[37] = .44$, respectively, $ps < .01$). Nor was it the case that the children of less educated parents were more likely to misunderstand the questions and/or to rate all of their responses indiscriminately high. The absolute levels of violence exposure and distress symptoms they reported did not differ significantly from the reports of children with better educated parents ($ts[73] = .51$ and $.57$, respectively). Although the association between violence exposure and distress symptoms was not significantly mediated by other demographic factors we examined, it is nonetheless worth noting that families with less educated parents were also characterized by higher levels of unemployment ($t[62] = 5.14$, $p < .001$) and use of public assistance ($t[59] = 4.10$, $p < .001$), and trends toward higher levels of mother absence ($t[63] = 1.46$, $p = .07$) and father absence ($t[63] = 1.31$, $p = .12$). Due to distributional and sample-size restrictions, however, it was impossible to determine the extent to which these variables, alone or in combination, contributed to the exposure–distress association in younger children.

Distress Symptoms in Older Children

Fifth- and sixth-graders' ratings of their distress symptoms on the CCDS were combined initially into two correlated scales of moderately high reliability: depression (alpha $= .71$) and anxiety (alpha $= .72$, $r[37] = .64$, $p < .001$). Identical analyses were conducted on the parent-report version of the CCDS, again yielding correlated scales for depression (alpha $= .75$) and anxiety (alpha $= .70$, $r[51] = .80$, $p < .001$). Analyses of variance revealed no significant differences between boys' and girls' depression and anxiety levels according to either parents' or children's own reports. As indicated in Table 14.8, overall children reported significantly higher levels of depression ($t[34] = 3.42$, $p < .01$) and anxiety ($t[34], = 3.79$, $p < .01$) symptoms than their parents reported about them. In light of the relatively

---

[4]Two bivariate outliers with extremely high exposure scores and extremely low distress scores were excluded from these analyses.

TABLE 14.8
Older Children's Distress Symptoms: Comparison of Parents' and Children's Reports

Distress Symptom	Parents' Ratings (n = 35)		Children's Ratings (n = 35)		t	p
	Mean	(SD)	Mean	(SD		
Trouble paying attention	2.75	(.96)	2.41	(.95)	1.53	ns
Daydreaming in class	2.38	(.95)	2.24	(.80)	.57	ns
Don't feel like doing fun things	2.05	(1.1)	2.36	(.96)	.26	ns
Don't care about anything	1.73	(.80)	2.16	(1.09)	2.21	< .05
Worry about safety	2.03	(1.18)	3.28	(.82)	4.88	< .001
Intrusive thoughts about upsetting events	1.78	(.90)	2.67	(.92)	3.96	< .001
Hard time getting/staying asleep	1.57	(.96)	2.43	(1.07)	3.22	< .01
Jumpy when hearing loud noises	1.88	(.98)	2.41	(.93)	2.18	< .05
Bad dreams/nightmares	1.70	*.85)	1.86	(.82)	.75	ns
Avoids upsetting situations	1.56	(.93)	2.50	(1.1)	4.07	< .001
Difficult time avoiding fear	1.61	(.90)	2.27	(.91)	3.22	< .01
Feel lonely	1.61	(.96)	2.22	(1.10)	2.25	< .05
Feel nervous, scared, upset	1.81	(.87)	2.32	(.74)	2.79	< .01
Easily bothered/upset	1.81	(.81)	2.24	(.86)	2.05	.05
Afraid might not live long	1.08	(.50)	1.75	(1.05)	3.28	< .01
Afraid might not have happy life	1.27	(.65)	1.67	(.97)	2.12	.05
Trouble remembering frightening events	1.35	(.59)	2.03	(.92)	4.21	< .001
Summary Scales						
Depression	1.66	(.48)	2.07	(.47)	3.42	< .01
Anxiety	1.88	(.46)	2.29	(.37)	3.79	< .01

high correlations between depression and anxiety for both children's and parents' reports, these scales were combined for each informant, yielding separate indices of children's distress based on parent and child reports.

For descriptive purposes, parent–child comparisons for individual distress symptoms are also presented in Table 14.7. As indicated, children reported significantly higher levels of distress than their parents reported about them in response to 22 (72%) of the 28 symptoms probed. These comparisons do not, however, adequately convey the extent to which parents underestimated the distress symptoms of their older children. For example, 49% of the parents reported that their children never worried about being safe, whereas none of their children said they never worried $X^2[1] = 48.57$, $p < .001$); only 16% of the parents reported that their children worried about being safe a lot of the time, compared with 50% of their children ($X^2[1] = 18.63$, $p < .001$). Similarly, 53% of the parents reported that their children were never bothered by intrusive thoughts about upsetting events, compared with only 8% of their children ($X^2[1] = 33.95$, $p < .001$); and 22% of the children reported being bothered by such intrusive thoughts, whereas none of their parents reported this ($X^2[1] = 16.96$, $p < .001$). Parents also significantly underestimated the extent to which their older children had problems either getting or staying asleep at night. Whereas only 27% of the parents reported that their children ever suffered from sleeping problems, 70% of their children reported sleeping problems at least some of the time ($X^2[1] = 25.31$, $p < .001$).

Parent–Child Agreement.   Consistent with our earlier report showing poor parent–daughter agreement about violence exposure (Richters & Martinez, 1993), agreement between parents and daughters about the daughters' distress symptoms was low and nonsignificant ($r[17] = .06$). In contrast, agreement between parents and their sons was moderately high and negative ($r[18] = -.56$, $p < .01$, not attributable to outliers). Boys who rated themselves *low* in distress, despite being rated *high* by their parents reported community violence exposure levels quite similar to the levels reported by other boys ($t[16] = .59$, *ns*), suggesting that they did not have a general tendency to withhold or underreport information. Moreover, although parents' CBCL-based anxiety ratings were strongly related to their ratings of their sons' anxiety on the CCDS distress questionnaire ($r(18) = .63$, $p < .01$), their association with mother-rated antisocial behavior was low and nonsignificant ($r[21] = .22$, *ns*). Thus, antisocial behavior was not a significant correlate of mother-rated anxiety in the boys. Nevertheless, boys who rated themselves *low* in distress, despite being rated as *high* in distress by their parents, were significantly more likely to have been rated by their parents as boastful and/or bragging on the CBCL (Item 7) than boys who agreed with their parents about high distress ($t[9] = 4.43$, $p = .001$). They were also rated as significantly more boastful/bragging than all other boys combined ($t[17] = 2.79$, $p < .01$). The partial correlation between parents' and sons' ratings of the sons' distress levels (when their bragging/ boasting scores were controlled for) was reduced to a nonsignificant, but still negative, level ($r[15] = -.34$, *ns*).

Violence Exposure and Distress Symptoms.   As indicated in Table 14.7, older children's reports of victimization and witnessing violence in the community involving persons known to them (family, friends, acquaintances) were significantly related to their self-reports of distress and depression (*r*s: .35–.42, *p*s $< .05$). The combined score reflecting victimization and witnessing violence in the community involving those familiar to the children was more strongly associated with self-reported distress symptoms ($r[37] = .48$, $p < .01$). Children's reports of victimization and witnessing violence involving strangers were not, however, related to their self-reports of distress or depression. Also, children's reports of violence (slapping, hitting, punching) within the home were significantly correlated with their reports of distress symptoms ($r[37] = .33, p < .05$).

The contributions of community and within-family violence exposure to the older children's reports of distress symptoms were examined using hierarchical multiple regression models. Results indicated that the significant community violence exposure correlates shared overlapping variance with distress symptoms. Once any of these variables was entered into the regression model as a predictor of distress symptoms, none of the remaining variables contributed significantly to the equation.

Exploratory analyses revealed that the association between violence exposure and distress symptoms based on children's reports was mediated by maternal education, such that exposure was more strongly predictive of distress symptoms in children of parents with little or no education ($r[10] = .64, p < .05$) than in children of parents who had graduated high school ($r[25] = .29, ns$). Thus, these results parallel the findings already reported for younger children.

To isolate the violence exposure variables most associated with high levels of distress symptoms, we compared children with the highest levels of self-reported distress (75th percentile and above) with those below the 75th percentile on each of the violence exposure variables. Children in the high-distress group were more likely than other children to have witnessed drug deals ($t[35] = 2.49, p < .01$); people being arrested ($t[34] = 2.02, p < .05$); someone being slapped, punched, or hit by a family member ($t[35] = 3.29, p < .01$); and someone carrying an illegal weapon ($t[35] = 2.17, p < .05$).

DISCUSSION

Violence Exposure

The data presented clearly indicate that, according to independent reports from children and their parents, both older and younger children in this sample were exposed to relatively high levels of violence in their homes and neighborhoods. Although a disturbing number of children had been direct victims of violence, they were 2 to 4 times more likely to witness violence to others and/or violence-related scenes involving others. Thus, although public health statistics concerning children (and adults) typically focus on direct victimization by violence (Christoffel, 1990), it is clear that witnessing violence by children also deserves attention as a public health issue. Much remains to be learned about the psychological consequences of exposure to violence in the community. There can be little question, however, that merely being in the presence of violence places children in harm's way.

Although we found impressive test–retest reliability for reports of violence exposure among a random subsample of the younger children, the study did not offer an opportunity to examine the test–retest reliability of reports from either parents or older children. Nonetheless, our confidence in the ability and willingness of children and parents to provide useful estimates of violence exposure is buttressed by their group-level agreement, their moderate and significant levels of pairwise agreement, and the details of violence exposure they often volunteered during face-to-face interviews. Moreover, the significant associations between summary exposure ratings based on parents' and their younger children's reports indicate that children as young as age 6 can provide useful information about violence exposure.

The poor pairwise agreement between parents and their daughters in both the younger and older samples raises questions about who provided the more accurate reports. Among older children, we are inclined to place more credence in the children's reports for two related reasons. First, the children were asked to report about violence that they themselves had experienced. Parents, on the other hand, were dependent for their knowledge of most types of children's violence exposure on what their children had reported to them. Therefore, it is not surprising that discrepancies between parent and child reports of violence exposure were almost always in the direction of children reporting more than their parents. To an unknown extent, this may have been due to children simply not reporting violence exposure to their parents. In some cases, reporting to parents may result in restrictions in children's activities and/or unwanted monitoring and supervision. In other cases, the violence exposure may not be sufficiently salient to the children to warrant reporting to parents. Relatively common events, such as drug deals in the neighborhood, may lose their signal value and, therefore, not be reported to others.

Parent–child discrepancies in reporting may also be due, to an unknown extent, to parents repressing information about their children's violence exposure as an active or passive coping strategy. We have seen anecdotal evidence of this process in follow-up interviews with selected families and in videotaped interactions between the parents and their children, in which some parents actively discouraged their children from talking about violence they had witnessed. Regardless of its origin, however, the fact that parents so consistently underestimated their children's violence exposure is significant for several reasons. Obviously, lack of parental awareness may place parents at a disadvantage in their efforts to monitor and effectively supervise their children's activities, and this disadvantage may decrease their effectiveness in protecting their children from subsequent violence exposure. Furthermore, the possibility that children may not be reporting more common forms of violence to their parents suggests that it may be beginning to lose its emotional impact for them. If true, this may have a range of important implications, not the least of which is the risk that desensitization may translate into a diminished ability to recognize and therefore avoid objectively dangerous situations and activities.

It is commonly believed that the likelihood of community violence exposure increases significantly when children begin attending school. Parents' reports of their children's violence exposure in this sample tend to confirm this expectation: Their ratings indicate a trend toward higher levels of exposure for older compared with younger children. The reports of younger children, however, suggest that a significant number of them had already witnessed high levels of violence by the time they entered first grade, significantly higher than indicated by their parents' reports. Moreover, those children with higher levels of violence exposure also reported significantly higher levels of distress symptoms.

Nonetheless, the absolute levels of exposure reported by the younger children were sufficiently high to raise questions about the veracity of their reports. Unfortunately, there is no absolute criterion against which to gauge the integrity of their reports. It is possible, of course, that the anonymity of responding in small groups may have engendered exaggerated response sets that would have been less likely in individual interviews. Also, younger children may have failed to discriminate sufficiently between violence that they had actually witnessed and violence that they had only heard about. We deliberately avoided requiring children to offer details of their exposure so as not to bias them against reporting violence they were uncomfortable talking about. In future research, it would be useful to probe for details of reported violence after all instances of exposure have been reported; such a procedure would allow researchers to explore the veracity of reports without risking such bias. In any event, whether one relies more on the reports of parents or on those of their children, the present data suggest that efforts to study the cumulative effects of violence exposure on children need to begin at very early ages.

As indicated earlier, we deliberately selected the study school because, according to DC police data on reported violent crimes, it is located in a moderately violent neighborhood, but we have no basis for estimating the extent to which the patterns of exposure reported here are representative of other schools in the District of Columbia, let alone in other cities around the country. It is worth noting, however, that a comparison of reported violent crimes in this neighborhood with reported violent crimes in other major U.S. cities during the year preceding the study indicated that violence in the study neighborhood was near the median for other major cities.

We are somewhat more confident about the representativeness of participating families in this study to the population of families with children attending the same grades in the study school. According to teachers' reports of family stability and violence, as well as their ratings of children's adjustment, there were no significant differences between the observed characteristics of the participating compared to the nonparticipating families and children. This is a very limited set of potentially biasing characteristics, however, and warrants expansion and scrutiny in future research.

Although the primary focus of this study was on children's exposure to community violence, parents reported disturbingly high levels of violence between adults within their homes. Prevalence rates of both minor and severe violence were between 5 and 6 times the national average. These data underscore the importance of supplementing measures of community violence exposure with assessments of within-family violence. They also underscore the fact that a significant number of children in violent neighborhoods are raised in a subculture of violence beginning at home. Being raised in a violent home within a violent neighborhood places children at an extraordinary disadvantage for normal development. This underscores the need to study the long-term consequences of chronic violence exposure on children's personality development. The high prevalence rates for within-family violence in this sample also have important implications for intervention programs designed to protect children from violence exposure and its consequences, because many such programs rely on working with parents who are not the perpetrators of violence.

The violence exposure survey instruments developed for this study yield only crude assays of the stimulus-rich violence to which the children had been exposed. They are a useful and necessary starting point for assessing violence exposure, but significant gains in our understanding of the consequences of exposure will require assessment strategies and instruments with a much higher degree of fidelity to violence phenomena and contexts than survey instruments afford. There are many types of shootings. They can result in wounds of many different types, body locations, and levels of severity; they can be witnessed at close proximity or at a distance; they can take place in contexts otherwise thought of as safe or dangerous; and they can involve persons with different relationships to and with a child. All forms of violence can vary along these and other important dimensions. Thus, there is probably little basis for the simplifying assumption that witnessing a shooting will be more severe in its effects on a child than witnessing someone being chased or threatened. Moving beyond such assumptions, however, will require the development of a taxonomy of violence exposure sensitive to a range of contextual factors. The importance and complexity of this task is already evident in the domain of child maltreatment, where issues of definition are receiving considerable attention (Cicchetti, 1991).

The limitations of sample size in this study, coupled with the limited breadth and depth of our assessments, precluded more than a cursory exploration of child and family factors associated with higher and lower levels of exposure to violence. To be sure, some differences in exposure are probably attributable to differences in the actual violence levels that characterize the children's neighborhoods, but it seems equally clear from our exposure interviews that children living on the same neighborhood blocks were often exposed to impressively different levels of violence. Thus, one of the most important goals for future research in this area should be the identification of personal as well as family and community factors associated with higher and lower levels of children's violence exposure.

Exposure-Related Distress

The data presented also indicate that violence exposure was associated with distress symptoms in both older and younger children. For children in both groups, victimization by violence in the community and witnessing violence or violence-related themes in both the community and at home were reliably related to greater levels of distress symptoms. Although the majority of violence experienced by the children took place outside their homes, reports from the older children indicate that the majority of those events involved persons familiar to the children, including family members, friends, and acquaintances. Moreover, older children's reports of distress symptoms and depression were significantly associated only with violence involving persons known to them. It was also the case that younger children with the highest levels of self-reported distress symptoms were significantly more likely than other children to report having seen guns and drugs in their homes. Thus, we know from the present data that reports of victimization by and witnessing violence in the community, as well as witnessing themes of violence in the home, are already associated with classic distress symptoms in very young children. Parents from the most violent homes were significantly less likely to agree with their children about their children's distress symptoms. To the extent that this reflects a genuine lack of parental awareness of the children's symptoms, it may place their children at an additional disadvantage for coping.

An equally striking finding was the extent to which parents underestimated levels of distress their children were experiencing. Certainly, the fact that parents tend to underestimate their children's feelings and emotions is a well-replicated finding in the child psychopathology literature (Achenbach, McConaughy, & Howell, 1987; Herjanic & Reich, 1982; Kashani, Orvaschel, Burk, & Reid, 1985), albeit one with largely unknown implications for children's social-emotional development, but this phenomenon may take on even added significance when the children's symptoms are associated with objectively dangerous experiences. Children whose parents are unaware of their distress symptoms may be at heightened risk for developing maladaptive coping responses and for overgeneralizing initially adaptive distress reactions to situations and contexts in which those responses are maladaptive. Parents who are unaware of their children's distress may miss important opportunities to offer counsel, to help their children cope with violence they have already experienced, and to develop strategies for avoiding violent situations in the future.

These parent–child discrepancies also underscore the need for researchers to interview children directly to assess their reactions to violent events. In this study, children as young as age 6 were able and quite willing to discuss their feelings and concerns about violence and distress when given the opportunity, yielding information that was unavailable from their parents' reports. In the case of older children, there was evidence that boys rated by their parents as highly anxious tended to deny those symptoms, and this denial was significantly associated with higher scores on bragging and boasting. This pattern, which was not present in the younger boys, may signal for a subset of boys a developmental shift toward bravado and the denial of anxieties and fears that are nonetheless recognized by their parents. The conditions under which this process develops and its implications for development, particularly among children living in dangerous environments, deserve careful attention in future longitudinal designs. Moreover, the fact that violence exposure was more strongly related to distress symptoms in both younger and older children from households with less educated parents suggests that these children may be at particularly high risk for developing maladaptive responses to violence exposure. Collectively, these data highlight the need for intervention programs in high-risk neighborhoods that can employ methods for helping children to talk about their distress and for helping parents to recognize and deal with symptoms of distress in their children.

In light of the cross-sectional nature of this study, it is impossible to examine the extent to which children's reported symptoms preceded and perhaps even gave rise to, rather than followed, their exposure to violence. One can easily imagine children who, for a variety of reasons associated with maladjustment, find themselves in situations in which they are exposed to higher than average rates of violence. For these children, it may be maladjustment that gives rise to violence exposure. It is also possible that some children, for reasons other than violence exposure, are suffering from symptoms of distress, and for that reason have a heightened sensitivity to actual as well as misperceived violence in their environments. Each of these possibilities deserves careful attention in subsequent research, and can be most easily studied using short-term longitudinal designs.

Beyond Distress

Finally, our focus in this report on children's distress symptoms associated with violence exposure should not obscure the fact that we know very little about either the immediate or long-term implications of these symptoms. To be sure, some symptoms can be seen as normal reactions to abnormal events. Certain types of fear, anxiety, intrusive thoughts, and even depression can serve adaptive functions in an objectively dangerous environment, particularly when they signal heightened vigilance and healthy emotional reactions to loss and pain, but just as clearly, they can signal maladaptive reactions with long-term negative consequences for normal social, emotional, and cognitive development. This can even happen when initially adaptive responses become entrenched, resistant to change, and overgeneralized to situations in which they are maladaptive. In the present study, parents' ratings of children's behavior problems were not significantly associated with either parent- or child-reported violence exposure. Given the pattern of disparities between parent and child reports, however, this should not be interpreted as evidence that distress symptoms are unrelated to children's behavior problems. An important task for future research will be to develop assessment strategies for discriminating more effectively between adaptive and maladaptive reactions to violence, and for detecting maladaptive response patterns before they become pathological. Obviously, the pursuit of these issues will also require sensitive strategies for combining data from multiple informants to assess children's distress symptoms and role functioning impairments.

Beyond distress symptoms per se, much remains to be learned about the impact of chronic violence exposure on children's ability to experience and modulate arousal; their images of themselves; their beliefs in a just and benevolent world; their beliefs about the likelihood of surviving into adulthood; their willingness to form and maintain affective relationships with parents, siblings, and peers who may not survive the violence; the value they place on human life; their sense of morality; and a range of other topics central to normal, adaptive development.

ACKNOWLEDGMENTS

This chapter was originally published as two companion papers in the February, 1993 special issue of *Psychiatry: Biological and Interpersonal Processes* devoted to research concerning children living in violent American communities (Martinez & Richters, 1993; Richters & Martinez, 1993). This research was supported by the National Institute of Mental Health and by a grant from the Early Childhood Transitions Network of the John D. and Catherine T. MacArthur Foundation. We thank Robert Emde, Marian Radke-Yarrow, and Peter Jensen for their encouragement and support throughout each phase of this research. We also thank Dante Cicchetti and Frank Putnam for their contributions to the early development of this project. Finally, we thank the principal, teachers, staff, and families of the Southeast Washington, DC elementary school (anonymous on request) in which this study was conducted.

REFERENCES

American Psychiatric Association (1987). *Diagnostic and statistical manual of mental disorders* (3rd ed., rev.). Washington, DC: Author.

Achenbach, T. M., & Edelbrock, C. S. (1983). *Manual for the Child Behavior Checklist and Revised Behavior Profile.* Burlington, VT: University of Vermont, Department of Psychiatry.

Achenbach, T. M., McConaughy, S., & Howell, C. T. (1987). Child/adolescent behavioral and emotional problems: Implications of cross-informant correlations for situational specificity. *Psychological Bulletin, 101,* 213–222.

Bodman, F. (1941). War conditions and the mental health of the child. *British Medical Journal, 2,* 486–488.

Brown, G. W., Harris, T. O., & Bifulco, A. (1986). Long-term effects of early loss of a parent. In M. Rutter, C. E. Izard, & P. B. Read (Eds.), *Depression in young people: Developmental and clinical perspectives* (pp. 251–296). New York: Guilford.

Burke, J. D., Borus, J. F., Burns, B. J., Milstein, K. H., & Beasley, M. C. (1982). Changes in children's behavior after a natural disaster. *American Journal of Psychiatry, 139,* 1010–1014.

Centers for Disease Control. (1988). *Premature mortality due to homicides: U.S., 1968–1985.* Washington, DC: Author.

Centers for Disease Control. (1990). *Homicide among young Black males: U.S., 1978–1987.* Washington, DC: Author.

Christoffel, K. K. (1990). Violent death and injury in US children and adolescents. *American Journal of Disease Control, 144,* 697–706.

Christoffel, K. K., & Christoffel, T. (1986). Handguns as a pediatric problem. *Pediatric Emergency Care, 2,* 75–81.

Cicchetti, D. (Ed.). (1991). Defining psychological maltreatment [Special issue]. *Development and Psychopathology, 3,* 1–124.

Cicchetti, D., & Rizley, R. (1981). Developmental perspectives on the etiology, intergenerational transmission and sequelae of child maltreatment. In R. Rizley & D. Cicchetti (Eds.), *New directions of child development* (pp. 31–56). San Francisco: Jossey-Bass.

Compas, B. (1987). Stress and life events during childhood and adolescence. *Clinical Psychology Review, 7,* 275–302.

Earls, et al. (1991, April). *Position paper: Panel on prevention of violence and violent injuries, solicited by the Division of Injury Control, Centers for Disease Control.* Paper presented at the Third Annual National Injury Control Conference, Atlanta, GA.

Emery, R. E. (1982). Interparental conflict and the children of discord and divorce. *Psychological Bulletin, 92,* 310–330.

Escobar, G. (1991, January 21). Washington area's 703 homicides in 1990 set a record. *The Washington Post,* p. 1.

Fingerhut, L. A., & Kleinman, J. C. (1990). International and interstate comparisons of homicide among young males. *Journal of the American Medical Association, 263,* 3292–3295.

Freud, A., & Burlingham, D. T. (1943). *Children and war.* London: Medical War Books.

Galante, R., & Foa, D. (1986). An epidemiological study of psychic trauma and treatment effectiveness for children after a natural disaster. *Journal of the American Academy of Child Psychiatry, 25,* 357–363.

Garmezy, N., & Rutter, M. (1985). Acute reactions to stress. In M. Rutter & L. Hersov (Eds.), *Child and adolescent psychiatry: Modern approaches* (2nd ed., pp. 152–176). Oxford: Blackwell Scientific Publications.

Gleser, G. C., Green, B. L., & Winget, C. (1981). *Prolonged psychosocial effects of disaster: A study of Buffalo Creek.* New York: Academic Press.

Glover, E. (1942). Notes on the psychological effects of war conditions on the civilian population: Part III. The blitz. *International Journal of Psychoanalysis, 29,* 17–37.

Handford, H. A., Mayes, S. D., Mattison, R. E., Humphrey, F. J., Bagnato, S., Bixler, E. O., & Kales, J. D. (1986). Child and parent reactions to the Three Mile Island nuclear accident. *Journal of the American Academy of Child Psychiatry, 25,* 346–356.

Herjanic, B., & Reich, W. (1982). Development of a structured psychiatric interview for children: Agreement between child and parent on individual symptoms. *Journal of Abnormal Child Psychology, 10,* 307–324.

John, E. M. (1941). A study of the effects of evacuation and air raids on children of pre-school age. *British Journal of Educational Psychology, 11,* 173–182.

Kashani, J. H., Orvaschel, H., Burk, J. P., & Reid, J. C. (1985). Informant variance: The issue of parent–child agreement. *Journal of the American Academy of Child Psychiatry, 24,* 437–441.

Kinzie, J. D., Sack, W. H., Angell, R. H., Manson, S., & Rath, B. (1986). The psychiatric effects of massive trauma on Cambodian children: I. The children. *Journal of the American Academy of Child Psychiatry, 25,* 370–376.

Kovaks, M. (1985). The Children's Depression Inventory. *Psychopharmacology Bulletin, 21,* 995–998.

Kristal, L. (1975). Bruxism: An anxiety response to environmental stress. In C. D. Spielberger & I. G. Sarason (Eds.), Stress and anxiety (Vol. 5, pp. 45–59). New York: Halsted.

Lacy, G. N. (1972). Observations on Aberfan. *Journal of Psychosomatic Research, 16,* 257–260.

Lebovici, S. (1974). Observations on children who have witnessed the violent death of one of their parents: A contribution to the study of traumatization. *International Review of Psychoanalysis, 1,* 117–123.

Lyons, H. A. (1973, Winter). The psychological effects of the civil disturbance on children. *Northern Teacher,* pp. 35–38.

Lyons, H. A. (1979). Civil violence: The psychological aspects. *Journal of Psychosomatic Research, 23,* 373–393.

Malmquist, C. P. (1986). Children who witness parental murder: Post-traumatic and legal issues. *Journal of the American Academy of Child Psychiatry, 25,* 320–325.

Martinez, P. E., & Richters, J. E. (1993). The NIMH Community Violence Project: II. Children's distress symptoms associated with violence exposure. *Psychiatry: Interpersonal and Biological Processes, 56,* 22–35.

McAuley, R., & Troy, M. (1983). The impact of urban conflict and violence on children referred to a child psychiatry clinic. In J. Harbison (Ed), *Children of the troubles* (pp. 33–43). Belfast, Northern Ireland: Stranmillis College.

McWhirter, L. (1982, November 4). Yoked by violence together: Stress and coping in children in Northern Ireland. *Community Care,* pp. 14–17.

McWhirter, L. (1983). Growing up in Northern Ireland: From "aggression" to the "troubles." In A. P. Goldstein & M. H. Segall (Eds.), *Aggression in global perspective* (pp. 367–400). New York: Pergamon Press.

McWhirter, L., & Trew, K. (1981). Children in Northern Ireland: A lost generation? In E. J. Anthony & C. Chiland (Eds.), *The child in his family: Children in turmoil. Vol. 7: Tomorrow's children* (pp. 69–82), New York: Wiley.

Milgram, N. A. (1982). War-related stress in Israeli children and youth. In L. Goldberger & S. Breznitz (Eds.), *Handbook of stress: Theoretical and clinical aspects* (pp. 656–676). New York: The Free Press.

Milgram, R. M., & Milgram, N. A. (1976). The effect of the Yom Kippur War on anxiety level in Israeli children. *Journal of Psychology, 94,* 107–113.

Public Health Service. (1990). Healthy People 2000: National health promotion and disease prevention objectives. Washington, DC: U. S. Department of Health and Human Services.

Pynoos, R. S., Frederick, C., Nader, K., Arroyo, W., Steinberg, A., Eth, S., Nunez, F., & Fairbanks, L. (1987). Life threat and posttraumatic stress in school-age children. *Archives of General Psychiatry, 44,* 1057–1063.

Richters, J. E., & Martinez, P. (1990a). *Checklist of Child Distress Symptoms: Parent report.* Rockville, MD: National Institute of Mental Health.

Richters, J. E., & Martinez, P. (1990b). *Things I Have Seen and Heard: A structured interview for assessing young children's violence exposure.* Rockville, MD: National Institute of Mental Health.

Richters, J. E., & Martinez, P. E. (1993). The NIMH Community Violence Project: I. Children as victims of and witnesses to violence. *Psychiatry, 56,* 7–21.

Richters, J. E., Martinez, P., & Valla, J. P. (1990). *Levonn: A cartoon-based structured interview for assessing young children's distress symptoms.* Rockville, MD: National Institute of Mental Health.

Richters, J. E., & Saltzman, W. (1990). *Survey of Children's Exposure to Community Violence: Parent report.* Rockville, MD: National Institute of Mental Health.

Rosenblatt, R. (1983). *Children of war.* New York: Anchor Press/Doubleday.

Sack, W. H., Angell, R. H., Kinzie, J. D., & Rath, B. (1986). The psychiatric effects of massive trauma on Cambodian children: II. The family, the home, and the school. *Journal of the American Academy of Child Psychiatry, 25,* 377–383.

Sanchez, C. (1989, March 21). Four youngsters wounded in NE schoolyard shooting. *The Washington Post,* p. 1.

Sanchez, R., & Horwitz, S. (1989, January 27). Four wounded in gunfire at Wilson High. *The Washington Post,* p. 1.

Sattler, J. M. (1970). Racial "experimenter effects" in experimentation, testing, interviewing, and psychotherapy. *Psychological Bulletin, 73,* 137–160.

Silber, E., Perry, S., & Bloch, D. (1958). Patterns of parent–child interaction in a disaster. *Psychiatry, 21,* 159–167.

Straus, M. A. (1979). Measuring intrafamily conflict and violence: The Conflict Tactics (CT) Scales. *Journal of Marriage and the Family, 41,* 75–88.

Straus, M. A., & Gelles, R. J. (1990). *Physical violence in American families: Risk factors and adaptations to violence in 8,145 families.* New Brunswick, NJ: Transaction Publishers.

Terr, L. C. (1979). Children of Chowchilla: A study of psychic trauma. *Psychoanalytic Study of the Child, 34,* 552–623.

Terr, L. C. (1981). Forbidden games: Post-traumatic child's play. *Journal of the American Academy of Child Psychiatry. 20,* 741–760.

Terr, L. C. (1983). Chowchilla revisited: The effects of psychic trauma four years after a school-bus kidnapping. *American Journal of Psychiatry, 140,* 1543–1550.

Tuckman, A. J. (1973). Disaster and mental health intervention. *Community Mental Health Journal, 9,* 151–157.

Valla, J. P. (1989). *Dominique: A cartoon interview for assessing young children's psychiatric symptoms.* Montreal: University of Montreal Press.

Watt, N. F., Anthony, E. J., Wynne, L. C., & Rolf, J. E. (Eds.). (1984). *Children at risk for schizophrenia: A longitudinal perspective.* New York: Cambridge University Press.

Werthamer-Larsson, L., Kellam, S. K., Dolan, L., Brown, C. H., & Wheeler, L. (1990). *The epidemiology of maladaptive behavior in first grade children.* Baltimore: Johns Hopkins University School of Public Health.

Ziv, A., & Israel, R. (1973). Effects of bombardment on the manifest anxiety level of children living in the kibbutzim. *Journal of Consulting and Clinical Psychology, 40,* 287–291.

IV PERSPECTIVES ON INTERVENTION

15 Children and Inner-City Violence: Strategies for Intervention

Steven Marans
Donald J. Cohen
Yale University, School of Medicine

The riots in Los Angeles in May 1992 brought a dramatic and explosive version of urban violence into the homes of all Americans, just as the riots in Watts did two decades earlier. However, many families that live in inner cities do not need to turn on their television sets to experience the threat of violence. They hear the sound of nightly gunfire, or witness shootings, stabbings, and fistfights in their homes and streets; both the assailants and the victims are their relatives and neighbors.

Community violence in the United States was not born in the late 20th century. However, the gangs no longer fight with fists, knives, and chains, but with semiautomatic and automatic weapons. The stakes are no longer determined by neighborhood pride, turf, and ethnic issues alone, but are driven by competitive market forces of a lucrative drug trade. Gone are the days of zip guns and "Saturday night specials"; they have been replaced by high-tech, 14-shot handguns that can be rented by the hour. The despair of unemployment, multigenerational poverty, and family dissolution contribute to a sense of helplessness and rage; for many urban youth, a measure of relief can be found in the power of fast money and the violent resolution of disputes. The combatants are not the only victims of violence. While ambulances rush the physical casualties to emergency rooms, the psychological victims—the children and their parents—are left to sleep on floors at night and to curtail activities during the day, hoping that these attempts to remain physically safe will help the threatening images, sounds, and thoughts of violence fade away. These images and fears do not fade, however, and the children, in particular, pay a high price for their forced attempts to adapt. Whole communities become captive observers and experience violence secondhand, always in fear about who the next intended or unintended casualty will be. The reality and specter of violence add potentially overwhelming force to the feelings of impotence, fear, and rage in the face of substandard housing, inadequate education, and the absence of jobs.

CHILD WITNESSES OF VIOLENCE

For children, the experience of acute, isolated, personal episodes of violence is often superimposed on chronic exposure to violence. Specific incidents of violence may lead to a range of emotional reactions, including the circumscribed symptoms of Posttraumatic Stress Disorder (PTSD): disrupted patterns of eating, sleeping, attention and relating, fearfulness, flashbacks, and the like. Repeated exposure to violence may also lead to a variety of persistent patterns of psychological maladaptation. Children may withdraw, turn inward, and appear depressed; they may display difficulties with attention, school achievement, and social engagement; or, they may assume the role of the oppositional, aggressive perpetrator, organizing their sense of self around the active involvement in just that type of experience that was initially so threatening.

The degree of a child's disturbance or traumatization is determined by an interplay of factors within the child and in his or her surroundings:

- Characteristics of the violence itself (e.g., the child's relationship to the perpetrator and to the victim, the proximity to the incident, the response of caregivers).
- The developmental phase of the child who is exposed (i.e., the status of the child's emotional and cognitive resources for mediating the anxiety associated with objective and fantasized dangers).
- The familial and community context of the violent incident (i.e., is the incident isolated and unusual or part of a chronic pattern of experience of daily life?).
- Recognition of and sustained responses to the possible effects of the child's exposure to violence by family members, school personnel, and community institutions.

All of these factors must be considered in developing strategies that may have an impact on the outcome of exposure to and perpetuation of violent behavior.

Children who witness violence do so in the context of developmentally shifting modes of expressing their own aggressive impulses and feelings. Aggressivity plays a central role in development as a means of achieving a sense of power and competence; it is also a source of conflict between love and hate. Over the course of development, the more direct enactments of the toddler's hitting, biting, and kicking shift to the preschooler's fantasies and play of destructive power, to the competition on the school-age child's sports field, to the vicissitudes of affection and anger that are a part of adolescent and adult relationships (Marans, Dahl, Marans, & Cohen, in press; Freud, 1972). However, this capacity to move from enactment to more sublimated expressions of aggressivity is undermined when the basic preconditions for feeling competent — including physical safety, stable relationships, and success in achieving desired goals — are overwhelmed by poverty, family dysfunction, overstimulation, and threatened or actual physical danger.

Feeling unsafe, helpless, and small runs counter to the developing child's desire and capacity to be in greater control of the self and to achieve increasing mastery of his or her environment. In addition to developing specific symptoms, a child may resort to turning passivity into action to regain the experience of power and control when the dangers of real violence provoke feelings of helplessness and fear. That is, rather than feeling the anxiety and humiliation of being the victim or feeling vulnerable to the aggression of others, the child may become the active perpetrator. Oppositional behavior at home and at school may be a transient means for the child to reassert his or her power at precisely the time when he or she is feeling most vulnerable. However, when the child is exposed to the dangers of violence on a regular basis, identification with the exciting and powerful role of perpetrator may become a chronic hedge against feeling helpless and afraid. When the most powerful models in the home and neighborhood exercise their potency at the end of a fist or gun, aggressive enactments, rather than sublimation, may be an adaptive response to both internal and external sources of danger.

A COLLABORATIVE RESPONSE TO URBAN VIOLENCE

Although New Haven is a small city (with a population of 140,000) and is the home of a major university, it is the seventh poorest city in the United States and is rated as the fifth highest in reported incidents of violent crime (New Haven Department of Police Services [NHDPS], 1992). The impact of violence has been experienced forcefully in New Haven, where the marked rise in homicides is one of the clearest social indicators of violence of inner city life. During 1991, there were 35 deaths by gunshot, 490 aggravated assaults, 100 rapes, 1,370 robberies, and 1,400 police dispatches to the call of "shots fired" (NHDPS, 1992). New Haven is relatively well endowed with mental health services for children and families, and approximately 1,200 minority, inner city children and families were seen in community mental health clinics during 1991. At lease one third of the inner city children receiving care in our outpatient clinic have witnessed or been involved in aggression and its consequences. (P. Armbruster, personal communication, 1992), yet the number of children who receive psychological care represents a fraction of the most vulnerable in the population who are exposed to violence. For example, in a survey conducted in 1992 of 6th-, 8th- and 10th-grade children in New Haven, at least 40% reported being witness to at least one violent crime during the previous year (R. Weissberg & M. Schwab-Stone, personal communication, 1992). By their teenage years, only a small minority of inner city children are free of direct exposure to violence—at home, on the street, or in school. The majority reported being afraid almost everywhere outside of home and many are fearful at home, as well. Studies published in the *Journal of the American Medical Association* reported high incidences of violence, and the characteristics of children and adolescents involved in violence, often with handguns (Callahan & Rivera, 1992; Fingerhunt, Ingram, & Feldman, 1992a, 1992b). In addition, other studies have reported alarming rates of children being directly exposed to episodes of violence (Garbarino, Dubrow, Kostelny, & Pardo, 1992; Taylor, Zuckerman, Harik, & Groves, 1992).

The social institutions in the inner city that are involved with children and families—the schools, social welfare and child- guidance agencies, churches, and police—) tend to focus on similar problems and, often, on the same individuals. Since the 1970s, clinicians in the Child Study Center have developed models for intervention, representing the application of concepts of child psychoanalysis and child development, that are based in schools and child-serving agencies. Through these programs, principles for collaboration among professionals and families have been developed and demonstrated to be useful in changing the atmosphere and functioning of child-serving institutions, such as the school and child welfare agencies (Adnopoz, Grigsby, & Nagler, 1991; Comer & Haynes, 1990; Comer et al., 1991; Goldstein, Freud, & Solnit, 1973, 1979; Goldstein, Freud, Solnit, & Goldstein, 1986). It is only quite recently that we have begun to understand and focus on the central role of the police in the lives of children and in the functioning of communities.

The police are the major representatives of societal authority in the inner city. With their uniforms, guns, and cars, they present an image of power and control, and they are the most visible governmental response to specific incidents of violence. Police officers have daily encounters with children and families in crisis (those involved in family violence, witnessing crimes, or suffering as victims of aggression), and they are increasingly confronted by very young children who are the perpetrators or victims of aggression.

At their best, police can provide children and families a sense of security and safety through rapid, authoritative, and effective responses at times of difficulty. All too often, however, children's contacts with police officers arouse far less comforting and more negative feelings. In the psychological lives of inner city children, the appearance of police officers in the context of aggression makes them objects for displacement of children's and families' rage; their arrival "after the fact" strengthens children's view of society as unprotective, and the role of police as symbols of the dominant culture may shape children's views of them as representatives of an alien, uncaring outside world. In fact, the contacts between police and children are sometimes harsh, and police officers, especially in the midst of a crisis, may not have time to be considerate of children's emotional needs. Negative encounters may further reinforce children's view of society as uncaring and aggressive. Thus, these experiences may strengthen a child's concept that hostile behavior—being rough and tough, bullying, and acting strong—is not only appropriate and reasonable in certain situations, but is the normative mode of adult functioning. There are too few countervailing models of social authority available in an inner city child's world.

The Child Study Center Program on Child Development and Community Policing is a collaborative effort aimed at facilitating the response of mental health professionals and police to the burdens violence puts on children, families, and the broader community. Through the application of the principles learned in work with schools and agencies, the program attempts to change the atmosphere of police departments in relation to children and to increase the competence of police officers in their varied interactions with children and families. Fundamentally, the program attempts to reorient police officers in their interactions with children to optimize the psychological roles that they can play as providers of a sense of security, positive authority, and models for identification.

As with other models for social change within institutions, such as schools, the Program on Child Development and Policing is based on the full engagement and philosophical agreement regarding goals and methods of the leadership of the New Haven police and the faculty of the Child Study Center. The program has three major components: the training of all incoming police recruits in principles of child and adolescent development, clinical fellowships for veteran officers who have field supervisory roles, and a 24-hour consultation service for officers responding to calls in which children are either the direct victims or witnesses of violence.

COMMUNITY-BASED POLICING

The Program on Child Development and Policing is closely related to and dependent on the reorientation of the New Haven Police Department, reflecting the philosophy of community-based policing. Community-based policing is an alternative to militaristic and highly hierarchical models of policing, which emphasize the response of police to crimes, the pursuit of criminals, and the making of arrests as primary missions. In this model, police officers are dispatched at times of crisis to neighborhoods where they are not known and with whom they have no relationship. In contrast, the concept of community policing emphasizes the major role of police in strengthening neighborhood social structures that deter crime and facilitate social functioning, in early detection of high-risk situations likely to lead to criminal activity, and in interrupting patterns of criminality at their roots. For community- based policing, the pursuit of criminals is seen within this broader context of prevention and early intervention in high-risk situations.

Major strategies of community policing include basing officers within neighborhoods, promoting decentralized functioning by police officers, empowering officers to deal creatively in solving problems, and encouraging regular and close collaboration between officers and community members, social service agencies, and institutions within the community. When it functions optimally, community-based policing integrates police officers into their communities: They become known as individuals, rather than by their role, and they know the people they serve as individuals.

The concepts and methods of community-based policing are still evolving, and each city must find and test its own best approaches. The chief and assistant chief of police in New Haven, Nicholas Pastore and Dean Esserman, have been at the forefront of national efforts to define and evaluate such approaches, with a particular focus on families, the roles of racism, and the impact of inner city violence.

Community policing brings police officers into regular, ongoing contact with children and families in a given neighborhood. This new approach requires a new type of police officer with special training.

CHILD DEVELOPMENT AND COMMUNITY POLICING

The Child Study Center and the New Haven Department of Police Services Program's collaborative model consists of several interrelated educational and clinical components that work toward sharing knowledge between police officers and clinicians.

Education of Police Rookies

In the past, the modal police recruit was 19 to 22 years old, had had some experience in the military or with a security organization, and had a high school or some college education. Increasingly, police officers being recruited in New Haven are somewhat older, are from inner city and minority backgrounds, and have a broader range of educational and professional experiences. However, there is no requirement that a recruit have any prior education in criminal justice. Academic preparation for police work is provided during 3 months of police academy training, where basic skills are acquired, and then in the field, where recruits receive supervised field training. The education of police officers in most cities (and, until recently, in New Haven) does not specifically and prospectively prepare them for much of the work in which they will be engaged, especially with the demands of community-based policing (i.e., dealing with the psychological impact of family violence, engaging with children and youth in situations of high risk, helping divert possible offenders, collaborating in neighborhood improvement, and assisting those who have been the victims of crime). The seminar for rookie police created by police officers and the faculty of the Child Study Center aims to provide young police officers with both knowledge and a sense of personal empowerment to think about and intervene positively with children and families.

A basic concept of the Program on Child Development and Community Policing is that rookies should be introduced to a mental health orientation while they are beginning to form a sense of their new professional identities. Thus, they attend a seminar that meets weekly during the first 10 weeks of field training. Exposure to child development principles early in their careers introduces young police officers to the importance of thinking about children's development and their own influence on children while they are, for the first time, encountering children and families in their daily work. Also, the course provides officers with the experience of working alongside mental health professionals and with concepts and methods for working cooperatively with other social services on behalf of children.

The major theme of the seminar is how police officers' direct experiences, enriched by knowledge from psychodynamic theory, can lead to useful understanding of the phenomenology of children's development in the inner city: the phases of child development, and how these are shaped by different types of experiences within the family and community; the structure and function of family life; the social structures that influence children's senses of themselves, their families, and social groups; sources of security for children and youth; the types of dangers, trauma, and stress children experience; varying patterns of coping; and how to communicate with and understand young children at different times, including when they are witnesses to and victims of violence and other trauma. In contrast with standard didactic courses, the seminar on children and families is interactive: The instructors try to use active discussion of individual cases and specific scenarios from the streets as starting points for teaching about general principles. In addition, videotapes of children and films about children (such as "John" by James and Joyce Robertson and "Boyz 'n' the Hood") make the theoretical concepts vivid and relevant to police work.

In addition to the involvement of the co-leaders, who are supervisory officers with 20 years of policing experience each, class discussions are enhanced by the participation of younger officers who have been on the job for at least 5 years. Also, the seminar groups are limited to 15 members to permit active discussion of the emotionally charged ideas and an increasingly rich sharing of personal experiences. During the first academic year of the program, 100 officers completed the course in child and adolescent development.

The knowledge gained in this program improves the effectiveness, positive impact, and safety of police officers interacting with young people in New Haven. It also enhances officers' self-image of serving positive roles within the community.

Child Development Fellowships

Community-based policing requires sergeants who direct substations to be committed to the philosophy of neighborhood policing and to be prepared to translate the concepts into actual practice. These sergeants supervise all the work of the substations, set the tone of police work within the community, and serve as models for younger officers. Especially during the transition to community-based policing, sergeants are faced with challenges in trying to implement goals in relation to prevention; early intervention; work with vulnerable children, youth and families; and collaboration with other agencies. The Child Development Fellowship Program of the Child Study Center aims to provide supervisory officers with special expertise in relation to these tasks.

Child Development Fellows are police sergeants who spend 4–6 hours per week for 3 months in the Child Study Center. With the guidance of a mentor from the clinical faculty, police fellows participate in a range of activities, similar to those of residents in psychiatry, that familiarize them with developmental concepts, patterns of psychological disturbance, methods of clinical intervention, and settings for treatment and care. Their program includes participation in the evaluations of inner city children with emotional and psychiatric problems; visits with a consultation team to community schools to learn about child–school issues and the functioning of Comer School Development Program; meetings with the Family Support Service Program to discuss families in crisis because of AIDS, cocaine, or family violence; participation in clinical discussions of children and adolescents who are brought to the Emergency Service or are psychiatric inpatients because of suicide, aggression, or serious accidents; and attendance at seminars and other teaching activities at the Child Study Center. A major goal of the fellowship is to establish relationships between the fellows and the child mental health professionals with whom they will be collaborating over the years. An important benefit of the fellowship is the knowledge that officers bring to the other mental health professionals within the Center.

Case Conference

Police officers, educators, and faculty of the Center (child psychiatrists, psychologists, social workers, pediatricians, and lawyers) meet weekly to discuss difficult and perplexing cases that arise from the officers' direct experience and from the Consultation Service (described further on). Cases are discussed by officers and clinicians from many different points of view: in relation to the specific problem of the child and the family, the reasons for their interaction with the police, the types of services they have used or might currently require, barriers to intervention, and specific problems posed to the police officers and other agencies involved. The case discussions emphasize the importance of trying to understand the inner experience and the meaning of events to children and adolescents; how psychological understanding can guide police and clinical work more effectively; the feelings aroused in the professionals by the children, families, or situations; and how the feelings of the professionals might interfere with or be used to inform intervention. Because the case conference often touches on sensitive issues, the format requires a progressively increasing sense of trust and collaboration among its participants. Through the case conference, the sergeants who have been Child Development Fellows are provided with a continuation and elaboration of their involvement with the clinical faculty of the Center.

The methodology for such case conferences that the Child Study Center has developed as part of "continuing education" includes collaboration with different disciplines. For example, one case conference has been functioning since the mid-1960s; it brings together mental health professionals and pediatricians for discussion of emotional issues that arise during the course of pediatric care. We anticipate that the case conferences for discussion of issues that arise in community-based policing will continue, as well, for many years, with a changing set of concerns that will reflect both the development of new collaborative relationships and the problems faced by police officers.

Consultation Service

When an officer comes into contact with a child or youth in great danger or distress, or becomes responsible for his or her disposition, that officer must make an immediate decision about whether to intervene and what action is in the child's best interest. At times, the path of intervention is clearly mandated, as when a child is believed to be the victim of abuse and the state child welfare agency must be notified. At other times, the critical nature of a medical condition (following an assault or a suicide attempt) dictates the involvement of emergency medical services. Quite often, however, officers are faced with more ambiguous situations or situations where there is no clearly mandated or available service. An officer who finds a child who has witnessed an accident or assault, who has a teenager confide in him or her about being worried about gang membership, or who observes a child becoming truant is offered clinical opportunities for intervention that are broader than those usually considered to be within the province of police work. It is within the officer's discretion as to how to proceed. As police officers work more closely with communities, these situations occur with greater frequency. Where might an officer turn for discussion, guidance, and an immediate clinical response? This is especially critical when the officer is faced with a child who is in great distress, as happens so often in relation to inner city violence.

The Consultation Service of the Program on Child Development and Community Policing (CS/CP) allows the police to make referrals and to have clinicians respond to police officers' immediate needs for guidance, especially following children's traumatic experiences. At the CS/CP, Child Study Center clinicians carry beepers and are on call 24 hours a day to discuss children and youth with police officers. At times, the consultation leads to a disposition to an available clinical program (e.g., the use of the child psychiatric emergency service, referral to the state child protection agency, an appointment at the Child Study Center or other child guidance services within the community, or engagement with the mental health teams within the child's school). At other times, a direct clinical response is needed, because of the urgency of the child's distress. At such times, CS/CP clinicians can respond immediately and see the child and youth at the Center, in the police station, or at their homes.

The first calls to the CS/CP involving children exposed to some form of violence were made by officers who had participated in the child development seminar, by officers who worked in neighborhoods supervised by the clinical fellows, or by the sergeants themselves. These incidents included:

- A 5-year-old girl was caught in the crossfire of a gang shooting and was struck by a .45 caliber bullet that lodged in her lower right mandible. She and her family were seen by a psychotherapist from the moment she entered the hospital and after she was discharged.
- A 12-year-old girl ran away from home when her mother and her mother's boyfriend began fighting at home. When she was 5 years

old, a similar situation had developed between her parents, which ended with the mother shooting the father after he repeatedly beat her. The girl and the mother were referred for psychotherapy, for the first time, by neighborhood police officers. When the mother was able to end her relationship with the abusive boyfriend, the police remained in close contact with the family and assisted the boyfriend in moving out of the home. The girl was able to return home.

- A 13-year-old girl was arrested and charged with murdering her newborn infant. The girl and her mother were referred for evaluation and treatment by the investigating police officers.
- A 16-year-old gang member was referred by the police after suffering a full-blown panic attack while being arraigned for the shooting death of a close friend. Despite his having spent 2 years in a correctional facility, this was the first time the boy had been evaluated by mental health professionals.

CHILDREN AS VICTIMS OF VIOLENCE: COLLABORATIVE INTERVENTION

Through the collaboration between police officers and mental health professionals, the Program on Child Development and Community Police has led to innovative methods for clinical intervention for children who have been victims of violence. Their cases reveal the depth of trauma to which inner city children are exposed, and the ways in which professionals can complement each other in trying to respond effectively.

Case 1: A Boy Shoots Himself

Sgt. Brown, a detective sergeant on the evening shift, called the on-call Child Study Center Consultant Service clinician to report that a 15-year-old boy had shot himself in the head after a fight with his mother. The boy, John Simmons, had been taken to the emergency room of the local hospital and was accompanied by his mother, his 17-year-old sister, and his 12-year-old brother. Sgt. Brown reported that the boy was not expected to live, and that he was concerned about the other two children, especially the sister, Carol, who had a history of psychiatric hospitalizations for attempted suicide. The on-call clinician spoke with the attending physician in the emergency room, who described the boy's status (he had been taken into the operating room) and reported that the mother had remained at the hospital, and the brother and sister had been taken home by a police officer. Given the sister's history, the clinician was concerned about the risk for another suicide attempt and phoned Sgt. Brown to suggest that an officer go to the family's home to determine whether the two children were adequately supervised.

The clinician and Sgt. Brown had never met, and the sergeant volunteered that he knew little about the collaborative Consultation Service other than that a memo suggested that this was the type of situation in which the Child Study Center should be notified. He added that he would pass on the suggestion of a police visit to the Simmons' home to the next shift, which would come on in 2 hours. The clinician was uneasy about this time frame, but was not in a position to press his concerns with an unfamiliar officer. The clinician contacted Sgt. Stone, a clinical fellow, who agreed that more immediate contact with the family was indicated. The clinician volunteered to go to the Simmons' home immediately, to determine whether there was adequate adult supervision of the children, and to assess their status. At 11:30 p.m., Sgt. Stone phoned the clinician to report that the 12-year-old was asleep and the 17-year-old was stable; she was concerned about her younger brother's condition, but did not exhibit any impulses to harm herself. However, by the time Sgt. Stone arrived, Ms. Simmons had returned home and had been drinking heavily, and was insisting that she would shoot herself with a gun that remained in the home. In consultation with the on-call clinician, Sgt. Stone arranged for a relative to come to the Simmons' home while he took Ms. Simmons to the emergency room for a psychiatric evaluation.

John Simmons survived and was sent to a local rehabilitative hospital following his recovery from surgery. Ms. Simmons was released from the psychiatric emergency room a day after the shooting, and the family was referred to the mental health center nearest their home. Despite Carol's previous brief hospitalizations, this was the first time that all the family members were seen by mental health professionals. Two weeks after the shooting, the on-call clinician contacted the therapists who became involved with the Simmons family at the local mental health center. What emerged was that each of the family members had experienced disruptions in sleeping and eating and were very eager to talk about the difficulties and anxieties that predated and followed the shooting incident. The family expressed surprise that the police had been so concerned about them. Their previous contact with the police had been around the arrests of Mr. Simmons, who was now serving time for armed robbery, and of a 19-year-old son, who had been involved in a gang-related shooting 2 years earlier.

Case 2: A Family is Witness to a Murder

Martin and Isabel Rodriguez lived in a public housing project in New Haven with their 2½- and 10-year-old sons, Manuel and George. Both Mr. and Ms.

Rodriguez were unemployed and lived on the Aid the Families of Dependent Children (AFDC) payments they received from the state.

On a Saturday morning, Martin's brother, Julio, raced into the apartment and claimed that four men with guns were chasing him. Ms. Rodriguez called the police and waited for them to arrive as the men attempted to batter down the apartment door. Julio tried to secure the door by leaning against it and pleaded with the men to let him come outside and talk, because there were children inside. As Ms. Rodriguez phoned the police again, Julio was shot through the door; he fell into the living room, bleeding profusely from a bullet wound to the chest. The shooter then battered the door down and walked around the apartment pointing his gun at everyone, including the children, who now stood over the body of their uncle. After ripping the phone off the wall, the assailant backed out of the room with his gun trained on Ms. Rodriguez. The police and an ambulance arrived moments later. The shooter and his three accomplices were arrested; Julio died en route to the hospital.

On the day of the shooting two New Haven police sergeants involved in the investigation referred the Rodriguez family to the Consultation Service. Both officers were part of the Child Study Center training program. Although the family initially declined immediate contact with a clinician, they were eager to have the officers' beeper numbers, and in the following days made frequent calls describing fears of further shootings, as well as multiple symptoms that both the children and the adults were experiencing. The officers were in daily contact with the psychiatric social worker assigned to the case, who advised them about gently pressing the idea of meeting with her. Six days after the shooting, Mr. Rodriguez left home, saying that he was unable to remain in the apartment where his brother had been killed. At this point, Ms. Rodriguez accepted the referral for services from the Child Study Center.

Because of transportation problems, the family was initially seen in their home. Ms. Rodriguez and her two sons were having difficulty falling asleep at night and were waking frequently during the night. Two-year-old Manuel was very clingy with his mother, demanding to be held and carried; he searched the apartment for his father and asked frequently where his father was. Ms. Rodriguez described Manuel as having previously been an active and independent child. She reported some success in soothing him by giving him a bottle, from which he had previously been weaned. Ten- year-old George was having nightmares, waking frequently, and checking that doors and windows were locked, and insisted on sleeping in his mother's bed. George also reported that he was nervous and scared all the time, that he couldn't stop thinking about the shooting, that he worried that the shooter would come back, and that he was afraid to be outside alone; this meant that he could not walk the few blocks to his aunt's house. Ms. Rodriguez reported sleeplessness, nervousness, and jitteriness; preoccupation with thoughts about the shooting; and worries that she and her children were not safe. During the interview, she was unable to sit still and was frequently tearful. Ms. Rodriguez had seen her primary physician, who had given her a prescription for a mild sedative to be taken at bedtime, but she had been afraid to take the medication lest it make her sleep so deeply that she would not be able to rouse herself in case of another emergency.

The family was seen on four occasions in their home. Most of the meetings took place with all three family members present, because there was little private space in the apartment. During some of the meetings, Manuel was either sleeping or was willing to play by himself in another room. It was apparent that Ms. Rodriguez and George had talked a lot about the incident and neither seemed surprised by anything the other said, although they did disagree about some details of the event.

The first meeting focused primarily on a description of the traumatic events and the witnesses' reactions. Both Ms. Rodriguez and George were quite eager to describe what had happened and to show the clinician where all the participants had been and the damage that remained in the apartment. According to Ms. Rodriguez' account, the most prominent details concerned her own helplessness and the helplessness of those around her. She repeatedly told of having been on the telephone trying to get help when the shot came through the door, and also focused on Julio's ineffective plea to the shooter not to come into the apartment, where there were children. Ms. Rodriguez also reported feeling afraid in her apartment but unable to go anywhere else. George's account of the shooting focused more on the gruesomeness of the scene. He was preoccupied with the images of blood on the floor, of blood on his own clothing, and of having been touched by Julio as he fell into the living room. George pointed out what was left of the blood stain on the rug and described feeling afraid to walk on the rug, especially on or near the stain. George was also preoccupied with concrete issues of physical security in the apartment (e.g., whether the spackle patching the bullet hole in the door might fall out). During the first meeting, the clinician responded by agreeing that the events described had really been horrible and overwhelming, and explained that the reactions the family described were expected reactions to a traumatic experience. The clinician discussed with Ms. Rodriguez the boys' experience of losing their father at the same time as witnessing the shooting and urged her to make some arrangement for them to have contact with their father.

In subsequent meetings in the home, Ms. Rodriguez was agitated, but more angry, than she had been initially. Her anger was directed at the landlord, who had not made needed repairs in the apartment and threatened to charge her for the cost of repairing the battered door, and at Mr. Rodriguez, who had not called her on Christmas, had not arranged to see

Manuel, and had chosen to stay with his father rather than her. She was also reexamining his actions during the shooting, and felt enraged that he had not provided any protection or assistance to her or the children, but had hidden himself in the bedroom.

During the later home visits George talked about his vengeful fantasies about what should happen to the shooter, his continuing fears about his own safety, his wish to live in an apartment with a security system, and his fantasies about dangerous and magical properties of the blood stained rug (e.g., its ability to make a battery-powered toy operate without batteries). The clinician encouraged both George and Ms. Rodriguez to differentiate their fantasies of danger and magic from what they knew was real, and recommended that Ms. Rodriguez come to the outpatient clinic with her children so that they could obtain longer term help in coping with this crisis than could be provided in their home.

In the course of this initial evaluation period, George was friendly, verbal, and engaging as he described his sleep difficulties; his anxious, intrusive thoughts about his safety; and his restricted activities following the shooting. He was pleased to be offered the chance for further discussions that might make him feel better; he had already felt some relief from his talks with the evaluating clinician. Although it appeared that George was very attached to his mother and sought comfort from her when he was scared, he was also burdened by her obvious distress and made frequent efforts to comfort her, especially when she cried.

Ms. Rodriguez was extremely anxious and sought constant contact and reassurance from the police and the clinician regarding her family's safety and emotional and physical needs. In spite of the on-call availability of both, Ms. Rodriquez was overwhelmed. She saw herself as passive, dependent, and helpless. She was unable to make realistic efforts to secure new housing for her family, and was unwilling to take prescribed medication that would help to diminish her level of immobilizing anxiety. Reassuring her about the safety of the medication, the clinician capitalized on Ms. Rodriquez' genuine concerns about her children and their need for her optimal stability to help them with the distressing events. In addition, the combined efforts of the clinician and community police officer involved in the case eventually guided Ms. Rodriquez to the appropriate public housing authorities for discussions about a possible change of neighborhoods.

During the clinician's initial contact with the Rodriquez family, it became apparent that George's acute, posttraumatic symptoms were predated by longstanding social and academic difficulties that had never been evaluated or treated. Although 2-year-old Manuel was able to give up the bottle once again and return to his previous good level of functioning on his father's return home, more extensive treatment for George and his mother was indicated. Both were referred to the outpatient clinic of the Child Study Center for individual and family psychotherapy. Transportation was arranged by the CP/CS clinician and the community-based police officer, who later engaged George in an after-school program sponsored by the police. As the posttraumatic stress symptoms abated for both George and Ms. Rodriquez, the emphasis of the clinical work shifted from the crisis that followed the shooting to longstanding difficulties with self-esteem, mutual dependence, and constriction of more age-appropriate autonomous functioning.

Case 3: A Father Kills Himself in His Son's Presence

Mark Jones was a 14-year-old boy who was spending the weekend with his father when, from a back room, he heard his father arguing with his girlfriend. Mr. Jones and Mark's mother had been divorced for 10 years; Mark lived at home with his mother and stepfather, and visited his father once a month. He had heard fighting on previous visits, and often worried about his father's drinking problem and frequent swings of depressive withdrawal, gregariousness, and volatile rage.

On this particular Friday evening, Mark tried to block the noise of the argument by turning up the volume on the television. When the shouting stopped, Mark was relieved until he heard the sound of the slide being pulled back on his father's automatic handgun. He prepared himself for what he thought would be the sound of the gun being fired into the wall. What he heard instead was his father saying goodbye to his girlfriend before shooting himself dead. Mark emerged from his room to see his father lying in a pool of blood on the living room floor. Mark phoned the police, screaming that his father had been hurt, and then began throwing objects around the room.

When police arrived on the scene, Mark was tearful and subdued. His mother and stepfather had been called, and were on their way to the father's house. The supervising sergeant phoned the CP/CS clinician on call who advised that the mother, Ms. Johnson, be informed that he would be available to meet with the family at their request. Both Mark and his parents asked to see the clinician immediately, and within an hour of the shooting they were seen in a quiet, private office in the police headquarters.

Accompanied by his mother and stepfather, Mark stared into the middle distance and, with tears in his eyes, slowly described what he had seen and heard. He stopped his story abruptly just before telling about the sound of the gunfire and looked around the room at his parents and then intently at the clinician, unable to go on. The clinician then asked if he would prefer speaking without his parents present. Mark nodded and, after the other adults left, he continued to talk about his wish that he had intervened when he heard the fighting. He sobbed as he acknowledged that he felt he was to blame for his father's death, but quickly composed himself. Again staring into space, Mark recounted his father's long history of difficulties with alcohol, drugs, and violence.

Mark repeated that he should have "done something to stop him" and said, "I wonder if he's all right." He then described feeling numb, as if in a dream that he wished would end soon. The clinician suggested that perhaps Mark knew for a long time that he was unable to control what his father did to himself, but that, especially now, when he felt so awful and overwhelmed, he wished that he could have been in control or only dreaming, or that he could believe that his father was not really dead but only wounded. Mark nodded and spoke of his hatred for his father's girlfriend, now blaming her for his death. "They always fought and she always started the fights . . . and he wasn't supposed to drink. What was she doing buying him alcohol?" His thoughts shifted rapidly as he described getting into trouble at school, including an incident in which he had stolen a hunting knife from his father and slashed a teacher's tires. Mark added, "Maybe that's why this happened . . . because I was bad . . . like this is my punishment." The clinician pointed out that perhaps the hardest person to be angry with right now was his father. Mark again stared out the window and, in a flat tone of voice, said that he always worried that his father might kill himself and that he alternated between getting into fights with other people and feeling miserable and depressed. "The scariest thing was with his guns. Sometimes when he got real upset, he would go and shoot at things in the basement. That's what I hoped he would do when I heard him loading his gun . . . but he didn't." With a deep sigh, Mark said that he didn't want to talk anymore, that he was tired and wanted to go home.

In a brief meeting, Mr. and Ms. Johnson said that Mark had been having troubles in school over the past year and was seeing the school social worker once a week. Ms. Johnson had little contact with her ex-husband, but expressed her guilt about allowing Mark to spend time with him over the years. She said that she knew how disturbed he was but did not want to deprive Mark of contact with him when Mark continued to want to continue the relationship. She blamed herself for what she concluded would be an indelible trauma for their son. The clinician pointed out that this issue of blame, and the wish that some aspects of the events could, somehow, have been controlled were similar to one ones with which Mark was currently, and would continue to be, struggling. In response to the parents' pleas for ways to help their son through this awful event, the clinician suggested that they recognize that Mark's responses would be varied and complicated, that they would need to follow his lead in how and when he wanted to discuss his thoughts and feelings with them. In addition, the parents requested that the clinician speak with the school social worker and make a referral for additional therapy services.

Meeting briefly with Mark and his parents, the clinician repeated what he had told the parents, and added that they could contact him at any time. During the next week, the clinician was called on several occasions by the family and by school personnel. The latter contacts were requests for ways of discussing Mark's loss with classmates and for input about how much the school social worker should push Mark to talk about his experience. The family wanted help in deciding whether to require Mark to go to a wake that he had no interest in attending. In addition to making a referral for psychotherapy outside of the school setting, the consulting clinician advised school personnel and the family regarding the wake on the basis of his follow-up phone contacts with Mark. Mark told the clinician, "Everybody keeps asking me a lot of questions and trying to tell me what will be best for me. It's as if they think that whether I go to the wake or talk all the time about my feelings, everything will be better. Everything will not be better . . . at least not for a very long time." In the ensuing weeks and months, Mark threw himself into the activities of normal life while pursuing his complicated thoughts and feelings about his life before and after his father's suicide, in the privacy of his therapy hours.

DISCUSSION

As the rate of violence in our inner cities has climbed, so has the number of children who are its direct and indirect victims. Previous work (Freud, 1956; Pynoos & Nader, 1988, 1989, 1990; Terr, 1989, 1991) has focused on the impact of exposure to isolated episodes of violence and the symptoms of PTSD that often follow. Although psychiatric services are frequently available to the victims of the most episodes of violence, children's exposure to random shootings, and to fighting at home and on the streets has not provoked a routine mental health response or suggested an obvious point of entry for intervention. In addition to suffering acute symptoms following observation of a shooting or stabbing death or the nightly sound of gunfire, children may respond to chronic exposure to violence by turning away from the frightening role of victim and, over time, assuming the exciting, but dangerous role of perpetrator.

Often, the families most affected by community violence have limited access to mental health services or are unable to take advantage of those that exist. A self-referral for psychiatric consultation may be low on the list of priorities for the families who struggle with chronic neighborhood violence, in addition to the hardships of unemployment, poverty, drug and alcohol abuse, and the like. Feelings of hopelessness conspire with the burdens of transportation and wariness of social service institutions to further limit utilization of existing clinical services.

Community-based policing offers a new approach to intervention for children and families exposed to inner city violence and its short- and long-term effects. The philosophy of community-based policing encourages police officers to detect vulnerable and distressed individuals and to help them obtain the services they need, and to collaborate with communities in establishing and making services available. For community-based policing to fulfill its expanded mission, police departments and police officers will need knowledge and methods, as well as a conceptual framework, to guide their interventions with children and their families. If community-based policing succeeds, even in part, police officers will be better able to collaborate with other professionals concerned with inner city children, such as clinicians, educators, and clergy.

We hope that the Program on Child Development and Community Policing in New Haven will increase the effectiveness of the outreach force of the 480 police officers who have the most direct, immediate, and sustained contact with the families hardest hit by community violence. Detecting vulnerable children and families and those in distress, offering referrals, arranging home visits, or providing transportation for appointments with mental health clinicians expand the role of the police officer responding to a call involving violence. This new role not only focuses the officer's attention on the children's experience of violence, but also supports the caregivers' attention to their own children's needs.

In each of the cases referred to the Consultation Service by the police, officers have commented that, in the past, their role would have ended with filing an incident report on the crime or complaint. They have described countless cases in which children may have been on the scene of violence and were never noticed by officers, who were only engaged in interviewing adult witnesses, collecting evidence, or coordinating arrangements with emergency services. In addition, previous police procedure would have viewed the adults only as suspects, witnesses, or subjects of arrest, not as parents or caregivers of the children who had been exposed to violence.

Veteran officers have described how, prior to the institution of the Child Development Program, even "the cops with the roughest edges always felt for the children" who became caught up in the scenes of violence. However, the earlier, more restricted definition of their job — "catching bad guys and making arrests" — and the absence of a resource for discussing the emotional needs of these young victims resulted in the "requirement" to not notice the children or to turn away from the painful and helpless feelings aroused when there was no active role for them to take in this area.

The shift to community-based policing introduces a different, or additional, role for police officers. With permanent assignments to specific neighborhoods, officers assume a proactive function that augments the traditional reactive one. Officers become known in the community. They are involved with individual families, as well as after-school activities for children, and attend meetings that address neighborhood concerns. All officers carry personal beepers, so that calls need not be routed through a central dispatcher. Instead, members of a neighborhood can now place a call directly to the officer with whom they are most familiar.

The introduction of courses on child and adolescent development for rookie officers, the clinical fellowship for veteran officers, and the Consultation Service are designed to address the needs of a police force seeking to play a more prominent, proactive role in the lives of the children and families in the inner city. In combination, these programs aim to equip officers with a broader frame of reference in dealing with the problems they confront in their daily work, and to provide a triage and referral service for specific cases in which children are the victims or witnesses of violence. Without interventions, the psychological victims of violence run the risk of never fully recovering, and will continue to pay a high price for their exposure. They may be unable to concentrate and learn, unable to feel safe and play, and they may eventually find some degree of safety and power only as the agent of violence, rather than as its victim. The Program on Child Development and Community Policing brings together police officers and mental health professionals who provide informed and consistent attention to the children at greatest risk for developmental difficulties, symptoms, and self-destructive responses, were their exposure to community violence to go unnoticed and untreated.

ACKNOWLEDGMENTS

The authors gratefully acknowledge the support of the Rockefeller Foundation and the Smart Family Foundation as well as the efforts of colleagues at the Yale Child Study Center and the New Haven Department of Police Service in the development of this project.

REFERENCES

Adnopoz, J., Grigsby, R. K., & Nagler, S. F. (1991). Multiproblem families and high-risk children and adolescents: Causes and management. In M. Lewis (Ed.), *Child and adolescent psychiatry: A comprehensive textbook* (pp. 1059–1066). Baltimore, MD: William & Wilkins.

Callahan, C. M., & Rivera, F. P. (1992). Urban high school youth and handguns: A school based survey. *Journal of the American Medical Association, 267,* 3038–3042.

Comer, J. P., & Haynes, N. M. (1990). Helping Black children succeed: The significance of some social factors. In K. Lomotey (Ed.), *Going to school: The African-American experience* (pp. 103–112). New York: State University of New York Press.

Comer, J. P., Haynes, N. M., Anson, A. R., Cook, T. D., Habib, F. G., & Michael, K. (1991). The Comer School Development Program: A theoretical analysis. *Urban Education, 26*(1), 56–82.

Fingerhut, L. A., Ingram, D. D., & Feldman, J. J. (1992a). Firearm homicide among black teenage males in metropolitan counties. *Journal of the American Medical Association, 267,* 3054–3058.

Fingerhut, L. A., Ingram, D. D., & Feldman, J. J. (1992b). Firearm and non-firearm homicide among persons 15 through 19 years of age: Difference by levels of urbanization, United States, 1979 through 1989. *Journal of the American Medical Association, 267,* 3048–3053.

Freud, A. (1956). Special experiences of young children, particularly in times of social disturbances. In K. Soddy (Ed.), *Mental health and infant development* (vol. 1, pp. 141–160). New York: Basic Books.

Freud, A. (1972). Comments on aggression. *International Review of Psycho-Analysis, 53,* 163–172.

Garbarino, J., Dubrow, N., Kostelny, K., & Pardo, C. (1992). *Children in danger: Coping with the consequences.* San Francisco, Jossey-Bass.

Goldstein, J., Freud, A., & Solnit, A. J. (1973). *Beyond the best interest of the child.* New York: The Free Press.

Goldstein, J., Freud, A., & Solnit, A. J. (1979). *Before the best interests of the child.* New York: The Free Press.

Goldstein, J., Freud, A., & Solnit, A. J., & Goldstein, G. (1986). *In the best interest of the child.* New York: The Free Press.

Marans, S., Dahl, K., Marans, W., & Cohen, D. (1992). Discussions with Oedipal children: Aggressivity in play. In A. J. Solnit, P. B. Neubauer, & D. J. Cohen (Eds.), *The many meanings of play in psychoanalysis.* New Haven: Yale University Press.

Pynoos, R. S., & Nader, K. (1988). Psychological first aid and treatment approaches to children exposed to community violence: Research implications. *Journal of Traumatic Stress, 1,* 445–473.

Pynoos, R. S., & Nader, K. (1989). Children's memory and proximity to violence. *Journal of the American Academy of Child and Adolescent Psychiatry, 28,* 236–241.

Pynoos, R. S., & Nader, K. (1990). Children's exposure to violence and traumatic death. *Psychiatry Annals, 20,* 334–344.

Taylor, L., Zuckerman, B., Harik, V., Groves, B. (1992). Exposure to violence among inner city parents and young children. *ADJC, 146,* 487.

Terr, L. C. (1989). Family anxiety after traumatic events. *Journal of Clinical Psychiatry, 50*(11), 15–19.

Terr, L. C. (1991). Childhood traumas: An outline and overview. *American Journal of Psychiatry, 148,* 10–20.

16 Israeli Children in the Gulf War: Problems of Masks and Peer Separation

Tiffany Field
University of Miami School of Medicine

When I asked an Israeli school teacher to identify the biggest problems for children during the Gulf War, the first one she mentioned was the gas masks. She elaborated that the masks were problems for all ages: Premature infants were transferred to tents and invariably experienced some degree of hypoxia. Mothers had bad experiences at the hospital and were like the "helpless taking the helpless home." The infants wore sealed masks, and when they cried, the masks clouded over, so that parents could not determine the reason for their infants' crying. Preschoolers wore "space suits," which were too hot and not very comfortable; they were also not very convenient, given the number of toileting regressions. Grade schoolers, in turn, had to assume many new responsibilities for the younger children in large families. High schoolers were reckless and refused to wear their masks. Many of them carried empty mask boxes instead. The high schools began to expel adolescents caught not wearing or carrying masks. She said the 12- to 17-year-olds were probably the most traumatized by the symbolism of masks, remembering the films they had seen of the Holocaust "showers." There were individual differences along the dimension of risk-taking about not wearing masks.

The second major problem she mentioned was having to stay home instead of attending school and being with friends. Although children in functional families loved the intimacy of being home for the curfews from 4 p.m. to the next morning with the rest of the family, kids in dysfunctional families "hated" it. The special children—the abused, neglected, psychiatrically disturbed and retarded children—who normally stayed at boarding schools, were sent home, and they had a different problem of being separated from their significant caregivers and returned to the parents who had abused or were not able to take care of them. Those children were soon returned to their schools. In any case, most children were separated either full time or part time from their best friends, as were their parents.

When I asked her if these were long-term problems, she said, "In some ways yes, and in some ways no." The test scores for eighth graders, for example, were no lower this year than last year. However, for the same-age children, a number of medical conditions, such as diabetes and other illnesses, worsened, suggesting that their immune systems may have been compromised by these stressors.

Looking to the children for answers on stress and coping with the war, there are several sources of information: drawings, dreams, letters, answers to questionnaires and interviews, and recorded telephone conversations with Kippy, the giant porcupine from "Rechov Sumsum," the Sesame Street-like television show that invited children to call and talk to him. There are also the psychologist-investigators, including Rachel Levy-Schiff, Abraham Sagi, Naomi Bat-Zion and Charles Greenbaum, who reported data, dreams, letters, questionnaires, interviews, and observations of the children. According to Levy-Schiff, the children manifested their stress behaviorally, in hand trembling, dysphoric faces, and temper tantrums; physiologically, in heart palpitations, diarrhea, eating changes, and sleep problems; and medically, in the form of immune system changes. These are not surprising inasmuch as they are universal symptoms in children's responses to multiple stresses, including separations from parents, hospitalization stress, separations from peers, and bereavement over loss, even for lost pets.

Although the Gulf War imposed a series of complex problems in stress and coping for young children, the problems of masks and peer separations loomed large in their reports to parents, teachers, and researchers, and were the topic of discussion with the television Kippy, as well as on the hotlines children were jamming to inquire about each other. Although limited, there are some related studies about masks and peer separations that place these problems in some context; they are elaborated, to some degree, in the remainder of this chapter.

THE PROBLEM OF MASKS

Masks pose a number of problems to children, including the imagined threat of suffocation, the presentation of an ugly face, and the disruption of normal activity, particularly that of social interaction.

Fear of Suffocation

One of the first fears experienced in life is that of suffocation. Indeed, built-in reflexes enable the newborn to ward off suffocation. The cloth-on-face reflex item of the Brazelton Neonatal Behavioral Assessment Scale is used to test the newborn's reflexive response to potential occlusion of the nose. The normal response is head turning and arching the back, along with hand swiping movements to remove the cloth. This reflexive action continues into childhood, when it is often necessary to use analgesic medication to prepare a child for an anesthesia mask. This fear of suffocation occurs across all ages, and generally produces a negative reaction to any application of sealed masks — a universal reaction that does not require references. It is interesting, in that light, that more people in Israel died from gas masks than from Scud attacks.

The Ugliness of Masks

A much less harmful, but nonetheless distressing, aspect of masks is their ugliness. For all of history and in all cultures, masks have been made ugly deliberately, to ward off evil spirits. Although intended to be functional, the masks worn by Israelis during the Gulf War will be placed in history alongside the ugliest of ceremonial masks intended to ward off evil spirits. It may be for this reason, more than any other, that Israeli adolescents (as opposed to younger age children) refused to wear their masks, and carried around empty mask boxes instead. Even very young infants can make discriminations between beautiful and ugly faces (Langlois, Roggman, & Rieser-Danner, 1990), but adolescence is the age of physical vanity, and wanting to appear attractive to one's peers is a normal feature of this stage. Not wanting to look ugly, they did not wear masks. Of course, this was not the complaint they registered, but rather that the masks interfered with their normal activities.

The kinds of concerns children expressed about the masks were more often about disruptions to their activities. In addition to complaints that, "Nobody will recognize me in this mask," they raised concerns such as, "What happens if I throw up in the mask?" and "What happens if people get married in masks. How can they kiss?" As early as infancy, investigators have demonstrated fear of masks and abnormal social interaction behaviors when infants cannot see their mothers' faces or when their mothers' faces are caused to go blank or still. Sroufe and his colleagues, for example, demonstrated infants' fear of their mothers when masks were placed on the mothers' faces (Sroufe & Wunsch, 1972). Even unfamiliar strangers' faces, which are not ugly the way masks typically are, have evoked fearful responses in infants in dozens of studies using a stranger approach paradigm. Fox (1985), for example, has demonstrated fearful faces, and even EEG activation changes, in infants presented a stranger's face.

Disruption of Social Interaction: Examples From Still-Face and Depressed-Face Paradigms

In other studies, mothers have been made to look strange by asking them to remain still-faced (Fogel, Diamond, Langhorst, & Demos, 1982; Stoller & Field, 1982; Tronick, Als, Adamson, Wise, & Brazelton, 1978) or to look depressed (Cohn & Tronick, 1983; Field, 1984). In all of these perturbations, the mother appears strangely unanimated to the infant. The infant makes several gestures and protest behaviors in an attempt to reinstate the normal social interaction and ultimately gives up and becomes distressed. In studies by Cohn and Tronick (1983) and Field (1984), the distressed and angry behavior shown by the infants whose mothers were asked to look still-faced or depressed persisted even after the mother returned to her normal, socially interaction behavior.

In fact, the mother's still face has been noted to be more stressful for the infant than a brief separation from her would be. In a recent study, my colleagues and I compared the effects of the mother's brief, still-faced interactions with the effects of brief separations. The mother and infant were positioned in a face-to-face interaction position, with the infant in an infant seat and the mother seated opposite him or her. Separation and still-face sequences were alternated. For the separation condition, the mother left her seat and went behind a curtain partition; for the still-face condition, she was asked to remain silent while looking at the infant's immobile face. Infant motor activity, gaze aversion, a distressed brow, and crying occurred more often during the still-face interaction than during the separation. Furthermore, the infants continued to be distressed following the reunion or the reinstatement of a normal interaction with the mother as manifested by increased motor activity, distressed brows, and crying (see Table 16.1).

It is not surprising that the infant would become distressed and disorganized in the absence of the mother, who is typically his or her primary source of stimulation and arousal modulation and who usually would not leave the infant alone during wakeful states. What is surprising is that the still-face paradigm appeared to be more distressing to the infant than the separation paradigm, as evidenced by motor activity, distress, and crying. Similar data have been reported for mothers' simulated depressed faces (Cohn & Tronick, 1983; Field, 1984). In these studies, mothers were asked to look depressed (rather than still-faced) in a similar paradigm. Again, the infants were significantly distressed and showed distress brows and fussy

TABLE 16.1
Mean Proportion Time that Mothers' and Infants' Interaction Behaviors Occurred During the Separation and Still-Face Perturbations

	Perturbation							
	Separation				Still Face			
Categories	Baseline	Separation	Reunion	F	Baseline	Still Face	Reunion	F
Infant Behaviors								
Smiling (.89)	08_b	01_a	11_b	6.11***	10_a	03_b	08_a	3.97
Vocalizing (.85)	05_a	06_a	05_a	—	05_a	09_a	10_b	3.17*
Motor activity (.80)	09_a	15_a	19_a	5.28**	08_a	21_a[1]	19_b	5.13**
Gaze aversion (.81)	35_a	00_b	35_a	8.43****	36_a	50_b[2]	38_a	4.99**
Distress brow (.81)	02_a	04_a	10_b	5.37**	01_a	09_b[3]	09_b	6.05***
Crying (.93)	01_a	04_b	07_b	4.08*	02_a	08_b[4]	07_b	5.27**
Mother Behaviors								
Smiling (.96)	29_a	—	46_b	8.12**	27_a	—	31_a[5]	—
Exaggerated faces (.84)	04_a	—	03_a	—	05_a	—	03_a	—
Vocalizing (.97)	43_a	—	48_a	—	41_a	—	45_a	—
Touching (.89)	43_a	—	18_b	7.42**	38_a	—	48_b[6]	5.09*
Moving limbs (.92)	10_a	—	02_b	7.17**	08_a	—	20_a[7]	7.58**

Means bearing different subscripts ;(a and b) are different as indicated by F values for repeated measures effects. Intercoder reliability coefficients in parentheses.

*$p < .05$.
**$p < .01, p < .005$.
***$p < .001$.

[1] Still-face > separation, $F = 4.26, p < .05$ in comparison of stress conditions.
[2] Still-face > separation, $F = 12.28, p < .001$.
[3] Still-face > separation, $F = 8.13, p < .01$
[4] Still-face > separation, $F = 7.63, p < .01$.
[5] Still-face < separation, $F = 4.19, p < .05$.
[6] Still-face > separation, $F = 9.11, p < .005$.
[7] Still-face > separation, $F = 12.17, p < .001$.

behaviors as they attempted to reinstate normal interactions (see Table 16.2).

It seems that the violation of expectancy in both the still-face and depressed-face situations, in which the mother suddenly becomes unresponsive in a typically interactive situation, and her emotional/affective unavailability are more distressing to the infant than simply being left alone with his or her own resources. Analogies in the literature are the anesthetized mother rat who is unresponsive to her pups (Schanberg & Field, 1987) and depressed mothers who, in a very adaptive way, tend to leave their infants physically alone in front of a television (Lyons, Zoll, Connell, & Grunebaum, 1986). Being left alone by a depressed mother may be less stressful for the infant than experiencing the mother as affectively unresponsive or emotionally unavailable, as in these still-face or depressed-face situations.

Although these paradigms have not been tried with older children and adults, preschool and kindergarten children have been anecdotally reported to become distressed in response to even clowns' faces, and parents have been noted to have more saddened affect in the presence of disfigured faces, such as those of children with cranio-facial anomalies (Field, Guy, & Umbe, 1985). Thus, the face, whether simply changed or made ugly by morphological anomalies or made less active and animated by instructions to remain still or look depressed, has significant effects on the interaction partner, from early infancy to adulthood. Although the muffling of the voice (another problem with masks) has not been studied in the same way, such alterations in vocal activity would, presumably, produce similar distress responses.

Fortunately, there may be a solution to this problem of masks with the design of other breathing devices (e.g., the astronaut's space helmet) that do not seem to have significant disruptive effects on face-to-face social interactions. Although the building materials, such as Plexiglass, may be more expensive, the cost savings in reduced stress may be considerable.

PROBLEMS OF CLOSED SCHOOLS, CURFEWS, AND PEER SEPARATIONS

Several pieces of evidence document the Israeli children's concern about not going to school and their missing their peers. According to Leavitt and Fox (this volume, Introduction), 80% of Israeli children were watching television during the Gulf War. One of the most popular programs for the younger children was "Rechov Sumsum," whose Kippy asked the viewing children to call him if they had "butterflies in their stomachs" and wanted to talk about things. Frequently, the children complained about longing to go back to school: "I want to go back to kindergarten." Similarly,

TABLE 16.2

Infant and Mother Behaviors During Spontaneous, Depressed, and Reunion Interactions

Categories	Nondepressed			Depressed			Effect and p Level
	Spontaneous	Depressed	Reunion	Spontaneous	Depressed	Reunion	
Infant Behaviors							
Positive facial expressions (frequency)	8.5	4.0_b	4.5_b	3.0_c	2.0_c	2.0_c	M^1I^1
Negative facial expressions (frequency)	1.5_a	8.0_b	6.5_b	5.5_b	5.0_b	4.5_b	I^1
Vocalizations (frequency)	7.0_a	3.0_b	3.5_b	2.0_c	1.5_c	1.5_c	M^2I_1
Looking away (% time)	21_a	48_b	39_b	38_b	32_b	33_b	I^2
Protesting (% time)	5_a	42_b	37_b	15_c	16_c	17_c	M^3I^3
Looking wary (% time)	7_a	36_b	31_b	11_c	14_c	13_c	M^3I^3
Activity	17_a	26_b	23_b	9_c	11_c	12_c	M^3I^1
Heartrate	148_a	159_b	154_b	140_a	142_a	145_a	M^1I^1
Mother Behaviors							
Positive facial expressions (frequency)	21.5_a	2.0_b	16.5_a	5.0_b	4.0_b	3.5_b	M^3I^4
Negative facial expressions (frequency)	2.5_a	8.0_b	3.0_a	9.0_b	11.5_b	10.5_b	M^1I^1
Vocalizations (frequency)	53_a	21_b	48_a	22_b	26_b	27_b	M^2I^2
Looking at infant (% time)	93_a	89_a	95_a	58_b	65_b	62_b	M^3
Tactile/kinesthetic stimulation (% time)	39_a	11_b	33_a	21_c	11_b	18_c	M^3R^3
Heartrate	79_a	87_b	81_a	71_c	73_c	74_c	M^1I^1

Means bearing different subscripts (a, b, and c) are different at $p < .05$ or less; SDs can be obtained from the author. M = mean, R = repeated measures, I = interaction effects.

[1] $p < .05.$
[2] $p < .01.$
[3] $p < .005.$
[4] $p < .001.$

questionnaires administered in the Scud zones and on the hotlines featured children's frequent expressions of concern about when the curfews would be lifted, when the schools would be re-opened, and expressions about how glad they would be to return to school, to talk to other children, to tell jokes with them, and so on. Evidence from several studies suggested that the anxiety levels of the children decreased on their return to school.

Parental Anxiety at Home

There are several interrelated aspects to the problem of not going to school and being separated from peers. By remaining at home, the children had more intensive and extensive contact with their parents and families, which, as already mentioned, was good in happy families, but less comfortable in dysfunctional families. Aside from that variability, Raviv (this volume, chapter 17) and others suggested that adults were more fearful than children, that children rated their parents as extremely fearful, that the children did not know what to do with them, and that these anxieties typically disappeared on the children's return to school. Thus, while schools were closed, children were exposed to their anxious parents more. This anxiety was presumably contagious, and was conveyed to the children, in turn affecting their own anxiety levels. An interesting comparison, then, would be to children on the kibbutzim going to shelters with their peers versus children going to shelters with their parents. It is one of the great egocentricities of parents to assume that their own negative affective states have very little influence on their children and, at the same time, to assume that they are central to the coping abilities of their children, discounting the fact that peers can often be very effective buffers to stress.

Disruption of Peer Relationships

Knowing that peers are effective buffers to stress offers some insight into the reportedly greater stress in Israeli girls versus boys, and in young adolescents versus younger and older children. Girls have been noted to be more relationship-oriented; thus, they might be expected to be more disturbed than boys by the disruption of all the relationships associated with not having school and curfews. Young adolescents were also noted to be more anxious, asking very socially oriented questions, such as how they would go to a birthday party if there was a Scud attack, or how they could get married wearing a mask. Peak anxiety at this age is understandable in the context of children turning away from their families and focusing more on their peers and friends. It was this age group that was jamming the phone lines seeking information about each other. During previous wars, children could attend school, so this was not a problem. Although the data in this book focuses on children more than adults, it is conceivable that peer separation was as big a factor for adults as it was for children; adults had lost their primary sources of social support both from extended family members staying in their own sealed rooms and from colleagues, whom they could not see when they were not going to work or taking their children to school.

Several conceptual models can be applied to the transitions and changes of remaining home from school, being physically constrained by curfews, and being separated from peers. These models include attachment theory, control theory, and others. One commonality that emerges from these models is the idea that children involved in a transition are faced with a number of tasks that place demands on their coping abilities. Some of these tasks are psychological, such as accepting separation from an important person, and others are social or interpersonal, such as having to establish new relationships. Still others are physical, such as having to perform new behaviors required in the new setting.

Separations: Examples From Parent and Peer Separation Paradigms

The most popularly studied transitions for children are those required for hospitalizations and those accompanying separation from school settings. Separations due to hospitalizations, for example, have been viewed as potentially disruptive to the attachment process (Rutter, 1981). One of the tasks faced by the hospitalized child is to maintain the security provided in a primary attachment during the hospitalization. The child's access to the attachment figure may be particularly important as the child faces a variety of new experiences, several of which are aversive and uncomfortable for the child. Studies of long hospital stays and repeated admissions have reported increases in behavioral distress, suggesting that children should have more continuous access to their primary attachment figure during hospitalizations (Rutter, 1981). The consensus is that separation from the primary caregiver is the key source of the stress. Other studies, in which the mother is hospitalized, instead of the child (e.g., for the birth of another baby), have similarly documented the significant stress for the child of being separated from the mother (Field & Reite, 1984). The stresses associated with separation from peers have rarely been studied.

Studies of monkey infants separated from their peers (Reite, Harbeck, & Hoffman, 1981; Suomi, Collins & Harlow, 1976), and those of peer separations in preschool children (Field, 1984) and infants (Field, Vega-Lahr, & Jagadish, 1984) suggest that the disorganizing effects of separations are not limited to mother–infant dyads. In a study by Reite et al. (1981), two infant pigtail monkeys who had been reared together showed behavioral and physiological disorganization following their separation. Similar to studies of infants separated from their mothers, agitated behavior followed separation, with increases in activity and vocalizations. Subsequently, both infant monkeys showed a decrease in play behavior and an altered cellular immune response. The impaired cellular immune function and agitated behavior noted in these infant monkeys suggested significant behavioral and physiological changes accompanying the separations of young primate peers.

Human infants and toddlers also appear to experience distress when separated from their peers. In the study reported by Field et al. (1984), following 14 months in an infant nursery, a group of 15-month-olds were transferred to a toddler nursery; at the same time, a group of 24-month-olds graduated from a toddler nursery to a preschool nursery. During the week immediately preceding the transfer and during the week following the transfer (as opposed to the baseline data collected 1 month prior to the transfer), infants and toddlers showed increases in activity level, in wandering about aimlessly, and in fantasy play (see Fig. 16.1). Increases were also noted in fussiness, physical aggression, and physical affection. Naptime sleep became more irregular, with longer latencies to sleep, more crying during sleep, and less time spent sleeping. Both parents and teachers noted changes in eating and sleeping patterns, and there was a greater incidence of absenteeism. A comparison between the infants and the toddlers suggested that the toddlers experienced greater changes in their behavior than the infants, including more anticipatory distress, during the period just prior to the transfer to the new nursery. This is not surprising, inasmuch as the older children had more sophisticated cognitive abilities. Their cognitive awareness of the pending separation may have been enhanced by preparatory remarks and discussions of their parents and teachers.

When a comparison was made between those infants and toddlers who were transferred to new nurseries without close friends versus those who were transferred with close friends, it became clear that being transferred with close friends served as a buffer against the stressful effects of separation. Infants and toddlers who remained with their close friends showed less fussing, less physical aggression, less wandering and watching other children during play, and more physical affection (see Fig. 16.2). During naptime observations, they also showed less crying and spent a greater percentage of naptime sleeping. Another difference that emerged was that children who were externalizers or who were verbally and facially expressive of their emotions had an easier time making the transition than children who were internalizers (see Fig. 16.3).

Thus, in both humans and monkeys, a similar constellation of behavioral and physiological responses occurred during separation from peers.

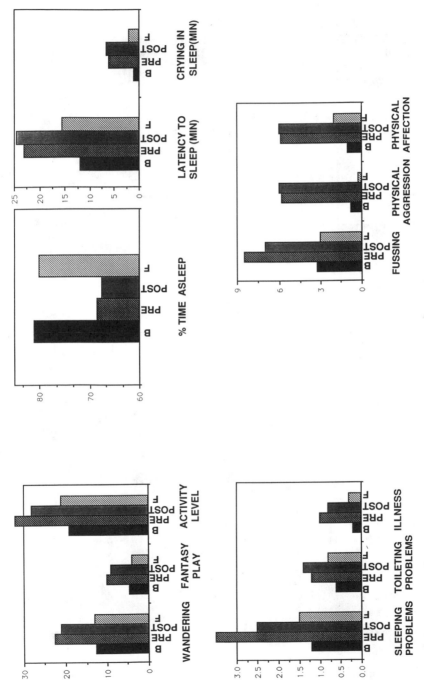

FIG. 16.1. Proportion of infant/toddler play time that wandering and fantasy play occurred, activity level (actometer measure), and proportion of time that fussing, physical agression, and physical affection occurred during baseline (B), preseparation (Pre), postseparation (Post), and follow-up (F) play observation periods. Percentage of naptime spent asleep, latency to sleep (minutes), and mean number of sleeping problems, toileting problems, and illnesses during these periods.

313

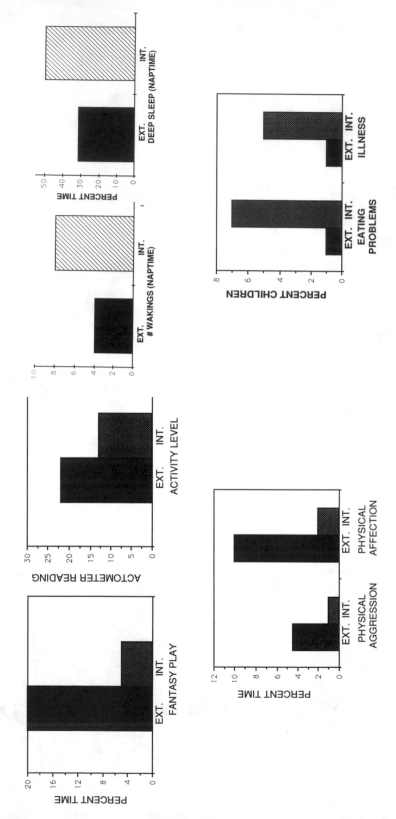

FIG. 16.2. Proportion of postseparation play time infants and toddlers who were externalizers (Ext.) or internalizers (Int.) spent engaged in fantasy play, mean activity level (actometer reading), proportion of play time spent engaging in physical aggression and physical affection, number of waking and deep sleep during naptime, and percentage of infants/toddlers who experienced eating problems and illness.

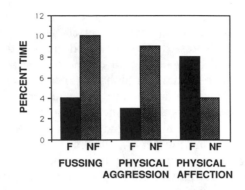

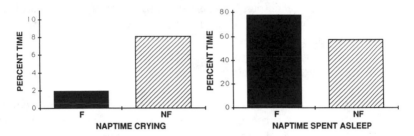

FIG. 16.3. Proportion of postseparation play time infants and toddlers transferred with close friends (F) or without close friends (NF) spent fussing and showing physical aggression and physical affection, crying during naptime, and sleeping during naptime.

Changes occurred in affect, play behavior, activity level, heart rate, sleep and eating patterns, and illness; and alterations were noted in the individuals' immune systems (Field, 1984, 1985; Field & Reite, 1984; Field et al., 1984; Reite & Capitiano, 1985). These are the same behavioral and physiological changes noted in the studies of Israeli children's responses to the Gulf War. It is not surprising that this particular constellation of changes was typically observed, because these functions are reputedly mediated by the hypothalamus and its extensive connections to other areas of the limbic system and the pituitary adrenal cortical system (Levine, 1983; McCabe & Schneiderman, 1985).

The only separation situations in which these changes seemed to be attenuated were those in which the infant or child was accompanied by an attachment object that appeared to buffer the child from separation stress. For example, the infants and toddlers who graduated to new nurseries with close friends experienced milder separation stress than those who were transferred without close friends (Field et al., 1984). The biphasic response to separation, with agitation followed by depression, also occurred in both the monkey and human infant studies, and was described in those studies as it was, earlier, by Bowlby (1969). The agitated reaction was accompanied by increased motor activity, frequent distress vocalizations, and elevated heart rate and body temperature immediately after the separation. This was typically followed by depressed behavior and decreases, to below baseline, in both heart rate and body temperature. The only separation situations that apparently did not feature this biphasic process of agitation followed by depression were moves to new places. For example, less depression has been noted in infant monkeys that are moved away from their social group to an isolation cage and in infants, toddlers, and preschoolers who are moved to a new classroom (Field et al., 1984) or a new school (Field, 1984). Remaining in an environment that reminds the child of the lost person may be more distressing than moving to a different environment. In addition, new stresses may present active coping opportunities, whereas being stuck in a "passive coping" or helplessness situation may continually remind the child of his or her missing peers through the environmental features that are associated with the missing peers.

Active Versus Passive Coping

The behaviors occurring during these agitation and depression phases appear to be similar to those noted during what have been called *active coping* versus *passive coping, helplessness, hypervigilance*, or *conservation-withdrawal* situations (McCabe & Schneiderman, 1985). This is worth mentioning, because one of the biggest stressors for both children and adults in Israel during the Gulf War was helplessness and a passive coping situation. Unlike during other wars, the Israelis were unaware of the locations of danger (i.e., the Scud attacks) and of missing relatives. Also unlike during other wars, the adults were confined to sealed-off rooms where they were helpless and inactive, and were forced to engage in passive coping. In active coping, the organism actively responds to stress, and the sympathetico-adrenal medullary system appears to be activated, as manifested in increases in activity, heart rate, and norepinephrine. In contrast, in a passive coping situation, active coping responses do not seem available; this state is characterized by helplessness, hypervigilance, or conservation-withdrawal. Activity levels and heart rate are depressed; epinephrine, ACTH, and adrenal-cortical secretions are elevated; and the immune response is suppressed. In a yoked-control experiment with adults (Lundberg & Frankenhauser, 1978), for example, some subjects were given a choice among various noise intensity levels while completing a mental arithmetic test. The others, the yoked controls, showed elevated levels of cortisol.

Active coping is considered more adaptive, because of associated elevations in norepinephrine (e.g., during exercise; Dimsdale & Moss, 1980) may offset the anxiety-related increases in epinephrine levels. Increased activity during agitation and associated increases in norepinephrine may also attenuate the suppressive effect of epinephrine on the immune system (Borysenko & Borysenko, 1982).

The physical constraints of remaining in crowded, sealed rooms (even though they may sometimes have been with their parents) for prolonged periods without activity are suggestive of passive coping situations. Larger shelters, instead of sealed rooms, in the company of friends and neighbors offering more active social experiences and in larger spaces offering more room to move around and get physical exercise might have alleviated passive coping situations of this kind. Having fantasy play opportunities for the very young children and social interaction opportunities for the older teenagers and their friends, both at school and in communal shelters, might have prevented some of the stresses experienced by Israeli children during the Gulf War.

SUMMARY

In summary, wearing masks and/or being isolated from significant partners or peers constrains, disrupts, and even prevents meaningful social interactions. This is bound to have negative consequences in any social context be it war or other forms of natural disaster. There are potential solutions to these problems—perhaps not simple solutions, but solutions nonetheless. Developing less aversive masks or oxygen delivery systems and insuring the continuation of normal activities of daily living, such as remaining in school and at the workplace, as well as being able to find shelters that are less physically constraining and more socially interactive, are potential solutions to these very stressful problems of masks and peer separations.

ACKNOWLEDGMENTS

This research was supported by a NIMH Research Scientist Award (#MH00331) and an NIMH grant (#MH40779) to Tiffany Field. I would like to thank all of the mothers and infants who participated in these studies.

REFERENCES

Borysenko, M., & Borysenko, J. (1982). Stress, behavior and immunity: Animal models and mediating mechanisms. *General Hospital Psychiatry, 4,* 59–67.

Bowlby, J. (1969). *Attachment and loss: Vol. I. Attachment.* New York: Basic Books.

Cohn, J. F., & Tronick, E. Z. (1983). Three-month-old infants' reaction to simulated maternal depression. *Child Development, 54,* 185–193.

Dimsdale, J. E., & Moss, J. M. (1980). Plasma catecholamines in stress and exercise. *Journal of the American Medical Association, 243,* 340–342.

Field, T. (1984). Early interactions between infants and their postpartum depressed mothers. *Infant Behavior and Development, 7,* 527–532.

Field, T., & Reite, M. (1984). Children's responses to separation from mother during the birth of another child. *Child Development, 55,* 1308–1316.

Field, T., Vega-Lahr, N., & Jagadish, S. (1984). Separation stress of nursery school infants and toddlers graduating to new classes. *Infant Behavior and Development, 7,* 277–284.

Field, T. (1985). Attachment as psychobiological attunement: Being on the same wavelength. In M. Reite & T. Field (Eds.), *The psychobiology of attachment and separation* (pp. 415–450). New York: Academic Press.

Field, T., Guy, L., & Umbe, V. (1985). Infants' responses to mothers' imitative behaviors. *Infant Mental Health Journal, 6,* 40–44.

Fogel, A., Diamond, G. R., Langhorst, B. H., & Demos, V. (1982). Affective and cognitive aspects of the two-month-old's participation in face-to-face interaction with its mother. In E. Tronick (Ed.), *Social interchange in infancy: Affect, cognition, and communication* (pp. 23–39). Baltimore: University Park Press.

Fox, N. (1985). Sweet/sour–interest/disgust: The role of approach–withdrawal in the development of emotions. In T. Field & N. Fox (Eds.), *Social perception in infants* (pp. 31–52). Norwood, NJ: Ablex.

Langlois, J. H., Roggman, L. A., & Rieser-Danner, L.A. (1990). Infants' differential social responses to attractive and unattractive faces. *Developmental Psychology, 26,* 153–159.

Levine, S. (1983). *A psychobiology approach to the ontogeny of coping.* Unpublished manuscript, Stanford University, Stanford.

Lundberg, U., & Frankenhauser, M. (1978). Psychophysiological reactions to noise as modified by personal control over stimulus intensity. *Biological Psychology, 6,* 51–59.

Lyons, R. K., Zoll, D., Connell, D., & Grunebaum, H. U. (1986). The depressed mother and her one-year-old infant: Environment, interaction, attachment and infant development. In E. Tronick & T. Field (Eds.), *Maternal depression* (pp. 61–82). San Francisco: Jossey-Bass.

McCabe, P., & Schneiderman, N. (1985). Psychophysiological reactions to stress. In N. Schneiderman & J. Tapp (Eds.), *Behavioral medicine: The biopsychosocial approach.* Hillsdale, NJ: Lawrence Erlbaum Associates.

Reite, M., & Capitiano, J. (1985). On the nature of social separation and social attachment. In M. Reite & T. Field (Eds.), *The psychobiology of attachment and separation* (pp. 223–250). New York: Academic Press.

Reite, M., Harbeck, R., & Hoffman, A. (1981). Altered cellular immune response following peer separation. *Life Sciences, 29,* 1133–1136.

Rutter, M. (1981). Stress, coping and development: Some issues and some questions. *Journal of Child Psychology and Psychiatry, 22,* 323–356.

Schanberg, S., & Field, T. (1987). Sensory deprivation stress and supplemental stimulation in the rat pup and preterm human neonate. *Child Development, 58,* 1431–1447.

Sroufe, L. A., & Wunsch, J. P. (1972). The development of laughter in the first year of life. *Child Development, 43,* 1326–1344.

Stoller, S., & Field, T. (1982). Alteration of mother and infant behavior and heart rate during a still-face perturbation of face-to-face interactions. In T. Field & A. Fogel (Eds.), *Emotion and early interactions* (pp. 57–82). Hillsdale, NJ: Lawrence Erlbaum Associates.

Suomi, S. J., Collins, M. L., & Harlow, H. F. (1976). Effects of maternal and peer separations on young monkeys. *Journal of Child Psychology and Psychiatry, 17,* 101–112.

Tronick, E., Als, H., Adamson, L., Wise, S., & Brazelton, T. B. (1978). The infant's response to entrapment between contradictory messages in face-to-face interaction. *Journal of Child Psychiatry, 17,* 1–13.

17 The Use of Hotline and Media Interventions in Israel During the Gulf War

Amiram Raviv
Tel Aviv University

At 2:05 a.m. on January 18, 1991, sirens were sounded throughout Israel. Awakened by the sirens, the residents of Israel fearfully donned their gas masks and closed themselves into their sealed rooms. Within less than 90 seconds, Iraqi Scud missiles descended on different areas of Tel Aviv and Haifa, causing injuries and extensive damage. Saddam Hussein's threats had become a reality, and the residents of Israel found themselves involved in the Gulf War.

The information provided by the media during the first hours of tension and uncertainty failed to mitigate the confusion and anxiety aroused by the totally unknown experience of missile attack and the threat of chemical warfare, which had been widely discussed in the media in the days preceding the outbreak of fighting. In a small portion of the population, there were extreme anxiety reactions, including unnecessary use of atropine injections, somatic reactions, and a frantic search for information through informal channels. Telephones rang with callers trying to ascertain the location and the extent of damage. Ironically, concerned Americans who called friends and relatives in Israel discovered that they had more information, based on CNN reports, than did the Israelis shut inside the sealed rooms. Within several hours, the "fog" lifted and it became clear that extensive physical damage had been caused by the missiles, forcing hundreds of families to evacuate their homes, to find alternative places of residence, and to receive physical and emotional assistance. However, it also became clear that the missiles did not carry chemical warfare, and that, relative to the force of the explosions and the degree of damage to property, human injuries were minimal.

The first missile attack was immediately followed by a massive intervention of mental health professionals who joined other official and voluntary emergency organizations that came to the aid of the evacuated families and the injured. Indeed, in comparison to previous wars, the Gulf War witnessed an unprecedented quantity and diversity of psychological interventions that stemmed from the unusual situation it created.

Israel's previous wars were characterized by a defined front line and a massive call-up of the male population. For the civilians, the threat was relatively defined and limited, lending a relative sense of security and confidence in the capacity of the Israeli army to repel its attackers. As a result, anxiety and concern during times of war were directed toward the soldiers at the front (Raviv & Klingman, 1983). The bulk of children's worries focused primarily on the welfare and security of their fathers at the front. In this sense, there was perhaps a greater similarity between the fears of American children whose fathers were drafted to fight in the Gulf War (DeAngelis, 1991) and those of Israeli children whose fathers fought against the Egyptians or the Syrians during previous wars than with those of Israeli children during the Gulf War.

In the Gulf War, almost the entire population of Israel was under the threat of a direct attack. The introduction of a new dimension to war — the use of long-range missiles — created an overwhelming feeling of helplessness in the face of the inevitable, yet always unexpected, next missile attack. Most terrifying was the prospect of chemical warfare, which aroused intense emotions among the population for whom the Holocaust continues to be a living memory. This situation gave rise to a wide range of fear and anxiety reactions among children and their parents (Klingman, 1992a, 1992b). In response to these reactions, mental health professionals provided a diverse range of interventions. These included: (a) crisis intervention counseling with parents and children, conducted on an individual and group level at treatment centers or at makeshift centers housed in hotels to which individuals were evacuated; (b) indirect interventions, including consultations with teachers, municipal staff, and emergency services staff, in addition to preventive interventions with the general population; (c) preventive measures, such as preparation of written material by school psychologists and teacher-counselors to be used by teachers and parents for the general population of children, as wells as for children of evacuated families; (d) hotlines — counseling over the telephone; and (e) interventions through the media.

This chapter focuses primarily on two relatively new and unique forms of intervention: telephone hotlines and the media. This choice was made for several reasons. First, both forms of intervention allow relatively easy access for individuals seeking help, particularly at times of war, when people are tuned to the media continuously in the expectation of receiving relevant information. Second, both place a strong emphasis on crisis intervention techniques, with a primary and secondary prevention approach (Klingman, 1988; Sandoval, 1991). Third, the massive use of these interventions during prolonged, large-scale crisis situations is a novel phenomenon. Finally, both are likely to be used in future emergency situations.

HOTLINE SERVICES

The provision of psychological help by means of the telephone to individuals in stressful situations is not a new phenomenon. The Samaritans in England was the first organization to use the telephone as a form of intervention in times of crisis. Chad Varah, an English priest, replaced the confessional booth with the telephone. Through the telephone, an anonymous caller was able to discuss his or her troubles with an unknown listener, who listened and counseled (Chad Varah, 1980; Lester & Brockopp, 1976).

There are several advantages to using the telephone in emergency situations:

1. It is easily accessible. The telephone is popular and easily reached.
2. It is immediate. The waiting line for the telephone is shorter, in many cases, than the waiting line at a clinic or an emergency room, and it saves travel time from one's home to the clinic.
3. One can talk from anywhere, an important characteristic of the telephone in times of war or emergency, when traveling is limited or when the caller is unable to travel because of his or her condition or because of others' dependence on him or her.
4. The caller tends to attribute greater authority to individuals providing help over the phone and is more likely to heed their advice.
5. The telephone encourages free and less inhibited speech.
6. The majority of intervention stages and processes are shortened significantly (Karon, 1991; Williams & Douds, 1976). Telephone interventions also have several disadvantages, however, including lack of eye contact, which prevents nonverbal communication; limited commitment on the part of the caller; and difficulties in applying certain intervention techniques.

Hotline Services During the Gulf War

The current survey is based on the initial reports of several organizations that provided hotline services during the war. Although it covers most of the services provided by these organizations, some of the data are still in the process of evaluation. Thus, the survey is limited to those reports so far submitted and analyzed. In addition, most of the hotlines were set up spontaneously, in response to the war, without a preconceived plan. As a result, notes and documentation were not formalized in a consistent manner and are, therefore, limited in their generalizability.

In the first 2 weeks of the Gulf War, several organizations operated hotlines. The hotlines were manned by mental health professionals, educators, and nonprofessional volunteers who were trained for the position by mental health professionals. Several hotlines were operated by organizations that provide similar services during peaceful times. The majority, however, were operated in response to the tension and stress reactions of the public. Most of the hotline services emphasized providing help to children. The following is a brief description of the salient organizations that provided hotline services during the war.

Information regarding these services was gathered from written and verbal reports, and reflects the general picture in the field.

Eran.   This was the first hotline organization in Israel. It was established in Jerusalem in 1971 and has grown to include seven additional branches throughout the country, answering more than 40,000 calls a year. Eran's phone numbers are publicized in the newspapers, and the most of the centers operate 24 hours a day. The organization operates with the help of approximately 500 volunteers who receive special training and supervision by mental health professionals (Gilat, 1991; Hertman & Gilat, 1991; Karon, 1991). During the war, Eran hotlines continued to operate as usual, often increasing their shifts.

The Ministry of Education.   An open line for pupils was opened at the beginning of the school year (September 1990), to serve as a center to which students could turn regarding their relationship with the school system. On Wednesday morning, January 16, 1991, schools were closed due to the declaration of a state of emergency. Immediately, the hotline altered its regular work and prepared itself for emergency calls. Additional phone lines were added daily in response to the large number of incoming calls, and personnel was increased substantially through the volunteer activities of counselors, educators, and psychologists. The goals of the open line included: (a) translating the information reported by the media to the level and the needs of the callers; (b) providing legitimization for the pupils' expressions of fear and anxiety, which were appropriate to their condition; (c) strengthening the pupils' faith in their ability to function appropriately; and (d) listening to pupils' feelings, thoughts, and ideas regarding ways to cope with the situation (Noy, 1991). In keeping with these goals, pupils' calls to the open line were treated as a normal response to anxiety states and did not receive stigmatic labels.

The Mental Health Clinic at Ramat Chen.   This clinic belongs to the General Sick Fund, which, during peace time, services a substantial portion of the Greater Tel Aviv population. In addition to providing professional help to Tel Aviv residents injured by the missiles, the center opened a hotline manned by its mental health professional staff, including psychologists, psychiatrists, and social workers. The hotline offered its services to all Tel Aviv residents, not only to members of the Sick Fund (Arazi, 1991).

The Tel Aviv School Psychological Services.   These services primarily came to the aid of the children and parents of evacuees. In addition to providing consultation and advice to city and educational personnel, many of the services' psychologists manned the hotline, which was opened immediately after the fall of the first missile on January 18, 1991.

Additional School Psychological Services.   The majority of the 124 School Psychological services throughout the country opened hotline services in response to the war.

Many were publicized in newspapers, and others advertised their services through informal channels. The scope of this phenomenon, and the extent of psychologists' involvement in manning hotlines, were assessed by means of questionnaires that were sent to 900 psychologists working in School Psychological Services (Raviv, Bar-Tal, & Wiesner, 1993). Of the 459 psychologists who returned questionnaires, 366 (approximately 80%) were involved in hotline counseling. The average number of hours spent manning the hotlines by each psychologist was 21.8. However, two points should be noted: First, the standard deviation obtained was large − 20.2 −, indicating a rather wide range of involvement; second, the distribution of the hours invested in hotline counseling during the war was probably uneven, with the majority of hotline consumption taking place during the first 2 weeks of the war.

Haga, the Civil Defense.   Haga opened a hotline several months before the onset of the war to provide information to the public on the technical aspects of the preparation for the potential war, such as distribution of gas masks, methods of sealing rooms against gas attacks, and so on. This was one of the busiest telephone centers. The Civil Defense phone line was not a typical hotline, in that it dealt primarily with logistical matters. One got the impression, however, that many of the callers who ostensibly requested information, did so out of a sense of anxiety and uncertainty. Moreover, before the war began, Haga added psychologists to its regular staff. The center documented brief and concise reports, referring to the period from December 15, 1990 to March 1, 1991.

The foregoing includes only hotline services that were operated by mental health professionals or volunteers and that had the declared goal of providing emotional assistance. Due to lack of documentation, the list is not exhaustive. It is a safe generalization that the majority of mental health professionals in Israel were involved in providing hotline services as part of their work, their army reserve duty, or as volunteers.

In addition, hundreds of telephone lines were set up by local municipalities and other organizations to provide callers with technical and logistical information, assistance in solving problems, and practical suggestions. Although these lines were usually not manned by mental health professionals, they undoubtedly served as support systems. As already pointed out, one can assume that, in many cases, calling these centers was motivated by anxiety and fear, in addition to a need for practical help.

Finally, it is important to note the supportive role fulfilled by the telephone, which served to connect family and friends under conditions of tremendous stress. Indeed, massive use of the telephone was another outstanding characteristic of Israelis' behavior during the war. Immediately after each missile attack, the phone lines became congested by calls made to inquire about the welfare of friends and family. The average usage of the telephone during January and February 1991 was 13% higher than that in January and February 1990, and 9% higher than that in November and December 1991 (D. Diamont, personal communication, July 1991). This represents a significant rise in usage given the fact that the usage of the telephone in the business sector, which is ordinarily the primary telephone consumer, dropped dramatically during this period.

Consumption of Hotline Services

The reported number of calls and the documented characteristics of callers varied among the different hotline centers. The Eran hotline, for example, reported an increase in the number of calls received during January and February, as compared to the previous months or the same period in the previous year. In January 1991, 5,216 calls were received, an increase of 58% over December 1990 and a 43% increase over January 1990. The distribution of calls throughout January was uneven. The largest increase in calls took place during the last 2 weeks of January, immediately following the first missile attacks. In February 1991, 4,430 calls were recorded, an increase of 25%, compared to February of the previous year. There were no differences in the proportion of calls made by children up to the age of 17 before and during the war. About 12% of the calls made to Eran were from children. However, during the war, there was a significant increase in the number of calls made by women and married adults with children, who required assistance for their children's anxieties. This type of call was very infrequent at Eran prior to the war. In response, many Eran volunteers worked with both parents and children. In addition, conversations with children during the war were longer than those before the war (Gilat, 1991; Hertman & Gilat, 1991).

The Ministry of Education's Open Line received over 6,000 calls. Differences were found between the number of calls during the first days of the emergency situation and later days. In general, the number of calls per day was in the hundreds, but there were days in which over 1,000 calls were received. These differences resulted not only from external events that took place on those days, but also from the amount of publicity the Open Line received in the media. One third of the calls were from adults, and two thirds were from children (Noy, 1991).

Two days after the first missile attack on Tel Aviv, it was announced that the Ramat Chen Center would serve as the national emergency hotline. Following advertisements on the radio and television and in newspapers, hundreds of phone calls were received from all over the country. Calls came in at all hours of the day, but increased in the evening hours. Toward the end of the first week of the war, the daily number of calls reached a record of 700. The majority of calls were from Tel Aviv and Ramat Gan, but included calls from throughout the country. Although there is no precise documentation of the total number of calls, it is estimated at several thousand. Callers included men, women, and children from all segments of the population; many parents called to get advice concerning their children (Arazi, 1991).

The Tel Aviv School Psychological Services' hotline, which opened on January 18, 1991, recorded 541 calls. However, many additional calls were received, but not recorded. Twenty-five percent of the recorded callers were children under the age of 15, and 50% were parents, especially mothers, who called concerning their children's problems. The largest number of recorded calls were received after the first missile attacks; this was followed by a rapid drop in calls (Shwartz & Wallach, in press).

The data obtained by Raviv et al. (1993) on psychologists' work in School Psychological Services throughout the country indicated that each psychologist manning a hotline received an average of 22.26 calls ($SD = 20.62$). Of the callers, approximately 57% were women, 16% were men, 17% were boys, and 10% were girls.

Haga's Information Center, which opened on October 8, 1990, received approximately 300,000 calls related to obtaining gas masks. It was only on December 15, 1990, that the Center began to accept questions of a more general nature and brought in consultants from the fields of medicine, chemical warfare, and psychology. Data based on the calls received between December 15, 1990, and March 1, 1991, were recorded on standardized forms by the female soldiers who received the calls. Unfortunately, due to time pressures and/or lack of professional skills, the gender of the caller was listed as *unknown* for 21.3% of the calls. The soldiers sorted the calls into 13 content categories. Although only 3.2% of the calls were recorded as belonging to the *psychology* category, it is clear that many additional calls, that were listed under categories such as *threat, family,* and so on, involved psychological issues, as well. Very few callers were below the age of 20, but many of them raised problems concerning their children and families.

The available reports do not allow for a precise estimation of the number of calls received by hotline services, because the collected information is based on notes recorded during the war that did not differentiate between callers who turned to the same hotline on several occasions or to several different hotlines. There were hours, particularly after missile attacks, during which the telephones at hotline centers rang incessantly, and the individuals manning the phones were overworked. However, there were also times when individuals working at the hotlines reported relatively few phone calls. An additional indication for the number of hotline consumers was provided, at my request, in a telephone survey conducted by the Dahaf Research Institute several months after the war. The survey included a sample of 832 individuals, including 203 mothers and 155 fathers of children under the age of 14. The participants were asked the following question: "During the Gulf War, did you call a psychological counseling center concerning issues related to children under the age of 14?" Twenty-nine individuals replied affirmatively, including 9 men and 20 women, representing 3.5% of the sample. These included 11 mothers (5.4%) and 5 fathers (3.2%) of children under the age of 14. These data indicate that more women than men called the hotlines, and, although they reveal a small percentage of callers, they undoubtedly represent the several thousand families who called the hotlines during the war.

The callers' demographic variables of age and gender indicate that the majority were adults and parents, particularly mothers. Children made a higher percentage of calls to hotlines geared specifically to them, such as the Ministry of Education's Open Line. However, it seems that they were well represented by their parents, who called for help concerning their children's problems. The greater number of women callers during the war appears to reflect the more general phenomena that women call radio psychological programs more frequently than men, in general (Raviv, Raviv, & Arnon, 1991) and that , even during peaceful times, they are more likely than men to turn to mental health agencies (Nadler, 1991).

Themes of Appeal

An examination of the content and characteristics of the hotline calls enables the elucidation of the problems and concerns that occupied Israeli families during this time (Arazi, 1991; Raviv et al., 1993). Most calls involved expressions of anxiety and fear, complaints of somatic symptoms that aroused anxiety, general tension, and a sense of helplessness. Calls from parents included requests for advice concerning children who expressed fears, had trouble sleeping, were not eating, refused to put on gas masks, vomited, and became aggressive. Many parents were concerned that their children's responses were abnormal. There were also many reports of children who took on the role of a support figure, taking on responsibility for their parents, grandparents, and younger siblings, such as ensuring that their parents donned their masks and entered the sealed rooms. In the children's calls, particularly those of the younger ones (ages 6–13), the most frequent topic was related to fears aroused by the war (Gilat, 1991).

All the calls expressed some degree of anxiety, although only occasionally was the anxiety of a paralyzing or helpless nature. Some calls attempted to camouflage anxiety under the guise of concern for another ("What should I do with my anxious brother?"), or through the search for information. There were also many expressions of direct anxiety that did not interfere with the ability to function. Some of the callers described extreme anxiety reaction; others described more mild reactions. The more extreme anxiety symptoms included: distressing fears, heightened sensitivity to sounds and noises, tremors, increased pulse rate, breathing problems, uncontrollable crying spells, contraction of the bowels, stomachaches, diarrhea, frequent urination, sleep disturbances, concentration disturbances, poor functioning, and difficulty in carrying out daily tasks and putting on the gas masks due to trembling hands. Callers also reported apathetic reactions, pessimism, lack of patience and tolerance, expressions of anger, and emotional outbursts. In addition, they complained about claustrophobic fears in the sealed rooms, feelings of strangulation when wearing the masks, fainting spells, and confusion. In essence, the entire range of anxiety and stress reactions mentioned in the professional literature was reported.

In many families, routine discipline and boundaries were disrupted. A conspicuous phenomenon that emerged in the calls was the intensification of previously existing problems within the family, indicating that communication problems exacerbated stress reactions. These cases should probably be viewed as at-risk populations for posttraumatic reactions.

Another common topic, which was more frequent at the beginning of the war, related to children's refusal to put on the masks, and physiological symptoms, such as vomiting and pains among children.

Arazi (1991) classified callers' anxiety reactions into three major types: (a) anxiety and fear related to missile attacks, damage and death, accompanied by a sense of helplessness; (b) fear of one's own intense anxiety reaction and the inability to control it, and loss of self-control, accompanied by an expressed fear of a mental breakdown or becoming psychopathological;

and (c) anger reactions and difficulty in accepting oneself as weak and vulnerable.

Ways of Helping

Although the majority of professionals who manned the hotlines were experienced professionals, the professionals at the Ramat Chen Center and at the Ministry of Education reported that many of them had had no previous experience with this type of psychological intervention. Even Eran volunteers, who were experienced in telephone interventions, were faced with unusual calls and unfamiliar problems.

In states of emergency, it is very important to encourage a feeling of normalcy and health among callers. In this regard, the Open Line of the Ministry of Education had an advantage over other hotlines since the Ministry is related to pupils' functioning in their "normal" lives, and no unhealthy stigma was associated with it, as was often the case with mental health stations. Thus, it was easier and more natural for a pupil in trouble to turn to an organization that he or she associated with normal daily functioning. In the majority of cases, it was possible to assist callers by means of conversation that included the following elements: provision of information, authoritative encouragement of coping, and the attribution of a "healthy" label to fear reactions (Noy, 1991).

The majority of calls to hotline centers were responded to by providing legitimization of the anxiety and stress reactions described by the callers. Each professional worked according to his or her individual, experience-based approach, with the goals of strengthening coping mechanisms and providing simple, common-sense advice. Certain hotlines provided forms of counseling, including behavioral guidance and concrete anxiety-reducing techniques. Others provided referrals to specific professionals for further assistance (Shwartz & Wallach, in press).

The general impression that arises from the written and informal reports is that the majority of interventions used by those who manned the hotlines were empathic listening, assurance and support, legitimization of anxiety, information about appropriate reactions, and giving meaning to what was happening. An important aspect of the intervention was helping callers create boundaries for their expressions of anxiety. For this purpose, various behavioral and cognitive crisis intervention techniques (Meichenbaum, 1985; Sandoval, 1985) were employed.

Callers' Reactions

To the best of my knowledge, there are no data on callers' satisfaction with the hotline services provided during the Gulf War. Some information can be obtained from hotline operators concerning the responses of some of the callers to the assistance they received over the hotlines. At Eran, for example, workers manning the phones reported feeling more efficient and helpful in response to questions related to the war situation than they did in general (66% vs. 47%), particularly in their conversations with children (Hertman & Gilat, 1991). Although these reports lack an empirical basis, they are consistent with studies on the helpfulness of hotlines in general (e.g., Gingerich, Gurney, & Wirtz, 1988; Hornblow & Sloane, 1980). Clearly, however, the assessment of callers' reactions to hotline interventions is an important issue that future research should address.

MEDIA INTERVENTIONS

In peacetime, the Israeli television operates a single television station. Its morning and afternoon programs are broadcast by the Israel Educational Television, under the direct auspices of the Ministry of Education; its evening and nighttime programs are broadcast by the Israel General Television, also under the auspices of the government. Israel does not have private television channels, although it is possible to receive a few outside stations that broadcast primarily in Arabic. It is only most recently, with the advent of cable television, that a greater variety of television channels has become available in some regions of the country. The majority of radio stations in Israeli radio are also under governmental auspices. They broadcast in Hebrew on several channels, approximately 18 hours a day, in addition to Arabic, English, and other language programs. In addition, there is a Hebrew language army station that broadcasts 24 hours a day. Most homes in Israel have a television and radio (Statistical Abstract of Israel, 1989).

The Gulf War was undoubtedly one of the greatest hours of Israel's electronic media. The media became the central source of information, giving meaning to the chaos and calming the public's fears. When the fighting in the Gulf began, all of Israel's radio stations were merged into a single station broadcasting continuously. The television also expanded its broadcasts, functioning around the clock, in an effort to alter and add programs in response to the war situation. Each warning siren was broadcast on radio and television, and was accompanied by instructions regarding appropriate behavior during the missile attack, given in all languages spoken by the heterogeneous Israeli population, intermingled with familiar and loved songs. The majority of Israel's residents were glued to the media in an unprecedented manner, especially during the first 2 days of the war, when they were directed by the military spokesman to remain in their homes. The radio and television appearance of the army spokesman (nicknamed "the national pacifier") was described repeatedly in newspapers and in several studies as one of the most important sources of support for the Israeli public. His clear instructions and explanations, given in a familiar and calm tone, can be viewed as a form of crisis intervention, in the classical sense of the term (Caplan, 1974). The army spokesman was assisted, behind the scenes, by several psychological and research organizations that provided guidance regarding what information should be emphasized in order to decrease the extent of the public's anxiety and encourage appropriate behavior.

Scores of mental health professionals were interviewed in the media before the war (at the time that gas masks were being handed out and preparation for the war had begun), during the war (with the onset of fighting), and after the first missiles fell on Israel. Psychologists in the media also served as hotlines, providing answers to hundreds of questions called in to the stations. Unfortunately, the interviews were conducted in a random manner, based on the choice of producers and other media professionals, and lacked comprehensive planning or provision of guidelines by a central psychological organization or other professional agencies.

A more systematic use of the media for psychological intervention in crisis situations is reflected in two programs — "Family Ties" and "Rechov Sumsum" — that are broadcast by the Israel Educational Television. "Family Ties," produced by D. Aviel, is a psychological educational program that provides parental guidance on various psychological problems, emphasizing family interactions and parent–child relationships. The program focuses on primary prevention by increasing parents' sensitivity, openness, tolerance, and flexibility in their relationships with their children, as well as by providing psychological knowledge on relevant topics. Usually, the program presents a previously recorded counseling session with families that volunteer to participate. In many programs, topics are drawn from viewers' letters asking for advice on specific matters. The program's hosts include several psychologists who use different therapeutic approaches.

A week after the onset of the war, the program's format was changed and broadcasts were filmed on the air. During the period from January 22, 1991 to March 10, 1991, 23 special programs were produced, dealing with war-related problems, including interviews with three real families, as well as with actors in role-plays. The psychological principles that guide the program during the year were adapted to the emergency situation (Rabinovitch, 1991). They included:

1. Interest and relevance: Each day a program relevant to the current situation was produced.
2. An ecological approach: The family mediates between the individual and the realistic threat; an improvement in any individual should improve the entire family system.

3. A holistic approach to the individual and the family, dealing with reciprocal family relations.
4. An educational approach, to increase awareness of coping processes to be used during times of stress and threat, and to explain that each family can find its own best solution.
5. Particular and pluralistic approach: There are many coping patterns and each family has its own patterns. The program does not present correct or incorrect coping patterns.
6. Historical approach: Every individual and family has previous experience in coping with stress situations that can be adjusted to the current threat.

"Rechov Sumsum," the Israeli Sesame Street produced by T. Steklov, is a well-known program geared toward young viewers, based on the U.S. program, but produced in Israel by local professionals in conjunction with colleagues in the United States. In the period before the war, the Israeli production staff was on vacation and reruns were being broadcast. With the onset of the Gulf War, the program was immediately renewed. The wartime programs sought to use the familiar characters and puppets that appeared regularly on the program to transmit to child viewers psychological messages aimed at helping them to cope with their fears and anxieties.

Twenty-five programs were produced, the majority on live broadcasts, dealing with topics related to coping with anxieties, reactions to stress situations, and the functioning of children during sirens and during the state of emergency. The puppet heroes of the program answered, on live television, the calls of viewers who described their experiences and asked for guidance. The following principles, formulated by Galia Rabinovitch, a developmental psychologist who served as the program's adviser before and during the war, were as follows:

1. The psychologist does not appear on the screen. The covert message is that all responses are normal; it is the situation that is abnormal.
2. Legitimization is provided for children's feelings of fear, dependence, anger, misunderstanding, boredom, and loneliness. Legitimization is provided for developmental processes: regression, lessening of independence, somatic complaints, aggression, and clinging to adults as a security base.
3. Expression of the listed principles is through dramatic means, so that the child can, through identification with the characters and their conflicts, arrive at a solution of his or her own conflict.
4. There is direct activation of the child at home through movement, song, games, or telephone conversation with the characters.
5. There is improvisation and actualization in relation to regular daily events.

Both programs planned their productions according to current events. This enabled the transmission of informative and supportive messages that served the immediate needs of their viewers and the creation of a positive anticipation for assistance from these programs.

Although the content of several children's programs was changed in response to war, these two programs were unique in their attempt to provide help to children and their families through the use of existing programs and with the guidance of psychologists. Although the programs were not planned in advance to serve as an official support system for crisis situations, they represent a form of intervention that took advantage of the existing infrastructure of production systems for providing psychological help during a crisis period. For this purpose, changes were made in program format, structure, and content during the war on live broadcasts. It is important to emphasize these points, because they seem to represent a worthwhile model to be adopted in preparation for future crisis situations. Indeed, this model of programming received very positive and appreciative responses from several sources through written letters and verbal feedback (Rabinovitch, 1991).

Unfortunately, an organized study on the effectiveness of these programs, in terms of viewership rates or the comprehension, absorption, and application of the psychological messages they transmitted, has not been conducted. However, one telephone survey was conducted during the war (February 11–14) to evaluate the perceived contribution of all the programs broadcast by the Israel Educational Television (Levinson, 1991). The results of the survey indicate that the programs were perceived as contributing to a better understanding of the situation (85%), providing constructive activity for children (84%), raising the morale (84%), fostering behavioral adjustment (83%), and reducing tension/stress (79%).

Several months after the war, I requested that the following question be included in the periodic survey conducted by the Dahaf Research Institute: "To what extent did the psychological advice provided by the media during the war help or disturb you?" The question was presented by telephone to a representative sample of men and women, aged 18 and above, who were asked to choose among seven options: *helped significantly, helped moderately, helped somewhat, did not help or disturb, disturbed somewhat, disturbed moderately,* and *disturbed significantly.* The sum totals (in percentages) of those who responded in a *help* or a *disturbance* category, were 40.4 and 2.8, respectively. A further analysis of the data revealed that parents of young children evaluated the advice received as more helpful than parents of older children (14+) or individuals without children. No differences between men and women were found in either category. The results provide merely a general impression obtained at a rather late date. However, their implications are of interest for future preparations and planning of media interventions. They are particularly interesting in light of the reactions to psychologists and psychological issues that appeared in the press during the war. Indeed, it is impossible to conclude this section without relating this puzzling phenomenon.

There are no exact records of the number of psychologists and their "presence" in the form of interviews, direct appearances, and responses to the public's questions on the radio and television. However, both the media and the written press were flooded with articles dealing with psychological counseling. In a survey of the three most popular newspapers in Israel, conducted during the period from January 15, 1991 to February 15, 1991, I found 114 newspaper articles that contained psychological advice and guidance, such as descriptions of psychological interventions, guidance to parents, advice regarding anxiety reactions, and so on. The large number of articles related to psychology and the tremendous flow of psychological information and intervention in the media during this period is unsurpassed. At the same time, a type of a boomerang effect seemed to take place, with the increasing appearance of newspaper articles rudely attacking the role of psychologists and their messages. The following are a few representative examples of segments from such articles that appeared during the war.

Referral to a Mental Health Officer — The hardest blow of the war to befall us thus far is the battalions of psychologists. They can be found on every inch of printed material and in every spare moment, on every radio frequency not occupied by crying Iraqis. A day does not go by in which tens of psychologists, sexologists, psychiatrists and social workers, in a variety of combinations, do not prattle on about fears during sirens, anxieties related to gas masks, atropine-linked paranoias, and above all — sex in the sealed room. What is going on? Have the members of the psychology department lost their ability to control themselves for a few minutes? (*Ma'ariv*, March 1, 1991, Gonen Gilat).

Surplus Calming — Each of Israel's wars is characterized by a particular phenomenon. The current crisis is characterized by a surplus of psychological counseling that appears from every direction and through all means. You open the newspaper, radio or television and immediately a male or a female psychologist is talking to the nation. Yet, a surplus of anti-fear means intensifies anxieties in the long run. When they continuously tell children and their parents "to let out their fears," the latter conclude that so much talk must imply a real reason for their fears (*Ha'aretz*, February 20, 1991, Dunevitch).

Suddenly Legions of Psychologists Appeared — The Scud war will be remembered as the great era of the mental health counselors. Telephone numbers for the anxious are publicized in newspapers and advertisements, and one can say that fear has received today greater legitimization than ever before. The current war appeared and released all inhibitions; the inhibition to turn to therapy no longer exists. Tens of phone lines are open, waiting for them to ring, hotlines are operating in every municipality, and the media is replete with the instant advice of professionals (*Ha'aretz*, February 8, 1991, Rali Sa'ar).

There were also psychologists who accused their colleagues of overexposure, of providing extreme legitimization of anxiety, and of weakening of coping mechanisms through extreme encouragement of the expression of anxieties and fears (Katzman, 1991). Although a systematic analysis of the amount and types of psychological messages transmitted to the public through the media is lacking, my own impression is that the majority of topics and information that were discussed in the media included "correct" theoretical elements that were in accordance with crisis intervention and coping approaches (Hobfoll et al., 1991). It is true that the Israeli population was never exposed so extensively to psychological topics, terminology, and analysis. However, it is also true that it was never exposed, as a group, to an experience characterized by such a high degree of threat and anxiety. Perhaps the gap between the threat of the anticipated disaster — primarily of chemical warfare — and the actual results — of a relatively low rate of casualties — aroused a feeling of embarrassment, shame, and anger at those who discussed their fears and anxieties. Clearly, this topic requires further discussion (Raviv, 1991). It is important, however, to note this phenomenon when attempting to generalize and learn from the lessons of the psychological interventions during the Gulf War, particularly because future wide-scale crisis situations are likely to require the intervention of psychologists through the electronic and written media and through the use of hotline services.

SUMMARY

Media interventions belong to the category of primary prevention in that they approach the target population before defined psychopathology arises (Alpert, 1985). In contrast, the hotline contains elements more similar to secondary prevention. The fact that individuals initiate calls to the hotline is indicative of the existence of a defined need or problem that causes them to seek help. The media enables access for a passive audience that refrains from seeking help for a variety of reasons. One can, however, also conceptualize the viewing of psychological counseling television programs as a way of receiving psychological help characterized by lower costs — perhaps one of its greater advantages (Raviv et al. 1991). However, the massive usage of psychological counseling and terminology like that made during the Gulf War, may carry within it certain dangers, such as overlegitimization of anxiety and, perhaps, the creation of an environment characterized by anxiety, or illness, anger, and resistance. It is, therefore, crucial to use correct doses of psychological interventions, that can be provided only by trained and experienced psychologists who can promote the use of coping mechanisms without focusing excessively on anxieties and difficulties.

Based on the experience of the Gulf War and clinical and research experience in coping with stress (Hobfoll et al., 1991), I suggest several recommendations that refer specifically to children and their families.

Recommendations for Hotline Services

1. To conduct systematic research and interviews of hotline operators to evaluate the types of problems they are presented with, their effectiveness, their reaction styles, and their helping techniques. In addition, it is important, although more difficult, to study the responses and feedback of individuals who receive help from hotline services.

2. To use this and additional information for training psychologists in providing help through hotlines, because not all clinical psychologists are trained to provide such types of help and may require additional theoretical and practical knowledge.

3. To develop a national plan that takes into account existing hotlines that operate on a daily basis and can be made available during emergency situations. In addition, the opening of additional municipal hotlines during emergency situations should be planned in advance.

4. To plan the opening of hotlines specifically geared toward consulting teachers and educators to improve their ability to cope with pupils' problems. It may also be possible to open several centers to which teachers can turn directly during peaceful times, as well, to get advice regarding pupils' crises beyond the well-developed school psychological services existing in Israel. It is important that these hotlines be brought to the attention of the general public.

5. To develop uniform and accepted procedures for documenting and reporting data that will enable follow-up research that will, in turn, promote the improvement of these services.

6. To develop supervision and support systems for individuals manning the hotlines, especially nonprofessional volunteers.

Recommendations for Media Interventions

1. To review the lessons of the experience, including feedback from listeners, viewers, and interviewed professionals from the fields of psychology and the media.

2. To prepare, perhaps through the initiative of the Ministry of Education, plans for using the media in emergency situations. Programs that aim specifically at children and operate through indirect means should be distinguished from those geared to parents and teachers, who have a greater capacity to make direct use of guidance and advice provided by psychologists, and to apply it to helping children.

3. To prepare, in advance, a list of experienced psychologists, including their areas of expertise, who agree to be at the service of the media during emergency situations.

4. To develop a special curriculum for training psychologists in counseling techniques and interventions through the media during crisis situations, with a specific emphasis on providing help for children and their parents.

5. To ensure that military and civilian research organizations are prepared for gathering information about the public's needs, moods, and concerns, as well as for evaluating the extent of viewership, during crises.

6. To standardize the systematic collection of data by mental health professionals, to be summarized and presented to radio and television professionals, enabling them to respond to pressing concerns and needs of the population.

In conclusion, although the foregoing discussion is specific to Israel, hotline and media interventions can undoubtedly be employed in national emergency situations in general. Both interventions can serve as large-scale support systems, providing easy access for the majority of the population, including children and parents. The interventions are particularly useful for those who are housebound or limited in their ability to travel. Moreover, their cost to individuals who seek help and to those who provide the services is relatively low compared to most other forms of intervention.

REFERENCES

Alpert, J. S. (1985). Change within a profession: Change, future, prevention, and school psychology. *American Psychologist, 40,* 1112–1121.

Arazi, S. (1991). *A summary of the activities of the National Hotline.* Unpublished manuscript. (in Hebrew)

Caplan, G. (1974). *Support systems and community mental health: Lectures on concept development.* New York: Behavioral Publications.

Chad Varah, J. (1980). *The Samaritans in the eighties: To befriend the suicidal and despairing.* London: Trinity Press.

DeAngelis, T. (1991, March). Psychologists take calls from kids about the war. *APA Monitor,* p. 8.

Gilat, I. (1991). *The characteristics of calls received at Eran during the Gulf War.* Unpublished manuscript. (in Hebrew)

Gingerich, W. J., Gurney, R. J., & Wirtz, T. S. (1988). How helpful are helplines? A survey of callers. *Social Casework: The Journal of Contemporary Social Work, 69,* 634–639.

Hertman, E., & Gilat, I. (1991, July). *Telephone emergency services in Israel during the Gulf War.* Paper presented at the XII International Congress of IFOTES, Noordwijkerhout, The Netherlands.

Hobfoll, S., Spielberger, C. D., Breznitz, S., Figley, C., Folkman, S., Lepper-Green, B., Meichenbaum, D., Milgram, N., Sandler, I., Sarason, I., & Van der Kolk, B. (1991). War-related stress: Addressing the stress of war and other traumatic events. *American Psychologist, 46,* 848–855.

Hornblow, A. R., & Sloane, H. R. (1980). Evaluating the effectiveness of a telephone counselling service. *British Journal of Psychiatry, 137,* 377–378.

Karon, M. (1991). Crisis intervention through the telephone [Special issue]. *Sichot, 5,* 22–24. (In Hebrew)

Katzman, A. (1991, March 8). Let's talk some more about it. *Ha'aretz Supplement,* pp. 16–17. (In Hebrew)

Klingman, A. (1988). School community in disaster: Planning for intervention. *Journal of Community Psychology, 16,* 205–216.

Klingman, A. (1992a). The effects of parent-implemented crisis intervention: A real-life emergency involving a child's refusal to use a gas mask. *Journal of Clinical Child Psychology, 21,* 70–75.

Klingman, A. (1992b). Stress reactions of Israeli youth during the Gulf War: A quantitative study. *Professional Psychology, 23,* 521–527.

Lester, D., & Brockopp, G. W. (Eds.). (1976). *Crisis intervention and counseling by telephone.* Springfield, IL: Charles C Thomas.

Levinson, H. (1991). *Viewing educational television programs during the first three weeks of the Gulf War.* Jerusalem: The Israel Institute of Applied Social Research. (In Hebrew)

Meichenbaum, D. (1985). *Stress inoculation training.* New York: Pergamon Press.

Nadler, A. (1991). Help-seeking behavior: Psychological costs and instrumental benefits. *Review of Personality and Social Psychology, 12,* 290–311.

Noy, B. (1991). *Pupils' calls to the Open Line during the emergency period of the Gulf War.* Jerusalem: Ministry of Education and Culture. (in Hebrew)

Rabinovitch, G. (1991, July). *Children and their families in the front line: The Israel experience.* Paper presented at the Third International Conference on the At-Risk Infant, Tel Aviv, Israel.

Raviv, A. (1991). *Why don't they like us? The psychologists' public image in Israel during the Gulf War.* Unpublished manuscript.

Raviv, A., & Klingman, A. (1983). Children under stress. In S. Breznitz (Ed.), *Stress in Israel* (pp. 138–162). New York: Van Nostrand Reinhold.

Raviv, A., Bar-Tal, D. & Wiesner, E. (1993). *School psychological services in Israel during the Gulf War.* Unpublished manuscript. (In Hebrew)

Raviv, A., Raviv, A., & Arnon, G. (1991). Psychological counseling over the radio: Listening motivations and the threat to self-esteem. *Journal of Applied Social Psychology, 21,* 283–300.

Sandoval, J. (1985). Crisis counseling: Conceptualizations and general principles. *School Psychology Review, 14,* 257–265.

Sandoval, J. (Ed.). (1991). Crisis counseling in the schools. *Resources in crisis intervention: School, family, and community applications.* Silver Spring, MD: National Association of School Psychologists.

Shwartz, Z., & Wallach, I. (in press). Psychological counseling by telephone during the Gulf War. In S. Levinson (Ed.), *Psychology in the school and in the community: Models of intervention.* Tel Aviv, Israel: Hadar Publishing. (in Hebrew)

Statistical Abstract of Israel (Vol. 40). (1989). Jerusalem: Central Bureau of Statistics.

Williams, T., & Douds, J. (1976). The unique contribution of telephone therapy. In D. Lester & G. W. Brockopp (Eds.), *Crisis intervention and counseling by telephone* (pp. 80–88). Springfield, IL: Charles C Thomas.

18 War-Related Stress and Family-Centered Intervention: American Children and the Gulf War

Charles R. Figley
Florida State University

Children can be exposed to violent conflict in many ways, as illustrated by the chapters in this book. The extent to which children are affected by this exposure—both short term and long term—is determined, in part, by reactions of parents and teachers (Figley, 1989b; Hobfoll et al., 1991). It is argued here that children not directly in harm's way experience mostly tertiary traumatic stress. Although this stress may be detrimental and may have negative consequences for many years, in most cases children recover quickly once the sources of stress are eliminated. However, children's primary sources of support—parents, teachers and other adults—may experience primary or secondary traumatic stress connected with the war and may require immediate assistance. Otherwise, their ability to work with their children may be greatly impaired.

The recent Persian Gulf crisis provides a useful context for examining the impact of traumatic stress. Although brief in duration as a national crisis, the ongoing military mobilization caused extreme hardship for children, marriages, and families of those who participated in some way.

BACKGROUND

My involvement with Gulf War families began shortly after American troops were mobilized at the start of Operation Desert Shield. The Marriage and Family Therapy Center/Clinic and Psychosocial Stress Research Program at Florida State University sponsored an emergency conference at the

339

Florida State Conference Center in Tallahassee on September 6, 1990, which I organized.

The purpose of the conference was to facilitate the work of professionals working with both military and hostage families most affected by the Middle East crisis. It was obvious from a phone survey of these professionals that they were under enormous strain. They were responsible for working with family members, including young children, of families whose members had been deployed suddenly.

The conference brought together those responsible for identifying and meeting the needs of American families most affected by the Middle East crisis, families of those activated or deployed as a part of Operation Desert Shield. The conference had three goals: (a) to identify the major needs of these military families, (b) to summarize the various programs being employed or needed to assist these families, and (c) to determine how to obtain additional resources to minimize the negative consequences of the mobilization on these families and those who served them (Figley, 1991b). Among the many recommendations emerging from this conference was the convening of a national conference to focus attention on the families affected by the Middle East conflict, especially the children, and to mobilize the private sector to assist in effective ways.

During the following 8 months, the Center produced a national conference (Figley, 1991a), two regional workshops (Figley, 1991b, 1991c), a community-based intervention program, and several other activities associated with helping these special families. More than 230 family members participated in the program in some way, and many more were affected indirectly. These efforts were undertaken with an appreciation for the immediate and long-term psychosocial consequences of war, not only the those who were exposed directly, but on those who supported or were supported by these combatants.

THEORETICAL ORIENTATION

War-related trauma and traumatic stress affects children in many different ways, as noted throughout this volume. Conceptually, the differences in human response to traumatic events across the life span are not well understood. One useful perspective is the traumatic stress theory (Figley, 1989a). This theory, based on several decades of research, assumes that highly stressful events are related, directly and indirectly, to a wide variety of stress reactions at the individual, interpersonal, and sociocultural levels. At each of these levels, individuals struggle to make sense of both the stressful event (e.g., a single, violent crime) or series of events (e.g., family abuse or hostage and war situations) and the consequences of these events (e.g., death, disability, or divorce).

Much of the conceptual work in the area of traumatic stress has focused on individual adults (Figley, 1988), although this trend is changing to include children, as well (Eth & Pynoos, 1985b) and families (Catherall, 1989; Figley & McCubbin, 1983). The key concepts include the following:

1. Traumatic Stressor: Frightening, sudden, overwhelming, extraordinary events or series of events that evoke stress.
2. Traumatic stress reactions: A set of conscious and unconscious actions and emotions associated with dealing with the stressors of the traumatic event and the period immediately afterward.
3. Primary traumatic stress: An emotional state of discomfort resulting from the memories of direct exposure and vulnerability to harm.
4. Secondary traumatic stress: An emotional state of discomfort resulting from concern for, and living in relationship affected by, a traumatized person.
5. Individual coping reaction: An effort by the individual to reduce both the sources of stress (e.g., avoiding the reminders and memories of the traumatic stressors) and the stress reactions (e.g., the various coping reaction strategies).

For adults, dysfunctional reactions include taking a drink, denying the trauma, and rejecting those who talk about the trauma: in children, such reactions might include regressions to earlier stages of development (e.g., bedwetting). Functional coping strategies for both adults and children include confronting the memories of the traumatic event and recognizing the wanted and unwanted consequences. Traumatized people generally attempt to answer five fundamental questions (Figley, 1985):

1. What happened?
2. Why did it happen?
3. Why did I act as I did then?
4. Why have I acted as I have since then?
5. Will I cope if it happens again?

For systems that are traumatized, there is a much more complicated pattern of response involving a consensus of the members regarding, among other things, the seriousness of the crisis, the resources necessary to cope, and the implementation of coping strategies that have worked in the past (Figley, 1989). Much more information is needed, however, to determine if these patterns are unique to Western-oriented, middle-class families.

Some traumatized people develop *posttraumatic stress disorder* (PTSD), an anxiety disorder produced by an emotional shock. It is characterized by (a) reexperiencing the traumatic event(s), (b) avoidance or numbing of reminders of the traumatic event(s), and (c) persistent arousal. *Primary traumatic stress disorder* (PSD) is an anxiety disorder produced by direct exposure to a shocking event; the individual displays symptoms of PTSD. This distinguishes those who were directly exposed to harm and threat from those who care for them. *Secondary traumatic stress disorder* (STSD; Figley, 1991c, in press) is an anxiety disorder produced by exposure to, and out of concern for, a traumatized person; the individual may display some of the symptoms of PTSD, or similar symptoms. Those most vulnerable to STSD are those most exposed to or dependent on the traumatized person. This includes spouses, older children, friends, and professionals, such as therapists and emergency workers who empathize with the victim, the person with the primary traumatic stress disorder. *Tertiary traumatic stress disorder* (TTSD) is an anxiety disorder produced by exposure to, and out of concern for, a secondary victim. This includes young children who are upset following a traumatic event that has caused major disruptions in his or her routine and sense of well-being. It also includes supporters of those with STSD, including spouses of trauma therapists, emergency workers, and others.

In the context of the Gulf War, parents, spouses, siblings, older children, and other family members and supporters of the troops were vulnerable to secondary or tertiary traumatic stress. In addition to being forced to deal with the absence of the missing trooper (e.g., a spouse or parent), family members were traumatized by imagining what might have been happening to that person (e.g., held as a hostage or engaged in the war). They were also traumatized by direct exposure to the family member's descriptions of his or her traumatizing experiences or the effects of his or her actions (Figley, 1989a; Hogencamp & Figley, 1983). Prevention and amelioration of systemic traumatization requires effective cognitive appraisal management. This is why information is so critical to traumatized families and individuals.

A family stress perspective, therefore, has several unique characteristics. It is important in considering the impact of war on children to identify for a family (a) its perceived sources of stress, (b) its methods of coping with these stressors, (c) methods that have previously resulted in reducing stress, (d) methods that had the opposite effect, and (e) patterns that have emerged within the family that were functional in managing the traumatic crisis, but may not be functional following the crisis.

IMMEDIATE SOURCES OF STRESS

Gulf War combatants were exposed to several major sources of stress, irrespective of their individual roles in the war (Brigham, 1991; Department of Veterans Affairs, 1991; Lindy, 1991; Ochberg, 1991). There was evidence of postwar stress and, for some, PTSD, despite the short duration and low intensity of the war.

During the War

In many ways, the Gulf War was like no other in American history (Hobfoll et al., 1991): (a) Many troops—and the rest of the world—were informed, with up-to-the-minute broadcasts, of the various developments via satellite television (including live broadcasts of Allied bombing raids even before the start of the war was officially declared); (b) there was a greater and constant threat of biochemical and nuclear warfare; (c) never before were so many troops massed so quickly to do battle with a single country; (d) never before was America threatened with terrorist attacks associated with a war; and (e) there was extraordinary support of the American people for the war effort, especially for the troops and their families. Other features of this war, though not unique, were no less stressful for those who had to serve and fight in the war zone: (a) changes in climate, routine, danger level; (b) the long period of anticipation of the war and individuals' roles in it; (c) the constant stress of being under attack by Scud missiles; (d) being away from home and family and all the associated comforts; (e) the dangerous preparation for war, including maneuvers and war simulations; (f) the war itself and the actual confrontations with the enemy, both alive and dead; and (g) the horrible and pathetic scenes during the mopping up phase.

Following the War

Conventional wisdom suggests that stress and anxiety disappear once a war is over. Research on the immediate and long-term psychosocial consequences of war, however, clearly suggests that the immediate postwar period is as stressful for both the troops and their families as the prewar period (Brigham, 1991; Department of Veterans Affairs, 1991; Figley, 1991a; Kulka et al., 1990). Among the many stressors for the troops are: (a) frustrations at not leaving for home fast enough; (b) the culture shock resulting from the short time lapse between being in the war theater and arriving home once troops finally leave (the "fox hole to front porch" period); (c) the conflicted emotions associated with the family reunion (happy to be home, but confused about the events in war and their various meanings); (d) the pressures of meeting others' immediate needs versus meeting one's own; (e) the pressures of returning to work versus enjoying life back home; and (f) the extraordinary contrast between being in the middle of an intense and huge war effort and dealing with the routine of life at home.

Families

Mental health professionals who traditionally focus on war veterans are less likely to be aware of stresses endured by the families of those veterans (Figley, 1978; Hogencamp & Figley, 1980; Stanton & Figley, 1978). Based on previous wars and other types of traumatizing events, especially those involving separation, it is likely that some family members of Gulf War combatants will experience postwar stress and, in small numbers, PTSD, despite the duration and intensity of the Gulf war.

Point of Deployment.   In a seminal paper, Amen, Jellen, Merves, and Lee (1988) showed that it is possible to reduce the impact of deployment separation on military children. Apparently, the key is focusing on those factors that most influence children's adjustment to parental absence. These include factors associated with various interactional patterns among family members during the predeployment, deployment, and postdeployment stages. The most critical factor is explicit, supportive communication that provides a rationale and clear understanding for the child about the deployment. During the Gulf War, however, the families and children most disrupted were not active-duty families, but those with members who were activated and deployed through the National Guard and reserve units.

During the War.   The Gulf War, which was unique in many respects, created specific stressors for the families of the war troops (Hobfoll et al., 1991). Perhaps the most profound impact occurred as a result of the media. Information transferred by way of conventional and satellite-transmitted television, commercial radio, computer modem, fax machine, and short-wave radio provided up-to-the-minute information about the war. As a result, many family members and friends felt compelled to monitor these sources of current information as much as possible. In doing so, they were exposed to rumors and misinformation and sacrificed other activities to maintain their vigil.

According to various sources (Figley, 1991a, 1991b; Hobfall et al., 1991), Gulf War families were exposed to a wide variety of stressors during the war, including: (a) the disruption of life patterns and routines; (b) the assumption of roles, tasks, and obligations vacated by the trooper; (c) the assumption of new roles associated with helping family members and friends cope with the crisis; (d) decreased income (especially among "reservist nuclear families"); (e) decreased quality of health care for dependents for families away from military medical facilities and CHAMPUS; (f) constant uncertainty about their trooper's welfare; (g) the inability to plan because of the uncertainty of the trooper's tour of duty; (h) concern about children's welfare (psychological, developmental, and medical) as a result of their being deprived of a parent for so long and the parent being in danger; (i) the confusion and frustration of military bureaucracy, policies, procedures, and expectations, especially for reservist families; (j) media reports associated with the length, outcome, and appropriateness of the war; (k) concern about the trooper's criticism or other comments associated with how things were being handled at home; and (l) concern about the long-term effects of the war on the trooper.

During the Homecoming.   Most people assume that the homecoming was a time of pure joy and satisfaction. Yet for most families, this period was extremely stressful (Hill, 1949; Hogancamp & Figley, 1983; Hunter, 1988; Wolfe, 1991). They shared with the returning trooper the relief of finally ending the separation, but soon faced a large number of challenges, which quickly intruded on the joy of reunion. These were challenges associated with the strains of reviewing what happened during the separation and of attempting to reorganize their lives as quickly as possible. Often, however, there was conflict over what was to be reorganized, by whom, and in what way.

The homecoming was a period of ambivalence, considerable relief mixed with exhilaration (Hunter, 1988). Among the many challenges faced by reunited Gulf War veteran families during this period were: (a) resolving family conflicts over what was done at home, how, and by whom; (b) evaluating the frequency and quality of letters, calls, and other communications from the trooper during his or her absence; (c) rearranging the family (following the reorganization of family roles, routine, and rules that took place in the trooper's absence); (d) making shifts in the friendship support network (e.g., troopers might have discouraged continuing contact with the family system); (e) resolving marital conflict over potential or real extramarital affairs; and (f) resolving conflicts over each person's homecoming fantasies (competition among family members over what activities to do, and when, where, and with whom).

LONG-TERM POSTWAR STRESSORS

After the parades, the delayed second honeymoons and vacations, and the good wishes to welcome the troops home, families had to settle down to face many issues, including issues unresolved at the time of deployment that may have been exacerbated. Other sources of stress may also have emerged as a result of the separation and the hardship associated with the war. Among these were: (a) struggling to get back to normal life, which may take longer than expected; (b) being forced to make decisions about careers and households that had been delayed; (c) confronting the long-term resentments of family members who were forced to assume new roles and responsibilities at home with little support from others; and (d) re-establishing personal relationships with family members who were affected by the war, especially marital relationship and trooper–child relationships.

STRESS REACTIONS

My observations of Gulf War families, based on my experiences at the FSU Center, are consistent with those reported in the literature (Figley & Southerly, 1980; Hill, 1949; Hogancamp & Figley, 1983; Hunter, 1982; Kuenning, 1991; Mason, 1988; Matsakis, 1988; Nice, McDonald, & Mc-Millan, 1981). These stressors manifested themselves in a variety of reactions during and following the war, including, but not limited to: (a) guilt about actions or lack of actions; (b) shame over some failure; (c) a depression or letdown that follows high levels of energy and activity; (d) poor reactions to changes, including those associated with the war; (e) excessive talking about stressors, especially that occurred during the war; (f) crying and extreme emotionality associated with the stressors; (g) difficulty sleeping; (h) undue suffering from minor illnesses; (i) having low energy; (j) overeating; (k) ruminating over minor issues; (l) an inability to concentrate; (m) overdependency on others or on activities that appear to relieve the stress; and (n) abusive actions against family members. These reactions have profound implications for family life, particularly for children.

METHODS OF COPING

As noted earlier, for both children and their parents, efforts to cope with war-related stressors can be successful and can result in avoiding stress reactions altogether. On the other hand, efforts to minimize the extreme stress of separation and uncertainty may not only be ineffective, but may add to the sources of stress.

Given the extraordinary stressors of the Gulf War, including the ones that emerged during the homecoming, family members and friends generally coped with the associated stressors and stress reactions. Most were able to endure and draw on their strengths and resources. Some appeared to become even more hardy, resilient, and functional, yet other families and family members, as a result of the war-related stressors, employed coping strategies that did more harm than good and became additional sources of stress. Figley (1989a) identified 11 characteristics that differentiate functional family coping from dysfunctional family coping. The following are examples of coping methods that have been found among Gulf War families. They are divided into those methods of coping that appear to be effective in reducing stress, and those that are ineffective.

Positive Coping Methods

Based on impressions of families seen at the Marriage and Family Therapy Clinic and findings from previous wars (Hunter, 1982), Gulf War families tended to cope with various war-related stressors effectively by: (a) talking to others (about everyday matters); (b) increasing their support networks; (c) channeling energy into doing something to help others and the troops (e.g., organizing the community to display yellow ribbons, volunteering as a Red Cross worker, or starting a newsletter for Gulf War families); (d) writing letters to the trooper and others to express their thoughts and feelings; (e) joining a support group; (f) engaging in appropriate exercise; and (g) becoming occupied with hobbies and other activities.

Negative Coping Methods

Similarly, according the experiences at the FSU Center and the literature (Hobfoll et al., 1991), negative or dysfunctional methods of coping included: (a) blaming oneself for all or most of one's negative life circumstances; (b) avoiding all responsibility for negative life circumstances while unfairly blaming others; (c) being overly cynical about one's life circumstances; (d) deciding to avoid various daily tasks and responsibilities; (e) taking frustrations out on others, particularly loved ones; (f) abusing drugs or alcohol; (g) excessively seeking information to clarify one's current situation (the "CNN syndrome"); (h) using alcohol or other substances excessively to control stress; or (i) exercising excessively to control stress or to avoid thinking about the stressors.

WAR-RELATED STRESS DISORDERS

A relatively small percentage of war veterans and family members who are unable to cope effectively will develop one or more associated mental disorders. There are standardized protocols to use in diagnosing the presenting problems (Carroll, Foy, Cannon, & Zwier, 1991).

Disorders Affecting Individuals

Harmless (1990) noted the developmental impact of combat exposure on adolescents, in contrast to adults. Structured interview and questionnaire data and diagnostic profiles collected from 56 patients at the Boston VA

Hospital were analyzed. The results indicate that younger individuals experienced greater difficulties later in life, including conflicted intimate and peer relations, inconsistent work histories, and significant histories of legal infractions. These difficulties were attributed to unsuccessful completion of adolescence. The author hypothesized that the traumas of war left the adolescent veterans unable to handle the multiple responsibilities of adulthood.

Hillenbrand (1976) suggested that children of military personnel, apart from dealing with the secondary or tertiary traumatic stress of war, must deal with an extraordinary set of psychosocial stressors (e.g., geographic mobility, transcultural experiences, and the father's episodic absence and early military retirement) that influence their developmental and life experiences. However, the majority of children do cope effectively with mobility and the changing quality of family relationships.

Moreover, Rosenheck and Nathan (1985), in analyzing a case history of the 10-year-old son of a war veteran, illustrated how a father's war experiences can be the primary cause of a child's traumatization. The son's symptoms included intense involvement in the emotional life of the father; deficient development of ego boundaries; high levels of guilt, anxiety, and aggressiveness; and conscious and unconscious preoccupation with specific events that were traumatic for the father. There are striking similarities with the patterns found among children of Holocaust survivors.

Initial findings (Department of Veterans' Affairs, 1991) suggested that few Gulf War veterans and family members were suffering from major mental disorders. However, this was also the initial conclusion during and immediately following the previous war (Borus, 1974). It is reasonable to conclude that children of troops who display the classic symptoms of PTSD are highly vulnerable to developing STSD or TTSD. The traumatology literature on children suggests that parents are extremely influential in the development of traumatic stress reactions and disorders (Donovan & McIntyre, 1990; Eth & Pynoos, 1985a, 1985b). This is especially true when the traumatic experiences emerge from within the family (Terr, 1989; Tsai & Wagner, 1978).

INTERVENTION IMPLICATIONS

What can be done to protect the children from war-related stress reactions? What methods are effective in ameliorating problems after they have emerged? As noted earlier, parents have considerable influence on the perceptions of their children. Thus, it is wise to view intervention with children from a systems perspective and, thus, to adopt a family therapy approach to intervention (Figley, 1989a, 1989b).

Jurich (1983) suggested that families of Vietnam veterans often exhibited an *enmeshed* parent–child relationship, in which the child (usually a boy) has difficulty separating where he begins and his dad ends. When the son reaches adolescence, his normal efforts to reach individualization is much more disruptive to the family. Jurich utilized a five-stage treatment method for veterans and their families that is broad enough to accommodate children's individual styles. The five stages are intake, ventilation, bridging, education, and home therapy. Figley (1989a) recommended a different five-phase approach to working with traumatized families of all types. The phases or tasks are building commitment to therapeutic objectives, framing the problem, reframing the problem, developing a healing theory, and closure and preparedness. Approaches that adopt a more traditional, child-centered approach are more prevalent (Donovan & McIntyre, 1990; Downing, Jenkins, & Fisher, 1988: Saigh, 1989; Sirles, Walsma, Lytle-Barnaby, & Lander, 1988; Terr, 1989; Tsai & Wagner, 1978).

The Florida State University's Marriage and Family Therapy Center offers other approaches: A national conference focusing on military family assistance by the private sector; a free family services program for family members of Gulf War veterans, especially those activated through the reserves and National Guard; and several in-service training workshops for those working with military families. In addition, in 1992 the Center contacted many other family-centered institutions and national mental health, professional organizations as consultants. Each was attempting to help as much as it could. It was obvious throughout this period that no plan of action existed on either a national or regional level. Few communities (Cleveland is a major exception) reacted to this emergency is a unified manner. As a result, many professionals were groping for direction in trying to coordinate their efforts with others in their area.

RESEARCH IMPLICATIONS

Enriched with the knowledged gained by the Gulf War, what should be the research agenda for helping children and others who have been traumatized or will be traumatized in the future? One approach is to consider a broader, contextual view of the study of people, in general, and children, in particular, exposed to stressful circumstances. Figley (1988), in the inaugural issue of the *Journal of Traumatic Stress*, presented a three-dimensional topology for studying the long-term psychosocial consequences of highly stressful events, such as war (Fig. 18.1).

This social context topology enables researchers and theorists to consider three critical sets of variables simultaneously: types of stressful events, levels of investigation, and recovery contexts. When applied to American

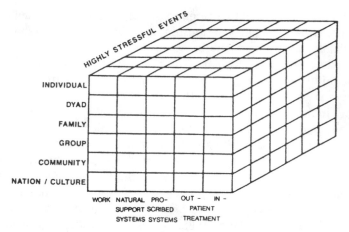

FIG. 18.1. A topology for studying the long-term psychosocial consequences of highly stressful events.

children and families of those who were part of the forces who participated in the Gulf War, the following questions become obvious.

Stressor Events

As noted earlier, the Gulf War involved a succession of stressors that began with notification — or anticipated notification — that the trooper family member would participate in the war, to preparation for departure of the family member; to the various changes in the family systems and lives of the family members, including the children, during the departure; and so on, as already discussed. The sources of stress for children were often different than those for parents. Participants at the FSU symposia, for example, talked about children being confronted by other children at their school about the war with questions such as "Is your dad dead yet?," "Ya know your head explodes when you smell poisonous gas?," and "Are you getting another mom while your mom's in Saudi?" Rarely do children talk about all of these events, yet collectively, they account for most of the stress and stress reactions these children exhibit.

Thus, a research question that deals with stressor events would be: What are the wanted and unwanted psychosocial consequences of various types of child traumatization on child, adult, and family functioning?

Levels of Investigation

Also noted earlier was the fact that most of the research reports on traumatic stress have focused on individual adults, as have the theoretical and clinical reports. Life-span developmental psychology has demonstrated the wide variation between the responses of children and adults and between those of the elderly and middle aged. Moreover, there are at least five additional levels of investigation beyond the individual level.

The dyadic level investigates the characteristic patterns that emerge through the interaction of two people, such as a marital relationship, a parent–child relationship, or a teacher–student relationship.

The family level investigates the characteristic patterns associated with an intimate group of people that includes at least one child. Although there is a vast literature dedicated to family studies, family social science, family sociology, and interpersonal attraction in social psychology, only a fraction focuses on familial responses to highly stressful events (Figley, 1989a, 1989b; Figley & McCubbin, 1983). If young children respond to stressful events based largely on the responses of their parents, the family provides a vital role in both interpreting stressful events and providing guidance in responding to and coping with these events effectively.

Unfortunately, the non-family group, has received much less attention in the last decade, compared to the 1960s and 1970s. Only a few studies have focused on group responses to stressful events. One of the earliest focused on flight crews during World War II (Grinker & Spiegel, 1943), and work-related traumatic stress has emerged recently as an important area of investigation (Mitchell & Everly, 1976), but most types of groups responding to most types of stressful events have not been investigated. An exception is Terr's (1983) study of the Chowchilla, California incident, in which children in a school bus were buried alive and survived.

Community responses to various types of traumatic events have received even less attention, with a few notable exceptions (e.g., the Buffalo Creek Dam disaster, the Three Mile Island nuclear mishap, and the contamination of the Love Canal neighborhood; Lystad, 1988). Most are connected with natural disasters or accidents. Obviously children are part of communities, but rarely are they the focus of investigation.

In addition, an entire *nation* and *culture* can be affected by a highly stressful event. Certainly, this was the case with the Los Angeles riots of 1992. Given the enormity of such an assignment, few researchers have focused at this level, especially in terms of stress and coping, yet this type of investigation could be very useful in predicting and accounting for an entire generation of attitudes, values, and reactions. The Vietnam War, lasting over a decade, affected an entire generation and has shaped not only foreign policy, but the entire political landscape of a nation with regard to war and government intervention (Kulka et al., 1990). Moreover, the Nazi Holocaust certainly had an impact on a generation of Jews world-wide and on their children (Danieli, 1985).

Thus, we can ask the following specific questions regarding levels of investigation:

1. What are the fundamental differences between adults and children — controlling for gender, race, culture, and geographic locality — in the perception of highly stressful events, functional and dysfunctional methods of coping, and the social support resources?
2. What are the relationships among children's cognitive appraisal of danger, levels of stress, and coping? McCormack, Burgess and Hartman (1988) studied 149 adolescents, who ran away from home due to alleged familial physical abuse, and found that the abuse was indirectly related to PTSD to the extent that the parent–child relationship was mediated by factors (e.g., perceptions of control of the stressor and of the availability of social support) that influence the adolescent's ability to cope with stressors.
3. Should there be a different set of symptom criteria for PTSD in children than for adults, including measurement differences? For example, in a review of the literature, Carroll et al. (1991) recently found that a "multiple-gating" model would be effective in assessing different aspects of family dysfunction. Rutter and Quinton (1984) found that children do not always show the same type of disorder as their parents, and that discord between parents and hostility toward children appear to be more important factors than exposure to a parent's disorder.

Recovery Environments

Even less attention has been devoted to the contexts within which individuals, couples, families, groups, communities, and even entire nations recover. These contexts — be they the natural support systems of the traumatized persons; work settings; proscribed systems, such as a support group, or psychotherapy treatment (either inpatient or outpatient) — already exist and are utilized for recovery. Knowing the best recovery environment for a specific type of trauma can have an enormous impact on preventing as well as ameliorating traumatic stress and stress disorders, in both the short and long term.

In this area, then, we can raise the following research questions:

1. What are the familial/social support contexts that most
2. "protect" the child from being traumatized? Mazon, Gampel, Enright, and Orenstein (1990), in their study of Holocaust survivors, noted the variations among those traumatized as children and

attempted to account for these variations in terms other than simply individual, characterological factors.

3. Similarly, what kind of familial/social support contexts most facilitate coping and recovery of children exposed to traumatic stressors and exhibiting symptoms of traumatic stress reactions? Doyle and Bauer (1989), in their study of the treatment of PTSD in children within a residential setting for emotionally disturbed youth, reported a major contributor to PTSD in children to be multiple out-of-home placements. This confirms the findings of Pynoos and Nader (1988) and others. Thus, the context of recovery is the same as the context of traumatization.

4. What kinds of treatment methods for preventing and ameliorating PTSD in children work with what types of traumatizing and recovery contexts? Terr (1989) noted that the techniques for treating psychic trauma in children are still at a very preliminary stage, and that no study has yet established a definitive treatment of choice that applies to all contexts.

CONCLUSION

In this chapter, I have tried to focus on the kinds of information that would assist mental health practitioners in working more effectively with Gulf War veterans and their families. In the process, I have stressed five fundamental points:

1. The psychosocial impact of the war on both families and troops has already been quite profound, in spite of the relatively short duration and limited intensity of the war, because duration and intensity are only two of many factors that cause posttraumatic stress.

2. By the time troopers were reunited with their families, the families may have endured more profound stress than the troopers.

3. The home coming, for both the troops and the families, may have been more stressful than the departure.

4. To help these troopers and families recover quickly from the war, we must understand the sources of stress and methods of coping, and their potential mental health consequences.

5. The research implications drawn should be sensitive to the broader context of the growing field of traumatology and the simultaneous search for understanding the interface of traumatizing context, recovery context, and unit of study. Fundamental questions focusing on children should be sensitive to these three elements.

Specialists in child mental health research have an extremely important role at this juncture in history. The Gulf War mobilized thousands of people worldwide. Our most precious possessions, our children, were highly vulnerable to the absurdities, cruelty, and capriciousness of war. We need to seize the opportunity in this natural laboratory to understand the developmental markers of trauma in children exposed to war.

Understanding the role of these stressors on children will not only enable us to help these children more effectively; it may also help us to recognize the enormous negative psychosocial consequences of war on children and to become even more cautious in using war as a means of solving disputes. Having studied thousands of families adversely affected by war, I can only hope war will be abandoned, although I doubt that it will.

REFERENCES

Amen, D. G., Jellen, L., Merves, E., & Lee, R. E. (1988). Minimizing the impact of deployment separation on military children: Stages, current prevention efforts, and system recommendations. *Military Medicine, 153,* 441–446.

Borus, J. F. (1974). The re-entry transition of the Vietnam veteran. *Archives of General Psychiatry, 30,* 554–557.

Brigham, D. (1991). Veterans benefits outreach to active duty military members. In the Department of Veterans Affairs, *War zone stress among returning Persian Gulf troops: A preliminary report* (pp. B1–B6. West Haven, CT: National Center for PTSD.

Carroll, E. M., Foy, D. W., Cannon, B. J., & Zwier, G. (1991). Assessment issues involving the families of trauma victims. *Journal of Traumatic Stress, 4,* 25–40.

Catherall, D. R. (1989). Differentiating intervention strategies for primary and secondary trauma in PTSD: The example of Vietnam veterans. *Journal of Traumatic Stress, 2,* 289–304.

Danieli, Y. (1985). The treatment and prevention of long-term effects and intergenerational transmission of victimization: A lesson from Holocaust survivors and their children. In C. R. Figley (Ed.), *Trauma and its wake: The study and treatment of PTSD* (pp. 295–313). New York: Brunner/Mazel.

Department of Veterans Affairs (1991). *War zone stress among returning Persian Gulf troops: A preliminary report.* West Haven, CT: National Center for PTSD.

Donovan, D. M., & McIntyre, D. (1990). *Healing the hurt child: A developmental contextual approach.* New York: Norton.

Downing, J., Johns, S. J., & Fisher, G. L. (1988). A comparison of psychodynamic and reinforcement treatment with sexually abused children. *Elementary School Guidance and Counseling, 22,* 291–298.

Doyle, J. S., & Bauer, S. K. (1989). PTSD in children: Its identification and treatment in a residential setting for emotionally disturbed youth. *Journal of Traumatic Stress, 2,* 275–288.

Eth, S., & Pynoos, R. (1985a). Developmental perspectives on psychic trauma in childhood. In C. R. Figley (Ed.), *Trauma and its wake: The study and treatment of PTSD* (pp. 36–52). New York: Brunner/Mazel.

Eth, S., & Pynoos, R. (1985b). *Post-traumatic stress disorder in children.* Washington, DC: American Psychiatric Press.

Figley, C. R. (1978). *Stress disorders among Vietnam veterans: Theory, research, and treatment.* New York: Brunner/Mazel.

Figley, C. R. (Ed.). (1985). *Trauma and its wake: The study and treatment of PTSD.* New York: Brunner/Mazel.

Figley, C. R. (1988). Toward a field of traumatic stress. *Journal of Traumatic Stress, 1,* 3–16.

Figley, C. R. (1989a). *Helping traumatized families.* San Francisco: Jossey-Bass.

Figley, C. R. (Ed.). (1989b). *Treating stress in families.* New York: Brunner/Mazel.

Figley, C. R. (1991a). *Strengthening military families: Mobilizing national resources. Proceedings of a conference held on October 4, 1990.* Tallahassee, FL: FSU Marriage and Family Therapy Center.

Figley, C. R. (1991b). Critical services for the veterans of the Gulf War. In the Department of Veterans Affairs, *War zone stress among returning Persian Gulf troops: A preliminary report* (pp. D3–D14). West Haven, CT: National Center for PTSD.

Figley, C. R. (1991c). *Investigation of war-related stress among families of Gulf War military service personnel.* Unpublished research proposal. FSU Marriage and Family Therapy Center, Tallahassee.

Figley, C. R., & McCubbin, H. I. (Eds.). (1983). *Stress and the family: Vol. II. Coping with catastrophe.* New York: Brunner/Mazel.

Figley, C. R., & Southerly, W. (1980). Psychosocial adjustment of recently returned veterans. In C. R. Figley & S. Leventman (Eds.), *Strangers at home: Vietnam veterans since the war* (pp. 167–180. New York: Praeger.

Grinker, R., & Spiegel, J. P. (1945). *Men under stress.* Philadelphia: Blakiston.

Harmless, A. (1990). Developmental impact of combat exposure: Comparison of adolescent and adult Vietnam veterans. *Smith College Studies in Social Work, 60*(2), 185–195.

Hill, R. (1949). *Families under stress.* New York: Harper & Row.

Hobfoll, S. E., Spielberger, C. D., Breznitz, S., Figley, C., Folkman, S., Lepper-Green, B., Meichenbaum, D., Milgram, N. A., Sandler, I., Sarason, I., & van der Kolk, B. (1991) War-related stress: Addressing the stress of war and other traumatic events. *American Psychologist, 46,* 848–855.

Hogancamp, V. E., & Figley, C. R. (1983). War: Bringing the battle home. In C. R. Figley & H. I. McCubbin (Eds.), *Stress and the family: Vol. II. Coping with catastrophe* (pp. 148–165. New York: Brunner/Mazel.

Hunter, E. J. (1982). *Families under the flag: A review of military family literature.* New York: Praeger.

Hunter, E. J. (1988). Long-term effects of parental wartime captivity on children: Children of POW and MIA servicemen. *Journal of Contemporary Psychotherapy, 18,* 312–328.

Jurich, A. P. (1983). The Saigon of the family's mind: Family therapy with families of Vietnam veterans. *Journal of Marital and Family Therapy, 9,* 355–363.

Kuenning, D. A. (1991) *Life after Vietnam: How veterans and their loved ones can heal the psychological wounds of war.* New York: Paragon.

Kulka, R. A., Schlenger, W. E., Fairbank, J. A., Hough, R. L., Jordan, B. K., Marmar, C. R., Weis, D. S., & Gradey, D. A. (1990). *Trauma and the Vietnam War generation: Report of findings from the National Vietnam Veterans Readjustment Study.* New York: Brunner/Mazel.

Lindy, J. D. (1991). Mental health needs of American veterans of Operation Desert Shield and Desert Storm. In the Department of Veterans Affairs, *War zone stress among returning Persian Gulf troops: A preliminary report* (pp. D29–D33). West Haven, CT: National Center for PTSD.

Lystad, M. (Ed.) (1988). *Mental health response to mass emergencies: Theory and practice.* New York: Brunner/Mazel.

Mason, P. (1988). *Warriors' wives.* New York: The Free Press.

Matsakis, A. (1988). *Vietnam wives.* Kensington, MD: Woodbine House.

Mazor, A., Gampel, Y., Enright, R. D., & Orenstein, R. (1990). Holocaust survivors: Coping with posttraumatic memories in childhood and 40 years later. *Journal of Traumatic Stress, 3,* 1–14.

McCormack, A., Burgess, A. W., & Hartman, C. (1988). Familial abuse and PTSD. *Journal of Traumatic Stress, 1,* 231–242.

Nice, D. S., McDonald, B., & McMillian, T. (1981). The families of U.S. Navy prisoners of war from Vietnam five years after reunion. *Journal of Marriage and the Family, 43,* 431–437.

Ochberg, F. M. (Ed.) (1988). *Post-traumatic therapy and victims of violence.* New York: Brunner/Mazel.

Ochberg, F. M. (1991). Readjustment services for Persian Gulf veterans. In the Department of Veterans Affairs, *War zone stress among returning Persian Gulf troops: A preliminary report* (pp. D36–D40). West Haven, CT: National Center for PTSD.

Pynoos, R. S., & Nader, K. (1988). Psychological first aid and treatment approach to children exposed to community violence: Research implications. *Journal of Traumatic Stress, 1,* 445–44.

Rosenheck, R., & Nader, K. (1988). Secondary traumatization in the children of Vietnam veterans with posttraumatic stress disorder. *Hospital and Community Psychiatry, 36,* 538–539.

Rutter, M., & Quinton, D. (1984). Parental psychiatric disorder: Effects on children. *Psychological Medicine, 14,* 853–880.

Saigh, P. A. (1989). The use of an in vitro flooding package in the treatment of traumatized adolescents. *Journal of Developmental and Behavioral Pediatrics, 10* 17–21.

Sirles, E. A., Walsma, J., Lytle-Barnaby, R., & Lander, L. C. (1988). Group therapy techniques for work with child sexual abuse victims. *Social Work with Groups, 11,* 67–78.

Stanton, M. D., & Figley, C. R. (1978). Treating the Vietnam veteran within the family system. In C. R. Figley (Ed.), *Stress disorders among Vietnam veterans: Theory, research, and treatment* (pp. 281–290). New York: Brunner/Mazel.

Terr, L. C. (1983). Chowchilla revisited: The effects of psychic of psychic trauma four years after a schoolbus kidnapping. *American Journal of Psychiatry, 140,* 1543–1550.

Terr, L. C. (1989). Treating psychic trauma in children: A preliminary discussion. *Journal of Traumatic Stress, 2,* 3–20.

Tsai, M., & Wagner, N. N. (1978). Therapy groups for women sexually molested as children. *Archives of Sexual Behavior, 7,* 417–427.

Wolfe, J. (1991) Preliminary report of a reunion survey on Desert Storm returnees. In the Department of Veterans Affairs, *War zone stress among returning Persian Gulf troops: A preliminary report* (pp. C1–C14). West Haven, CT: National Center for PTSD.

Author Index

Note: Page numbers in italics refer to bibliography pages.

Subject Index